CONTEMPORA

World History

A.D. 1215.

MAGNA CARTA
Regis Johannis.

Matthew T. Downey

McGraw Hill **Wright Group**

The McGraw·Hill Companies

Author

Matthew T. Downey received his Ph.D. in American History from Princeton University. He served as Director of the Clio Project in History-Social Science Education in the Graduate School of Education at the University of California, Berkeley. He also directed the U.C. Berkeley site of the California History-Social Science Project. He has taught at the University of Colorado, the University of California at Los Angeles, and at Louisiana State University. Currently, he directs the Social Science Program and the William E. Hewitt Institute for History and Social Science Education at the University of Northern Colorado.

Senior Editor: Mitch Rosin
Executive Editor: Linda Kwil
Composition: Matt McCarthy
Cover Design: Tracy Sainz
Interior Design: Linda Chandler

Reviewers

Jeffrey J. Johll
  K–12 District Social Studies Supervisor
  Dubuque Community School District
  Dubuque, Iowa

Jill DeLuccia
  Social Studies Instructor
  Atlanta, Georgia

Jill Mott-Smith
  Social Studies Instructor
  Giddings, Texas

Eleanor Nangle
  Social Studies Instructor
  Chicago, Illinois

Brian Silva
  Social Studies Instructor and Technology Coordinator
  Long Beach, California

About the Cover

The images on the cover include (from left to right): Charlemagne, Queen Elizabeth I, Nelson Mandela, Simón Bolívar, Empress Wu, Leonardo da Vinci.

Photo credits are on pages 474–475.

Wright Group

ISBN: 0-07-704447-9 (Student Softcover Edition)
ISBN: 0-07-704449-5 (Student Softcover Edition with CD)
ISBN: 0-07-704519-X (Student Hardcover Edition)
ISBN: 0-07-704520-3 (Student Harcover Edition with CD)

Send all inquiries to:
Wright Group/McGraw-Hill
P.O. Box 812960
Chicago, IL 60681

Printed in the United States of America.

1 2 3 4 5 6 7 8 9 10 QUE 09 08 07 06 05

The *McGraw-Hill* Companies

Contents

To the Student

This textbook is a history of the world's people and major cultures from early times to the present. It begins with Stone Age people of prehistoric times. Prehistory is that time before people made written records. We know about these people mainly from the artifacts they left behind.

The book next looks at the early civilizations that developed writing, agriculture, and towns and cities. It traces the rise of the ancient Middle East, North Africa, Asia, and the Americas. These civilizations developed separately with little or no outside contact.

However, at the beginning of what we call the Global Age, the people of Asia, Africa, Europe, and the Americas came into contact with one another. Some of these contacts were peaceful, with people trading goods. Often contact led to wars, the enslaving of people, and death by diseases brought by the invaders.

World history is a story of change. Civilization began as the change from hunting and gathering to farming and town life. As towns grew into cities, the way people lived changed again. More people lived by making and selling goods. That led to the Industrial Revolution as people worked in factories instead of at home. We continue to live in a changing world. Many of these changes have brought us a higher standard of living and a better life.

While change brings opportunities, it also causes problems. This book examines many world problems of the past and of today. These include revolutions, brutal dictatorships, world wars, economic hard times, and environmental disasters.

Fortunately, world history is more than the story of disasters and defeats. It also is an account of how people solved or learned to manage the problems they encountered. I hope that this book helps you to better understand the opportunities and problems of the world in which you live.

Matthew T. Downey

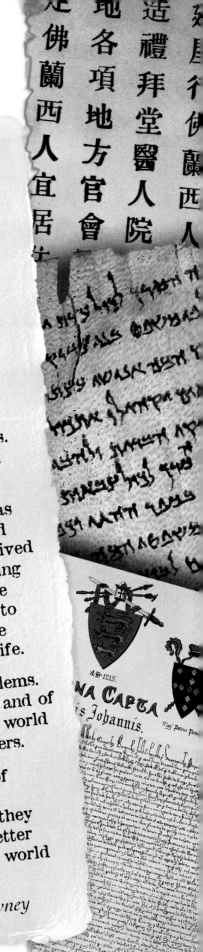

UNIT 1

THE BEGINNING OF CIVILIZATION

The earliest humans appeared about 250,000 years ago. It took about 240,000 years for people to domesticate plants and animals. Before this, people picked grains and berries and dug roots for food. They also hunted, but they did not know how to plant and harvest crops. Once they mastered farming, changes came very quickly. Why did farming make such a difference in the way people lived?

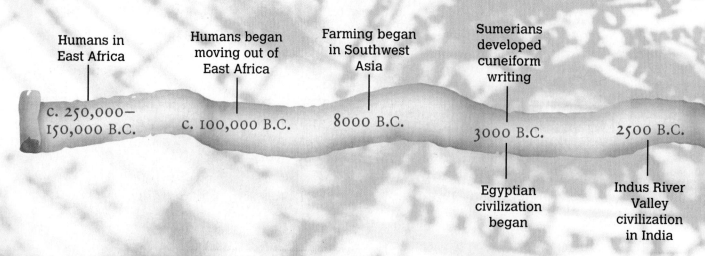

Humans in East Africa
c. 250,000–150,000 B.C.

Humans began moving out of East Africa
c. 100,000 B.C.

Farming began in Southwest Asia
8000 B.C.

Sumerians developed cuneiform writing
3000 B.C.

Egyptian civilization began

2500 B.C.

Indus River Valley civilization in India

c. stands for *circa*, which means "about" in Latin

How did irrigation systems help the people of Mesopotamia grow food?

Why do you think early hunting people painted pictures of animals?

Why was Hammurabi's Code of laws so important?

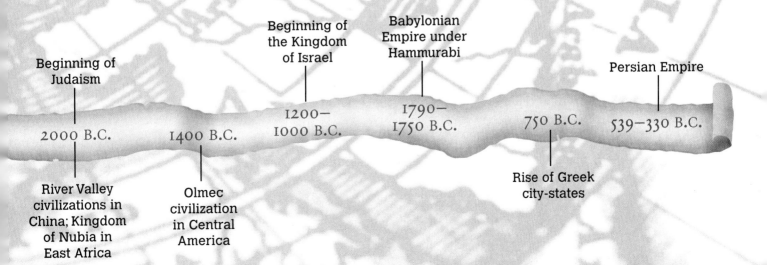

Beginning of Judaism

Beginning of the Kingdom of Israel

Babylonian Empire under Hammurabi

Persian Empire

2000 B.C.

1400 B.C.

1200–1000 B.C.

1790–1750 B.C.

750 B.C.

539–330 B.C.

River Valley civilizations in China; Kingdom of Nubia in East Africa

Olmec civilization in Central America

Rise of Greek city-states

Chapter 1

THE EARLIEST HUMANS

(PREHISTORY TO 2500 B.C.)

Getting Focused

Skim this chapter to predict what you will be learning.
- Read the lesson titles and subheadings.
- Look at the illustrations and read the captions.
- Examine the maps.
- Review the vocabulary words and terms.

What do you think this chapter is about? Do the subheadings and pictures raise any questions for you? In your notebook, write at least two questions you want answered as you read this chapter.

LESSON **1**

Prehistory

Thinking on Your Own

Read the vocabulary words on this page. While you read this lesson, use each vocabulary word in a sentence. Write the sentences in your notebook. Share your sentences with a partner.

The time before writing was invented is called **prehistory**. Writing is only about 5,200 years old. The earliest humans evolved on Earth between 150,000 and 250,000 years ago. If there was no writing for most of this time, how do we learn about the earliest people? Answering this question is the work of specially trained scientists.

focus your reading

How do people learn about prehistory?

What do anthropologists think are the stages of human development?

How did early people live?

vocabulary

prehistory	artifacts
anthropologists	fossils
culture	hominids
archaeologists	nomads

How We Know About Early Life

Anthropologists study the beginnings and development of humans and their **cultures**. In this context, *culture* does not mean movies or music. As anthropologists use the word, *culture* means the way of life of a group of people. It includes their beliefs, traditions, government, religion, and social classes. A way of life is what makes a group unique.

Archaeology is a branch of anthropology. **Archaeologists** study past societies by examining the things people made and left behind. These things are

Archaeologists dig for artifacts in Egypt.

called **artifacts**. An artifact can be anything from a building to an earring. Anthropologists use both artifacts and **fossils** in their work. Fossils are the remains of humans, plants, and animals that have become hard like stone.

Over the years, scientists have set up scientific methods for finding and studying artifacts and fossils. The search begins with a dig, or excavation. Scientists carefully remove layers of dirt looking for evidence of human activity. They use a small hand tool called a trowel and different-sized brushes. Each find, or discovery, is labeled and packed for later study.

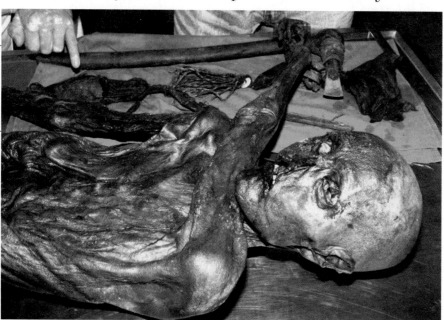

The remains of Otzi, the world's oldest mummy, have been preserved for study of what life was like 5,300 years ago.

Back in the lab, scientists carefully examine the artifacts and fossils. To understand human developments, scientists need to date their finds. Anthropologists try to figure out if one culture lived earlier than, later than, or at the same time as another culture. To date items, they often conduct radiocarbon dating. Other methods of dating include tree-ring dating and stratigraphic observations.

Early Stages of Development

Anthropologists have found evidence in Africa of the ancestors of modern humans. These early humanlike creatures are called **hominids**. They walked upright and made stone tools. Anthropologists believe that hominids went through three stages of development.

Hominids used stone hand axes as tools.

The first hominids are called *Australopithecus*. They lived in eastern and southern Africa, possibly 3 to 4 million years ago. They walked upright and made a few simple tools from stone.

Evidence of later hominids has also been found in Africa—as well as in Europe and Asia. They are known as *Homo erectus*. They appeared about 1.5 million years ago. *Homo erectus* walked upright, too, and made more advanced stone tools. Anthropologists believe *Homo erectus* began in Africa and moved to Asia and Europe over time. It was during this period that fire was discovered. Lightning could start a fire and so could sunlight on dry branches. But these fires started naturally. *Homo erectus* figured out how to start fires and keep them burning. This was an important turning point in history.

The last stage of development is called *Homo sapiens*. Anthropologists have found evidence of these humans in East Africa between 150,000 and 250,000 years ago. One branch of *Homo sapiens* became modern humans, known as *Homo sapiens sapiens*. About 100,000 years ago, *Homo sapiens sapiens* began moving out of Africa. By 50,000 years ago, humans had reached Australia. By 40,000 years ago, they were living in Europe. Humans also moved east, reaching Asia 25,000 years ago. From Asia, humans moved into North America and then South America. By 10,000 years ago, they had reached the tip of South America.

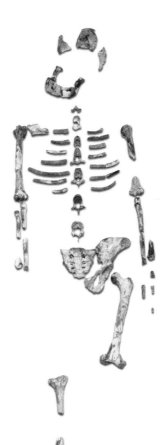
Lucy, a member of the *Australopithecus* genus, lived about 3.3 million years ago in Ethiopia, Africa.

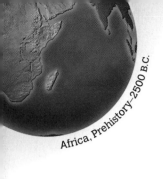

Stone tools help archaeologists to learn about ancient cultures.

Hunters and Gatherers

The earliest people were **nomads**. They lived in groups of 20 to 30 people. Nomads do not live in one location. They move from place to place. The earliest people had to move around because they lived by hunting and gathering their food. The men hunted big-game animals like woolly mammoths and bison. They also hunted smaller game like deer and rabbits. If a group lived near water, the men might also fish. The women dug up plants and roots, and gathered berries, nuts, fruits, and grains to add to the meat. All the plant foods grew wild. The earliest people did not know how to farm. People who live this way are called hunters and gatherers.

stop and think

Why do you think learning to make tools for grinding grain and killing animals was important? Talk over your ideas with a partner. Write a sentence to answer the question.

Many ancient burial sites contain items for the deceased to use in the afterlife.

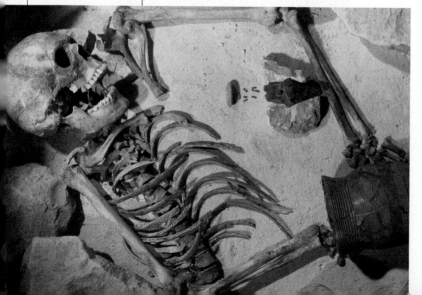

Prehistoric people spent most of their time finding and preparing food. As a result, there was little time for anything else. Over thousands of years, however, people made discoveries that made

their lives easier. They invented speech so they could communicate plans for the hunt. They learned to make tools from stone and fishhooks from bone. The invention of the spear made it easier to bring down large animals on the run. So did the invention of the bow and arrow. As people moved into colder areas, they learned to make clothing from the skins of animals. They invented needles and used thin strips of animal sinew as thread to sew skins together.

Women had a central role in prehistoric groups. Like men they were responsible for finding food. Archaeologists also speculate that women prepared the food and took care of the children. Some archaeologists think that women had a role in running the groups and making decisions.

Putting It All Together

Choose one photograph from the lesson. Write a paragraph to explain what it shows. Use information from the text and the caption. Share your paragraph with a partner.

The Leakeys: Time Travelers

The Leakeys are a family of anthropologists who work in East Africa. The first anthropologist in the family was Louis (1903–1972). His wife, Mary Douglas Nicols, (1913–1996) soon joined him in looking for fossils. Their son, Richard, (1944–   ) found his first fossil when he was six. Richard married a fellow scientist, Meave Epps. Their daughter Louise has also joined in the family's work.

The Leakeys' work has changed the way science describes the ancestors of modern human beings. Louis and Mary made their first important discovery in 1959. Each discovery pushed the age of human ancestors farther and farther back in time.

After her husband's death, Mary Leakey continued their work. Her discoveries have been dated to 3.6 million years ago. Richard Leakey also worked in East Africa and made important finds. He dug up what may be a separate group of human or humanlike creatures.

Biography

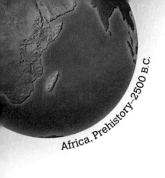

LESSON 2

Farming and the Beginning of Civilization

Thinking on Your Own

Once people learned to grow their own food, they knew that food would be available to eat. How do you think their lives changed? Write your prediction in a sentence. As you read this lesson, check your prediction against what you learn.

Early people were hunters and gatherers. Farming did not develop until about 10,000 years ago. When people were able to give up roaming in search of food, dramatic changes occurred in their lives. The development of farming created so much change that it is considered a revolution. Anthropologists call it the **Neolithic revolution**.

focus your reading

How did people learn to farm?

How did new technologies affect early people?

What is a civilization?

vocabulary

Neolithic revolution

domesticate

surplus

deities

social hierarchy

artisans

civilization

The practice of farming evolved over many thousands of years.

First Farmers

Farming began about 8000 B.C. in Southwest Asia. Some scientists think farming spread from there to other regions. Other experts think that people in different regions figured out on their own how to farm. Experts do agree that people began farming in different regions at different times. There is also agreement that people were farming in Africa, Europe, Asia, and Central America by 5000 B.C.

Experts can only speculate at how people initially learned to

domesticate, or tame and control, seeds. It is possible that someone noticed that the same plants came up in the same place each year. People might have tried throwing some seeds on the ground and putting dirt over them. Or maybe they dug holes and placed seeds in the holes. No one knows for sure. But over time people in Southwest Asia began growing wheat and barley. By around 5000 B.C., people in China were growing rice, while people in Mexico and Central America were growing beans, squash, and maize—a form of corn.

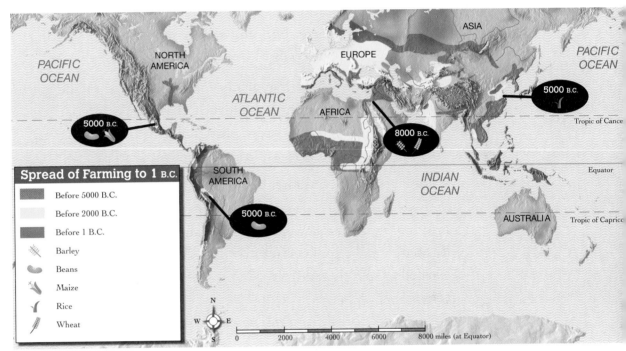

Spread of Farming to 1 B.C.

- Before 5000 B.C.
- Before 2000 B.C.
- Before 1 B.C.
- Barley
- Beans
- Maize
- Rice
- Wheat

Along with learning how to grow crops, people learned to domesticate animals. Instead of moving from place to place to hunt animals, hunters captured them alive. The hunters penned up the animals and fed them. The animals were killed as their meat was needed. The first evidence of domesticated animals is in Southwest Asia. By 8000 B.C., people there were keeping cows, goats, pigs, dogs, and sheep.

In time, people found that animals provided other sources of food besides meat. Cows and goats provided milk. People also found other uses for animals besides food. Horses, reindeer, camels, and even dogs could be trained to carry loads. The wool from sheep could be woven into clothes. The skins of cows, goats, pigs, and sheep could be used as blankets and made into clothing and bags.

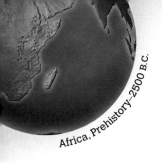

New Ways of Life

By farming and raising animals, people were able to control the sources of their food. Once they could control their food, people did not have to be nomadic. Instead, they settled where they grew their crops. If they were going to stay in one place, people could build permanent homes. They would no longer have to abandon their shelters when they moved. Nor would people have to take down their shelters and move them to another camp. People began building sturdy homes of long-lasting materials like mud bricks.

Ancient civilizations, including the Aztec, developed calendars to keep track of the seasons.

Calendars

A calendar is a way of measuring the passage of time. Many cultures and religions have developed calendars over the centuries. Today, the Gregorian calendar is the one used by nations around the world. It measures time backwards and forwards from the year 1.
• Time before year 1 is indicated as B.C.
• Time since year 1 is indicated as A.D.

The phrase "about 10,000 years ago" means about 8000 B.C.
Today is about 2,000 years since the year 1. To find the date, subtract 2,000 from 10,000. The date is about 8000 B.C.

With a steady food supply, people began to have more children. The population of villages grew. Little villages became bigger villages and then towns and cities.

With a larger population, not everyone had to farm. People with special skills became craftworkers. For example, some people learned to make baskets from reeds and pots from clay. Some learned to spin thread from certain plants and to weave cloth.

Around 4000 B.C., craftworkers in Asia learned to make bronze. Copper was already in use in some places in the world. Bronze is a combination of copper and tin and is a very soft metal. With the development of bronze, metalworkers could make a living by creating bronze weapons and jewelry. Other people became traders. They made their living by exchanging **surplus** food and other goods like jewelry.

stop and think

What changes resulted when people began to farm? List the changes in your notebook. Check them with a partner to be sure you listed at least five.

Bronze was used to make goods like weapons, jewelry, and mining tools.

These skills developed in different regions at different times. Like the knowledge of farming, some of these skills may have spread from one region to another. Or some may have developed independently in different parts of the world. Archaeologists are still working to solve these mysteries.

The Six Characteristics of Civilization	
Cities	As populations grew, cities became the centers of early civilizations.
Central government	Large numbers of people need a single government. Government keeps order and helps people work together.
Religion	Early people developed religions to explain nature. Early people also believed that **deities**–or gods–would help them. Rulers said their right to rule came from the deities.
Social and economic classes	As people began to do different kinds of jobs, some became wealthier than others. A **social hierarchy** was set up based on wealth. At the top was the ruler and his family. They were the wealthiest and the most important people. Next came priests and warrior nobles. Merchants and craftworkers were the third level. Farmers were the least wealthy. Below them were slaves.
Arts and architecture	Large buildings such as palaces for the ruler and temples for the deities were built. Craftworkers and **artisans** decorated them with statues, paintings, and beautiful furniture.
Writing	Not all civilizations developed writing, but many did. Writing was used to keep tax records for the government.

Africa, Prehistory–2500 B.C.

What Is a Civilization?

Civilization is a term that anthropologists and archaeologists use to describe a complex culture. Lesson 1 explained that culture is the way of life of a group of people. It includes their beliefs, traditions, government, religion, and social classes. The early farming people had simple cultures. They lived in small groups and worked their fields together. Women took less part in decision making for the group than they had during the hunting and gathering stage. Male heads of families began to meet as councils and make decisions for the village.

As villages grew, they needed more leadership and more organization. The result was the development of civilizations. Historians have studied early civilizations and found that most share the same six developments: cities, central government, religion, social and economic classes, art and architecture, and writing.

Putting It All Together

In three or four paragraphs, describe how early people went from hunting and gathering to farming to living in cities. First, list information about each step in your notebook. Then check your list with a partner.

The remains of the granaries at Harappa, Pakistan.

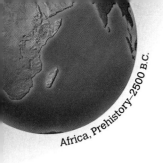

Africa, Prehistory–2500 B.C.

Chapter Summary

- The time before writing is known as **prehistory**.
- **Anthropologists** study the beginnings and development of humans and their **culture**. They use **fossils** and **artifacts**.
- **Archaeologists** study the past by examining artifacts.
- Anthropologists believe that the first **hominids** lived in Africa about 3 to 4 million years ago.
- An important turning point in prehistory was the discovery of how to start a fire and keep it burning.
- Prehistoric people were **nomads** who lived by hunting and gathering their food.
- The development of farming is called the **Neolithic revolution** because it changed the way people lived.
- Early people learned to **domesticate** animals and crops.
- Because of farming, people (1) were able to control their food supply, (2) stopped moving from place to place, and (3) built permanent homes. (4) Populations grew and (5) cities developed. (6) Not everyone had to farm. A **surplus** of food allowed artisans to create other goods.
- **Civilizations** are complex and have the following six characteristics: (1) cities, (2) central government, (3) religion based on **deities**, (4) social and economic classes, (5) arts and architecture created by **artisans**, (6) writing.
- The development of social and economic classes is a **social hierarchy**.

Chapter Review

1 Write a paragraph to describe what life was like for a group of hunters and gatherers.

2 Language had to be invented. The first people did not have words to speak to one another. Imagine you are a hunter. Make a list of words you would need to talk to another hunter.

3 Select one characteristic of civilization. Write a paragraph about the characteristic.

Skill Builder

Identifying the Main Idea and Supporting Details

The main idea is the theme or idea that a piece of writing is mostly about. Look at the organization of this textbook. It has chapters and each chapter has lessons. Each chapter has a main idea; so does each lesson. Each section within a lesson also has a main idea.

The chapter title tells you the main idea of the chapter. The lesson title tells you the main idea of the lesson. Each paragraph also has a main idea. Often it will be stated in the first sentence of the paragraph. This is similar to the way a chapter title states the main idea of a chapter. Sometimes the main idea of a paragraph is unstated. Then you have to figure out the main idea from the details in the paragraph. The details explain or describe the main idea. For this reason, they are called supporting details.

> To find a main idea of a paragraph or a piece of writing, ask yourself the following:
>
> 1. Is there a single sentence that states what the piece is about? If there is, then you have found the main idea. To be sure, restate the sentence in your own words. Does it tell what the paragraph is mainly about?
>
> 2. If there is no single sentence main idea, what does the piece seem to be about? What are the details describing or explaining? When you think you know, restate the main idea in your own words. This will help you be sure you have the main idea.

1 What is the main idea of (a) Chapter 2? (b) Chapter 6? (c) Lesson 1 of Chapter 4? (d) Lesson 3 of Chapter 19?

2 Read the section "How We Know About Early Life," pages 5–6. Identify the main idea in each paragraph. Decide whether the main idea is stated or unstated. Then write a bulleted list of supporting details.

Chapter 2

SOUTHWEST ASIA: BEGINNINGS

(1200 B.C.–500 B.C.)

Getting Focused

Skim this chapter to predict what you will be learning.
- Read the lesson titles and subheadings.
- Look at the illustrations and read the captions.
- Examine the maps.
- Review the vocabulary words and terms.

Sumerians lived in city-states. Israelites spent many years moving from one place to another. Create a T-chart. Label one side "Sumerians" and the other side "Israelites." Think about what ancient city dwellers might need in order to live. Think about what ancient nomads might need. Review Chapter 1 for ideas if necessary. Then complete your T-chart.

LESSON 1

Mesopotamia: The Land Between the Rivers

Thinking on Your Own

Turn each of the subheadings into questions. Write them in your notebook. As you read the lesson, answer each question in your notebook. Compare your answers with those of a partner.

Mesopotamia means "land between the rivers." The rivers are the Tigris and Euphrates. They are located in what is now Iraq in Southwest Asia. Each year the rivers flooded their banks. This flooding left **fertile**, or rich, soil on the **floodplain** in the river valleys. The floodplain is the area the rivers flooded. People began to settle on the floodplain and farm around 8000 B.C.

People soon realized that they needed to control the rivers. The floods were good for the soil, but they were also destructive. The floods did not come at exactly the same time each year. In order to be sure to have enough food, the people

> **focus your reading**
>
> How did people use the Tigris and Euphrates Rivers?
>
> Why was the development of writing important?
>
> Why is Hammurabi remembered?
>
> What did Darius do?
>
> **vocabulary**
>
> | | |
> |---|---|
> | fertile | deities |
> | floodplain | ziggurat |
> | city-states | cuneiform |
> | scribes | codify |

Farming was an important part of the culture in Mesopotamia.

Southwest Asia, 1200 B.C.–500 B.C.

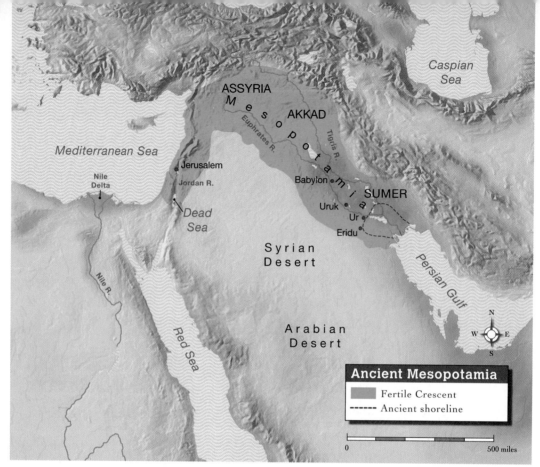

Ancient Mesopotamia

▨ Fertile Crescent

----- Ancient shoreline

0   500 miles

had to plant by a certain time of the year. The crops also needed water while they grew. Mesopotamia had little rainfall and the summers were very hot.

The Mesopotamians figured out how to build dikes to hold back the flood waters. They also learned to use irrigation to bring river water to their crops. By building dams with gates, the people could direct water to their fields.

To build the dikes and the dams, the people had to cooperate. As they learned to work together, they began to gather in villages, towns, and cities. The formation of cities is one characteristic of civilization.

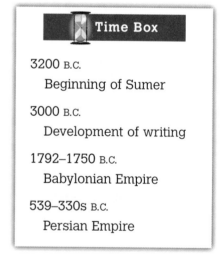

Time Box

3200 B.C.
    Beginning of Sumer

3000 B.C.
    Development of writing

1792–1750 B.C.
    Babylonian Empire

539–330s B.C.
    Persian Empire

Sumer

Sumer was the southern region of Mesopotamia. The people of Sumer were the first to build a civilization. Sumer was a series of **city-states**. A king ruled over each city-state. The armies of rival kings often battled each other for power over a city-state.

Bricks made from mud were used to build houses and buildings in the Sumerian city-states.

The cities were walled. Houses and the walls were made of mud bricks. The bricks were made by shaping mud into long, thick rectangles. The bricks were then left in the sun to bake, or harden. Most Sumerians were peasants, or farmers. They lived in small houses just outside the city walls. In the city were a number of larger houses and large buildings. Most of the larger buildings were temples to the gods and goddesses. The Sumerians worshiped several gods and goddesses.

Although most people were farmers, there were other social classes. Below the ruler were priests and soldiers. Next were **scribes**, merchants, and craftworkers. Priests were both men and women. Their task was to hold ceremonies to honor the Sumerian gods and goddesses. Their **deities** were very important to the Sumerians. The deities oversaw the well-being of a city. They made sure that the harvests were good and the people were prosperous. The Sumerians believed that the king received his power to rule from the deities. The Sumerians developed the **ziggurat** as a special temple to honor their deities. Ziggurats were built of mud bricks and shaped like a pyramid.

The ziggurat of Ur, Iraq, was built to honor Sumerian gods and goddesses.

One of the most important inventions of the Sumerians was a form of writing. As towns and cities grew, a system for

record keeping was needed. The ancient Sumerians developed **cuneiform** writing around 3000 B.C. *Cuneiform* means "wedge-shaped." The Sumerians did not use an alphabet like ours. Their writing was based on pictures. Scribes used a reed, or stick, to draw the shapes on clay tablets. The tablets were then allowed to bake, or harden, in the sun. Only men could be scribes. They were the people who kept the records for the king. They also wrote down the stories, songs, and poetry of the people. The *Epic of Gilgamesh* is one of these early stories. Gilgamesh was a Sumerian king.

Cuneiform is one of the earliest systems of writing.

The Babylonian Empire

In 1792 B.C., Hammurabi decided to create an empire. He was the ruler of Babylon, a city-state in Sumer. He and his army set out to unite Mesopotamia under his rule. He succeeded in taking over much of central and southern Mesopotamia. Many other kings attempted to control parts of Mesopotamia before and after Hammurabi. He is remembered, however, because of his code of laws.

Hammurabi was the first ruler to **codify**, or bring together, a set of laws. He did not write the laws. He gathered them from the many parts of his empire. The 282 laws were then carved on stone pillars and placed throughout the Empire. By reading the laws, Hammurabi's subjects would know what was and was not lawful.

The laws set up a strict system of justice. Those who broke the law were punished. Often the punishment was severe. Punishments were worse for public officials and wealthy men than for peasants. The laws also

Hammurabi is remembered for arranging the first written set of laws, now known as Hammurabi's Code.

stop and think

Make up symbols to stand for the letters A, B, C, D, and E. Then use your symbols to write four simple English words. Show your symbols and words to a partner. Ask your partner to figure out the words using the symbols. Have your partner read the words aloud or write them in English.

regulated marriage and the family. Every marriage was governed by a marriage contract. Fathers had absolute rule over the family. Women had fewer rights than men.

Achievements of Mesopotamia

Many different people lived in Mesopotamia over the centuries. They made important discoveries. They also developed many important concepts, or ideas.

DISCOVERIES	CONCEPTS
• the arch • the dome • the wheel • bronze and copper for tools, weapons, and jewelry • iron for tools and weapons	• cuneiform writing (Sumerians) • alphabet (Phoenicians) • division of the circle into 360 degrees • geometry concepts for measurement • calendar • code of laws

The Persian Conquerors

The power of city-states rose and fell in Mesopotamia. First, one ruler would take control of other city-states and perhaps even large parts of Mesopotamia. He would die and the next king might be powerful enough to keep the Empire together. Then later kings would be weak and the Empire would fall apart. That is what happened to the Babylonian Empire after Hammurabi's death.

It took an outsider to create another large empire in Mesopotamia. Between 559 and 539 B.C., Cyrus the Great of Persia created a large empire in what is today southwestern Iran. In 539 B.C., he and his army invaded Mesopotamia. Within nine years, Cyrus added Mesopotamia to his Persian Empire. Cyrus was known as Cyrus the Great because of his just treatment of the people he conquered.

Several years after Cyrus, Darius took command of the Persian Empire. He ruled from 521 B.C. until 486 B.C. Darius enlarged the Empire so that it reached from Europe to

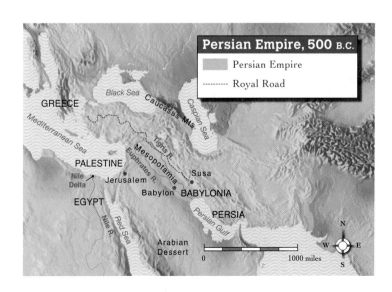

Persian Empire, 500 B.C.
- Persian Empire
- ------- Royal Road

India. Mesopotamia became a small part of the Persian Empire.

Darius made an important contribution to the development of ideas about government. He set up a centralized government to rule over his empire. He organized his empire into 20 provinces called satrapies. A governor, or satrap, ruled each one. A royal road linked the parts of the empire to Susa, the capital of the Persian Empire. The satraps reported to the emperor. Each one collected taxes and paid the royal army in his satrapy. The royal army protected the Empire from invaders. It also maintained the power of the emperor.

The Persian Empire was the first to use a uniform system of coins.

Putting It All Together

Create a concept map to help you remember the information in this lesson. Draw a large circle and label it "Mesopotamia." Label three smaller circles "Sumer," "Babylonian Empire," "Persian Empire." As you review the lesson, add information to your concept map.

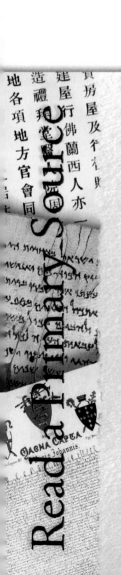

Read a Primary Source

The Code of Hammurabi

The following are some laws from the Code of Hammurabi. Subjects of the Babylonian Empire could find a law to govern just about everything they did.

1. If a man brings accusation against another man, charging him with murder, but cannot prove it, the accuser shall be put to death.

4. If he bear [false] witness concerning grain or money, he shall himself bear the penalty imposed in that case.

22. If a man practices robbery and is captured, that man shall be put to death.

195. If a son strikes his father, they shall cut off his hand.

233. If a builder builds house for a man and does not make its construction sound, and a wall cracks, that builder shall strengthen that wall at his own expense.

reading for understanding

What is another way to say "bear false witness"?

What is the punishment for Code 233?

Do you think the punishments are fair? Use the laws to support your opinion.

The Israelites and the Beginning of Judaism

Southwest Asia, 1200 B.C.–500 B.C.

Thinking on Your Own

Look at the pictures and read the captions. Do you know anything about any of the objects or events shown? If you do know something, write a sentence to tell what you know about each object and event. If they are all unfamiliar to you, list what you want to know more about.

The Jewish religion, or Judaism, began in Mesopotamia. It is one of the oldest of the world's religions. What we know about its beginnings comes from the Hebrew Bible, known as the **Torah**. Christians call it the Old Testament. Archaeologists have also helped us to learn more about the historical beginnings of Judaism.

focus your reading

What was the historical beginning of Judaism?

What are some basic beliefs of Judaism?

How were Jewish beliefs different from other early people's beliefs?

vocabulary

Torah   monotheistic

Yahweh   covenant

famine   prophets

The Israelites

Judaism began around 2000 B.C. with a leader named Abraham. He and his family moved from Mesopotamia into a region called Canaan. Later, this area was called Palestine. Hebrew writings state that **Yahweh**, the Hebrew word for God, promised this land to them. Since the third century B.C., the Jewish people have avoided saying *Yahweh*. Out of respect, they use the term *Lord* or *God*.

The Hebrews were nomadic herders. They raised sheep and goats. When a **famine** came, the Hebrews migrated to Egypt in search of land and water for their herds. In the 1300s B.C., the Egyptians enslaved the Hebrews. In the 1200s B.C., a Hebrew leader named Moses led them out of Egypt and back into Canaan. This journey is called the

The Torah is the Hebrew Bible.

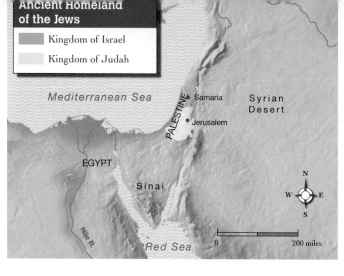

Ancient Homeland of the Jews

	Kingdom of Israel
	Kingdom of Judah

Mediterranean Sea

Samaria

Syrian Desert

PALESTINE

Jerusalem

EGYPT

Sinai

Nile R.

Red Sea

0   200 miles

Exodus. It is honored in the Jewish holy time of Passover.

Sometime between 1200 and 1000 B.C., David united the twelve Hebrew tribes into the Kingdom of Israel. His son Solomon built a temple to God in the city of Jerusalem. The temple became the center of the Israelite religion. Soon after Solomon's death, the kingdom split apart. By about 922 B.C., the two southern tribes had become the Kingdom of Judah. Jerusalem remained their capital. The ten tribes of the north kept the name of Israel. They set up their capital at Samaria.

In 722 B.C., invaders from Assyria, an empire in northern Mesopotamia, moved into the Kingdom of Israel. They forced out the Israelites. Over time, the Israelites married into other groups and were lost as a distinct people.

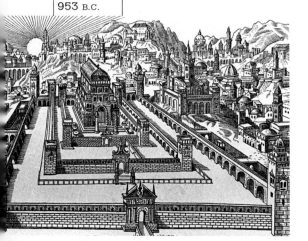

Solomon's temple in Jerusalem, Israel, was built in 953 B.C.

stop and think

The northern and southern tribes split because of differences over how Solomon ruled the kingdom. The northern tribes objected to high taxes and forced labor on building projects. With a partner write a letter to King Solomon. Ask him to stop his huge building projects and to lower taxes.

In 586 B.C., new invaders overran the Kingdom of Judah. They destroyed Jerusalem and the temple. These invaders took many Jews as captives to Babylonia in Mesopotamia. Some 50 years later, the Persians conquered Babylonia. It was Cyrus the Great who allowed the Jews to return to their homeland. They were able to rebuild Jerusalem and the temple.

Jewish Beliefs

There are certain beliefs that are central to Judaism.

1 Judaism is **monotheistic**. This means that Jews believe in one true God.

2 God and the Jews entered into a **covenant**, or agreement. Under the agreement, they would be protected if the Jews obeyed the Ten Commandments. This covenant gave the Jews their sense of being God's chosen people.

Over time, holy leaders known as **prophets** arose among the Israelites and later the Jews. The people believed that the prophets transmitted and interpreted God's teachings to them. These teachings included a strong sense of right and wrong, both for individuals and for the community. The idea of social justice—looking out for others—became a core value of Judaism. The rich and powerful had a duty to help the poor and needy.

The Ten Commandments

1. Thou shalt have no other gods before me.
2. Thou shalt not make unto thee any graven images.
3. Thou shalt not take the name of the Lord thy God in vain.
4. Remember the Sabbath day, to keep it holy.
5. Honor thy father and mother.
6. Thou shalt not kill.
7. Thou shalt not commit adultery.
8. Thou shalt not steal.
9. Thou shalt not bear false witness against thy neighbor.
10. Thou shalt not covet any thing that is thy neighbor's.

Differences with Other Early Religions

Judaism	Other Early Religions
Judaism was monotheistic.	Other early religions were polytheistic. They worshiped many male and female gods.
Judaism believed that the things of the natural world—sun, moon, stars, rain, thunder, trees, and so on—were examples of God's work. God was far greater than any of these things. The things of the natural world were not deities and were not to be worshiped.	Other early religions believed that the things of nature—sun, moon, stars, and so on—were deities. These religions worshiped the things of the natural world.
Jews remained faithful to their religion. Their belief in the one true God and their sense of being the chosen people separated them from their neighbors.	Other people put aside their own deities and worshiped those of their conquerors.

Putting It All Together

Create a T-chart. Label the left side "Event" and the right side "Importance." Choose four events in the history of the Israelites and Jews. List them on the left side of the chart. On the right side explain why each one was important.

Chapter Summary

- The earliest civilization began in Mesopotamia in Southwest Asia. It arose along the **fertile floodplain** in the river valleys of the Tigris and Euphrates Rivers.
- Sumer was in the southern part of Mesopotamia. It was made up of **city-states** ruled by kings.
- The top social class was the king-ruler. Then there were priests, soldiers, **scribes**, merchants, and craftworkers. Most people were peasants.
- The people worshiped many **deities**. They built temples shaped like pyramids to honor their deities. These temples were called **ziggurats**.
- A form of writing called **cuneiform** developed around 3000 B.C. in Mesopotamia.
- In 1790 B.C., Hammurabi created a single set of laws for the Empire. It was the first time laws were **codified**.
- Judaism began in Mesopotamia around 2000 B.C. When a **famine** struck, the Hebrews migrated into Egypt. In the 1300s B.C., they were enslaved by the Egyptians, but Moses led them out of Egypt and back to Canaan.
- The Hebrew Bible is known as the **Torah**.
- The Jews believed they had a **covenant** with **Yahweh**. It was part of their obedience to the Ten Commandments.
- Judaism was a **monotheistic** religion whereas other early religions were polytheistic.
- The Jews believed that **prophets** were sent by God to transmit and interpret his teachings.

Chapter Review

1 Imagine you are writing laws for Hammurabi's empire. Write laws that teenagers would have to obey. Write a paragraph to explain why you think the laws are important. Share and discuss your laws and your paragraph with a partner.

2 Write a bulleted list that compares and contrasts the people of Sumer or Babylonia with the Israelites. Then write a short paragraph including key concepts.

Skill Builder

Analyzing Timelines

Sequence is the order in which things happen. Knowing the sequence of events can help you understand the causes of events. Sequence can also tell you the effects of events. If you know when something happened in one place, you will be able to tell if it was before or after a similar event in another place. For example, writing developed in Mesopotamia around 3000 B.C. The Chinese developed their writing system about 2000 B.C. By knowing the dates, you can see that writing developed in Mesopotamia first.

A timeline is a quick way to see the sequence of events. A timeline arranges dates and events in chronological order. Chronological order is time order. The earliest dates are first.

The following timeline was created from the dates in the section titled "The Israelites."

Use the timeline to answer the following questions:

1 When did the Egyptians enslave the Hebrews?

2 How many years did the Kingdom of Judah exist after the Kingdom of Israel was destroyed?

3 Which happened first: Moses leading the Hebrews out of Egypt or the founding of the Kingdom of Israel?

4 Which of these events happened after the destruction of the Kingdom of Israel: the Hebrews were enslaved or the Jews were sent to Babylonia?

5 What is the time span of the events shown on the timeline?

Southwest Asia, 1200 B.C.–500 B.C.

2000 B.C. Beginning of Judaism

1300s B.C. Egyptians enslaved Hebrews

1200–1000 B.C. Hebrews united into Kingdom of Israel

722 B.C. Assyrians destroyed Kingdom of Israel

539–530 B.C. Cyrus the Great conquered much of Mesopotamia; Jews returned to homeland

2000 B.C. — 1500 B.C. — 1000 B.C. — 500 B.C.

1200s B.C. Moses led Hebrews out of Egypt

922 B.C. Southern tribes separated and formed Kingdom of Judah

586 B.C. Kingdom of Judah captured; Jews sent to Babylonia

THE FIRST CIVILIZATIONS

UNIT 2

The earliest civilizations developed in river valleys. The first civilization was Mesopotamia. It grew up around the Tigris and Euphrates Rivers. Other important river valley civilizations arose along the Nile River in North Africa, the Indus River in India, and the Huang He and Chang Jiang Rivers in China.

Geography was also important in the development of Roman and Greek civilizations. The city of Rome developed on seven hills near the banks of the Tiber River. However, the area of ancient Greece did not have any great rivers. The Greeks lived in mountainous areas and on islands. The sea helped to shape Greek civilization.

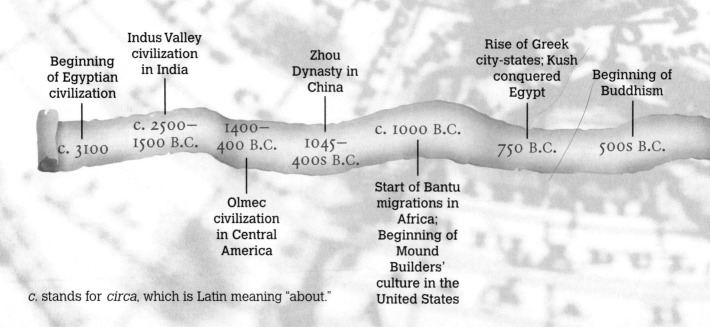

Beginning of Egyptian civilization
c. 3100

Indus Valley civilization in India
c. 2500–1500 B.C.

Olmec civilization in Central America
1400–400 B.C.

Zhou Dynasty in China
1045–400s B.C.

Start of Bantu migrations in Africa; Beginning of Mound Builders' culture in the United States
c. 1000 B.C.

Rise of Greek city-states; Kush conquered Egypt
750 B.C.

Beginning of Buddhism
500s B.C.

c. stands for *circa*, which is Latin meaning "about."

Why did the Greeks build city-states?

Why is Egyptian civilization called the "Gift of the Nile"?

How did the new ruling dynasties come to power in ancient China?

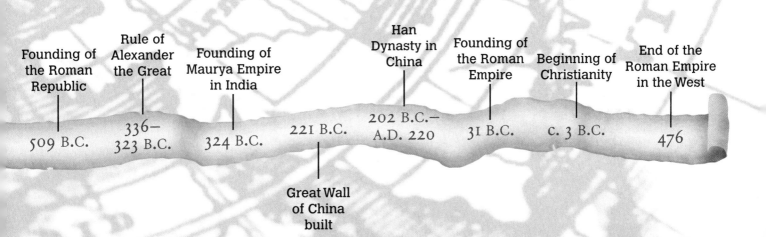

Founding of the Roman Republic
509 B.C.

Rule of Alexander the Great
336–323 B.C.

Founding of Maurya Empire in India
324 B.C.

Great Wall of China built
221 B.C.

Han Dynasty in China
202 B.C.—A.D. 220

Founding of the Roman Empire
31 B.C.

Beginning of Christianity
c. 3 B.C.

End of the Roman Empire in the West
476

Chapter

3 ANCIENT CIVILIZATIONS OF NORTH AFRICA

(2700 B.C.–500 B.C.)

Getting Focused

Skim this chapter to predict what you will be learning.
• Read the lesson titles and subheadings.
• Look at the illustrations and read the captions.
• Examine the maps.
• Review the vocabulary words and terms.

Imagine you are the ruler of an empire. What would you do as emperor? Would you go to war against your neighbors? Would you have laws written for your people? Would you use tax money to build more palaces for yourself? Make a list of five things you would do as emperor. Share your list with a partner. Discuss whether your decisions would be fair and just.

Pharaohs and Egypt

Thinking on Your Own

Make a three-column chart in your notebook. Label the first column, "What I Know About Ancient Egypt," the second column, "What I Want to Learn About Ancient Egypt," and the third column, "What I Learned About Ancient Egypt." Fill in columns one and two now, and column three as you read. Discuss what you learned with a partner.

The Egyptian civilization grew up along the banks of the Nile River. Ancient Egypt is sometimes called the "gift of the Nile." The Nile River Valley is located in the Sahara, a huge desert in North Africa. The climate is hot and dry. Without the waters of the Nile, the Egyptians could not have planted and harvested crops.

Like the Tigris and Euphrates Rivers, the Nile flooded each year. When the river flowed back within its banks, it left rich soil behind. The Egyptians planted their crops in this soil.

Like the ancient Mesopotamians, the Egyptians learned to build dikes to control the flooding of the Nile. They also learned to build dams and irrigation ditches to bring the river water to their fields.

focus your reading

What features did the Old, Middle, and New Kingdoms have in common?

Why were pyramids built?

What was daily life like in ancient Egypt?

vocabulary

dynasty   pyramids

pharaoh   scribes

mummified   hieroglyphics

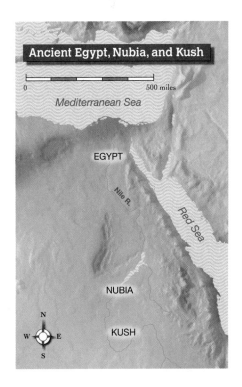

Ancient Egypt, Nubia, and Kush

0   500 miles

Mediterranean Sea

EGYPT

Nile R.

Red Sea

NUBIA

KUSH

N
W   E
S

Pharaohs

Around 3100 B.C., Menes united the peoples along the Nile into the Kingdom of Egypt. He began the first **dynasty**, or family of rulers. Over time the Egyptian ruler became known as

North Africa, 2700 B.C.–500 B.C.

the **pharaoh**. Pharaohs had absolute and unquestioning authority over their subjects. Egyptians believed that the pharaoh's power came from the sun god Ra. The pharaoh represented the god on Earth and was considered divine.

Historians divide ancient Egyptian history into three periods. See the time box on this page for the names and dates of these periods. These periods have the following features in common: (1) strong pharaohs, (2) peace with Egypt's neighbors, (3) large building projects, and (4) great cultural and scientific achievements.

Between these periods, Egypt suffered from weak pharaohs and invasions by stronger neighbors like the Hyksos. The region was in a state of chaos, and as a result, there were few intellectual achievements. There was also little money and time to build temples for the deities and palaces for the pharaohs.

Ramses II was pharaoh when Moses led the Hebrews out of Egypt.

> ⌛ **Time Box**
>
> 2700–2200 B.C.
> Old Kingdom
>
> 2050–1652 B.C.
> Middle Kingdom
>
> 1567–1085 B.C.
> New Kingdom

Biography

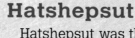

Hatshepsut

Hatshepsut was the daughter of Pharaoh Thutmose I. Egyptian royal families could marry only among themselves. As a result, she married her half-brother who in time succeeded their father. When Thutmose II died, Hatshepsut's stepson became Thutmose III. However, Hatshepsut seized power and had herself crowned pharaoh. She ruled for the next 30 years, from 1503–1482 B.C..

Statues show Hatshepsut both as a woman and as a figure with a beard. Like male pharaohs, she sometimes taped a long narrow beard to her chin. She was called "His Majesty."

During Hatshepsut's reign, Egypt expanded its power and wealth. She sent a trading expedition south along the Nile, possibly as far as present-day Somalia. She may even have commanded the trip. Hatshepsut had a huge temple built near the capital to house her tomb.

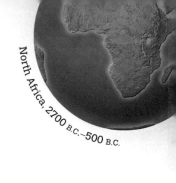

Egyptian Religion

Religion was a very important part of Egyptian life. Like most ancient people, the Egyptians were polytheistic. They worshiped deities in the natural world around them and in the sky above them. The sun gods and land gods became the chief deities of the Egyptians. Ra was the sun god. Osiris was the god of the Nile. He brought the annual flood. His wife Isis was also a deity. Together, they represented resurrection, or a new beginning.

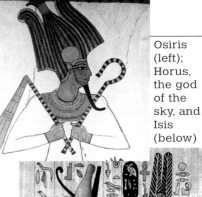

The Egyptians believed in life after death. They thought it was similar to life on Earth. As a result, the pharaohs had themselves buried with all the things they would need in the afterlife. Their tombs were filled with food, clothing, and jewels. Their servants and even their pets were killed and buried with them.

Osiris (left); Horus, the god of the sky, and Isis (below)

Because they would need their bodies in the afterlife, pharaohs were **mummified**. Mummification is a process that preserves, or saves, the body. The internal organs were removed and spices were placed in the body. Then the body was dried and wrapped in linen cloth. In the beginning, only pharaohs and nobles were allowed to be mummified. Later the custom spread to other Egyptians.

The Great Pyramid at Giza

The pharaohs were buried in tombs within large structures called **pyramids**. The Great Pyramid at Giza contains the tomb of King Khufu and was finished about 2540 B.C. It is made of over two million blocks of limestone. Each block weighs about two tons. The pyramid stands 481 feet high. Each side is 756 feet long. The whole structure covers 13 acres. That is about the size of 12 football fields. The pyramids are one of the greatest achievements of the Egyptians. They built these huge structures without any of the labor-saving equipment of today like cranes and other construction equipment.

Paint and goldwork adorned the coffinettes of many pharaohs, such as King Tutankhamen.

Egyptian Society and Daily Life

At the top of Egyptian society was the pharaoh and other members of the royal family. Next came the upper class of priests and nobles. The priests took care of the temples and celebrated religious ceremonies. The nobles oversaw the government. The ruling, or upper class, was small in number.

The middle class was slightly larger and made up of merchants, craftworkers, scribes, and tax collectors. The **scribes** kept records using **hieroglyphics**. This was the writing system that the ancient Egyptians developed.

stop and think

The lesson says that there was little money and time to build during certain periods in ancient Egyptian history. How would invasions and war affect what went on in Egypt? With a partner think about the effects of invasions and war. Write a paragraph to answer this question.

Hieroglyphics was an early form of Egyptian writing.

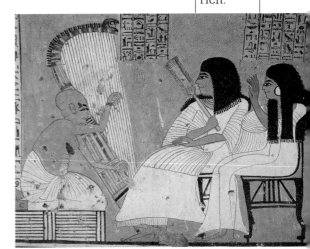

Egyptian life was culturally rich.

The largest class of people were peasant farmers. Land belonged to the pharaoh who gave some of it to the nobles and priests. The farmers worked the fields for the upper class. They also maintained the irrigation systems. Both men and women worked in the fields. The women were also responsible for taking care of the home and children. During nonfarming seasons, farmers worked on the pharaoh's building projects. Slaves were the lowest social class, below the peasants.

Achievements of the Ancient Egyptians

Some concepts, such as writing, did not develop in one region and spread to other world regions. Often, a concept developed independently in different parts of the ancient world.

INVENTIONS	CONCEPTS
• papyrus, a paper-like material • pyramid • mummification • medical advances such as surgery and the use of splints for broken bones • metal working in copper, bronze, and gold	• hieroglyphic writing • geometry concepts for measurement • calendar of 12 months, each containing 30 days with 5 days at the end

Putting It All Together

Women in ancient Egypt had many rights. However, they could not become scribes or work for the government. With a partner, discuss reasons why you think women were kept from these jobs. Write a paragraph to explain your ideas. Conclude by stating whether you think this was fair or unfair.

The Kingdom of Kush

Thinking on Your Own

Find the general location of ancient Kush and Nubia on a world map. Find the following areas: North Africa, West Africa, Southwest Asia (Arabian Peninsula), and South Asia (India). Create a T-chart to organize bulleted notes about each region.

The land of Kush lay to the south of Egypt. The area is today part of the nation of Sudan. The kingdoms of Egypt and Kush were connected for many centuries through trade and politics.

focus your reading

Why was Nubia important to Egypt?

Why was the location of Meroë ideal?

vocabulary

trade   trade routes

iron   export

Nubia

The area that became Kush was first called Nubia. Like the Egyptians, the people of Nubia and later Kush were mainly farmers. However, over time, some Nubians became wealthy through **trade**. As early as 2000 B.C., Nubian merchants were providing Egypt with such luxury items as ivory, ebony (a black wood), leopard skins, and slaves.

Farming was an important part of life along the Nile River.

During the New Kingdom, 1567–1085 B.C., Egypt conquered Nubia. Egypt wanted to control Nubia's rich trading network. By about 1000 B.C., Nubia fought for and won its independence from Egypt. It became known as the Kingdom of Kush.

The Expansion of Kush

In 750 B.C., King Piankhi of Kush succeeded in conquering Egypt. The Kingdom of Kush spread its power all the way to the Mediterranean Sea. A dynasty of Kushite pharaohs took over the Egyptian throne. The rule of the five Kushite pharaohs lasted for about 100 years.

The pyramids at Meroë held non-mummified remains of the Kush.

In 663 B.C., the Assyrians from Mesopotamia invaded Kush. They easily defeated the Kushites. The Assyrians had mastered **iron** working and were using iron weapons. Iron is a metal that is much stronger than bronze. The bronze and stone weapons of the Kushites were no match for the Assyrians' iron swords and spears. The Kushites had not yet learned how to make things from iron. The Kushites were pushed back into their own lands south along the Nile.

stop and think

The use of iron changed the ways of life for the Kush. With a partner, write a bulleted list of five reasons why iron was important.

Around 500 B.C., the Kushites built a new capital at Meroë. The location was ideal for two reasons. First, it was where two **trade routes** crisscrossed. One route went north and south along the Nile. The other route went east and west from the Red Sea across North Africa and into West Africa.

Over time these routes connected Kush with the Roman rulers of Egypt. The routes also connected Kush with the Arabian Peninsula in Southwest Asia and with India in South Asia. Merchants carrying gold, ivory, ebony, jewelry, slaves, and iron goods traveled along these routes.

Iron was the second reason that Meroë's location was ideal. Meroë was built near large deposits of iron ore. The Kushites had learned iron working from their enemies, the Assyrians. The Kushites then turned to making iron tools, weapons, and other iron goods for their own use and for **export**. *Export* means "to trade or sell goods to other nations."

The Kingdom of Kush ended around A.D. 350. It was invaded and conquered by the neighboring kingdom of Axum.

Iron tools and weapons were introduced by the Assyrians.

Putting It All Together

Make a timeline of important dates in this lesson. With a partner, figure out how many years passed between sets of dates.

Chapter Summary

- Early civilizations were built in river valleys.
- The Egyptians used irrigation ditches to water their crops.
- Egyptian rulers were called **pharaohs** and were part of **dynasties**.
- Egyptian history is divided into three kingdoms: the Old, Middle, and New.
- The three periods had the following features in common: (1) strong pharaohs, (2) peace, (3) large building projects, and (4) cultural and intellectual achievements.
- The Egyptians were polytheistic.
- Egyptian pharaohs were **mummified** and buried in **pyramids.**
- Egyptians developed **hieroglyphics**.
- The pharaoh and royal family were at the top of the social structure. Next came nobles and priests. Then were merchants, craftworkers, **scribes**, and tax collectors. Peasant farmers were the largest class. At the bottom were slaves.
- Conquering Nubia gave Egypt control of Nubia's **trade**.
- The Assyrians' **iron** weapons defeated the Kushites and drove them out of Egypt.
- Kush built its new capital, Meroë, on two **trade routes** and near iron deposits. Iron tools, weapons, and other iron goods became important **exports**.

Chapter Review

1 Go back to the world map you used for "Thinking on Your Own" in Lesson 2. Write sentences using directions to tell where Kush was in relation to (1) Egypt, (2) the Arabian Peninsula, and (3) India.

2 Using the same map, write sentences using directions to tell where Egypt was in relation to (1) Kush, (2) the Red Sea, and (3) Central Africa.

3 Create a timeline to combine important dates for ancient Egypt, Nubia, and Kush.

Skill Builder

Comparing and Contrasting Information Using a Table

To compare information is to look for similarities. To contrast information is to look for differences. Tables are very useful tools for comparing and contrasting information. By reading down the columns and across the rows, you can determine how things are the same or different.

To use a table for comparison and contrast, follow these steps:

- Read the title of the table to learn what it is about.
- Read across the first row to learn exactly what people, places, or events are being described in the table.
- Read down the first column to see what category, or type, of information is given for the people, places, or events.

Ancient Mesopotamian and Egyptian Civilizations

Category	Mesopotamians	Egyptians
Geographical location	• Southwest Asia	• North Africa
River valleys	• Tigris River Valley • Euphrates River Valley	• Nile River Valley
Political organization	• city-states ruled by kings	• empire ruled by pharaoh
Economy	• mainly farming • some trade	• mainly farming • some trade
Religion	• polytheistic • kings considered divine	• polytheistic • pharaohs considered deities
Social structures	• king and royal family • priests and nobles • merchants, craftworkers, scribes • peasant farmers • slaves	• pharaoh and royal family • priests and nobles • merchants, craftworkers, scribes, tax collectors • peasant farmers • slaves
Writing system	• cuneiform	• hieroglyphics

1 What is this table about?

2 List five things that the Egyptians and Mesopotamians had in common.

3 List five things that were different about the two civilizations.

Chapter 4

THE INDIAN SUBCONTINENT

(2500 B.C–A.D. 500)

Getting Focused

Skim this chapter to predict what you will be learning.
• Read the lesson titles and subheadings.
• Look at the illustrations and read the captions.
• Examine the maps.
• Review the vocabulary words and terms.

Studying world history takes the reader all over the world. To help you remember where you have been and where you are going, use an outline map of the world. Start a map key. To indicate different regions, use shading or a design. Choose two ways to show regions and mark the two world regions you have studied so far: Mesopotamia, Egypt, and Kush. Label the two boxes in your map legend.

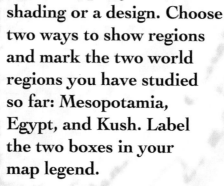

LESSON 1

Civilizations Along the Indus and Ganges Rivers

Thinking on Your Own

Create a concept web. In the center write "Indian Subcontinent." As you read this lesson, add information to your web. Include all the factors that influenced life on the Indian subcontinent.

The large Indian **subcontinent** is part of the larger continent of Asia. It is called a subcontinent because it extends out from the continent. Today, India, Pakistan, and Bangladesh are the major nations of the Indian subcontinent. To better understand the history of the region, it is important to know something of its geography.

focus your reading

How did monsoons affect people on the Indian subcontinent?

What were Harappa and Mohenjo-Daro like?

How did Aryans affect Indian society?

vocabulary

subcontinent   monsoons

plains   Brahman

plateau   castes

Geography of the Indian Subcontinent

The Indian subcontinent is shaped like a huge triangle. The base of the triangle lies in the north along the Himalaya Mountains. These are the tallest mountains in the world. Below the mountains lie **plains**, or flat land. The plains are watered by the Indus River to the west and the Ganges River to the east.

South of the plains is the Deccan **Plateau**, an area of high, mostly flat land. The sides of the triangle face the Arabian Sea on the west and the Bay of Bengal on the east. To the south is the Indian Ocean. The climate is hot and dry in winter and

warm and wet in summer. The change in climate is caused by **monsoons**. These are seasonal winds that blow across the Indian Ocean. The winter monsoons begin in October. The summer monsoons begin in late May or early June.

Monsoons have played an important role in the history of the subcontinent, and they still affect people living there today. The farmers of the subcontinent have always depended on the monsoons to bring rain to grow their crops. The monsoons are both life-giving and life-threatening. Without the rain, crops wither and die. With too much rain, the rivers flood. Thousands of people die and crops are destroyed in the swirling flood waters.

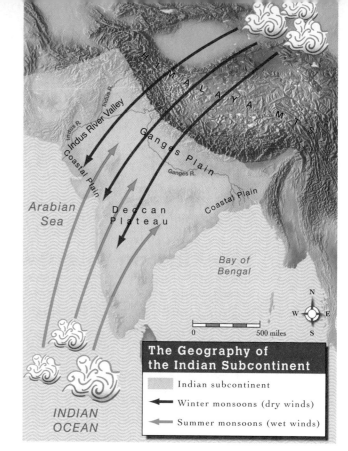

The Geography of the Indian Subcontinent

- Indian subcontinent
- ← Winter monsoons (dry winds)
- ← Summer monsoons (wet winds)

The summer monsoon floods still impact life in India.

The First Civilization

The earliest civilization on the subcontinent began in the Indus River Valley. Archaeologists have found more than one thousand sites there. They date the civilization around 2500 B.C. to 1500 B.C. Much of what is known is based on two cities, Harappa and Mohenjo-Daro. More is still to be discovered as archaeologists continue to study other settlements.

Harappa and Mohenjo-Daro are 400 miles apart and may have been twin capitals. The two cities were carefully planned and very similar. Both were laid out on a grid pattern. Wide streets ran north and south and smaller streets ran east and west.

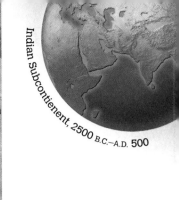

Mohenjo-Daro was located in the Indus River Valley in what is today Pakistan.

Private homes and public buildings were made of mud bricks. Some houses were three stories tall. All houses had a center courtyard. Rooms were built around the courtyard and opened onto it. Houses had running water and indoor plumbing that drained into a citywide sewage system.

A combined temple, palace, and fort stood over each city on a nearby hill. Both cities had villages and fields scattered around them. Farmers lived in the villages and worked the fields. Each city had large warehouses where the crops were stored.

The economies of Harappa and Mohenjo-Daro were based on farming. Like the Tigris, Euphrates, and Nile Rivers, the Indus flooded each year. Farmers used the rich soil left behind to grow crops such as wheat and barley. The farmers of the Indus Valley were the first to grow cotton. Spinners turned the cotton boll, or seed pod, into thread. Weavers wove the thread into fine cloth.

A carving found at Mohenjo-Daro

Cotton cloth became one of the trade goods of Indus merchants. Other trade goods included grain, copper, and pearls. A trading network developed between the Indus Valley and the city-states of Sumer. Merchants sent trading ships along the coast of the Arabian Sea to the Persian gulf. The ships then sailed north through the Gulf as far as Sumer.

Evidence tells archaeologists that Harappa and Mohenjo-Daro had some form of central government. A strong,

organized government was needed to plan and lay out the cities. The government was probably headed by a king or priest-king. No one has been able to decipher the written language of the Indus Valley people. All we know about life in these cities comes from archaeological records.

The people of the Indus Valley were polytheistic—meaning they worshiped many gods. A major deity was a god of creation. They also worshiped animals.

stop and think

Look back at the table on page 39 of Chapter 3. Draw a fourth column in your notebook. Label the new column "Indus Valley People" and add information from this lesson. Work with a partner to complete this column.

The Impact of Aryan Invaders

Around 1500 B.C., Aryans from Central Asia invaded and conquered the Indus Valley. They were nomadic warriors. Over time they moved eastward into the plain around the Ganges River and then south into the Deccan Plateau.

Most of what is known about the Aryans comes from the *Vedas*. The *Vedas* are a collection of books containing prayers, songs, and other writings of the Aryans. The Aryans brought with them their own language, religious beliefs, and social system. They spoke an Indo-European language known as Sanskrit. English, German, Persian, Spanish, and French are some of the languages that are based on the Indo-European language.

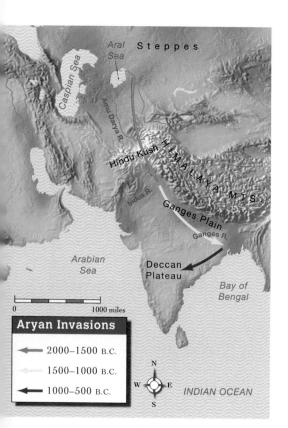

Aryan Invasions

⬅ 2000–1500 B.C.

⬅ 1500–1000 B.C.

⬅ 1000–500 B.C.

Like other ancient people, the Aryans were polytheistic. Their chief deity was Indra, the god of war. Other deities represented the natural world such as the sky, air, and water. Priests called brahmans offered sacrifices to the deities. Over time, the people began to worship a single force or power in the world known as **Brahman**.

The Aryans developed a social system that has had a lasting impact on Indian culture.

Mahabharata, an Indian epic, details basic Indian culture.

They divided the population into four major categories, or **castes**. These four castes were further divided into thousands of subcastes. The castes determined a person's occupation and social class. Those not included in the caste system were called Untouchables.

Over time, Aryan culture and its caste system expanded across much of the Indian subcontinent. Aryan kingdoms grew up in several areas, especially on the vast plain around the Ganges River. These became important centers of farming and trade.

Five Major Categories of Aryan Society

Caste	Characteristics	Work
Brahman	• priests • highest caste and smallest in number	• oversaw religious ceremonies
Kshatriya	• warriors	• defended kingdom
Vaisya	• commoners, or ordinary people	• mostly farmers or merchants
Sudra	• largest group of people • non-Aryans	• earned a living by doing farm work and other manual labor
Untouchable	• outside the caste system • about 5 percent of the people	• did jobs no one else would do, such as garbage collecting • lived separate from others

Putting It All Together

Imagine you are a member of the Sudra caste or an Untouchable. The only reason you are not a member of a higher caste is that you are not an Aryan. The Aryans conquered your people. How would you feel (a) about your life and (b) about the Aryans? Discuss the questions with a partner. Write a bulleted list of notes as you talk. Use your notes to write a paragraph that answers the questions.

LESSON 2

The Beginning of Hinduism

Thinking on Your Own

Skim the lesson by reading the subheadings, captions, and vocabulary words. Write five questions that you have about this lesson. Share your questions with a partner. As you read, answer all of the questions.

Hinduism is one of the two major world religions that began on the Indian subcontinent. The other religion is Buddhism.

Hinduism developed from a blending of Aryan religious beliefs with those of other people who lived on the subcontinent. Unlike Judaism or Buddhism, no one person founded Hinduism. The teachings, prayers, hymns, and ceremonies of Hinduism developed over centuries. In time, they were collected in four long *Vedas* and three other works.

focus your reading

How did Hinduism develop?

What are the basic beliefs of Hinduism?

vocabulary

Hinduism	karma
atman	dharma
reincarnation	mobility

The Ganges River is sacred to people of the Hindu faith.

Basic Beliefs of Hinduism

Hinduism is a very complex religion with many deities and different rituals and practices. However, Hindus share certain beliefs.

1 Brahman is the supreme and eternal spirit, or force, of the universe.

Because this is a difficult idea to understand, Hinduism has a large number of lesser deities. People find it easier to worship deities that are shown as humans or animals. Hindus believe that these deities are all forms of Brahman.

2 The goal of every soul is to become part of Brahman.

Brahma

Shiva

The Hindu word for soul is **atman**. The goal of every atman is to unite with Brahman after death. Before it can achieve this, the soul must free itself from earthly desire, such as wanting to be wealthy or popular. It may take many lives to complete this journey. This cycle of birth and death is called **reincarnation**.

3 **Karma** determines a soul's next life.

Karma is the sum of a person's actions in life. These actions determine whether a soul is reborn into a higher or lower life or whether it has to be reborn at all. The answer depends on how close the soul comes to freeing itself from earthly desire. For example, a commoner who has worked hard at being good could be born into the warrior caste.

Vishnu

4 Karma is determined by following **dharma**.

Dharma refers both to divine law and to a person's obedience toward divine law. Dharma sets up certain moral and religious duties for every person. These duties depend on one's caste, job, gender, and age. A person is supposed to behave according to his or her dharma. How well a person performs these duties helps in his or her journey toward union with Brahman. If a person behaves according to one's dharma, then he or she will move toward union with Brahman. Disobey one's dharma and move backward on the cycle of reincarnation.

Hinduism has social as well as religious importance. Hinduism links union with Brahman to behavior on Earth. For centuries, this link encouraged people to stay within their castes, behave better, and work hard. Social **mobility** is the ability to move from social class to social class and better one's life. Hinduism made this difficult, if not impossible. It supported keeping things the way they were. The ruling caste and the wealthy did not have to worry about being pushed out by people working their way up. The promise of reincarnation gave hope to the poor. Their lives could be better the next time.

> ## The Hindu Trinity
>
> Brahma, Vishnu, and Shiva make up the Hindu trinity, or Trimurti. These are not separate gods, but three faces of the same god.
>
> **Brahma:** the creator, who breathes out the universe to make it come into existence.
>
> **Vishnu:** the preserver or caretaker of the universe, who must balance everything that exists, and whose constant action–karma– keeps everything running.
>
> **Shiva:** the destroyer: god of opposites–light and darkness, good and evil, creation and destruction, rest and activity, mild and terrible, male and female.

Putting It All Together

The last paragraph says that Hinduism "supported keeping things the way they were." What two basic beliefs of Hinduism were most important in supporting the caste system? Talk this question over with a partner. Write your answer in a sentence in your notebook.

LESSON 3

The Beginning of Buddhism

Thinking on Your Own

Look through the lesson for vocabulary words in bold type. In your notebook, write the words you do not know. Read the definitions in the text and in the Glossary. Write a sentence for each word. Be sure you use the word in context and spell it correctly.

Unlike Hinduism, **Buddhism** was founded by a person. It began in the 500s B.C. by Siddhartha Gautama. Much of what we know about him comes from **tradition**, or stories passed from one generation to the next. According to tradition, Siddhartha was born around 563 B.C. His father was the **rajah**, or ruler, of a small kingdom in what is today Nepal.

Siddhartha lived the life of a prince until he was about twenty-nine years old.

focus your reading

What was Siddhartha searching for?

What are the four basic principles of Buddhism?

Why is Asoka one of India's greatest rulers?

Why is the Gupta period in Indian history important?

vocabulary

Buddhism	nirvana
tradition	dynasty
rajah	missionaries
meditation	

Buddha sitting under a banyan tree meditating

One day while out riding, he came upon a sick person, then an old person, and finally a dead body. He wanted to know why people like this suffered and died. Siddharta gave up his life as a prince to search for the answer to his question.

Indian Subcontinent, 2500 B.C.–A.D. 500

He spent six years wandering India. At some point in his journey he took up **meditation**. Meditation is intense thinking about spiritual things. One day while sitting under a tree and meditating, he was enlightened to his question. He learned the answer. In time, his followers called him Buddha, meaning the "Enlightened One."

Buddha takes many forms around the world.

The Four Noble Truths and the Eightfold Path

Buddha lived to be about eighty years old. He spent his life teaching the answer he had learned. His words became the basis for Buddhism. Its basic principles can be summed up in the Four Noble Truths and the Eightfold Path.

The Four Noble Truths

1 Life is filled with suffering, pain, and sorrow.

2 Suffering is caused by our desires.

3 The only way to end suffering is to conquer desire.

4 The way to conquer desire is to follow the Middle Path.

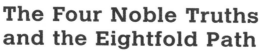

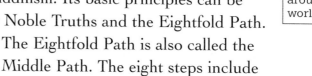

The Eightfold Path is also called the Middle Path. The eight steps include having the

(1) right belief: A person must know the Four Noble Truths.

(2) right intention: A person must commit to living by the Four Noble Truths.

(3) right speech: A person must always speak the truth and must not gossip or use bad language.

(4) right behavior: A person must not kill, steal, or do anything that is not moral and right.

(5) right occupation: A person must quit a job that is not good for him or her and find one that will help the person live according to Buddhism.

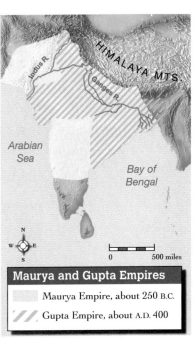

(6) right effort: A person must develop good attitudes and behaviors and keep bad ones from developing.

(7) right mindfulness: A person must be constantly aware of the senses in order to control the body.

(8) right concentration: A person may receive enlightenment by meditating.

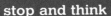

stop and think

Use a Venn diagram to compare and contrast Hinduism and Buddhism. Work with a partner to make sure that you include all the information from Lessons 2 and 3.

Buddha accepted the Hindu ideas of karma and dharma. However, he rejected the many deities of Hinduism. Like Hindus, Buddha believed in reincarnation. The goal of Buddhists is to reach union with the universe. However, Buddha did not accept the caste system. He taught that a person could achieve **nirvana** without having to move upward through the caste system in each new life. Nirvana was Buddha's name for release from the cycle of reincarnation. Over time, Buddhism spread throughout Asia as far as Korea and Japan. Hinduism remained an Indian religion.

Buddhism and the Maurya Empire

A major reason that Buddhism spread so far was Asoka. He was the grandson of Chandragupta Maurya. In 324 B.C., Chandragupta founded the first **dynasty**—or ruling family—to unite much of the Indian subcontinent. He began his conquest in the Ganges Valley.

Asoka continued his grandfather's struggle against the other rulers of India. However, after one very bloody battle, Asoka gave up fighting. He converted to Buddhism and committed himself to living by the Four Noble Truths. He used these principles to rule his empire. Among other actions, he improved medical care by setting up hospitals. To aid travelers, he built roads and rest houses along the roads. He had his laws carved on stone pillars so everyone could see them. His laws followed Buddhist teachings. Asoka also sent **missionaries** throughout

Maurya and Gupta Empires

Maurya Empire, about 250 B.C.

Gupta Empire, about A.D. 400

Asoka had rules carved on pillars.

India and to other places to preach Buddhist teachings. Missionaries go out to preach to and convert people to their religion.

Missionaries often went along on trading expeditions. The Maurya Empire was part of a large trade network that reached from the Pacific Ocean to Southwest Asia and the Mediterranean. The Empire grew wealthy under Asoka and later rulers. Asoka is considered one of India's greatest rulers.

The Golden Age of the Gupta

The Maurya Empire lasted only 50 years after Asoka died. The period between 186 B.C. and A.D. 320 was marked by invasions and warfare. Nomads from Central Asia overran parts of the subcontinent. Rival Indian kingdoms fought for power. In the year 320, a new Indian dynasty, the Gupta, rose to power in northern India. It lasted until the end of the 400s.

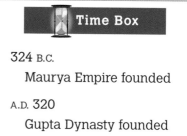

Time Box

324 B.C.
　Maurya Empire founded

A.D. 320
　Gupta Dynasty founded

Unlike the Maurya, the Gupta were Hindus, not Buddhists. Like Asoka, the Gupta rulers encouraged trade. Their trade network spread to include China and Southeast Asia as well as the Mediterranean. Their rule is known as the "Golden Age of the Gupta." The name honors the important contributions made during this time. The Arabic number system was

Murals at the Caves of Ajanta show life during the Gupta period.

developed. When Arab scholars adopted the system in the A.D. 800s, its use spread to Europe. Discoveries in one world region often spread to other places.

Achievements of Maurya and Gupta Empires

- smallpox vaccination
- medical advances such as surgery and setting of broken bones
- Stupa, a large dome-shaped shrine
- Arabic number system

- idea of zero (0)
- decimal system
- mapped the stars and planets
- discovered that Earth was a sphere, rotated on its axis, revolved around the sun

Putting It All Together

To review this lesson, write five questions and answers using important information from this lesson. Read an answer to your partner. He or she has to give you the question. Take turns giving answers and questions.

From the *Arthashastra*

The *Arthashastra* was written during the rule of Chandragupta who founded the Maurya dynasty around 300 B.C. The *Arthashastra* is considered a major work of political policy. The following explains the duties of a ruler.

"[The ruler] should facilitate mining operations. He should encourage manufacturers. He should help exploitation of forest wealth. . . . He should construct highways both on land and on water. He should plan markets. He should build dikes for water. . . .

"The ruler should maintain adolescents, the aged, the diseased, and the orphans. He should also provide livelihood to deserted women . . . and protection for children born to them . . . .

"He should protect cultivation from heavy taxes, slave labor and severe penalties, herds of cattle from cattle lifters, wild animals, . . . and diseases. . . .

"He should not only conserve existing forests, buildings, and mines, but also develop new ones."

reading for understanding

Which of the duties listed relate to businesses?

Which of the duties listed relate to making people's lives better?

Are any of the duties similar to things that government does in the United States? If yes, list them.

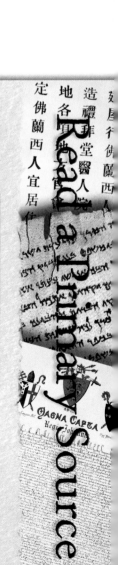

Read a Primary Source

Chapter Summary

- The Indian **subcontinent** is part of the continent of Asia. Its northern **plains** are home to the Indus and Ganges River Valleys. The Deccan **Plateau** is in the south.
- **Monsoons** greatly affect the climate of the subcontinent.
- The earliest civilization was in the Indus River Valley. Two important sites were Harappa and Mohenjo-Daro.
- Aryans from Central Asia invaded the subcontinent around 1500 B.C. They brought with them the Sanskrit language, their belief in Brahma, and the **caste** system. Their priests were called **Brahmans**.
- **Hinduism** and **Buddhism** are two world religions that began on the Indian subcontinent.
- Hindus believe that the goal for the **atman**, or soul, is union with Brahman. **Karma** and **dharma** guide Hindus on this journey toward **reincarnation**.
- Hinduism reinforced the caste system and limited social **mobility**.
- Much of what we know about Siddhartha Gautama, the Buddha, comes from **tradition**. He was the son of a **rajah** and gave up his life as a prince to find the answer for human suffering. He found his answer through **meditation**.
- The basic principles of Buddhism are found in the Four Noble Truths and the Eightfold Path.
- Buddhists believe in reincarnation and union with the universe in **nirvana**.
- Asoka of the Maurya **dynasty** converted to Buddhism. He sent **missionaries** to preach and convert people.

Chapter Review

1 Choose five people, ideas, or events from this chapter. Write a two-line headline for each one.

2 Add the geographic features of the Indian subcontinent to the world map that you began at the beginning of the chapter. Be sure to add to the map's key.

Skill Builder

Outlining Information

An outline is like the skeleton of a piece of writing. It lists the basic information in the piece. Making an outline is a good way to organize information when you study. To make an outline, look for the main idea—the most important information—in a section. Then look for the details that support it.

An outline has a standard format of levels, letters, and numerals. Each level is indented.

I. Main ideas are listed with Roman numerals.
   A. The most important details are listed with capital letters.
      1. Less important details are listed with Arabic numerals.

An outline for part of Lesson 1 looks like this:

I. Civilizations along the Indus and Ganges Rivers
   A. Geography of the Indian subcontinent
      1. Deccan Plateau—high, flat land
      2. Monsoons—winter and summer
   B. The first civilization
      1. Mohenjo-Daro developed around 2500 B.C.
      2. Economy based on farming
   C. The impact of Aryan invaders

This outline makes it easy to answer the question, "What influenced the development of civilizations along the Indus and Ganges Rivers?"

Complete the following outlining activities.

1   Outline "Basic Beliefs of Hinduism," pages 47–48.

2   Outline Lesson 3. Use each subheading in the lesson as a main idea. Your outline will have Roman numerals I through III for main ideas. The number of other lines in your outline will depend on how many supporting details you list.

Chapter 5

EARLY CHINESE CIVILIZATIONS

(1750 B.C.— A.D. 200)

Getting Focused

Skim this chapter to predict what you will be learning.
• Read the lesson titles and subheadings.
• Look at the illustrations and read the captions.
• Examine the maps.
• Review the vocabulary words and terms.

What do you know about China and the Chinese people? Make a list of things you know. Then look through this chapter at the illustrations and headings. What questions do they raise in your mind about Chinese civilizations? Write at least three questions about early China that you want answered by the end of the chapter. Be sure to add China to the world map you began in Chapter 4.

The First Chinese Civilizations

Thinking on Your Own

Read the Focus Your Reading questions and the vocabulary words. Write the vocabulary words in your notebook. Discuss the possible meanings with a partner. As you read, write the meanings next to the words. Then use each word in a sentence that shows the word's meaning.

Like early civilizations in Mesopotamia, Egypt, and the Indian subcontinent, the first civilization in China began in a river valley. The Huang He Valley is in eastern China. It was here that farming began in China. Like the Tigris, Euphrates, Nile, and Indus Rivers, the Huang He River flooded. When the river returned to its banks, it left rich soil behind.

Like other people, the Chinese had to learn to build dikes to control the river. They also learned to dig irrigation systems to water their fields. Every few years, the floods of the Huang He were very destructive. There was so much water that the dikes could not hold back the river. The river roared out of the dikes and over the land. Thousands of people and farm animals drowned. Houses, tools, and crops were destroyed. The Chinese began to call the Huang He the "river of sorrows."

focus your reading

How is early Chinese civilization similar to early civilizations in other world regions?

Why are the Xia and Shang Dynasties important?

What was the Mandate of Heaven?

What was the traditional Chinese family like?

vocabulary

ancestor worship

mandate

dynastic cycle

filial piety

extended family

The First Dynasties: Xia and Shang

The earliest Chinese dynasty was the Xia (SYAH), which began around 2200 B.C. It was a prehistoric civilization, as there is no written record. What is known about the Xia comes from the work of archaeologists. The Xia built their civilization in the Huang He region. The economy was based on farming.

However, at least some of the people lived in cities. The Xia knew how to make bronze tools. Archeologists have also found pottery and large tombs.

Legend says that Tang, the leader of the Shang (SHAHNG) people, overthrew the last Xia ruler. Tang established the Shang Dynasty around 1750 B.C. Like the Xia, the Shang were farmers. But many people lived in large, walled cities. Like the Xia, the Shang knew how to make bronze.

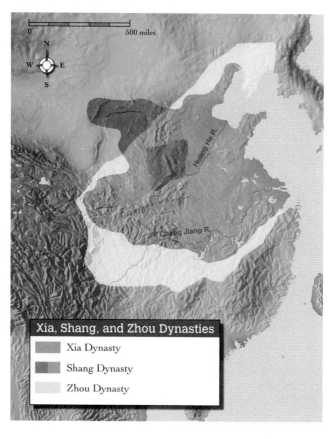

Xia, Shang, and Zhou Dynasties

- Xia Dynasty
- Shang Dynasty
- Zhou Dynasty

The Shang left their impact on future generations of Chinese in two important ways. It was the Shang who developed a writing system for the Chinese language. The Shang also began what is called **ancestor worship**. Ancestors are members of a family who have lived and died. Like other early people, the Shang believed in life after death. They buried the dead with things that the person might need in the afterlife. The Shang also believed that the dead could either help the living or bring them bad luck. As a result, the living

This bronze elephant represented the trustworthy and peaceful Shang government.

Time Box

C. 2200–1750 B.C.
Xia Dynasty

C. 1750–1122 B.C.
Shang Dynasty

1045–256 B.C.
Zhou Dynasty

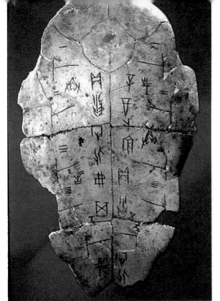

Oracle script, shown here on a tortoise shell, is the oldest writing in China.

began to offer sacrifices to their ancestors. This form of religious worship continued for thousands of years.

The Zhou Dynasty and the Mandate of Heaven

The Zhou (JOH) people rebelled against the Shang in 1045 B.C. The Zhou set up their own dynasty and ruled in central China.

To explain why they overthrew the Shang, the Zhou developed the principle of the **Mandate** of Heaven. A mandate is a command. The Zhou said that the deities in heaven ordered the Zhou to replace the Shang ruler. The Zhou used this principle to justify, or support, their overthrow of the Shang. According to the Mandate of Heaven, the king—and all later emperors—ruled by divine right. Their power came from the gods.

In time, the Chinese expanded the theory. Rulers did not always act in the best interests of the people. Then the Mandate of Heaven gave the people the right to rebel against their ruler. The result was the development of the **dynastic cycle**. This is the rise, rule, and then fall of a dynasty over a number of years. Over time, the Mandate of Heaven became the basis for the way the Chinese changed their rulers.

stop and think

The Chinese language uses characters or groups of characters to make words. With a partner, think of six words that you could make by drawing pictures. Three of the words should be persons, places, or things. Three should be ideas. Draw your characters and under each one write its meaning in English.

Chinese Writing

Written Chinese first developed during the Shang Dynasty. English is based on a 26-letter alphabet. To read English, a person has to learn those 26 letters and their 43 phonetic sounds. Chinese is based on characters, not letters. Each character stands for a picture of something or an idea. There are thousands of characters in Chinese. An elementary school student knows at least 1,500 characters.

Translation: Studying old history helps in the learning of new ideas.

Chinese Civilizations, 1750 B.C.–A.D. 200

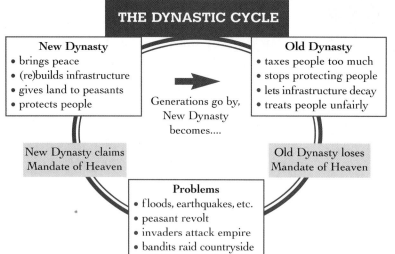

THE DYNASTIC CYCLE

New Dynasty
- brings peace
- (re)builds infrastructure
- gives land to peasants
- protects people

Generations go by, New Dynasty becomes....

Old Dynasty
- taxes people too much
- stops protecting people
- lets infrastructure decay
- treats people unfairly

New Dynasty claims Mandate of Heaven

Old Dynasty loses Mandate of Heaven

Problems
- floods, earthquakes, etc.
- peasant revolt
- invaders attack empire
- bandits raid countryside

The Importance of the Family in China

The family was the basic unit of Chinese society and the most important. Each member of a family had a duty and responsibility to every other member. This duty was known as **filial piety**. It governed the relationships among family members. Sons and daughters were to obey their parents. Parents were to obey their parents.

All family members were to obey the oldest male of the family. He was the head of the **extended family**. An extended family contains all the related members of a family — grandparents, parents, children, aunts, uncles, and cousins. The oldest male member of an extended Chinese family might have been a great-great-grandfather.

Filial piety governed life in the extended family.

Putting It All Together

The extended family was an important part of Chinese life. Discuss the importance of the extended family with a partner. Then write a paragraph to compare and contrast the extended family in ancient China to your modern family.

Chinese Philosophies

Thinking on Your Own

To help you study this lesson, create a three-column chart. Label the columns "Confucianism," "Daoism," and "Legalism." As you read, take bulleted notes about each of these Chinese philosophies.

By A.D. 100, Buddhism had spread to China. Over the next 300 years, many Chinese adopted Buddhism. Buddhism in turn adopted teachings of the Chinese. One of the features that it adopted was filial piety. By then, filial piety had become an important part of a Chinese philosophy known as **Confucianism**.

Philosophy is the search for knowledge about the world. It studies the natural world, human behavior, and thought. Philosophy is not the same as **religion**. Religion is the belief in and worship of a divine or superhuman power. Judaism, Hinduism, and Buddhism are religions. Confucianism was a philosophy.

focus your reading

What are the Five Constant Relationships?

What was the lasting effect of Confucianism?

How is Daoism different from Legalism?

vocabulary

Confucianism	civil service
philosophy	Daoism
religion	Legalism

The Teachings of Confucius

Confucianism was based on the teachings of Confucius. He was a wandering scholar who lived from 551 to 479 B.C. Confucius tried to interest the rulers of local Chinese states in his ideas. He never succeeded with the rulers. But his ideas impressed other Chinese.

Confucius and some of his followers

A group of students began to gather around him. They collected his teachings and began to teach others.

Confucius was not interested in studying spiritual or religious questions. He wanted to bring harmony—peace and order—to this world. Filial piety played an important role in his plan for maintaining harmony. Confucius taught that duty to the family and the community was more important than a person's own needs and wants. Confucius illustrated his idea of duty with the Five Constant Relationships:

- parent and child
- husband and wife
- older brother or sister and younger brother or sister
- friend and friend
- ruler and subject

stop and think

Choose one of the five relationships that Confucius listed. Do you think Confucius was right about how to create a good relationship between these two people? Talk over your ideas with a partner. Then write two or three paragraphs to explain why you agree or disagree.

Achievements of the Ancient Chinese

- how to make paper—around A.D. 100. This knowledge spread to India in the 700s. It then spread to Europe in the 1100s.
- how to grow silk worms and weave silk cloth
- iron blades for plows to break up hard-packed dirt
- wheelbarrow
- compass—a device to find direction
- new ways to rig sails on ships so ships could sail against the wind
- rudder—a device to steer ships
- acupuncture—a way to treat disease using needles

Except for friendship, each relationship involved one person with authority over the other. However, friendship was between equals unless there was an age difference. Then, the older person was considered superior to the younger person. In the other relationships, the older person or person of higher rank was superior. Men were always on a higher level than women.

Confucius taught that the higher ranking person had a loving responsibility to care for the lesser person. The lesser person, in turn, had a duty to give loving obedience to the higher person. If everyone lived by his or her duty, then harmony would rule the family and the community.

Influence of Confucianism

Confucius thought the ruler of China was like the head of a family. All Chinese owed the ruler loving obedience. In turn, the ruler was responsible to heaven for the well-being of his subjects. The ruler must provide peace and order so the people might become wealthy.

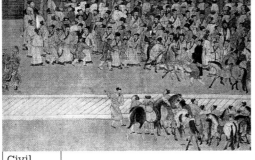

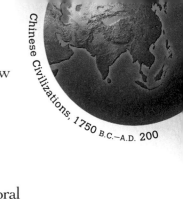

If the ruler failed, heaven would allow his subjects to overthrow him.

The ruler had to be of good moral character and be an example to his subjects. This was also true of the officials who ran the government under the ruler. Confucius believed that public officials had to be moral and well-educated. Their only goal was the well-being of the people.

Civil servants had to pass an exam during the Han Dynasty.

In time, Confucianist ideals came to control China's government. During the Han Dynasty, the rulers set up a school to train men who wanted to do government jobs. They had to pass a test known as a **civil service** examination. Civil servants work for the government. This system was the way public officials were chosen in China for 2,000 years.

Daoism and Legalism

Between 500 and 200 B.C., two other important philosophies developed in China. One was **Daoism** and the other was **Legalism**.

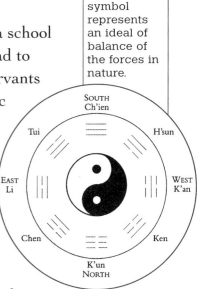

The Yin Yang symbol represents an ideal of balance of the forces in nature.

The name Daoism comes from the word *dao* meaning "the way." Daoism is based on the teachings of Laozi (LOW•DZUH). He probably lived at the same time as Confucius. Laozi taught that the way to happiness was to live in harmony with nature. One could not control it nor describe it. A person simply had to "be" in nature. In terms of government, a good ruler was one who did little.

Laozi

Legalism was very different from both Confucianism and Daoism. It began with the teachings of Hanfeizi (HAHN•FAY•DZEE) who lived in the 200s B.C. Legalists believed that people were naturally bad. A strong ruler, a long list of laws, and harsh punishments were necessary. This was the only way to bring order to society.

Putting It All Together

Do you agree or disagree with the Legalists' viewpoint about people and government? To answer the question, talk with a partner. Then write a paragraph explaining your ideas about Legalism.

The Rise and Fall of Dynasties

Thinking on Your Own

Create a Venn diagram to help you remember the differences and similarities between the Qin and Han Dynasties. Label the part where the two circles overlap "Similarities." Label the left circle "Qin." Label the right circle "Han." As you study the lesson, complete the diagram.

The Zhou had seized power of a large part of China by 1045 B.C. However, local chiefs known as **warlords** ruled states within the empire. By the 400s B.C., these warlords had seriously weakened the power of the Zhou rulers. The warlords fought one another for power and territory. As time went on, more and more wars broke out among these local chiefs.

> ### focus your reading
>
> Why was Qin Shihuangdi hated?
>
> What were the long-term effects of the Han Dynasty?
>
> ### vocabulary
>
> warlords   bureaucrats
>
> emperor   censors
>
> centralized government

The period from the 400s to the 200s B.C. is known as the Warring States Period. That is the reason that Confucius tried to get the warlords to accept his ideas. He wanted to bring peace and stability to the empire.

A battle between Chinese warlords

Qin Dynasty

Confucius was unsuccessful in his effort to change the ideas of the warlords. The Qin were more successful with their iron swords. By 221 B.C., the people of the Qin state had won control of most of China. The Qin ruler, Qin Shihuangdi (CHIN SHUR•HWONG•DEE), declared himself China's first **emperor**.

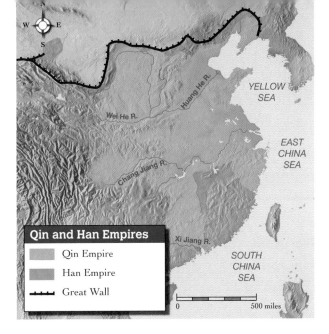

Qin and Han Empires

Qin Empire
Han Empire
Great Wall

0   500 miles

For the first time, China had a single **centralized government**. Before Qin Shihuangdi, local lords ruled their own states. The new emperor removed the local lords. He divided China into provinces and counties. **Bureaucrats** were appointed to oversee the new regions. A bureaucrat is a government official who enforces the rules of the government. Under the Zhou Dynasty, government positions had been passed down from father to son. Qin Shihuangdi ended this practice. He also set up the censorate. The members of this department were known as **censors**. Their job was to check up on the bureaucrats.

Qin Shihuangdi established an army to keep order and to protect China. A system of roads was built to make it easier to move troops quickly from place to place. One area that needed protection was the northern frontier. The Xiongnu (SYEN•NOO) were threatening the region. They were nomadic herders who raised sheep, cattle, and goats. They were also fierce fighters. To keep them out of China, Qin Shihuangdi had the Great Wall built across the northern region.

Time Box

c. 400–221 B.C.
Warring States Period

221–206 B.C.
Qin Dynasty

202 B.C.– A.D. 220
Han Dynasty

The Great Wall was one of the reasons that the peasants turned against the Qin Dynasty. The wall was built with the forced labor of peasants. It was also an expensive project. Qin Shihuangdi placed heavy taxes on his subjects to pay for the wall and for his armies.

Han Dynasty

The leader of the peasant revolt against the Qin was Liu Bang (LYOH•BONG). He was a peasant himself. His victory over the Qin gave him great power. He took the name Han Gaozu

The Great Wall of China

(HAHN GOW•DZOO) and declared himself the first Han emperor. The Han Dynasty lasted for 400 years. For more than 300 years, China was peaceful and prosperous under the Han.

Han Gaozu kept the government structure that Qin Shihuangdi had set up. China remained divided into provinces and counties. Han Gaozu also adopted the Qin's use of appointed bureaucrats. Over time, the Han developed a civil service exam to find the best qualified civil servants. Han rulers set up a school to train candidates for government work. The students learned Confucianism and Chinese history and law.

Han Gaozu replaced the harsh laws and punishments of the first emperor. Qin Shihuangdi had forbidden the teaching of Confucianism. Han Gaozu adopted Confucianism. The Five Constant Relationships supported peace and order in Chinese society. They also strengthened the position of the emperor.

During the Han Dynasty, the population of China tripled. It went from 20 million people to 60 million. The empire also grew in land area. Han armies extended the empire north, south, and west.

Piece of carved jade from the Han Dynasty

Qin Shihuangdi

Before he became emperor, Qin Shihuangdi's name was Zhao Zheng. *Shihuangdi* means First Emperor. He declared himself the First Emperor of the Qin, or Chin. This is how the name "China" began.

Calling himself emperor is just one example of Qin Shihuangdi's boasting. He also claimed that his dynasty would last for 10,000 generations—about 250,000 years.

Qin Shihuangdi was a ruthless emperor. He based his rule on Legalism. He governed with harsh laws and severe punishments. He forced his subjects to pay high taxes and to work on his building projects. He was described as having "the heart of a tiger and a wolf . . . he punished men as though he were afraid he would never get around to them all." After his death, the peasants rebelled against the next Qin emperor. The dynasty that was supposed to last 250,000 years lasted only 11 years.

By A.D. 170, Han control over China was slipping. There were peasant revolts over living conditions. Rival military leaders fought for power. In 220, a rebel general seized power. However, his rule did not last. For the next 400 years, China was the scene of civil wars and invasions by nomadic people from the north.

The Silk Road and Sea Routes

Beginning around 200 B.C., China became part of the international trade network. Chinese merchants traded along land routes and sea routes. Their ships sailed throughout Southeast Asia and into the Indian Ocean. The land route became known as the Silk Road. This was because China's most important trade good on this route was silk. The Silk Road stretched 4,000 miles from eastern China to the Roman Empire.

Besides silk, Chinese merchants traded spices, tea, and porcelain—a type of fine pottery. Ivory, cotton cloth, pepper, and gems flowed east and west from Indian merchants. Roman merchants sent woolen and linen cloth, glass, and gems to the east.

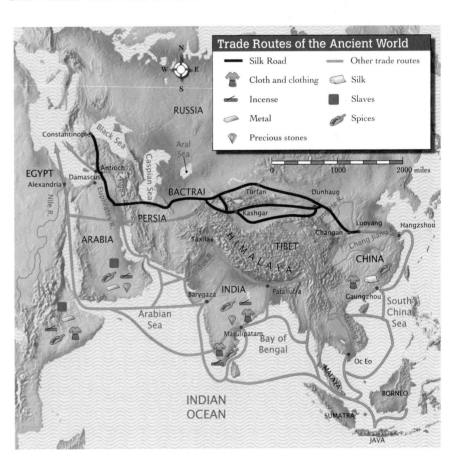

Putting It All Together

Review the Venn diagram you filled in as you read this lesson. Write two or three paragraphs to explain how the Qin and Han Dynasties were the same and how they were different.

Chapter Summary

- During the Shang Dynasty, the Chinese developed a writing system based on characters, not letters. The Shang also practiced **ancestor worship**.
- The Zhou overthrew the Shang ruler.
- The **Mandate** of Heaven explains the **dynastic cycle** that developed in China.
- The family was the basic unit of Chinese society. The **extended family** included all related family members. Each family member had a duty and responsibility to every other family member. This duty was known as **filial piety**.
- During the early period of Chinese history, three important **philosophies** developed: **Confucianism**, **Daoism**, and **Legalism**. A philosophy is different from a **religion**.
- After the Zhou were overthrown, China entered the Warring States Period. Rival **warlords** fought for power.
- Qin Shihuangdi united and expanded China. He declared himself China's first **emperor**. He set up a **centralized government** and used **bureaucrats** to run it. **Censors** made sure that officials did their jobs.
- Qin Shihuangdi began the building of the Great Wall of China.
- The Qin Dynasty was overthrown by the Han. The Han adopted Confucianism. They kept the idea of appointed civil servants and set up **civil service** exams.
- Trade became important under the Han. Many trade goods flowed back and forth along the Silk Road.

Chapter Review

1 Review the questions that you wrote at the beginning of the chapter. Talk with a partner about your questions and possible answers. Then write an answer for each question.

2 Imagine you are a headline writer for a Chinese newspaper. Write a two-line headline for each of the following: (a) the overthrow of the Zhou, (b) the Mandate of Heaven, (c) the teachings of Confucius, (d) a trading trip on the Silk Road.

Skill Builder

Using Special-Purpose Maps

There are many kinds of maps. There are road maps, historical maps, land-use maps, natural-resources maps, and the list goes on. Most of the maps in this book are historical maps.

To read and use the information on the map, follow these steps:

1. Read the title of the map to find out what it is about.
2. Look at the map to see what colors and symbols are used.
3. Match the colors and symbols to the map key. This explains what the colors and symbols represent.
4. Read the map scale. This tells you the distance between places shown on the map.

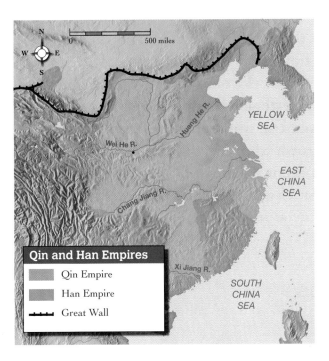

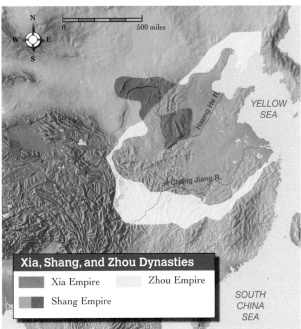

1 What is the title of each map?

2 What symbol is used to show the Great Wall?

3 How do you know which area was ruled by the Zhou?

4 What is the greatest distance from east to west that the Shang ruled?

Chapter 6

ANCIENT GREEK CITY-STATES

(1750–133 B.C.)

Getting Focused

Skim this chapter to predict what you will be learning.
- Read the lesson titles and subheadings.
- Look at the illustrations and read the captions.
- Examine the maps.
- Review the vocabulary words and terms.

All the civilizations that you have studied so far had one thing in common. They all developed in river valleys. Ancient Greece, however, developed on a mountainous peninsula and on many rocky islands. How do you think its geography affected the way ancient Greece developed? Write a brief paragraph to predict how geography affected the development of ancient Greek civilization. As you read the chapter, check your prediction. Remember to add Greece to your world map.

LESSON 1

The Development of Greek City-States

Thinking on Your Own

Create a three-column chart to compare and contrast Sparta and Athens. Label the first column "Categories." Write topics in this column, such as "Government" and "Role of Women." Label the other columns "Sparta" and "Athens." Fill in the columns as you read the lesson.

Much of the Greek peninsula and nearby islands are mountainous. In some areas, river valleys cut through the mountains. Small, low plains dot the region. At some time in the ancient past, groups of people settled in these valleys and plains. The mountains kept these groups separate from one another. Over time, people living in the groups developed independent, self-governing city-states.

Many Greeks earned their living from the sea. They became expert sailors. Their trading network spread the length and width of the Mediterranean Sea. Eventually, people moved from Greece to set up colonies in other parts of the Mediterranean. Merchants moved to the new colonies to start trading businesses. Other Greeks went to find better farmland. Between 1100 B.C. and 750 B.C., people left Greece to escape invaders.

focus your reading

What forms of government were developed by the Greek city-states?

What was life like for Spartans?

Why is Athenian democracy called limited democracy?

vocabulary

polis	tyrants
agora	democracy
aristocrats	ephors
oligarchy	helots

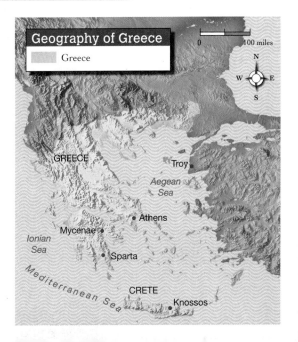

Geography of Greece

☐ Greece

0   100 miles

N W E S

GREECE

Troy

Aegean Sea

Athens

Mycenae

Ionian Sea

Sparta

Mediterranean Sea

CRETE

Knossos

Greek City-States

The Greek city-state was called a **polis**. It was both a place and a governing body. The English word *politics* comes from the Greek word *polis*. City-states were built around a hill. At the top of the hill was an area called the acropolis. Temples and public buildings were built there. The rest of the city was built below the acropolis on flat land. One area of the city was kept as open space. It was called the **agora**. Citizens assembled there for meetings and used it as a marketplace. Over time, the area surrounding the city came under the control of the city-state.

The earliest city-states were monarchies ruled by kings. Some men became wealthy because of the amount of land they owned. Their wealth gained them power. In some city-states, these **aristocrats** were able to overthrow the king and set up rule by **oligarchy**. An oligarchy is a state that is ruled by a few people. Generally, the rulers of the oligarchy were elected by other aristocrats and ruled only for a certain period of time. When their terms ended, another group was elected.

Time Box

2800–1450 B.C.
   Minoan civilization

1600–1100 B.C.
   Mycenaen civilization

1100–750 B.C.
   Dark Ages

The Minoan civilization developed on the island of Crete. It was ruled by a king and its economy was based on trade. The details of Minoan paintings tell much about their lives. The Minoans were probably conquered by Mycenaen people from the Greek mainland.

Mycenae was made up of a number of independent royal centers. Each was ruled by a king who lived in a walled palace-fort on a hill. The people lived in scattered settlements around the forts. The Mycenaen civilization was based on trade. They traded gold, bronze daggers, beads, and pottery. Mycenae collapsed because of warfare among rival kings and invaders from the north.

The next 350 years is called the Dark Ages because few records have been found. *The Iliad*, however, may be rooted in truth. It is an epic poem by Homer about the Trojan War. Archaeologists have not been able to prove or disprove its story. The Greeks won the war by hiding soldiers in a huge wooden horse that was sent to Troy as a gift. The Trojans wheeled the horse inside their city walls. At night, Greek soldiers crawled out of the horse and seized the city. They burned it to the ground.

The Erechtheion on the Acropolis in Athens, Greece

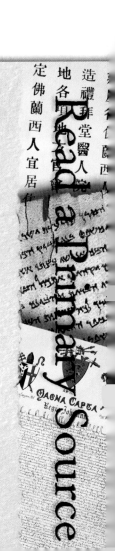

Ancient Greek City-States, 1750–133 B.C.

stop and think

Greece and its colonies had large resources of silver, gold, iron, and timber. How would these help the Greeks become successful traders? Talk over possible answers with a partner. Then write a paragraph to answer the question.

The 500s B.C. marked the rise of **tyrants**. A tyrant was not always a cruel ruler, as the word means today. In ancient Greece, a tyrant was a government ruled by one man. Rule by tyrants was the first step toward democratic rule, as they were often caring and fair rulers. In some cities like Athens, tyrants made important reforms to help the poor. But overall, Greeks turned away from absolute rule and toward **democracy**. They wanted a say in how they were governed.

Sparta: The Military Polis

Over time, Sparta and Athens became the most important city-states in Greece. During the 700s B.C., Sparta became a military polis. Harsh laws governed all parts of Spartans' lives. Boys were trained from childhood to be soldiers. At age seven, they were sent to live in barracks. Discipline was severe and punishments were harsh. At age twenty, Spartan men became soldiers and could marry.

Sparta

The Greek historian Xenophon describes one way Spartan boys prepared to become soldiers.

"Instead of softening their feet with shoe or sandal, . . . [they went] barefoot. This habit . . . enabled them to scale heights more easily and clamber down precipices with less danger. In fact, with his feet so trained the young Spartan could leap and spring and run faster unshod than another [in shoes]. . . .

"Spartan boys were given little food. They were expected to steal more. This was to train them to find food when they were fighting. The Greek historian Plutarch describes the process.

" '[Spartan youths were required to steal . . .], which they did by creeping into the gardens, or . . . into the eating houses; if they were taken in the act, they were whipped without mercy, for thieving so poorly and awkwardly. They stole, too, all other meat they could lay their hands on, looking out and watching all opportunities, when people were asleep or more careless than usual. If they were caught, they were not only punished with whipping, but hunger, too.' "

reading for understanding

What were Spartan boys able to do easily without shoes?

Why were boys whipped when they were caught stealing?

What do you think about the reason for teaching Spartan boys to steal food?

Read a Primary Source

Women and girls also had roles in this military state. Their job was to marry and have strong, healthy children. As a result, women, too, had to take part in vigorous exercise. Because husbands lived in barracks for many years, Spartan women had more authority and responsibility than women in many cultures.

Sparta's government and army were headed by two kings. However, the real power lay with a council of five men called **ephors**. These men managed the government on a daily basis. There was also a council of elders made up of the two kings and 28 citizens over the age of sixty. There was an assembly of citizens who voted on issues put before them by the council of elders. The assembly was not allowed to discuss the issues, only to vote. Only native-born men thirty years of age and older were citizens.

The only job for a Spartan citizen was soldier. All other work such as farming was done by **helots**. These were people captured in battle and enslaved.

To protect its way of life, Sparta cut itself off from the rest of the world. Travel was forbidden. Visitors from the outside were not welcome. The study of literature, the arts, and philosophy was not encouraged. New ideas could be dangerous.

Spartan pottery illustrates the importance of military training.

Athens: An Experiment in Limited Democracy

The earliest government of Athens was a monarchy. In the 700s B.C., an oligarchy of aristocrats replaced the king. Nine members of the wealthiest families in Athens made up this ruling council. An assembly of citizens elected the nine oligarchs who served for a certain period of time. Otherwise, the assembly had little control over the government.

Democracy was an important aspect of Athenian life.

Between 560 B.C. and 510 B.C., tyrants ruled Athens. By 512 B.C., Cleisthenes had the support of enough Athenians to gain control of the government.

He reorganized Athens' government. Cleisthenes is regarded as the founder of Athenian democracy. Native-born Athenian women were citizens, but they could not vote. Slaves and foreign residents were not citizens.

Government Set Up by Cleisthenes		
Government Body	**Members**	**Duties**
Assembly	• all male citizens of Athens, eighteen years of age and older	• debate and pass laws • elect public officals • decide all matters of war and foreign policy
Council of 500	• 500 citizens chosen by lottery to serve for one year—50 from each of the ten tribes that made up Athens city-state and surrounding area	• prepare laws for debate by the Assembly • carry out decisions of the Assembly
Law Court	• 6,000 citizens chosen by lottery from the Assembly	• serve as judge and jury for criminal and civil trials
Board of Generals	• ten generals elected by the Assembly	• advise the Assembly • lead the army and navy

Most families in Athens could afford a slave or two. Many worked in homes doing cooking and cleaning. The enslaved were also used for farm work. By the 400s B.C., Athens was an important trading center. It grew much of its own food, but also imported grain in large amounts. Some of its trade goods were wine and olive oil. Slave labor was used to manufacture these goods.

Slaves often worked in Athenian homes.

Putting It All Together

Imagine you are a Spartan in 507 B.C. An Athenian visits your family and talks about the government of Athens. How could this be dangerous for the rulers of Sparta? Talk about it with a partner. Then write a paragraph to explain how learning about the government in Athens might be dangerous. Use examples from the lesson to support your opinion.

LESSON 2

Classical Greece

Thinking on Your Own

Create two columns in your notebook. Title one "War with Persia," and the other "The Peloponnesian War." As you read, fill in the columns with key information about each war and its effect on ancient Greece.

Between about 500 B.C. and 338 B.C., the Greeks developed what is called **classical** Greek civilization. They made great contributions to the arts and sciences. Also during this period, Athens increased its power and fought two long and costly wars.

War with Persia

By the mid-500s B.C., Persia had taken control of the Greek colonies of Iona in what is now Turkey. The war between Persia and Greece began over the control of these colonies. In 499 B.C., the Athenian navy helped the Ionian colonies to rebel. The Persians crushed the revolt.

Darius, the Persian king, was angered that Athens had sent ships to help the rebels. In 490 B.C., he sent the Persian army to destroy Athens. The smaller Athenian army met the Persians on the plain of Marathon. In a deadly battle, the Athenians defeated the Persians.

Wars were a common theme of Greek pottery.

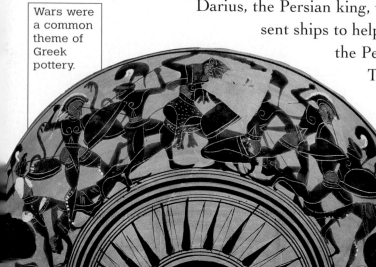

Pheidippides died after gasping out the news of Athens' victory after the Battle of Marathon.

In 480 B.C., Darius' son Xerxes ordered the Persian army and navy to go to war against Athens again. In 479 B.C., the Athenian army and its **allies** defeated the Persians at Plataea.

The following year, Athens formed the Delian League, or alliance, with other Greek city-states. The purpose of this alliance was to take back control of the Greek colonies from Persia. In time, the League was successful.

The Age of Pericles

Athens reached its greatest glory in the years between the Persian Wars and the Peloponnesian War. This period in Greek history is often called the Age of Pericles.

Pericles was a general of the board of generals and a forceful public speaker. His position gave him great influence over public policy. Although an aristocrat, Pericles focused on the poor in guiding reforms. Reforms were passed that helped poor citizens participate more fully in Athens' government. Citizens who did not own property were allowed to hold public office. In addition, those who served on juries and held office were paid for their time. Pericles was also a supporter of the arts. It was during this period that the Parthenon was built. It and other public works projects gave jobs to the poor.

Stone relief depicts democracy crowning the people of Athens.

The Parthenon was constructed in Athens between 447 B.C. and 432 B.C.

One of the greatest glories of Athens at this time was its government system. Under Cleisthenes, Athens had become a direct democracy. Citizens took part in governing Athens directly. The Athenian Assembly met every 10 days to discuss and vote on issues. All 43,000 citizens did not show up for each meeting, but the meetings were held and citizens could attend. Today, we would call Athens a limited democracy because women and slaves could not vote.

The Peloponnesian War

While the Delian League was freeing Greek colonies, Athens was using the League to create an empire. Athens' leaders held the major positions of power in the League. As a result, they were able to move the League's treasury to Athens. Each city-state contributed money to the treasury, which was to be used for the League's expenses. Instead, the leaders of Athens used the money to rebuild their city. If a city-state tried to leave the League, Athens sent soldiers to stop it.

Athens' power soon divided the Greek city-states into allies and enemies. Sparta was its chief rival. With its own allies, Sparta formed the Peloponnesian League. In 431 B.C., Sparta and Athens and their respective allies went to war.

Time Box

499 B.C.
Uprising of Greek colonies in Persian Empire

490–479 B.C.
Persian Wars against Greek city-states

461–429 B.C.
Age of Pericles

431–405 B.C.
Peloponnesian War

Mural depicting the Peloponnesian War

Athenian leaders decided to keep its army within the city's walls and wait out the Spartans. The Spartans were stronger fighters. Spartan soldiers surrounded the city and waited for two years. In the second year, a **plague**, or deadly disease, broke out in Athens. About a third of Athens' population died. However, the conflict continued.

In 405 B.C., Persia joined with Sparta to destroy Athens' navy. They also **blockaded** Athens' port. Food and other supplies could no longer reach Athens. The city finally surrendered in 404 B.C. As a result of its defeat, Athens lost its empire. It was no longer a powerful force in Greek affairs. Other city-states fought Athens and one another for power. The Greek mainland was torn by conflict for the next 100 years.

stop and think

How did the desire for power and territory cause both the Persian Wars and the Peloponnesian War? Write down some notes to answer this question. Share your ideas with a partner. Then write two or three paragraphs to answer the question.

Cultural Achievements of Classical Greece

Since the earliest times, the Greeks had composed stories and poetry and made artworks. The Age of Pericles marked the peak of ancient Greek culture. One of the most important contributions of classical Greece to Western civilization was the development of written history. History is the study of past events in an organized way. Herodotus, who lived from about 484 B.C. to 425 B.C., is considered the first Western historian. He traveled widely to interview eyewitnesses to events.

Greek literature began with Homer's two epics about the fall of Troy—the *Iliad* and the *Odyssey*. The ancient Greeks are also known for their development of drama. Greek **tragedies** dealt with themes such as good and evil and the rights of individuals. Some of these plays are still performed today. Greek **comedies** used humor to criticize society, especially politicians. The ancient Greeks, like the ancient Chinese, were also interested in understanding the universe and humans' place in it. Greek philosophers such as Socrates, Plato, and Aristotle developed ideas about the world.

Masks depicting tragedy and comedy

Important Greek Philosophers

Philosopher	Teachings	Lasting Contributions
Socrates, c. 470–399 B.C.	• "The Unexamined life is not worth living." • He used questions to get people to think about issues.	• Teaching by asking questions is known as the Socratic method. It is still used today in schools and colleges.
Plato, c. 427–347 B.C.	• Reality is made up of ideal, eternal Forms. • The ideal government would have three groups: philosopher-king as ruler, soldiers to protect the people, and workers (all other men and women). • Men and women should be treated equally.	• *The Republic* is Plato's writings about the ideal government.
Aristotle, 384–322 B.C.	• He rejected Plato's concept of ideal Forms. • Analysis, observation, and investigation are needed to answer questions about life and human nature. • Based on his research, he found monarchy, aristocracy, and constitutional government to be the best ways to govern people. • Constitutional government was the best form to use.	• Aristotle's work on government and other areas such as astronomy, biology, and physics influenced Western thinking until the A.D. 1600s.

Putting It All Together

This lesson discusses many events. Create a timeline to put the dates and events in sequence. Share your timeline with a partner. Ask questions about when one event happened in relation to another. Was it earlier, later, or at the same time?

LESSON 3

Alexander the Great and Hellenism

Thinking on Your Own

Read the Focus Your Reading questions. Then write three more questions you have about the lesson. Share your questions with a partner and answer all the questions as you read.

The Peloponnesian War greatly weakened all the Greek city-states, not just Athens. Over the next 60 years, the city-states fought one another for more power. They were further weakened by almost constant conflict.

King Philip II of Macedonia took advantage of the conflict. Macedonia is located to the north of

focus your reading

How did Philip II gain control of Greece?

How large was Alexander's empire?

What is Hellenism?

vocabulary

conquer   Hellenism

Philip II

Greece. Philip ruled Macedonia from 359 B.C. to 336 B.C. He formed alliances with some Greek city-states by using bribery and threats of force. Athens would not agree, however. It formed an alliance with the city state of Thebes instead. In 338 B.C., Philip's army defeated Athens and Thebes. Philip then seized control of all Greece. Philip's next plan was to **conquer** the Persian Empire. However, he was assassinated before he could attack.

Alexander's Army on the March

Philip's son Alexander became king at age twenty. He had been well trained by his father to be a soldier and a general. Alexander was also a student of the great philosopher Aristotle. In 334 B.C., Alexander launched an invasion of the

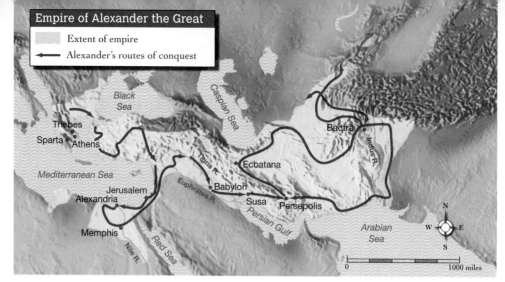

Empire of Alexander the Great

Extent of empire

Alexander's routes of conquest

Persian Empire. He led Macedonian and Greek forces into battle.

Between 334 and 326 B.C., Alexander brought under his control all or part of what are the modern nations of Iran, Egypt, Syria, Lebanon, Israel, Turkey, Iraq, Pakistan, Afghanistan, Turkmenistan, Uzbekistan, and Kazakhstan. In 326 B.C., Alexander led his army across the Indus River into India. Fighting Indian soldiers who were on war elephants, combined with being away from home for a long time, was too much for his troops. They refused to continue. Alexander agreed to turn back.

Alexander died three years later from a fever. His empire was split among four generals. One general took Macedonia and Greece and set up his own kingdom. The glory of Greece was dimmed but not dead. Greek culture continued to influence other cultures and to be influenced by them.

Time Box

359–336 B.C.
  Rule of Philip II as king of Macedonia

336–323 B.C.
  Rule of Alexander the Great

stop and think

Locate the world map at the end of this book. With a partner, figure out where Alexander's military campaigns took him. Use the information in your textbook to help you. What obstacles did his army face? Make a bulleted list of geographic obstacles.

Alexander the Great in battle

Hellenistic World

Hellenism was the adoption of the Greek language and culture by the peoples that Alexander conquered. His march across Southwest Asia and into North Africa and South Asia left

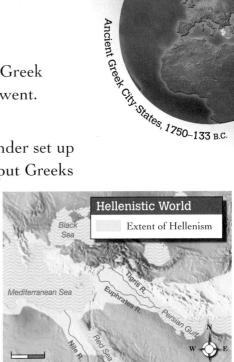

its mark. Alexander's army spread the Greek language and Greek ideas wherever it went. The result was the Hellenistic Era.

As each area was conquered, Alexander set up his own government to oversee it. He put Greeks in positions of power. The kings who followed him continued this practice. Only Greeks were allowed to govern, and Greek was the language of the government. In time, non-Greeks were able to gain government jobs. However, they, too, had to use the Greek language in their work.

Hellenistic kings spent money on architecture and sculptures such as *Winged Victory.*

Hellenistic World

Extent of Hellenism

Black Sea

Mediterranean Sea

Tigris R.

Euphrates R.

Persian Gulf

Nile R.

Red Sea

0   200 miles

N W E S

Alexander also set up new settlements in the areas he conquered. They were settled by Greeks from the mainland. This practice of sending Greeks to settle in conquered territory continued after his death. Some of the colonists were soldiers. Most were ordinary citizens. They did all the jobs that a city needed—merchant, farmer, artisan, actor, architect, and so on.

The temples and other public buildings in these new cities were based on the plans of Greek architects. Statues and wall paintings looked like ones in Athens or Corinth. The colonists held religious festivals and sporting contests as though they were in Greece. Over time, local people picked up Greek styles and customs. Greek colonists, in turn, picked up local ideas. The result was a vast merging, or blending, of Greek, Persian, Egyptian, and Indian cultures.

Achievements of the Hellenistic Era

Mathematics and Science

- Pythagoras figured out how to find the sides of a right triangle—Pythagorean theorem.
- Euclid developed the basic principles of geometry.
- Archimedes determined the value of *pi*, which is used in geometry. He also invented the pulley.
- Eratosthenes determined that the earth was a sphere and figured out its circumference.
- Aristarchus determined that the earth rotated on its axis and orbited the sun.

Putting It All Together

Write two-line headlines for each of the following: (1) Philip's taking control of Greece, (2) Alexander's plan to invade the Persian Empire, (3) Alexander's death, (4) the Hellenistic Era.

Chapter Summary

- The basic unit of Greek government was the **polis**, or city-state. It had two levels: the acropolis, or hilltop, and the **agora**, or open market and assembly place.

- In general, city-states went through four stages of political development: monarchy, **oligarchy** made up of **aristocrats**, rule by **tyrants**, and **democracy**.

- Sparta was a military city-state. Its male citizens were trained to be soldiers. All other work was done by **helots**, or enslaved peoples. Five men called **ephors** ran the city.

- The years between 500 B.C. and 338 B.C. are known as the **classical** period in Greek history. The three great Greek philosophers—Socrates, Plato, and Aristotle—lived during this period. Dramas of **tragedy** and **comedy** developed as well.

- Athens and its **allies** defeated Persia in a series of wars.

- Athens and Sparta and their allies fought one another in the Peloponnesian War. Athens' loss was partly due to a **blockade** of the city and a **plague** that wiped out many of its citizens.

- Philip II of Macedonia **conquered** the Greek city-states. His son Alexander the Great joined Greek and Macedonian forces to seize the Persian Empire.

- After Alexander's death, the new rulers continued his policies. Greek influence, or **Hellenism**, spread throughout the regions.

Chapter Review

1 Write lead newspaper paragraphs for each of the following: (a) Persian Wars, (b) Peloponnesian War, (c) Cleisthenes' reforms, (d) Socrates, (e) Alexander the Great. Be sure to include *who*, *what*, *where*, *why* and *when*.

2 You want to attract residents to Athens. With a partner, design a logo or write a slogan about Athenian democracy. A slogan is a phrase or sentence that describes the most important point about a product.

Skill Builder

How to Write a Persuasive Essay

An essay is a composition of several paragraphs. An essay may explain or describe something. An essay can also attempt to persuade the reader. This is a persuasive essay.

To write a persuasive essay, you must do some work before you begin writing.

- First, decide what you think about the issue. For example, suppose the issue is whether the United Nations should send peacekeepers to a particular region. What might happen if the peacekeepers are sent? If they are not sent? What might be the long-term results?
- Write notes about your ideas as you think about the issue.

Now you can start the writing process.

- Review the notes you wrote. Cross out ideas that do not fit your point of view. Add ideas that support your viewpoint.
- Put your ideas in the order that you will use them in your essay. Do not rewrite your ideas. Number them so you can find each one when you are ready to use it.
- Write your topic sentence. This should contain your viewpoint. This viewpoint is the main idea of your essay.
- Add other paragraphs that support your viewpoint with more evidence. Each paragraph should include one piece of evidence that supports your viewpoint.
- End with a strong concluding paragraph. Restate your point of view. Briefly restate your strongest evidence.

1 Think of an issue in your school. (a) State the issue in a sentence. (b) What is your point of view about the issue? Follow the steps above to decide on your viewpoint. (c) Write an essay to persuade someone else to adopt your viewpoint.

2 Sparta trained its male citizens to be soldiers. It was their only job. Foreigners and slaves did every other kind of work. Was this a practical and efficient way to set up a society? Write a persuasive essay to answer this question.

Chapter 7 ANCIENT ROME

(500 B.C.–A.D. 500)

Getting Focused

Skim this chapter to predict what you will be learning.
• Read the lesson titles and subheadings.
• Look at the illustrations and read the captions.
• Examine the maps.
• Review the vocabulary words and terms.

The Roman Empire was one of the world's largest empires. Many different groups lived under its rule. You have studied several empires in this book. Based on what you know, what do you think helped to keep the Roman Empire together? List your ideas. As you study the chapter, check your list. Add to or cross out ideas. Also, remember to add Italy to the world map you are making.

The Roman Republic

Thinking on Your Own

Look at the lesson subheadings. Use these to create an outline for the lesson in your notebook. As you read the lesson, fill in the outline.

I taly is a peninsula that extends out into the Mediterranean Sea. The Roman Republic began along the banks of the Tiber River in Italy. The river runs through the plain of Latium, which is about halfway down the west side of the peninsula. A peninsula is a piece of land that is surrounded on three sides by water.

Sometime around 1500 to 1000 B.C., people began moving into the Italian peninsula from the north. Some were Latins who settled on the plain of Latium. The plain takes its name from these people. By 800 B.C., they had set up small villages on seven hills along the Tiber River.

Etruscan murals often depict daily life.

focus your reading

How was Rome founded?

How was the government of the Roman Republic organized?

How did the Republic gain control of the Mediterranean region?

Why was Rome able to keep the territory it conquered?

vocabulary

republic

patrician

plebeian

consuls

diplomacy

Roman Confederation

Around 650 B.C., Etruscans moved into Latium from the north. They seized control of much of central Italy. They turned the seven villages into the city of Rome. The Etruscan state was a monarchy. In 509 B.C., the Romans overthrew the Etruscan king. Romans considered this act the beginning of their nation.

Rome's location was ideal because it was near the sea but far enough away from it to avoid pirates.

The Government of Rome

Instead of a monarchy, the Romans set up a **republic**. In a republic, citizens elect representatives to govern. This is different from the democracy that Athens developed. In Athens, citizens voted directly in their Assembly on running the government.

At first, **patricians** decided who would govern Rome. Patricians were wealthy landowners and were the most important social class in the Republic. They were also the soldiers of the Roman army. The small landowners, farmers, craftworkers, and merchants, who were known as **plebeians**, had little say in deciding who would govern. Both patricians and plebeians were citizens. For much of the history of the Republic, patricians and plebeians clashed for political power.

The government was headed by two **consuls**. Until the 300s B.C., the office of consul was open only to patricians. They were elected by the Centuriate Assembly, which the patricians controlled. The consuls issued laws and orders and could veto each other's decisions. They did not have to send their laws to the Senate for a vote, although they could.

The Senate was also made up mostly of patricians. The Senate's duties included seeing that the laws and orders of the consuls were carried out and advising the consuls on issues.

In time, the plebeians gained a larger voice in Roman government. In 471 B.C., they won the right to set up their own assembly called the Council of Plebs. The council passed laws for plebeians. By 409 B.C., plebeians had gained the right to hold public office. Before this, only patricians could be elected to office. However, unlike Athens, Rome did not pay its officeholders. This meant that plebeians were less likely to serve in government. After 287 B.C., the Assembly of the People, which included all male citizens, could make laws that all Romans had to obey.

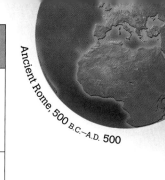

Government Office/Body	Members	Duties
• Consul (509 B.C.)	• two citizens elected by the Centuriate Assembly • until the 300s B.C., office of consul open only to patricians	• issue laws and orders with or without sending them to the Senate for a vote • veto each other's decisions • command the army
• Dictator	• appointed by the consuls and the Senate • hold power for six months	• rule during an emergency • hold absolute power
• Praetor (197 B.C.)	• six male citizens • elected	• second in power to the consuls • act as judge in civil cases
• Senate (509 B.C.)	• around 300 members, including former office holders • mostly patricians	• see that the laws and orders of the consuls are carried out • advise the consuls
• Centuriate Assembly (509 B.C.)	• army of Rome • patrician majority in the assembly	• elect consuls and praetors • pass laws
• Council of the Plebs (471 B.C.)	• all male plebeians	• elect 10 tribunes to represent plebeians' issues • pass laws for plebeians • after 287 B.C., pass laws for all Romans
• Assembly of the People (447 B.C.)	• all male citizens of Rome	• at first, only proposed laws • after 287 B.C., pass laws for all Romans

Government of the Roman Republic

The Roman Army on the March

The Romans gradually extended their control over Italy and the Mediterranean. By 261 B.C., the entire Italian peninsula was under Roman control. Rome had conquered some city-states and made alliances with others. By 146 B.C., the Roman army had gone far beyond Italy. It had reached as far west as what is today Spain. By 129 B.C., the army had taken control of the Greek peninsula to the east. Farther east it had seized territory in what is today Turkey. By 44 B.C., Rome controlled the Mediterranean.

The three Punic Wars were fought between Rome and Carthage. Carthage was an important trading rival in North Africa. By the 200s B.C., Carthage had set up colonies in Spain and on islands in the Mediterranean near the Italian peninsula. This was threatening to Rome. In 264 B.C., Rome attacked the Carthaginian colony in Sicily, beginning the First Punic War. It took 23 years, but the Romans defeated the Carthaginian navy and seized Sicily. This was the first of Rome's foreign territories, or provinces. As a result of these wars, Rome also controlled an area in North Africa.

Ancient Rome, 500 B.C.–A.D. 500

The Roman Republic, 44 B.C.

Roman Republic

Twenty-three years after the end of the First Punic War, the Carthaginian general Hannibal invaded Italy. Hannibal had been only six when Rome defeated Carthage the first time. Hannibal decided on an overland route to surprise the Romans. Carthaginian ships carried 46,000 soldiers, horses, and battle elephants to Spain. Hannibal then marched his army across what is today France and over the Alps mountains.

At Cannae, the Roman and Carthaginian armies faced off. By the end of the battle, almost 40,000 Roman soldiers had died or been wounded. Those who were left retreated. Hannibal and his remaining soldiers continued to harass the Italian peninsula. Rome had not finished the fight, however. Its generals put together another army and invaded Spain. The Romans defeated the Carthaginian colonies there and then sailed to North Africa. They took the war to the walls of Carthage itself. Hannibal and his army hastily returned from Italy, but the Romans overwhelmed them.

As a result of its victory, Rome added Spain to its provinces. Rome also allowed Carthage to remain. This was a mistake. In 149 B.C., a third war broke out between Rome and Carthage. This time Rome destroyed and burned Carthage so

Time Box

Roman Conquests

264–241 B.C.
   First Punic War;
   Rome won

218–202 B.C.
   Second Punic War;
   Rome won

149–146 B.C.
   Third Punic War;
   Rome won

148–146 B.C.
   Controlled Macedonia
   and Greece

129 B.C.
   Seized territory in Asia

44 B.C.
   Controlled
   Mediterranean region

that it could never threaten Rome again. Its citizens were sold into slavery. The area was renamed Africa and became another Roman province.

stop and think

Create a chart to compare and contrast Carthage and Rome. Work with a partner to fill in details. Then write a short paragraph explaining the similarities and differences.

Reasons for Rome's Success

Rome used both force and **diplomacy** in gaining control of the Mediterranean. The **Roman Confederation** is an example of its use of diplomacy. This example also helps explain why Rome was able to keep control for centuries.

The Roman Confederation set up a series of alliances between Rome and other areas in Italy. In return for loyalty, member city-states could run their own governments. They also received many benefits from their relationship with Rome:

1 Rome ended the rivalry among city-states on the peninsula. The result was a period of peace and prosperity.

2 Rome granted citizenship to member city-states. This gave them special privileges in the Roman Republic.

3 Member city-states were granted trading rights with Rome. The road system that Rome built throughout Italy helped the spread of trade.

4 In return, member city-states had to provide soldiers for the Roman army. However, Rome did not require that the city-states pay to support the army.

Putting It All Together

Create a concept web to describe the Roman Republic. At the center draw a large circle and label it "Roman Republic." Then add lines and smaller circles for each of the important subtopics: "Government," "Wars," and "Reasons for Success." To fill in the concept web, draw more lines and smaller circles and fill with additional information.

The Appian Way, built in the 300s B.C., was the first major Roman road.

Politics and Society

Thinking on Your Own

As you read this lesson, make a timeline of important dates and events. This will help you remember the sequence, or order, in which events happened.

Over time, the government of the Republic changed. The plebeians had gained many rights. However, these rights came to mean little. By the 100s B.C., the real power lay with wealthy patricians in the Senate. The result was a growing gap between rich and poor.

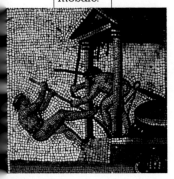

Roman slaves at work are depicted in this mosaic.

> ### focus your reading
>
> What caused the end of the Roman Republic and the rise of the Empire?
>
> What kind of rulers were the Roman emperors?
>
> What was Roman life like during the Empire?
>
> ### vocabulary
>
> | | |
> |---|---|
> | successor | gladiators |
> | hereditary | adopted |
> | Pax Romana | adapted |

Reformers attempted to help the poor but had little support in the Senate. Meanwhile, there were riots among the poor and rebellions among slaves. Ambitious generals took advantage of the uncertain times. They used the armies they commanded to fight one another for power. The result was a series of civil wars between 82 and 31 B.C.

The Rise of the Empire: The First Triumvirate

In 60 B.C., three rival forces joined together—Julius Caesar, Pompey, and Crassus, the richest man in Rome. They formed the First Triumvirate, or an alliance of three people. By using their combined political power, they had Caesar elected consul. The three then took command of armies in different regions. In 53 B.C., Crassus was killed in battle. Then Pompey turned against Caesar. Prompted by Pompey, the Senate tried to force Caesar to give up his command.

Statue of Julius Caesar

Caesar and his army had just fought and won much of Gaul—modern-day France. Instead of returning alone, a victorious Caesar marched his army to Rome. A civil war with Pompey's troops broke out. Caesar defeated Pompey and became dictator in 45 B.C. Caesar attempted a series of reforms, including taking land from the wealthy and giving it to veterans of his army. He also put the jobless to work on public building projects. In an effort to reduce the Senate's power, Caesar enlarged the Senate to 900 members. Angered by his actions, a group of senators killed him in 44 B.C.

The Second Triumvirate

Allies of Caesar formed the Second Triumvirate after his death. Caesar's nephew Octavian joined with Mark Antony, who had been consul with Caesar in 44 B.C., and Lepidus, who had been an officer under Caesar's command. The Second Triumvirate lasted only a short time. By 37 B.C., Octavian and Antony had defeated Lepidus. They split the Roman territory into two regions. Octavian ruled the western part and Antony ruled the eastern part.

Tiberius and Gaius Gracchus

The Gracchus brothers, Tiberius (163–133 B.C.) and Gaius (154–121 B.C.), belonged to one of the most important patrician families in Rome. However, they chose to work on behalf of the poor. They saw the declining number of small farmers as the basis of the Republic's problems. The solution was to give public land to small farmers who had lost their land. However, much of the public land was already divided among senators.

In 133 B.C., Tiberius was elected a tribune. He made a proposal to the Council of Plebs to redistribute land. The Council passed the law and the government began turning over land to people without land. However, Tiberius had made enemies among the senators. When he tried to run for a second term, he and 300 supporters were killed in an election riot.

In 123 and 122 B.C., Gaius was elected tribune. Like his brother, he wanted public land given to the poor. He also sponsored a program to buy grain and sell it to the poor at a reduced price. His ideas cost him re-election in 121 B.C. The Senate then attempted to repeal, or undo, his reforms. Riots broke out and he was killed. Some 3,000 of his supporters were executed.

Biography

Ancient Rome, 500 B.C.–A.D. 500

But there was to be no peace between the rivals. In 31 B.C., Octavian defeated Antony and seized power for himself. Octavian was given the title "Caesar Augustus," meaning "honored one." The year 31 B.C. marks the end of the Republic and the beginning of the Empire.

Augustus changed the way leaders were chosen. The Senate and the Centuriate Assembly had elected two consuls yearly. Augustus established a new system. The emperor would choose his **successor** from his own family. The title of emperor would be **hereditary**. It would be passed down from one man to another within a family. No longer would a man have to earn the right to be elected. The Senate would never again be so powerful.

stop and think

Julius Caesar, Pompey, and Octavian were all ambitious men. How did they use their ambition to gain power? Talk over your ideas with a partner. Then write a bulleted list of ideas to explain how ambition caused these men to act in a certain way.

Expansion and Peace

Under Augustus and later emperors, Rome continued to expand its borders. Emperor Claudius, who ruled from A.D. 41 to 54, added Britain to the Empire. He also granted Roman citizenship to people in the Roman provinces. The Empire reached its largest territory under Emperor Trajan, who ruled from 98 to 117.

One of the greatest achievements of the Roman Empire was the **Pax Romana**. This is the name given to about 100 years of peace and prosperity. It began with Emperor Nerva in 96 and ended in 180 with the death of Emperor Marcus Aurelius. During this time, people, trade goods, and ideas moved freely back and forth along the Empire's trading network. The peace ended with another civil war. The next 300 years saw periods of war and peace and a slow decline of Roman power.

One of the most important and lasting

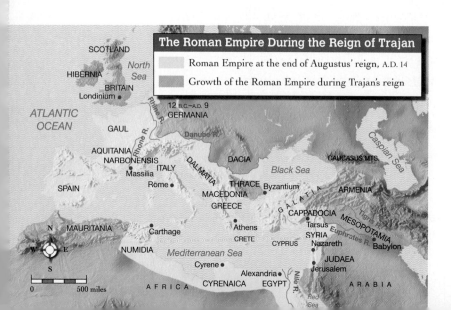

The Roman Empire During the Reign of Trajan

Roman Empire at the end of Augustus' reign, A.D. 14

Growth of the Roman Empire during Trajan's reign

Achievements of the Romans

- dome
- first to use concrete for large buildings
- improved on design of Etruscan arch
- improved on Greek designs for columns
- aqueduct, a bridge-like stucture to carry water great distances
- roads and bridges—The Roman Empire was connected by 50,000 miles of roads.

contributions of the Roman Empire was its law code. As Rome extended its rule beyond the borders of Italy, it developed the Law of Nations. Among its basic principles were (1) people are innocent until proved guilty and (2) people may defend themselves before a judge. In the early 200s, Roman judges put together law books for use by judges in all parts of the Empire.

Roman Society and Culture

Under the Republic, the father and husband had absolute authority in the family. Over time, this changed and women gained more freedom.

Upper-class boys and girls were taught to read and write. In addition, boys learned Roman law and moral principles. For girls, education ended when they got married. Most girls married between the ages of 12 and 14. By law, boys could marry at 14 but were usually older.

Romans enslaved people that they captured in war. Slaves were used for entertainment in Roman arenas. Trained as **gladiators**, they fought each other to the death while Romans cheered. Most slaves, however, labored on farms or on public building projects. They are the ones who built the Roman roads, bridges, aqueducts, temples, and arenas.

The Romans borrowed much from Greek civilization. Greek styles in sculpture and architecture were **adopted** by the Romans and **adapted**, or changed, to make them their own. In literature, the Romans borrowed Greek ideas, too. The poet Virgil wrote the *Aeneid* to give Romans the same kind of epic story as the Greeks had in the *Odyssey*. The Roman historian Livy wrote a 142-volume history of Rome.

Hadrian's Wall marked the northern boundary of the Roman Empire in Britain.

Putting It All Together

At the beginning of this lesson you began creating a timeline of events. Use this timeline to develop a short essay about the Roman Empire. Select several key events and use them as the main ideas of your essay.

LESSON **3**

The Fall of the Roman Empire

Thinking on Your Own

Create a table with four columns. Label the table "Causes for the Fall of the Roman Empire." Label the columns "Military," "Political," "Social," and "Economic." As you read the lesson, fill in the columns with information about the decline of the Empire.

The decline and fall of the Roman Empire in the west took place over a long period of time. It was more a gradual loss of its power over the centuries than a quick collapse in a few decades. There were many reasons for the slow loss of Rome's power: economic, social, political, and military. All of these reasons mixed together to create trouble for the Empire.

focus your reading

How did the tax policies of the emperors weaken the Empire?

Why did the lack of traditional values weaken the Empire?

How did political problems weaken the Empire?

How did nomadic people weaken the Empire?

vocabulary

plague   values

Economic Causes

As the Roman Empire expanded, so did its expenses. The new provinces had to be governed, and this meant new public officials. Roman soldiers had to keep the newly conquered people from rebelling. To pay these expenses, emperors imposed high taxes.

At the same time, the population of the Empire was declining. Civil wars, invasions by nomadic people, and **plague** killed many people. Plague is a deadly disease that spreads quickly. As a result, there were fewer people to pay taxes. More and more small farmers lost their lands when they could not pay their debts or their taxes. Toward the end of the Empire, they moved to cities.

The Colosseum in Rome was the site of "bread and circuses."

To keep the poor and jobless in the cities from rebelling, emperors began to give out food. They also arranged entertainment for city residents. This practice of giving food and entertainment came to be known as "bread and circuses." All this free food and entertainment cost money. The result was higher taxes, which meant more farmers became landless, and so the cycle continued.

Upper-class women in ancient Rome had slaves do their work.

Social Causes

Loyalty and duty to one another and to the government had been two important **values**—or principles—of the early Republic. Over the centuries, such values became less important.

For example, the Roman army had once been made up of citizen soldiers. After the 200s, many soldiers were non-Romans. They worked for pay, not out of loyalty to the Empire. As new provinces joined the Empire, many local officials remained in place. This meant that in many provinces, there were few Romans in the government. In time, even the emperor was a non-Roman.

The lack of traditional values was also evident among the wealthy. With increased trade, wealthy patrician families became wealthier. Eventually the men of these families became less interested in providing leadership for the government. They were more interested in leading lives of luxury and idleness.

Political Causes

By the time of Emperor Diocletian, the Empire had become too large to rule efficiently. In 293, he divided it into an eastern and a western empire. He ruled the eastern part. Constantine succeeded him in 312. By 324, Constantine had become the sole ruler. However, he did not rule from Rome. He built a new capital in what is today Turkey. His city, Constantinople, became the gateway to trade with Asia. It grew wealthy while the western part of the Empire became poorer and weaker.

stop and think

Romans valued loyalty and duty to one another. What do these values mean? Write a definition of each value and give an example for each one. Share your ideas with a partner and revise your definition if needed.

Civil war also weakened the Empire. Between 235 and 284, Rome had 22 emperors. The civil wars that raged during the later years of the Empire had serious results. First, the civil wars cost the government precious tax money. Second, they killed thousands of soldiers that could have been better used against the Empire's outside enemies. Third, they left the borders open to those enemies.

Military Causes

Emperor Constantine

Beginning in the A.D. 200s, Germanic peoples from the north and east migrated into the Empire. Among the first nomadic invaders were Visigoths from around the Black Sea. They moved south and west through much of the Roman Empire, settling on land from Greece to Spain. In the 400s, the Vandals moved west across the Empire to Spain. Then they took their campaign into the Roman provinces in North Africa. From there they sailed to Italy and invaded Rome in 455.

Other invaders of the 400s were the Angles and Saxons from what is today Germany. They crossed the North Sea to invade Britain and defeat the Roman army.

Perhaps the fiercest invaders were not Germanic peoples, but the Huns from Central Asia. Between 441 and 450, they swept into Gaul, Italy, and Greece under their leader Attila. Unlike the Germanic peoples, the Huns did not stay.

The final blow came from the Visigoths. In 410, they had invaded Rome. In 476, Odoacer overthrew the emperor and proclaimed himself king. This event marks the end of the Roman Empire.

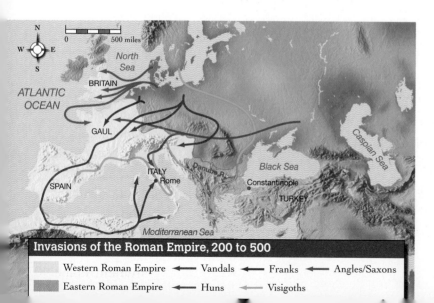

Invasions of the Roman Empire, 200 to 500

| Western Roman Empire | ← Vandals | ← Franks | ← Angles/Saxons |
| Eastern Roman Empire | ← Huns | ← Visigoths | |

Putting It All Together

Create a T-chart to show the events and outcomes for the decline and fall of the Roman Empire. Fill in your chart. Share it with a partner to make sure that you listed all the reasons.

The Rise and Spread of Christianity

Thinking on Your Own

Look at the subheadings in this lesson. Turn each into a question. Write the questions in your notebook. Write the answers as you read the lesson.

Jupiter and his wife Juno are Roman dieties.

The Roman government supported an official state religion. It centered on the worship of various male and female deities. The Romans borrowed many of their deities from the people they conquered. For example, the chief Roman god was Jupiter, the god of thunder and the skies. He was similar to Zeus, the chief god of the Greeks.

focus your reading

What was the central message of Jesus' teachings?

Why were early Christians persecuted by the Romans?

Why did Christianity appeal to so many people?

vocabulary

messiah   martyrs

Gospels   tolerance

apostles   charity

persecute

The Romans allowed the people they conquered to keep their own religions. As a result, the Jews in Judaea continued to practice Judaism after the Roman conquest. Many Jews were awaiting the coming of the **messiah**, the one sent by God to lead the Jews to freedom. He would fulfill the promise made to the Jewish people by God.

Jesus and His Teachings

Some Jews believed that a man named Jesus, a humble carpenter's son from Nazareth, was the messiah. Jesus began preaching around the age of 30. Most of what we know about him comes from the **Gospels**. These records of Jesus' life and teachings were written by four of his closest followers, who were known as **apostles**. The Gospels make up the first four

books of the New Testament of the Christian Bible.

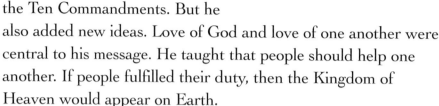

Followers of Jesus believe he performed miracles.

Jesus' message was based on the teachings of Judaism. He preached belief in one God and obedience to the Ten Commandments. But he also added new ideas. Love of God and love of one another were central to his message. He taught that people should help one another. If people fulfilled their duty, then the Kingdom of Heaven would appear on Earth.

Jesus' teachings attracted large crowds wherever he went. In time, he came to the attention of Roman officials. They feared he might lead the Jews in a revolt. Finally, one of Jesus' apostles, Judas, betrayed him to the authorities. Jesus was arrested, tried, and crucified. His followers declared that Jesus had risen from the dead and ascended into heaven.

St. Peter

The Beginning of the Christian Church

The apostles spread the message of Jesus. At first, they continued his work among the Jews in Judaea. Within a short time, however, they moved throughout the Roman Empire spreading Jesus' word and converting non-Jews. Jesus became known as the Christ from the Greek word meaning "anointed one, the messiah."

At first, Christians attracted little attention from Roman officials. However, during the reign of Emperor Nero from 54 to 68, the policy changed. The government began to **persecute** Christians. The Romans thought they were disloyal. Many Christians, known as **martyrs**, met horrible deaths from torture. During the next two centuries there were fewer persecutions.

The Christian Church continued to grow and make converts. One of the most important was the Roman Emperor Constantine. In 313, by the Edict of Milan, he made **tolerance** of Christianity the official policy of the Roman Empire. Then in 381, Theodosius the Great made Christianity the official religion of the Roman Empire.

stop and think

Create a concept web that explains the beginnings of Christianity. Include names and important events. Share your web with a partner.

Spread of Christianity

Even while Christians were being persecuted, many people converted to Christianity. Once the persecutions ended, Christianity spread quickly. The system of Roman roads, the Roman trading network, and the size of the Empire itself helped Christian missionaries spread the word.

The appeal of Christianity was based on three main causes. First, the message of Jesus attracted the poor and the persecuted. Jesus preached **charity**, or kindness to one another, on Earth and promised equality and a better life after death.

Second, some of the teachings were similar to the ideas of Plato and other Greek philosophers. They appealed to educated people because they were already familiar with the ideas.

Third, people have a need to belong to groups. The Christian Church offered a way to fill this need. Christians built a sense of community by worshiping together and by working together to help the poor and sick.

The Spread of Christianity

Areas largely Christian by A.D. 600

Main areas of Christian growth to A.D. 325

Putting It All Together

Write a short essay about the beginning and spread of Christianity. Use details from the questions and answers you wrote at the beginning of this lesson, as well as the information from your concept web.

Chapter Summary

- The Romans set up a **republic. Patricians** and **plebeians** fought for political power.

- Two **consuls** ran the government of Rome. The Senate ensured that the laws and orders of the consuls were carried out.

- Rome used **diplomacy** and force to extend its power. An example of its diplomacy was the **Roman Confederation**.

- For a time, Julius Caesar took control as a dictator. He was killed by opponents in the Senate.

- The **Pax Romana** was a period of peace.

- Romans **adopted** many ideas from the cultures they conquered and **adapted** them to their needs. **Gladiators** were used for entertainment.

- Power was taken away from the Senate and emperors chose their own **successors**. The title of emperor was **hereditary**.

- The decline and fall of the Roman Empire took place over many years. The major reasons were military, political, social (**values**), and economic.

- The **plague** killed many in the Empire.

- Jesus was considered the **messiah** by some Jews. Much of what we know about Jesus comes from the **Gospels**. His teachings about **charity** and **tolerance** for one another attracted many people.

- The **apostles** and other followers spread Jesus' teachings. For a time, Christians were **persecuted** by the government. Many died as **martyrs**.

Chapter Review

1 Write two-line headlines to describe (a) the end of Etruscan rule, (b) right of the plebeians to hold office, (c) Punic Wars, and (d) end of the Republic.

2 Imagine you are a senator who supports Tiberius Gracchus' land proposal. Write a speech asking your fellow senators to vote for the proposal.

Skill Builder

Analyzing Cause and Effect

The cause is what makes something happen. The effect is what happens—or the outcome of the cause. For example:

The rivalry between Rome and Carthage resulted in the Punic Wars.

Cause: rivalry   Effect: Punic Wars

It is easy to identify the cause and the effect in this sentence because the verb *resulted* signals the relationship between rivalry and Punic Wars. The word *because* in the last sentence is another cause-and-effect signal word. But in this case, the cause and the effect are not easy to identify.

Cause: the verb *resulted* signals   Effect: easy to identify the
      the relationship   cause and effect in this
                                           sentence

The concept webs you created in this chapter are one way to determine cause-and-effect relationships. Another way is to use a flowchart. Sometimes the effect of one event is the cause of another. Then your flowchart would look like this:

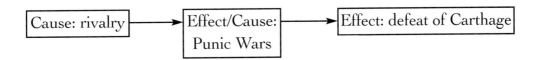

Cause: rivalry → Effect/Cause: Punic Wars → Effect: defeat of Carthage

Use the information about the decline and fall of the Roman Empire to complete these activities.

1 Write a sentence for each of the three Punic Wars. Explain the cause and effect for each war.

2 Write three sentences describing three cause-and-effect relationships that weakened the Roman Empire. Create a cause-and-effect flowchart for each one.

3 Write sentences explaining three causes of the appeal of Christianity. Create a flowchart to show the causes and effect.

UNIT 3

LATER WORLD CIVILIZATIONS

After the fall of the Roman Empire, new empires and kingdoms rose and fell in Europe. The Roman Empire in the East, known as the Byzantine Empire, continued for another thousand years. Kingdoms and empires also began and ended in other parts of the world. In West Africa, mighty empires grew up along trade routes. China spread its influence east to Korea and Japan while continuing to trade with Europe. Mongols, a fierce warrior people from Central Asia, swept across China and seized power for a time.

During the 600s, the prophet Muhammad began to preach a new religion, Islam. In less than a century, his followers spread Islam throughout the Arabian Peninsula and were moving throughout the Mediterranean region.

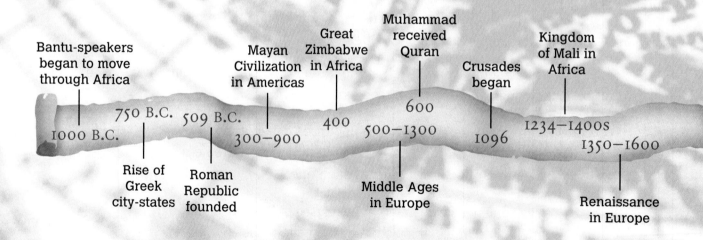

Bantu-speakers
began to move
through Africa

1000 B.C.

750 B.C.

Rise of
Greek
city-states

509 B.C.

Roman
Republic
founded

Mayan
Civilization
in Americas

300–900

Great
Zimbabwe
in Africa

400

Muhammad
received
Quran

600

Middle Ages
in Europe

500–1300

Crusades
began

1096

Kingdom
of Mali in
Africa

1234–1400s

Renaissance
in Europe

1350–1600

How did the West African kingdoms become wealthy?

How do the Five Pillars of Islam guide the life of Muslims?

How did the Incas rule over their vast empire?

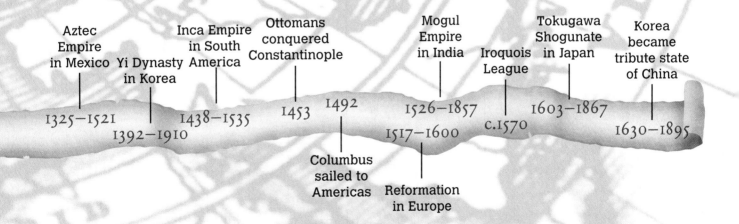

Aztec Empire in Mexico

Yi Dynasty in Korea

Inca Empire in South America

Ottomans conquered Constantinople

Mogul Empire in India

Iroquois League

Tokugawa Shogunate in Japan

Korea became tribute state of China

1325–1521

1392–1910

1438–1535

1453

1492

1526–1857

1517–1600

c.1570

1603–1867

1630–1895

Columbus sailed to Americas

Reformation in Europe

Chapter 8

THE BYZANTINE EMPIRE

(330–1618)

Getting Focused

Skim this chapter to predict what you will be learning.
- Read the lesson titles and subheadings.
- Look at the illustrations and read the captions.
- Examine the maps.
- Review the vocabulary words and terms.

This chapter is about the Byzantine Empire and its neighboring areas. Create a concept web with "Byzantine Empire" in the center. As you read, add notes about Constantine, Justinian, religion, daily life, and the development of Russia. Remember to add the Byzantine Empire and Russia to the world map you began in Chapter 4.

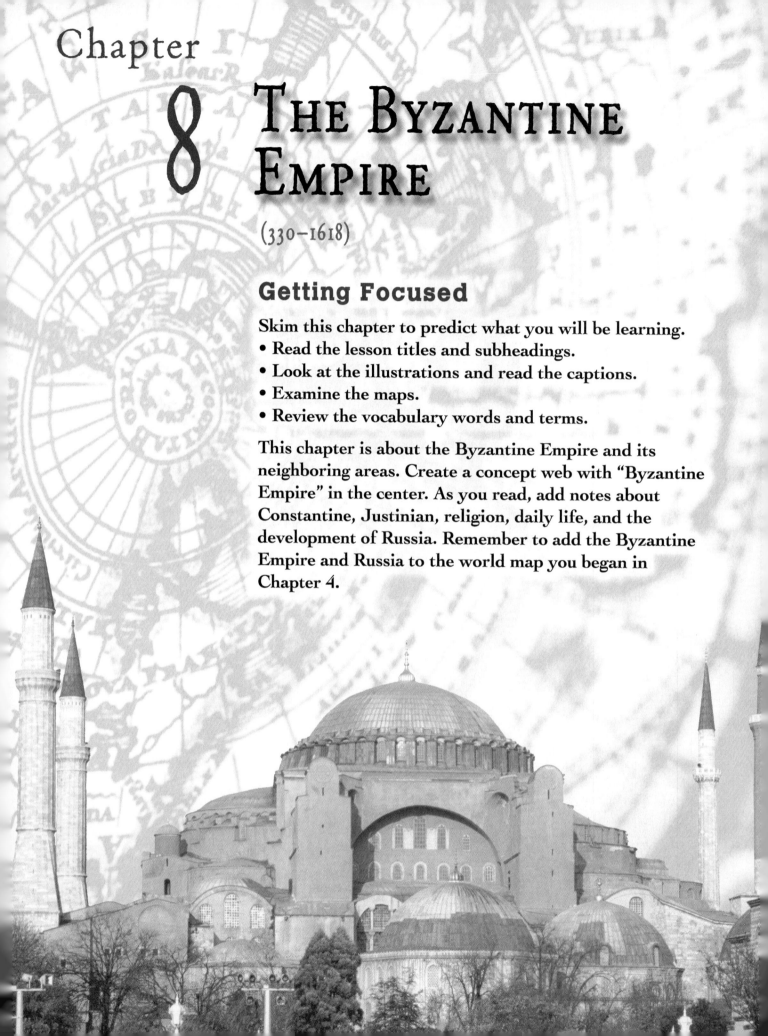

LESSON **1**

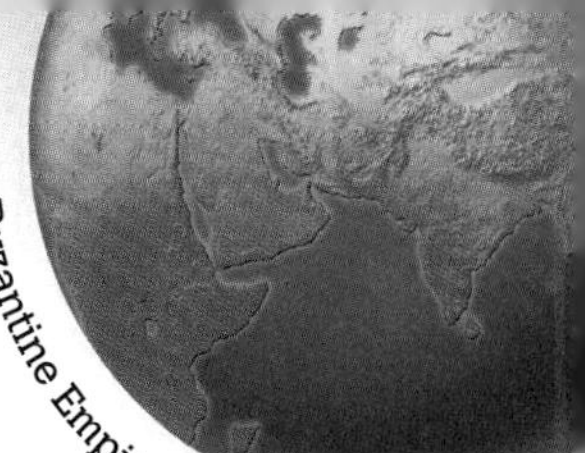

The Byzantine Empire— Successor to Rome

Thinking on Your Own

Create an outline as you read this lesson. The outline will include the Roman numerals I, II, III, and IV—one for each subheading. Be sure to include important facts and details.

Constantine was the Roman emperor from A.D. 306–337. He granted freedom of worship to Christians. Constantine himself had converted to Christianity. Before this time, both Christians and Jews were often persecuted for believing in only one God. He also moved the capital in 330 to Byzantium, which he renamed Constantinople.

Emperor Constantine

The original name of the town survived because the Empire itself was called Byzantine.

focus your reading

Why did Constantine choose Byzantium as the new capital?

What did Justinian accomplish for the Empire?

What were the reasons that Constantinople became an important trade center?

Explain the argument that took place over the use of icons.

vocabulary

aqueducts   Orthodox

civil law   textiles

customs duties   mosaics

schism   icons

Constantine's New Capital

Constantine decided to move the capital of the Roman Empire. He moved the capital away from the city of Rome because Germanic people frequently attacked the city.

Constantine also wanted to keep track of the rival Sassanid Empire in Persia. The site of the new capital was located further to the east than Rome.

Byzantium was a fishing village and market town when Constantine decided to make it his capital. It was located in a strategic position on a peninsula. The location made the city easy to defend against invading armies. The city also had a natural harbor known as the Golden Horn. The town offered the chance to control sea traffic in the Mediterranean and Black Seas. Constantine had new walls built to enlarge the city, which he named Constantinople after himself. To fill the new capital, Constantine offered free grain to people who came to live there.

Hagia Sophia was built as a Christian place of worship and later became a Muslim mosque.

Like many emperors, Constantine loved to build. To his new capital, he added palaces, churches, two theaters, a university, and four courts of law. In addition, he brought statues and art from other places in the empire. He called Constantinople the "New Rome." Rome itself fell to invading Germanic people in 476.

The Empire Expands

Several emperors ruled after Constantine's death. One of the greatest was Justinian. He became emperor in 527. Under the rule of Justinian, the Empire grew to its largest extent.

Time Box

320
Constantinople becomes the Roman capital

476
Rome falls to the Visigoths

527
Justinian becomes emperor

532–537
Justinian rebuilds Hagia Sophia

1054
The Great Schism divides the Church

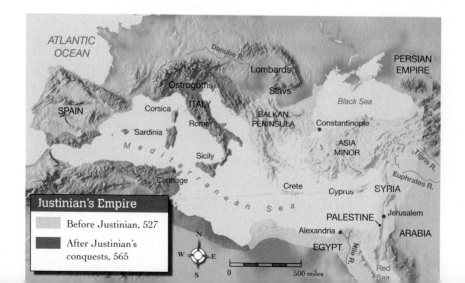

Justinian's Empire

Before Justinian, 527

After Justinian's conquests, 565

ATLANTIC OCEAN

Danube R.

Lombards

Ostrogoths

Slavs

PERSIAN EMPIRE

Black Sea

SPAIN

Corsica

ITALY

BALKAN PENINSULA

Constantinople

Rome

Sardinia

ASIA MINOR

Tigris R.

Mediterranean Sea

Sicily

Euphrates R.

Carthage

Crete

Cyprus

SYRIA

PALESTINE

Jerusalem

Alexandria

ARABIA

EGYPT

Nile R.

Red Sea

0   500 miles

The Byzantines used Greek fire against their enemies. This twelfth century image has the inscription, "The fleet of the Romans firing on an opposing fleet."

However, not everyone approved of his reign. In 532, a protest broke out during a chariot race at the hippodrome, or the circus. It was called the Nika Riot—*nika* is the Greek word meaning "to conquer." That was the word that people shouted during the fighting. Rioters set fire to buildings and crowned a new emperor. When Justinian decided to fight rather than to run away, thousands of rioters were killed. Justinian won the battle and rebuilt Constantinople. He added 25 churches as well as bridges and **aqueducts,** which supplied the city with water.

Justinian is perhaps best known for codifying—or standardizing—Roman laws. The original laws had been added to for centuries. Justinian reviewed the laws and simplified them. These **civil law** codes influenced the laws in many parts of Western Europe.

Daily Life in the Byzantine Empire

For most of its existence, Constantinople was the largest city in Europe. Nearly one million people lived there. The population relied on farmers to supply the grain they needed. These farmers were often free peasants who worked on their own land. There was also a class of citizens who owned large amounts of land. Although the peasants there were not slaves, they

Justinian's Code

When Justinian reviewed all of Roman law, he divided it into 7 sections, containing a total of 50 chapters. The code covered matters such as contracts, property and inheritance laws, slavery, marriage, child guardians, and wills.

Here are some of the laws in Justinian's code:

- Women cannot adopt children after they have lost their own children without the permission of the emperor.

- Males at puberty and females at a marriageable age receive appointed curators until they are 25. Curators are people who protect the interests of those they serve.

- If someone is captured in war and is made a slave, then escapes, that person is again free when he is with his own people.

- If you find a precious stone or gem along the seashore, it is yours.

were bound to the land and could not leave. Some of these peasants were sharecroppers. Part of their harvest went to the owner of the land. Very few of the sharecroppers could ever earn enough money to buy their own land.

Farming was important to the economy of the Byzantine Empire.

Constantinople was an important trade center. The city was the crossroads of trade going both north-south and east-west. Its gold coin, the *bezant*, was the standard form of money for traders from the 500s to the 1200s.

Many people in Byzantine society could read and write. In 425, a school of higher learning in philosophy, medicine, and law was established by Theodosius II. The school, known as

Biography

Empress Theodora

Imagine a love so great that it changed the law. Before he became the emperor, Justinian fell in love with Theodora. She was a wool spinner who had been an actress. However, Roman law did not allow government officials to marry actresses. Justinian had the law changed so that he could marry Theodora.

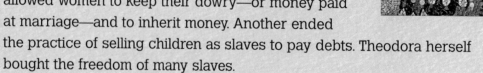

Theodora was very intelligent. She helped Justinian write some laws to help women. One law allowed women to keep their dowry—or money paid at marriage—and to inherit money. Another ended the practice of selling children as slaves to pay debts. Theodora herself bought the freedom of many slaves.

During the Nika Riot, Theodora encouraged Justinian not to run away. She said, "For a king, death is better than dethronement and exile."

Theodora also met with foreign diplomats who came to court. She took part in Councils of State as well. She died of cancer in 548. Justinian ruled alone for almost 20 more years. No major laws were passed after her death.

Constantinople University, lasted for more than one thousand years. Greek literature was also studied and valued. Many of the manuscripts—or written works—we now have are Byzantine copies of Greek works.

The city was also part of the famous Silk Road. The road was used by traders to transport goods between Asia and Europe. All of the goods that came through the city were subject to taxes. These taxes, called **customs duties**, helped make the city rich. In addition, artisans in Constantinople bought goods and added to their value. For example, they made jewelry out of raw gems from India and dyed wool from Europe. Then they resold these items to make a profit.

After Justinian's death, the Byzantine Empire began to weaken. It lost territory that had originally been part of the Roman Empire. Land that had been reclaimed by Justinian was soon lost to other growing powers. The Empire continued until the mid-fifteenth century, however, when it was conquered by the Turks. They renamed the capital city Istanbul. The church of Hagia Sophia became a center of Islamic worship. The influence of the Empire is still felt in nations such as Greece, Serbia, Russia, and Turkey.

Religion and Art of the Byzantine Empire

Just as there were political tensions between the capitals of Rome and Constantinople, disagreements over religion also occurred. Two groups formed within the Christian Church, and they argued over beliefs and practices. Some of these, such as whether a priest should have a beard, seem less important to us now.

There was also disagreement about the power of Rome over the Eastern churches. The pope claimed to rule over all the Christian churches. Not surprisingly, the head of the Church at Constantinople, called a patriarch, disagreed. In 1054, the pope and the patriarch broke their relationship. This was known as the Great **Schism**. The Eastern church became known as the

Eastern **Orthodox** Church. The Western church was the Roman Catholic Church. The split continues to this day.

Textiles were woven by women.

Istanbul was well known as a center for artisans. People worked in gold and silver, made glassware, and wove **textiles**. The textile, or fabric, industry grew even more when silkworms were illegally imported from China. Soon, silk from Constantinople was known for its high quality.

Along with their magnificent architecture, the Byzantines are well known for **mosaics** and **icons**. The Romans made mosaics from bits of marble. Beginning around 330, the Byzantines began decorating the floors, ceilings, and domes of their churches with pictures made of bits of colored glass.

Religion was often the focus of intricate mosaics.

Religious icons—or pictures of religious figures—could be painted on wood or made of mosaics. The Church had arguments about whether icons should be allowed. Some people were afraid that the icons were being worshiped instead of God. Others believed it was wrong to make any image of God, as was written in the Ten Commandments. Islam, which was becoming important in the East, did not allow images either. Many of the icons were burned or painted over. The church finally agreed in 843 to allow icons as long as they were not worshiped.

Achievements of the Byzantine Empire
• street lights • table forks • gunpowder • silk making • Justinian's code of laws • mosaics • icons • architecture

Putting It All Together

Look back at the laws of Hammurabi's Code in Chapter 2. Use a Venn diagram to compare the laws of Hammurabi with the laws of Justinian. Under which ruler would you prefer to live? Write a short paragraph supporting your decision with facts and details.

The Rise of Russia

Thinking on Your Own

Create a T-chart in your notebook. Label the left column "Invaders and Leaders" and the right column "Details." As you read, make a list of all the different countries that invaded Russia and the leaders involved. In the right column, take bulleted notes about each invasion and leader. Share your list with a partner.

The Byzantine Empire continued to influence other nearby lands. The land we know as Russia was settled by nomadic people from eastern Europe around A.D. 500. These people, originally from central Asia, were known as Slavs. Later, Vikings explored Russia. They came from what is now Scandinavia. They set up trade routes along some of the major rivers of Russia.

focus your reading

What groups of people first settled in Russia?

Explain the contributions Cyril and Methodius made to Russia.

What were some of the contributions of the Byzantine Empire to Russia?

Discuss the importance of the Golden Horde.

vocabulary

principalities   tribute

feudal   horde

The Mission to the Slavs

Two brothers from Greece, Cyril and Methodius, went to the Slavic people as missionaries in the ninth century. The Slavs, who settled in the region northwest of Kiev, had no system of writing. Cyril and Methodius developed the Cyrillic alphabet. It allowed the people to learn how to read and write.

Viking Trade Routes

    Extent of Kievan Rus

—— Viking trade routes

0   500 miles

Cyril and Methodius with their Cyrillic alphabet

The Greek alphabet influenced the Cyrillic one, which is still used in Russia today.

The Cyrillic alphabet represents the sounds of Slavic languages more accurately than the Greek alphabet could. After the brothers created this alphabet, they translated the Bible into the Slavic language.

Kievan Rus

During the ninth and tenth centuries, the Slavs began forming territories ruled by powerful princes. These territories were called **principalities**. A group of them banded together as a confederation called Kievan Rus. Kiev, located north of Constantinople, was their major city. The Dnieper River and the Black Sea connect the two cities.

The rulers of the Kievan Rus were Vikings. The Vikings used the rivers as trade routes for slaves, amber, and furs. They also raided the Byzantine Empire. In 862, Rurik became a prince of Novgorod, a city farther north of Kiev. It may be that his clan name, Rus, is where Russia got its name. Oleg, who followed Rurik as prince, enlarged the rule to include more land. Rurik's descendants ruled over Russia until 1598.

Kiev became very rich through its trade with Constantinople and other regions. By the eleventh century, Kiev was reported to have 400 churches and eight large market centers. Nearly 30,000 people lived in Kiev by the early twelfth century.

Early Russia, 879–912

Vladimir I was the ruler of Kievan Rus from 980 until 1015. In 988, he converted to Christianity. One legend says that he sent people to observe other religions. The group was most impressed with the beauty of worship in Hagia Sophia. This was the start of the Russian Orthodox religion. Kiev's Saint Sofia was built in 1037 to rival Hagia Sophia.

Vladimir I also adopted the **feudal** system—a form of government used throughout the Byzantine Empire. The Kievan Rus had been ruled by clans. In a feudal system there is a powerful ruler to whom everyone owes honor and loyalty. Like the Byzantines, the Rus developed a written code of laws. Eventually, the Rus claimed that the city of Moscow was the Third Rome.

The Golden Horde

East of Kievan Rus was a tribe known as Mongols. The Mongols were originally from an area known as Mongolia in East Asia. These men were fierce fighters and were becoming more powerful. They were especially known for their skill with archery and horses. Genghis Khan, who ruled from 1206–1227, led an Asian army against Russia in 1223.

Gold and silver domes crown the cathedral of St. Sofia.

One of Khan's grandsons, Batu Khan, led an invasion of Russia in 1237. The Mongols, however, did not remain in Russia. They continued moving to the southwest and eventually conquered what are today Poland, Hungary, and Austria. In 1242, Batu Khan withdrew his armies from Europe. However, they still demanded military service from the people and **tribute**, or taxes. Batu ruled over an area that stretched from the Caspian and Black Seas to western Siberia's plains. It was known as the Golden Horde. A **horde** was the name for a political division, similar to a principality. It has come to mean "a large crowd."

Putting It All Together

Work with a partner to create a timeline of events in early Russian history. Include invasions, leaders, and other important events. Use the notes you took at the beginning of this lesson to help you develop your timeline.

Chapter Summary

- Constantine moved the capital of the Empire from Rome to Byzantium, which he renamed Constantinople.
- Justinian created a summary of Rome's **civil laws**.
- Justinian rebuilt the church of Hagia Sophia, one of the oldest churches in the world. He also added **aqueducts** to Constantinople.
- The Byzantine Empire was known for its **mosaics** and **icons**.
- Constantinople was an important trade center and farming region. **Customs duties** helped the city become wealthy. Artisans created beautiful objects, including silk **textiles**.
- Disagreements between Rome and Constantinople led to a split in the Christian Church known as the Great **Schism**. The Roman Catholic Church became the Western church. The Eastern church is known as the **Orthodox** Church.
- The Byzantine Empire ended in the mid-fourteenth century with the Turks' victory.
- Viking and Eastern Slavic people settled in Russia.
- Missionaries Methodius and Cyril developed an alphabet for the Russians and translated the Bible.
- Strong rulers led **principalities** in Russia.
- Russians adopted many Byzantine ways of life, including the **feudal** system.
- Mongol invaders attacked Russia and demanded **tribute** money. They ruled an area known as the Golden **Horde**.

Chapter Review

1 Choose one of the events of the chapter and retell the story using cartoon storyboards.

2 Write a news article about something from the chapter, using at least five of the vocabulary words.

Skill Builder

Analyzing Special-Purpose Maps

Maps can do more than tell you about the geography of an area. Some maps have special purposes. When reading a special-purpose map, be sure to:

- Read the titles carefully to determine what they can teach you.
- Look at the key for helpful symbols and colors used.
- Examine the map's scale, which tells you how to measure distances.

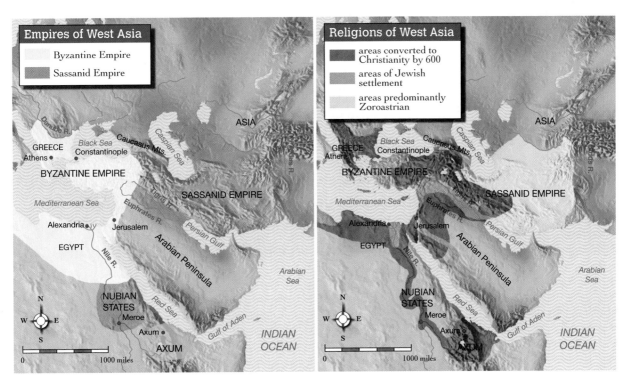

Use the maps to answer the following questions:

1 What different information does each map contain?

2 Which map would you use to find out where Jewish settlements were located in West Asia?

3 Where was the Zoroastrian religion strongest?

4 How far south did the Byzantine Empire spread?

5 What seas did the Byzantine Empire touch?

Chapter 9

ISLAM AND MUSLIM CIVILIZATIONS

(622–1699)

Getting Focused

Skim this chapter to predict what you will be learning.
- Read the lesson titles and subheadings.
- Look at the illustrations and read the captions.
- Examine the maps.
- Review the vocabulary words.

What changes have you seen in your school this year? How did these changes happen? Did one person make the change? A group? Make a concept web with "effective ways to bring about change" in the center. Write your observations about the changes you have seen. Also write your ideas about ways to bring about change. Then discuss and compare your ideas with a partner. Remember to add the Islamic Empire to your world map.

The Beginnings of Islam

Thinking on Your Own

What do you already know about the history and practice of Islam? What would you like to know? Create a K-W-L chart. In the first column, list "What I Know." In the second column, list "What I Want to Know." In the third column, list "What I Learned." Fill in the first two columns as you skim the lesson and the last column as you read the chapter.

M ost of the major religions of the world began with the thoughts and teachings of one person. In some areas of the world these men are called prophets. Judaism began in 2000 B.C. with the Mesopotamian leader, Abraham. Christianity appeared around A.D. 0 with Jesus of Nazareth. Islam's beginnings are traced to Muhammad Ibn Abdallah in A.D. 620. Like the others, Muhammad was a simple man who cared about the people of his country.

focus your reading

Why was Muhammad concerned about the Arabic society of his day?

Why did Muhammad and his followers go to Madinah?

Describe the conflict that divided the followers of Islam.

vocabulary

Quran	caravans
boycott	hajj
monotheists	caliphs

The Life of the Prophet Muhammad

When he was forty years old, an Arab merchant named Muhammad Ibn Abdallah heard a voice that changed his life. Muhammad was in a cave on Mount Hira outside Makkah (Mecca). Makkah is located in what is now the western part of Saudi Arabia. Muhammad usually went there during the month of Ramadan to fast and pray.

Picture by www.Artislamic.com

The prophet Muhammad would retreat to a cave in Mount Hira to meditate.

Muhammad was worried about the Arabian people. They were more concerned with making money than with traditional Arabic values such as caring for one another. They sometimes mistreated slaves and children. They were also worshiping many gods instead of the one true God, Allah. At the shrine known as the Kaaba, there were 360 pagan gods. The Kaaba was thought to have been built by Adam. It was associated with a meeting of Abraham (Ibrahim) and his son Ishmael (Ismail), who was considered the father of Arab tribes.

According to legend, an angel appeared to Muhammad in the cave. The angel carried a scroll which he commanded Muhammad to read. Like most of his tribe, Muhammad could not read or write. The angel insisted he recite the words on the scroll. Muhammad recited words that are now part of the **Quran** (KUH•RAHN). The Quran is the sacred scriptures of Islam.

Muhammad doubted the source of his experience. For two years he told no one except his wife, Khadija, and a few close friends. Over the next several years, Muhammad received the full text of the Quran.

At that time, people were used to memorizing large pieces of literature. They trusted their memories more than they did written words. The text of the Quran was not written down until after the prophet's death. Muhammad became unpopular in Makkah because he spoke out against injustice. The ruling clan placed a **boycott** on Muhammad's tribe. No one would sell them food. This boycott lasted for two years.

Time Box

610

The prophet Muhammad receives the first parts of the Quran (Koran) in Makkah (Mecca). The Quran will become the holy book of Islam.

622

Muhammad and 70 families of his followers go to Madinah (Medina).

632

Muhammad dies.

638

Muslims capture Jerusalem, which becomes the third holiest Muslim city after Makkah and Madinah.

The Five Pillars of Islam

These five rules are required of all devout followers of Islam:

1. Believe in Allah as the only God.
2. Pray five times a day.
3. Give to the poor.
4. Fast during Ramadan.
5. Go to Makkah on pilgrimage.

Madinah is the second holiest city in Islam.

In 622, a group of 70 families who believed the words Muhammad preached left Makkah to settle in Yathrib, in what is now western Saudi Arabia. They renamed Yathrib, Madinah (Medina). They became known as the Muslim—the followers of Islam. Such a move was a major decision. The people were leaving their old tribal loyalties, not just changing locations. They were giving their first loyalty to the ideals of Islam rather than to blood ties. This move was so important that the Islamic calendar considers it Year 1.

Muhammad did not at first think he was founding a new religion. He thought he was a Christian or Jewish prophet. He respected both Jews and Christians. They were also **monotheists** and "people of the Book." He had prayers on Friday nights, as the Jewish people did, and called for a fast on their Day of Atonement. However, the Jews did not believe Muhammad was a prophet. They did not accept his version of their scriptures.

Muhammad finally realized that the Muslims were not going to be a part of the Jewish faith. He had his followers switch the direction of their prayers away from Jerusalem and toward Makkah.

stop and think

Think about how Islam was different than other religions of the time. Make a bulleted list of how Muhammad's ideas and beliefs set Islam apart from other religions.

Muhammad's Ideals

Perhaps because he had been orphaned by the age of six, Muhammad was very concerned about helping others. He was interested in the equality of women. The Quran addresses both women and men and sees them as equally responsible before Allah. Muhammad mended his own clothes, helped with household tasks, and consulted his wives for advice. Islam also allowed women to divorce and to inherit property.

The Quran is the holy book of Islam.

This was hundreds of years before nations in Europe allowed these rights.

Muhammad was interested in peace. Arabic tribes had long been at war over the scarce resources of the desert region. The raiding of **caravans** was customary. Caravans were groups of people who traveled together. Strict rules governed the practice. For example, if your tribe or clan had made a treaty with another tribe, you could not raid that tribe's caravans. The battles that occurred after the Muslims went to Madinah were necessary. If the Muslims did not win the battles, they would be killed and the faith of Islam would die. The rule of the desert was to kill or be killed.

Muhammad tried to end the warfare by going on a **hajj**, or pilgrimage to Makkah, in 628. The hajj was a long-standing custom in the region. People came to Makkah to the Kaaba to worship. There were rules that forbade warfare or any killing. The pilgrimage was successful and led to a treaty between the ruling tribe of Makkah and the Muslim.

People were impressed with Muhammad's courage and his attempts at peace. More and more people converted to Islam. In 630, when the ruling tribe of Makkah broke the treaty, Muhammad led an army of ten thousand against the city. The people of Makkah knew they could not defeat the Muslim. They opened the city gates and surrendered.

Terms to Know	
imam	leader of a Muslim congregation
Islam	surrender to God's will
jihad	effort, struggle
mosque	Muslim holy building
Muslim	one who accepts the teachings of Islam
Ramadan	month of fasting
salat	ritual prayer made five times a day
zakat	gifts to the poor

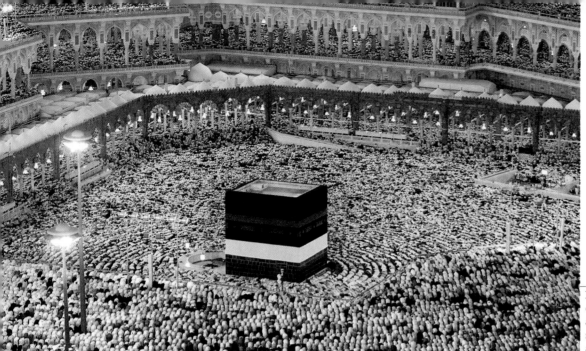

Pilgrims in Makkah circle the Kaaba, a sacred black stone covered by a beautiful cloth.

The Spread of Islam

By the time of Muhammad's death in 632, most of the Arabian tribes had become converts or allies of the Muslim. Four men who were relatives or friends to Muhammad ruled during the next thirty years. They were known as **caliphs**, or deputies. They did not claim to be prophets, but they guided the community in Muslim beliefs. As a group, they were known as the *Rashidun*, or the "rightly guided" caliphs.

The Rightly Guided Caliphs				
	Abu Bakr	**Umar**	**Uthman**	**Ali**
Relationship to Muhammad	• father-in-law	• friend	• son-in-law • member of the Umayyad family	• first cousin • son-in-law
Career	• merchant	• merchant	• merchant	• soldier • writer
Caliphate	• 632–634	• 634–644	• 644–656	• 656–661
Achievements as Caliph	• spread Islam to all of Arabia • restored peace after death of Muhammad • created code of conduct in war • compiled Quran verses	• spread Islam to Syria, Egypt, and Persia • redesigned government • held a census • made taxes more fair • built roads and canals • aided poor	• spread Islam into Afghanistan and eastern Mediterranean • organized a navy • improved the government • built more roads, bridges, and canals • distributed text of the Quran	• reformed tax collection and other government systems • spent most of caliphate battling Mu'awiyah, the governor of Syria

Under the Rashidun, the Muslim Empire expanded. The Persian and Byzantine Empires had been fighting one another for many years. Their armies and resources were exhausted. Their lands came under Muslim control.

Each of the last three caliphs was assassinated. When Ali, who was Muhammad's cousin and son-in-law, was killed, the Muslim became divided. Some people believed that only Ali's descendants should rule. These people were known as the supporters of Ali, the *Shiah i-Ali*. The term was contracted to Shia or Shiite. At that time, people felt that the spirit and wisdom of one person could be passed on to his or her descendants.

The Names of Allah

The Quran gives 99 names to describe Allah, including:

The Guide	The Merciful
The Mighty	The Protector
The Creator	The Majestic
The Provider	The All Knowing
The Great One	The Judge

Another group believed that Muhammad's successors did not need to be his direct descendants. Following the way of Muhammad and being from his clan was enough. The way of Islam was called the *Sunna*. These people became known as the Sunni Muslims.

One of the clans, the Umayyad, refused to recognize Ali as ruler. They believed his clan had something to do with the murder of one of the earlier caliphs. The conflict did not lead to war, however. Muslims refused to fight against other Muslims. A group of judges decided who would be the next leader. They chose Mu'awiyah, the governor of Syria, as the leader. He was the choice of the Sunnis.

The split between Shia and Sunni Muslims continues to the present. Sunni Muslims make up the majority of Muslims around the world.

Putting It All Together

Look at the concept web that you made at the beginning of this chapter. Using what you have learned in this lesson and your bulleted notes from Stop and Think, write a paragraph that explains how Muhammad tried to bring about change.

LESSON 2

Empires and Legacies

Thinking on Your Own

What are some of the problems that come with having a large empire? Make a list and then work with a partner to see how your lists compare. Based on what you know about the Roman Empire, write a paragraph predicting what you think will happen to the Islamic Empire.

The Islamic Empire was a vast region. It was difficult to rule. Different problems confronted people in very different regions. Communication and transportation networks were slow. Eventually, the Empire broke apart.

Dynasties and Crusades

The Umayyad Dynasty, which included fourteen caliphs, lasted from 661 until 750. These rulers moved the capital to Damascus in Syria. Under the Umayyad, Islam continued to expand. The Empire reached as far west as Spain, where the Muslim conquests ended in 732. In addition to gaining the eastern and southern parts of the old Roman Empire, the Muslims moved northwest into central

focus your reading

Explain why the capital of the Islamic Empire was moved to Damascus, Baghdad, and Cairo.

What event caused Europe to see Islam as a world power?

What were the Safavid and Ottoman Empires?

Discuss some of the contributions of Islam to the world.

vocabulary

crusades	astrolabe
chieftain	calligraphy
tribute	minarets

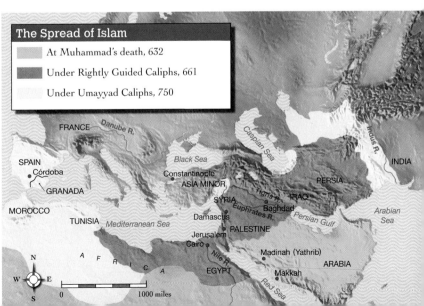

The Spread of Islam

- At Muhammad's death, 632
- Under Rightly Guided Caliphs, 661
- Under Umayyad Caliphs, 750

The Great Mosque at Cordoba is an example of Islamic architecture in Spain.

Asia and east into Persia and Mesopotamia.

In 750, a descendant of Muhammad's uncle founded a new dynasty, the Abbasid. The Abbasid Dynasty was the result of a revolution and the massacre of more than 70 Umayyad leaders. The leaders were killed by an Abbasid general while they were attending a banquet. The new Abbasid capital was Baghdad—the capital of modern-day Iraq. Located on the Tigris River, it was a crossroads for caravan travel.

This was a time of peace within the Empire. Warriors had been the ideal citizens during the Umayyad Dynasty. Now, judges and merchants were respected. During the ninth century, the caliphs supported writers and artists.

Different parts of the Empire soon began to break away. Spain, Egypt, and Morocco on the African north coast each formed independent dynasties. The Seljuk Turks grew stronger, eventually taking over Baghdad in 1055. They defeated the Byzantine army. Then the Byzantine Empire asked the governments of Europe for help.

Beginning in 1096, the Christian nations of Europe mounted a series of **crusades** against the Turks. The Christians wanted to regain control of the holy sites under Muslim control. They had limited success.

A powerful Muslim ruler, Saladin, invaded Jerusalem in 1187. His army destroyed the Christian forces there. Saladin allowed Christian worship to continue and did not massacre the Christian invaders.

The Mongols of China and central Asia posed a greater threat to the Islamic Empire. In 1258, an invading force destroyed Baghdad after sweeping through Persia and Mesopotamia. Cairo, a city in Egypt, then became the new center of Islam.

Sufi mystics believe that dancing brings them closer to Allah.

Time Box

661–750
Umayyad Dynasty

1096
Crusades begin

1258
Mongols invade Baghdad

1453
Ottomans conquer Constantinople

1683
Ottomans attack Vienna

The Safavid Empire

The Islamic Empire became divided geographically. Two of the most successful empires were the Safavid and Ottoman Empires.

From 1500 until 1722, the Safavids ruled in Persia, now known as Iran, in southwest Asia. Their name comes from a leading brotherhood among Islam, the Safawiyya. The term means "red heads." They were called this because of the red caps they wore. The Safavids had originally been Sunni. During the fifteenth century, however, they became extremist Shia. They fought against the Ottomans to gain territory. The hatred between Sunni and Shia Muslims dates from this era.

The Poetry of Rumi

The Sufis were the religous mystics of Sunni Islam. They focused on close personal relationships with Allah. They were also known for their ecstatic dancing and chanting.

Rumi was a poet who composed as he danced. In the following poem, Rumi imagines the call of Allah to Muhammad.

reading for understanding

Discuss the descriptive images used by Rumi.

What does God encourage Muhammad to do?

One Who Wraps Himself

God called the Prophet Muhammad Muzzammil,
"The One Who Wraps Himself,"
  and said,
"Come out from under your cloak, you so fond
  of hiding and running away.

Don't cover your face.
The world is a reeling, drunken body, and you
  are its intelligent head.
Don't hide the candle
  of your clarity. Stand up and burn through
  the night, my prince.

Without your light
  a great lion is held captive by a rabbit!

Be the captain of the ship,
Mustafa, my chosen one,
  my expert guide.
Look how the caravan of civilization
Has been ambushed.
Fools are everywhere in charge.
Do not practice solitude like Jesus. Be *in*
  the assembly,
  and take charge of it.
As the bearded griffin,
  the *Humay*, lives on Mt. Quf because he's
  native to it,
  so you should live most naturally out in public
  and be a communal teacher of souls."

Read a Primary Source

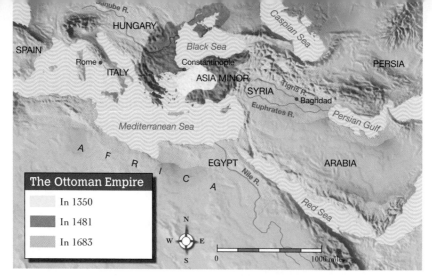

The Ottoman Empire

In 1350

In 1481

In 1683

N W E S

0   1000 miles

Islamic scholars made many contributions in science, literature, and architecture.

The Ottoman Empire

In the early fourteenth century, Osman, a Turkish tribal **chieftain**—or leader—founded a principality in western Turkey. The empire he built is called Osmanli in the Turkish language. It is known in English as the Ottoman Empire. This empire grew from a Turkish nomadic tribe. Members of the tribe fled after the Mongol invasion destroyed Seljuk rule.

Osman and his son moved into Europe. Rulers in the Balkans of Eastern Europe paid **tribute**—or monetary payment—to them each year. The Ottomans fought against many European powers, gaining and losing territory. As a result of the development of cannons, the design of forts and other military buildings changed. Battle formations also changed.

Using this new military technology, the Ottomans captured Constantinople in 1453. They changed the city's name to Istanbul. It became the capital of the Ottoman Empire for the next 469 years.

The Empire continued to grow. Everyone except the Safavids in Iran saw the Ottomans as the heirs to the caliphs.

Under Süleyman the Magnificent, the Ottomans became a world power. However, after his death, the Empire declined. Taxing farmers, using slaves for the army, and keeping a large army all contributed to the decay.

stop and think

Discuss with a partner the contributions of the Muslim rulers and scholars. Then write a bulleted list of the ten most important contributions by Muslim rulers and scholars. Add to your list as you finish reading the lesson.

Islamic Science and Art

Islamic scholars had translations of texts from Greek and Indian sources. From these, they developed an interest in astronomy and astrology. Knowledge of medicine came from Persian Christians, one of whom became a court physician. Other medical knowledge came from Jewish physicians.

During the early ninth century, one of the caliphs founded the "House of Wisdom." Here, Muslim and Christian scholars translated scientific and literary works from Greek into Arabic. Through their efforts, the learning of ancient cultures was preserved and later passed to Europe.

Islam also made great advances in mathematics. They invented algebra and borrowed the Hindu number symbols of 0 to 9. Today we call these symbols Arabic numerals. Muslim scientists improved the **astrolabe**. Sailors used the astrolabe to figure out their position at sea based on the location of the stars. Using the astrolabe to measure distances, Muslims discovered that the earth was round. The Arabs also pioneered work in chemistry and medicine. They were the first to learn that blood moves to and from the heart.

An early astrolabe

Muslims are also known for their literature and their **calligraphy**. *Calligraphy* means "beautiful writing." Because Islam forbids images in worship, calligraphers decorated mosques with verses from the Quran. Calligraphy was also used on books, carpets, and porcelain.

Because it became important to be able to study the Quran, schools were established and many people learned to read and write. Muslim writers created books of history, poetry, biography, and stories such as *The Arabian Nights*.

The Muslims built beautiful mosques and other buildings. The mosques have **minarets**, or towers, from which to call the faithful to prayer.

Putting It All Together

Make a Venn diagram comparing the Ottoman and Safavid Empires. List at least three distinct differences between the empires and three similarities.

Minarets are towers from which people are summoned to *salat*, or prayer.

www.Artislamic.com

Chapter Summary

- Muhammad had a series of revelations. People were angry and called for a **boycott** against his clan.
- Muhammad's followers were **monotheists** who worshiped Allah and followed the **Quran**.
- Muhammad tried to make peace among the tribes who raided each other's **caravans**. A treaty was created after Muhammad went on a **hajj**.
- After Muhammad's death, the community was led by a series of four **caliphs**.
- Sunni and Shia Muslims disagreed over who had a right to rule.
- Beginning in 1096, European nations sponsored **crusades** to try to regain Christian holy sites.
- Mongols invaded the Islamic world in the thirteenth century.
- The Ottoman Empire, led by **chieftains**, expanded into Europe. In 1453, Ottomans conquered Constantinople, which they renamed Istanbul. Conquered people paid **tribute** to the Ottoman rulers.
- Muslim scientists made advances in science and medicine, including using the **astrolabe** to determine the size of Earth.
- The **calligraphy** of Islamic artists is a way to decorate without using images.
- Islamic mosques are easily identified by their prayer towers, or **minarets**.

Chapter Review

1 Choose one event from Muhammad's life and illustrate it. You may use any artistic style to depict the event.

2 Write a three-paragraph essay explaining the importance of one of the empires discussed in the chapter.

3 Create a flowchart that illustrates the changes that took place in the Islamic Empire.

Skill Builder

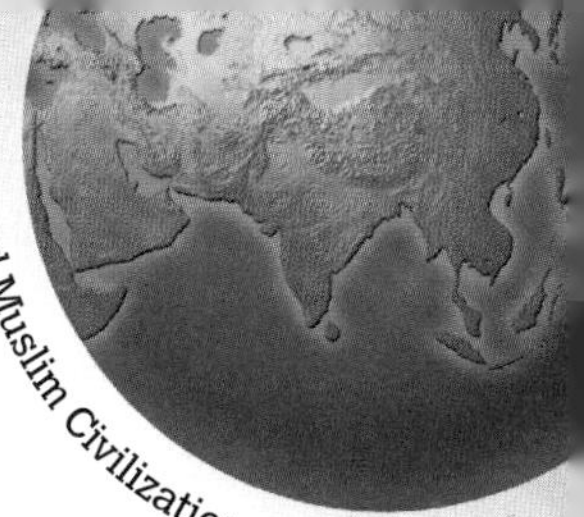

Reading a Circle Graph

Graphs represent data visually. They condense large amounts of information so that people understand it more easily. Graphs often show relationships. For example, a circle graph represents parts of a whole as percentages. To read a graph, follow these steps:

- Read the title of the graph so you know what it is about.

- Look at the labels of each segment.

- Study the colors and patterns used and compare them with the key.

- Compare the parts of the circle to find the relationships and draw conclusions.

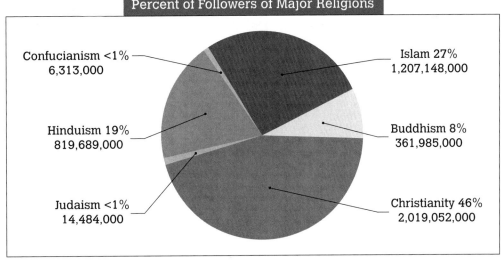

Percent of Followers of Major Religions

Confucianism <1% 6,313,000

Islam 27% 1,207,148,000

Hinduism 19% 819,689,000

Buddhism 8% 361,985,000

Judaism <1% 14,484,000

Christianity 46% 2,019,052,000

Use the circle graph above to answer the following questions:

1 Which religion has the largest percentage of followers? What is the percentage?

2 What percentage of people follow Islam?

3 Do Hindus or Buddhists represent a larger portion of the whole?

4 How could you state the percentage of Jewish followers in relation to Confucian followers?

Chapter 10

CIVILIZATIONS OF AFRICA

(750 B.C.–A.D. 1570)

Getting Focused

Skim this chapter to predict what you will be learning.
- Read the lesson titles and subheadings.
- Look at the illustrations and read the captions.
- Examine the maps.
- Review the vocabulary words and terms.

Make a four column chart. Label the columns "Geography," "People," "Places," and "Events." Then make a list of at least five things that you know about Africa. They might be facts about geography or about famous African people, places, or events. Review your list with a partner and add them to your chart. As you read the chapter, add at least twenty new facts to the chart. Be sure to find facts for each column. Remember to add Africa to your world map.

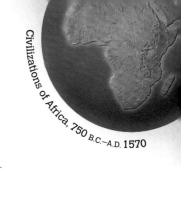
LESSON 1

The Bantu Migrations

Thinking on Your Own

Examine the subheadings and illustrations in this lesson. Write four questions in your notebook that you would like answered by studying this lesson. After you finish reading the lesson, answer the questions.

The African continent has many different **environments**. A region's environment includes all the outside factors that influence the development of a people. Among these factors are the physical geography and the climate where the people live. Climate is the weather that a place has over a long period of time. It is important to learn about the geography of Africa in order to understand the different kingdoms and empires that developed there.

focus your reading

Explain the land and climate zones in Africa.

Who are the Bantu-speakers?

Why did the Bantu-speakers migrate throughout Africa?

Describe African society during the Bantu migration.

vocabulary

environment

vegetation

savanna

rain forest

slash-and-burn

ethnic group

river basin

Geography of the African Continent

Africa has bands, or zones, of different kinds of climates and vegetation. **Vegetation** includes grasses, plants, bushes, and trees. The desert zones include the Sahara in the north and the smaller Kalahari in the south. Together, they make up about 40 percent of the African continent. Beginning in ancient times, traders set up a network to link sub-Saharan Africa with the Mediterranean region. Sub-Saharan Africa includes the regions located south of the Sahara Desert. Traders moved back and forth across the Sahara on camels.

Olokon was a sea god to the people of the Ife Kingdom.

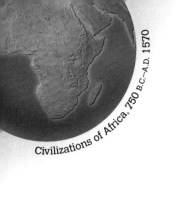

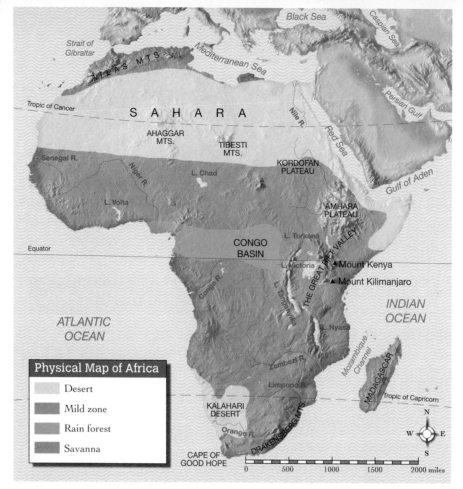

Another large area is the **savanna**. This is a region of grasslands with small trees and bushes scattered here and there. Usually it rains enough in the savanna for farming and herding. However, a stretch of dry years without rain results in droughts and famine. Beginning in the 500s, wealthy kingdoms and empires developed in the savanna region of West Africa. Their wealth came from trade.

About 10 percent of the African continent is **rain forest**. This is the area bordering the equator. The region is very hot and receives a great amount of rain. As a result, vegetation is thick, but some farming has been possible since early times. Africans developed the **slash-and-burn** method to clear the forest. They would cut down trees and plants and then burn them to open land for planting crops.

Africa's geography includes savanna (left) and rain forest (right).

Civilizations of Africa, 750 B.C.–A.D. 1570

stop and think

Write a description of the various climates of the African continent. Use as many directions in your description as you can. Besides east, west, north, and south, try to use the intermediate directions northeast, northwest, southeast, and southwest. Share your description with a partner. Quiz one another on the climate zones of Africa.

Both the far northern region and the southern tip of the continent have areas with mild, rainy winters and hot, dry summers. In the north, this region is along the Mediterranean Sea.

Bantu-Speaking People

The Bantu-speaking people are not an **ethnic group**, like Italians, Chinese, Serbians, or Hispanics. An ethnic group shares the same culture. Bantu-speakers belong to many ethnic groups. What they have in common is their language family, or group of languages. There are over 300 Bantu languages or dialects. Today, over 180 million Africans speak a Bantu language.

The Bantu on the Move

Historians think that the first Bantu-speakers lived in what is today the nation of Cameroon. Bantu-speakers were farmers who moved and settled in small family groups. They lived in the region around the Niger River. Possibly as early as 1000 B.C., the Bantu began to move south into the Congo River basin. A **river basin** is a large area that includes a major river and its tributaries. Sometime around 500 B.C., Bantu-speakers also moved east. Over time, they spread throughout central Africa. By the 1200s, the Bantu were in much of southern Africa.

Archaeologists think that two events made it possible for Bantu-speakers to move out from the area of the Niger River. First was the discovery of iron-making. Someone figured out how to make iron into axes and hoes. With iron axes, men could cut down trees, and with iron hoes they could farm. Second, a trade network linked the Niger River area with the east coast. Traders along this route brought yams

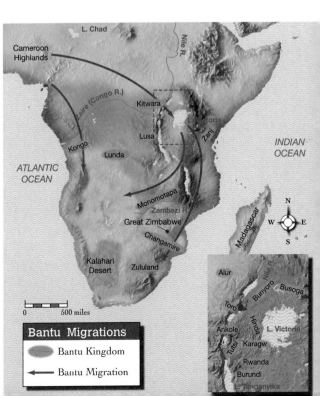

Bantu Migrations

⬭ Bantu Kingdom

⟵ Bantu Migration

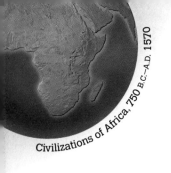

and bananas from Malaysia in Southeast Asia. These crops were especially suited to growing in hot, wet climates.

But why did the Bantu move? Archaeologists think that the population in the Niger River area was growing too large. The pressure of too many people caused some family groups to move to a new place. Over time, the population increased in the new area. Again, some families would decide to leave and look for a new place to settle. This cycle was repeated until Bantu-speakers had migrated to southern Africa. This movement took place over hundreds of years.

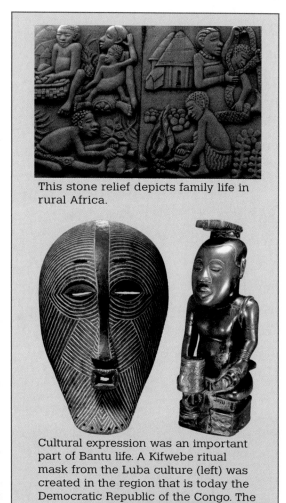

This stone relief depicts family life in rural Africa.

Cultural expression was an important part of Bantu life. A Kifwebe ritual mask from the Luba culture (left) was created in the region that is today the Democratic Republic of the Congo. The Ndop carving of King Mishe miShyaan maMbul Kuba was created in Zaire.

The environments were different in new areas where the Bantu settled. As a result, their previous ways of life did not always work in the new region. The Bantu-speakers had to adapt. For example, as the Bantu moved out of the rain forest and into the savanna, some gave up farming. They took up herding cattle. Other Bantu-speakers still farmed but with different crops. In East Africa, Bantu-speakers became part of a trade network that reached across the Indian Ocean.

Often the migrants learned new skills and how to grow new foods from people already living in the new areas. For the most part, the mixing of Bantu-speakers with native populations was peaceful. In many areas in central and southern Africa, large states and empires developed from the mixing of Bantu-speakers with others.

Putting It All Together

Use a modern political map of Africa to trace the migration of the Bantu-speakers. Work with a partner to make a list of all the modern nations that the Bantu moved through and the places in which they settled.

LESSON 2

The Trading States of East Africa

Thinking on Your Own

As you read each section in this lesson, create a concept web of the people who lived in East Africa. Include important details, facts, and dates.

The history of East African cultures features the mixing of different people. Many, of course, were African. But others were from the Arabian Peninsula, India, Persia, and even Greece. Trade was an important factor in the development of East African kingdoms and states.

focus your reading

Why did Axum fight with its neighbors to the south?

Decide why Great Zimbabwe is famous. Explain your decision.

How did the Swahili culture develop?

vocabulary

mortar   intermediaries

vassals   Swahili

The Kingdom of Axum

Around 700 B.C., Arabs set up a colony in what is today the East African country of Ethiopia. This was about the same time that the Greeks started colonies in Asia. Like the Greeks, the Arabs were interested in trade. By 300 B.C., Arabs and Africans had joined to create the rich trading kingdom of Axum.

The city of Adulis, located on the Red Sea, became the chief trading center of Axum. Trade goods from the interior of Africa passed through Adulis on their way to the Arabian Peninsula, the Mediterranean region, and Asia. Axum was part of a trade network that reached as far as India. The monsoon winds made it possible for early trading ships to sail across the Indian Ocean. African trade goods included ivory, slaves, and spices. Cloth, wine, and olive oil were among the goods imported by Axum's traders.

The barter system was replaced by shells, trinkets, and eventually, coins.

In A.D. 300, Axum defeated the kingdom of Kush, which was its trading rival. The king at the time was Ezana. In 324, he converted to Christianity and made Christianity the official religion of Axum.

A church built from solid rock in Lalibela, Ethiopia

Beginning in the 1100s, conflict broke out between Axum and the Muslim trading states to the south. The issue was control of the slave and ivory trade. The Muslim city-states were trying to take over the trade from Axum. Fighting occurred over the next few centuries. By the 1500s, Axum was a trading partner with, and an ally of, Portugal. It appealed to Portugal for help. In 1543, the allies defeated their southern rivals. Axum, however, split into several kingdoms. It was not until the 1880s that it would come together again as one nation, Ethiopia.

The Zimbabwe Region

Some Bantu-speakers moved east and then south along the eastern coast of Africa. The earliest Bantu-speakers were in the area by 400. Later groups came between 900 and 1500.

One of the places they settled came to be called Zimbabwe. The word means "great stone houses." It refers to the huge stone buildings that were built over many centuries. There are a number of these ruins, but the largest is known as Great Zimbabwe. It has a palace, towers, a fort, and fences all made from pieces of stone. The stones were laid one on top of another without any **mortar**, or cement, to keep them together. Archaeologists believe that Great Zimbabwe was the center of a huge trading kingdom. Zimbabwe was on the trade route that linked the interior of Africa with the East Coast and beyond to Asia. Zimbabwe's major export was gold.

By the early 1400s, the Shona, a Bantu-speaking clan, had seized power in the region and driven out other groups. The

The stone walls of Great Zimbabwe were constructed without the use of mortar.

leader Mutota, and later his son Matope, gained control over their rivals. All traders traveling through their territory had to pay a tax on their goods.

Matope further enlarged his lands and set up the Monomotapa Empire. He developed a feudal system of government. Under feudalism, lesser nobles called **vassals** owed loyalty, service, and sometimes a yearly payment of money to a higher noble or king. Matope's vassals were relatives and allies. He divided the Empire into provinces, each governed by a vassal.

In the 1500s, the Monomotapa rulers began to lose power to the Portuguese. The Portuguese were slowly moving into the interior of East Africa from cities along the coast. They were looking for the gold mines that supplied the gold trade. In the 1620s, the forces of the Monomotapa king were defeated by the Portuguese.

stop and think

Write three important facts that you learned about Axum and three important facts about the Zimbabwe region. Turn the facts into questions. Take turns with a partner asking and answering questions.

Trading City-States

The trade from the interior passed through a few cities on the east coast of Africa on its way to Arabia or India. Eventually, coastal cities such as Kilwa, Mombassa, and Zanzibar became independent states with their own rulers, governments, and armed forces.

At one time or another, Persian, Arab, Indonesian, and Indian traders all settled in the cities along Africa's east coast. However, by 1000, Arab merchants had become the most important to the economy. They grew wealthy from international trade. They lived luxurious lives in huge houses with rugs from Persia and porcelain from China. They wore silk clothes from Asia and jewels set in gold. Their diets included coffee and fruits from the Arabian Peninsula.

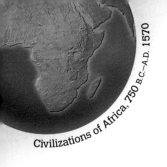

The wealth of the merchants was built on trade in iron ore, ivory, slaves, and gold from the interior of Africa. The merchants exchanged these for their own luxuries, and other trade goods such as cloth, glass, and metal goods for customers in the interior. Through **intermediaries**, or middlemen, trade goods flowed back and forth between East Africa and India, Malaysia, Indonesia, and China.

In time, the population of the city-states began to change. Bantu-speaking Africans and Arabs mixed and intermarried. Many Africans converted to Islam. New customs and a new language called **Swahili** developed. Swahili means "people of the coast" in Arabic. Today, Swahili is the most widely spoken language in East Africa. It is the official language of the modern nations of Kenya and Tanzania.

The arrival of the Portuguese brought an end to centuries of relatively peaceful trade. The Portuguese were determined to take control of the East Coast trade. Beginning in 1505, the Portuguese fought the Arab city-states for power. For the next 300 years, conflict between Arabs and Portuguese on the East Coast was common.

East African Trading States, 400–1500

Legend:
- Axum, 900 B.C.–A.D. 600
- Swahili settlement, c. A.D. 1300
- Trade route

Map labels: Mediterranean Sea, Baghdad, Cairo, EGYPT, Nile R., Red Sea, ARABIAN PENINSULA, Persian Gulf, To India, Makkah (Mecca), Meroe, AXUM, Gulf of Aden, Arabian Sea, L. Turkana, Mogadishu, Congo R., Victoria, INDIAN OCEAN, L. Tanganyika, Mombasa, Zanzibar, Kilwa, L. Nyasa, Zambezi R., Great Zimbabwe, Limpopo R.

Scale: 0 — 500 miles

The dhows used today are very similar to ancient Arabian trading ships.

Putting It All Together

Rivalry over trade caused conflict throughout East Africa. Create a cause-and-effect flowchart for conflict in each of the three kingdoms or regions described in this lesson. Be sure to indicate the cause and the result of each conflict. Share your flowchart with a partner and review the cause-and-effect relationships.

LESSON **3**

West African Kingdoms

Thinking on Your Own

As you study this lesson, create a table in your notebook to help you remember information about the three important kingdoms in West Africa. Use the following categories for your table: "Name of Kingdom," "Dates," "Location," "Trade Goods," and "Key Facts."

Between 500 and the late 1500s, three important **kingdoms**—or areas governed by a monarch—rose and fell in the savanna region of West Africa. Each one was based on trans-Saharan trade. Trade goods passed north to south and east to west along a series of trade routes. The network joined West Africa with the Mediterranean region and the Arabian Peninsula.

focus your reading

How did Ghana become wealthy?

Why is Mansa Musa remembered?

Explain how Songhai become so powerful.

vocabulary

kingdoms	scholars
merchants	rebel
Berbers	

Gold, ivory, slaves, leather goods, cattle, sheep, and jewelry were sent north along the trade routes. Salt, cloth, wheat, dried fruit, horses, and metal goods were shipped south. Muslim **merchants**—or businessmen—slowly took control of the trade. They bought trade goods from West African traders. The merchants then sold these goods to **Berbers**, or desert nomads, who ran camel caravans across the Sahara. The Berbers sold the goods to merchants in North Africa. These merchants either sold the goods there or to other traders who carried them farther east, even to the Arabian Peninsula. Like the goods that traveled along the Silk Road, each time the goods were resold, they became a little more expensive.

Camel caravans are still used as a means of transporting goods.

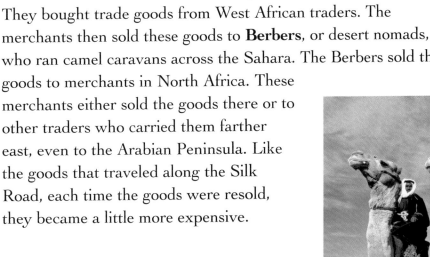
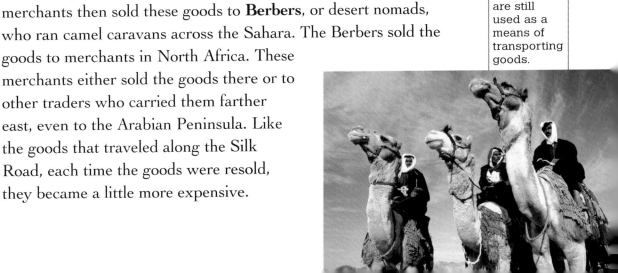

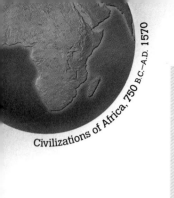

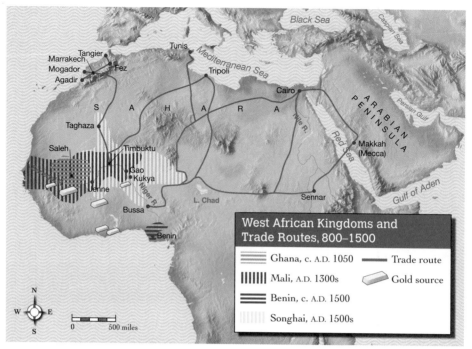

West African Kingdoms and Trade Routes, 800–1500

Ghana, c. A.D. 1050	Trade route
IIIIII Mali, A.D. 1300s	Gold source
Benin, c. A.D. 1500	
Songhai, A.D. 1500s	

0   500 miles

The Kingdom of Ghana

The first of the great West African kingdoms was Ghana. The kingdom reached into parts of what are today Mauritania, Mali, Senegal, and Guinea. Most of the people were farmers, but the wealth of the kingdom came from trading gold.

Ghana was located near a huge gold field. Ghanians mined the gold and traded it for goods from North Africa and beyond. Another important trade good was salt. Ghana had gold; North Africa had salt. The kings taxed the salt coming into the kingdom and the gold going out. They grew wealthy from the taxes placed on trade.

Beginning in the 600s, Islam became a major influence in West Africa. Invading armies spread Islam among the people they conquered. Muslim merchants also spread Islam. As merchants began to settle in market towns and cities, Islamic **scholars** followed them. The scholars soon began teaching about Islam. City dwellers, including the advisers to

stop and think

Imagine that you are an Arab merchant living in Ghana. What would you import that the people of Ghana wanted? What would you export for sale outside of Ghana to help pay for your imports? What other expenses would you have? Work with a partner to develop a list of imports, exports, and expenses.

Ghana's kings, became Muslims. West Africans living in farming villages, however, did not convert to Islam. They tended to continue practicing their traditional religions.

Ghana began a slow decline in the 1100s. The kingdom never recovered from invasions by Islamic armies from North Africa. Rebellious states began to break away from the kingdom. The final blow came in 1240 when King Sundiata of Mali conquered what was left of the "land of gold," as Ghana was known.

The Kingdom of Mali

According to the *Epic of Sundiata*, Sumanguru, the ruler of the Kingdom of Kaniaga, seized power over part of the Kingdom of Ghana. In an effort to increase his power, Sumanguru invaded Mali and killed 11 princes who were the older brothers of Prince Sundiata Keita. When he grew to manhood, Sundiata Keita avenged the death of his brothers by killing Sumanguru. Like Sumanguru, Sundiata Keita then went on his own campaign to enlarge Mali. Over time, Mali spread its rule as far west as the Atlantic coast and as far east as what is today Niger.

The burnt-brick mosque in Timbuktu, Mali

Most people in Mali were farmers who lived in villages. However, Mali's wealth was built on the gold and salt trade. The kings of Mali taxed all goods being exported and imported. They also collected taxes from their own people.

The kings of Mali became Muslims. Muslims are supposed to make a pilgrimage to Makkah (MECCA) once in their lifetime. Mansa Musa, who ruled from 1312 to 1337, made a

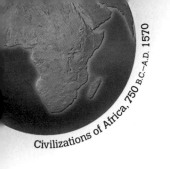

pilgrimage like no other. In 1324, he brought together 60,000 people for his trip across Africa and the Arabian Peninsula. Among them were 12,000 slaves. Of these slaves, 500 carried staffs, or walking sticks, made of gold. Eighty camels carried 300 pounds of gold each. Because of Mansa Musa's lavish spending and generosity in giving away so much gold on his trip, the price of gold fell sharply. It took 12 years for the price to rise to where it had been in 1324.

The great Islamic cities that Mansa Musa visited made an impression on him. He brought back architects and Islamic scholars to Timbuktu, the capital of Mali. He had mosques, palaces, and schools built. Timbuktu became the center of Islamic learning in West Africa.

Shortly after Mansa Musa died, Berbers from North Africa invaded Mali. At the same time, **rebel** states fought for power. Rebels often fight against a government and try to gain power. In 1359, Timbuktu and Gao broke away. Mali quickly lost its importance.

⧗ Time Box
500–1240
Kingdom of Ghana
1234–1400s
Kingdom of Mali
1450–1600s
Kingdom of Songhai

The Kingdom of Songhai

The city of Gao eventually became the trading center for the Songhai Kingdom. In 1464, Songhai's leader, Sunni Ali, set out to conquer more territory. But he was not interested in territory for the sake of expansion. He wanted the regions around Timbuktu and Jenne in order to gain control of the salt and gold trade.

After Sunni Ali's death, fighting broke out over who would rule. His son lost the struggle to Muhammad Ture. In 1493, Ture took command and changed his name to Askia Muhammad. Like Sunni Ali, he extended the borders of Songhai. Askia Muhammad also divided the kingdom into provinces managed by governors. He continued the practice of collecting taxes on all goods entering and leaving the kingdom.

Plaque of a Nigerian Edo bodyguard from the sixteenth century

A devout Muslim, Askia Muhammad also made an impressive pilgrimage to Makkah. He supported the building of mosques and schools and attempted to convert everyone in Songhai to Islam. Islamic principles became the basis of the court system and of social reforms.

Askia Muhammad's rule was a period of peace and prosperity. However, fighting among rivals and the invasion by the sultan of Morocco's army put an end to Songhai. By 1600, the glory of Songhai had faded like that of Ghana and Mali before it.

Putting It All Together

This lesson uses the comparison-and-contrast signal word *like* several times. Find three examples and write them in your notebook. Then review the information in the table that you created as you read this lesson. Write five comparison-and-contrast sentences using information from the table. Share your sentences with a partner.

A Visit to Timbuktu

In the early 1500s, Leo Africanus, a visitor from Morocco, described Timbuktu. The following is an excerpt from his writings. *Barbary* refers to North Africa, which was overwhelmingly Muslim by this time.

reading for understanding

Based on this reading and information from the lesson, how do you think the king gets money to pay for doctors and other services?

What does the high price of manuscripts and books tell you about the people of Timbuktu?

Describe Timbuktu in one sentence.

"Here are many shops of artificers and merchants, especially of such as weave linen and cotton cloth. And hither do the Barbary merchants bring the cloth of Europe. . . . The inhabitants . . . are exceedingly rich. . . . Here are many wells containing most sweet water. . . . Corn, cattle, milk, and butter in this region yields in great abundance. . . . The inhabitants are people of a gentle and cheerful disposition. . . . Here are great store of doctors, judges, priests, and other learned men, that are bountifully maintained at the king's cost and charges. And hither are brought diverse manuscripts or written books out of Barbary, which are sold for more than any other merchandise."

Read a Primary Source

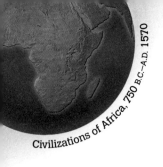

Civilizations of Africa, 750 B.C.–A.D. 1570

Chapter Summary

- Africa has many different **environments**. They include desert, **savanna**, and **rain forest**. Africans developed **slash-and-burn** agriculture to clear **vegetation**.
- Bantu is a language family, not an **ethnic group**.
- Bantu-speakers migrated into the Congo **River basin** around 1000 B.C.
- The buildings of Great Zimbabwe were made without using **mortar**.
- The Monomotapa kingdom was based on feudalism. The king made his relatives and allies **vassals**.
- Trade goods flowed through **intermediaries** along the network that linked the interior of East Africa, the East African city-states, India, Malaysia, Indonesia, and China.
- East African city-states were a mix of Bantu-speaking Africans, Arabs, Persians, and Indians. Arab **merchants** became economically important. Over time a new culture and language called **Swahili** developed.
- The **kingdoms** of Ghana, Mali, and Songhai developed in the savanna region of West Africa.
- Islam became an important influence in West Africa. Islamic **scholars** helped make the city of Timbuktu a center of Islamic learning.
- **Berbers** ran camel caravans across the Sahara and sold goods in North Africa.
- **Rebels** fought for power in Mali.

Chapter Review

1 Use the table you created in Lesson 3 as the basis for an essay about the differences and similarities among the three West African kingdoms.

2 Write two-line headlines for (a) the migration of Bantu-speakers into the Congo basin, (b) the arrival of the Portuguese in East Africa, (c) the completion of the palace in Great Zimbabwe, (d) Mansa Musa's arrival in Makkah, (e) Askia Muhammad as ruler of Songhai.

146 | Chapter 10

Skill Builder

Summarizing and Paraphrasing

A summary is a short description of something. For example, if a classmate asks you what happened on a TV show the night before, you explain the important points but leave out most of the details. You make it short. In other words, you summarize the show.

When you write a report, you often need to paraphrase what you have read. When you paraphrase, be careful not to write word-for-word what you have read. Use your own words and keep the important details as well as the main idea. A paraphrase may be about the same length as the original. Read the following paragraph from Lesson 2:

> The arrival of the Portuguese brought an end to centuries of relatively peaceful trade. The Portuguese were determined to take control of the East Coast trade. Beginning in 1505, the Portuguese fought the Arab city-states for power. For the next 300 years, conflict between Arabs and Portuguese on the East Coast was common.

The following is a paraphrase of that paragraph. It restates the main fact and important details in different words.

> The Portuguese wanted to control trade along the east coast of Africa. They started their campaign to take it over by fighting Arab city-states in 1505. For 300 years the Portuguese and Arabs fought on the East Coast.

Summarizing—a short restatement of the main idea

Paraphrasing—restating a passage in your own words, including the main idea and details

Complete the following activities.

1. Paraphrase paragraphs 2 and 3 under the subheading "The Geography of the African Continent."

2. Reread the section "The Kingdom of Ghana." Find the main idea of each paragraph. Then write a summary of "The Kingdom of Ghana."

Chapter

11 THE AMERICAS

(1400 B.C.—A.D. 1570)

Getting Focused

Skim this chapter to predict what you will be learning.
• Read the lesson titles and subheadings.
• Look at the illustrations and read the captions.
• Examine the maps.
• Review the vocabulary words.

This chapter is about Native Americans. Based on
your knowledge of how people moved from place to
place and how civilizations developed, what do you
think this chapter will tell you about Native Americans?
Predict the topics or categories of information that you
think it will discuss. Make a list of the topics that you
think you will learn about Native Americans. Remember
to add North and South America to your world map.

LESSON 1

Cultures of Central and South America

Thinking on Your Own

Chapter 1 presented the six characteristics of a civilization. Make a table with four columns. In the first column, list the six characteristics. Label the other columns "Mayan," "Aztec," and "Incan." As you read the lesson, fill in each column with facts.

The first humans arrived in the Americas thousands of years ago. Archaeologists disagree on exactly when the first migrants came and where they came from. However, they have found no evidence dating earlier than about 12,000 to 15,000 years ago. During the last Ice Age many people crossed a **land bridge** that connected North America to Asia. As the ice melted, the land bridge was slowly covered by water. Today, this area is the Bering Strait. Some archaeologists think that early Americans came from Europe, Africa, or the South Pacific.

focus your reading

Summarize how North and South America became populated by the first Americans.

What happened to Mayan civilization in the Yucatán?

How did the Aztec rule their empire?

Explain how the Inca ruled their empire.

vocabulary

land bridge

Yucatán Peninsula

ceremonial centers

overfarmed

prophecy

commoners

quipu

terraced

Early Americans

The first Americans migrated in small groups across the continents. It took thousands of years, but they spread from the Arctic to the southern tip of South America. Wherever they settled, the first Americans had to adapt to their environment.

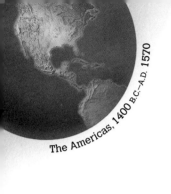

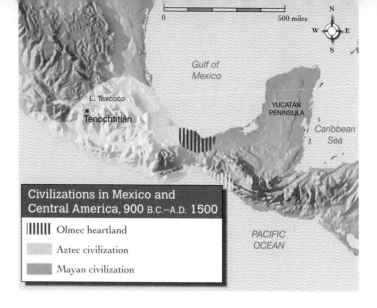

The Americas, 1400 B.C.–A.D. 1570

Civilizations in Mexico and Central America, 900 B.C.–A.D. 1500

‖‖‖‖ Olmec heartland

░ Aztec civilization

▓ Mayan civilization

The first Americans were hunters and gatherers. They followed wild herds of big game like mastodons and mammoths. As the big-game herds died out, the men turned to hunting bison and smaller game like rabbits and deer. To add to their diet, the women gathered plants, nuts, and berries, and dug roots.

Some hunters and gatherers in Mexico and South America learned to domesticate plants and began growing food crops. This Neolithic revolution, as historians call it, had far-reaching effects. Farming produced a surplus of food, which freed some people to become craftworkers, full-time soldiers, and priests. In the Western Hemisphere, as well as in Europe and Asia, it made living in villages year-round possible. From that, came cities and civilization.

The first civilization in Mexico and Central America was the Olmec. It developed in the rain forest along the Gulf of Mexico. Instead of cities, the Olmec built large religious centers. People lived in nearby villages. They came to the centers to worship in huge pyramid-shaped temples. This is one of the 40-ton carved heads that stood in the centers.

Mayan Civilization

The largest civilization in Mexico and Central America was the Mayan. Much of it was centered on the **Yucatán Peninsula** in what is today Mexico. The area is mainly rain forest.

The Mayan civilization reached its height between 300 and 900. Like the Olmec, the Mayans did not build cities. They built large religious centers, known as **ceremonial centers**. The centers had temples dedicated to the deities and palaces for the ruler and other nobles. There were also huge ball courts and marketplaces. Each center and its nearby villages made up an independent city-state. Rival city-states often warred against each other.

The temples were several stories high and were built in the shape of pyramids. However, the tops

Early ball games were played by hitting the ball with the body, not hands or feet.

were flat. Priests carried out human sacrifice on this flat space. The Mayans believed that they had to make sacrifices to the gods in order to satisfy them. If the gods were not happy, they would cause harm. Players on the losing side in a ball game were sacrificed. Enemies captured in battle were also sacrificed. Sometimes battles were fought just to get prisoners for sacrifice.

The ruler and his family were at the highest level of Mayan society. Below them were other nobles, and priests. Some nobles ran the government and collected taxes. Others were warriors who led soldiers into battle. Below this class were a small number of craftworkers, merchants, and traders. Like other early civilizations, most Mayans were farmers. They lived in villages outside the centers. Their chief crops were beans, corn, and squash. Mayan society also included slaves.

The Mayans developed a form of hieroglyphic writing and a very accurate calendar. Because the Mayan economy was based on farming, the calendar was very important. Mayans used the calendar to know when to plant their crops each year.

Sometime around 900, the Mayans left their centers in the Yucatán. Archaeologists do not know why but offer several reasons. The Mayans may have **overfarmed** their land. As a result, they migrated in search of new land. Enemies may have invaded their territory. Farmers may have rebelled under the burden of high taxes. Today, descendants of the Mayans live in Guatemala, the Yucatán Peninsula, and northern Mexico.

Time Box

300–900
  Mayan Civilization
1325–1521
  Aztec Empire
1438–1535
  Inca Empire

The Aztec Empire

During the 1200s, the Aztec migrated from the northwest into the Valley of Mexico. They were pushed out of their homeland by groups moving south. In 1325, the Aztec settled on islands in Lake Texcoco. There they built the city of Tenochtitlán (tay•NAWCH•teet•LAWN). In time it became the capital of a huge empire.

Montezuma (c. 1466–1520) was the Aztec ruler when the Spanish arrived.

The Americas, 1400 B.C.–A.D. 1570

The Empire was made up of city-states that the Aztecs had conquered. At the top of the Empire was the Aztec king in Tenochtitlán. The states were ruled by local leaders. Each state paid a yearly fee or tax, known as tribute, to the king. As long as the states paid their tribute, they were left in peace. If they tried to revolt, Aztec warriors would be sent to put a brutal end to the rebellion. By the time the Spanish arrived in 1519, the Aztec ruled approximately 5 million people.

Like the Mayans, the Aztec practiced human sacrifice. They believed it was necessary in order to keep the world from being destroyed. According to the Aztec religion, four worlds had already been destroyed by fighting between good and evil. It was only by making human sacrifice to Huitzilopochtli (wee•tsee•loh•POHKT•lee), the god of the sun and war, that the end of the fifth world—the current world—could be prevented. Wars were sometimes fought just to take prisoners for sacrifice.

stop and think

Create a Venn diagram to compare and contrast the Aztec and Inca Empires. Work with a partner to fill in the details.

Aztec Society

Aztec society was divided into social and economic classes. At the top were the monarch and his family. Next were nobles, which included priests, government officials, war chiefs, and wealthy merchants. The largest group were the **commoners**. This group included everyone who was not a noble or a slave, and who owned property. Small merchants, craftworkers, and farmers were commoners. Farmers were the largest section in this group. Below commoners were farm laborers. Slaves were at the bottom of the group.

Aztec legends explain why they chose their island home. Huitzilopochtli, the god of war, had made a **prophecy**. He said that they should settle down where they came upon a certain sign. The sign was an eagle sitting on a cactus that was growing out of rock. The word *Tenochtitlán* means "place of the cactus in the rock." The Spanish destroyed Tenochtitlán (above) in 1521 and built Mexico City over it. The eagle and cactus can be seen on the flag of Mexico.

Similar to the Mayan, the Aztecs developed a form of hieroglyphic writing and a calendar. They built palaces and huge pyramid-like temples. The tops of

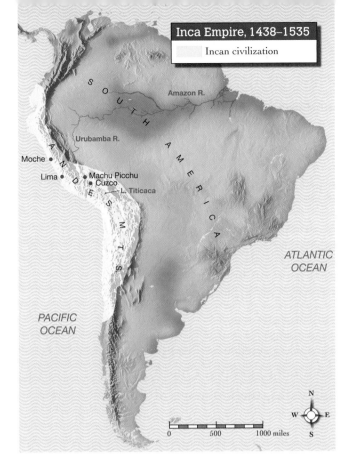

Inca Empire, 1438–1535

Incan civilization

SOUTH AMERICA

Amazon R.

Urubamba R.

Moche •

Lima •
Machu Picchu •
Cuzco •
L. Titicaca

ANDES MTS.

ATLANTIC OCEAN

PACIFIC OCEAN

0   500   1000 miles

N W E S

Aztec pyramids were also flat for conducting human sacrifices and other ceremonies.

The end of the Aztec Empire came in 1521. Tribute states and the Spanish joined together to overthrow the Aztec king.

The Inca Empire

The Inca began as a small group in the mountains of Peru. Their center was Cuzco, a city 11,000 feet above sea level. Beginning with the rule of Pachacuti (pah•cha•KOO•tee) in 1438, the Inca set out to conquer surrounding groups. By 1527, the Inca had spread their rule over a vast area.

The Inca Empire was divided into four provinces. As soon as a group was conquered, their land was taken over by the government. Some of it was given back to the people. Some land was turned over to the Empire, and some was given to

Pachacuti (?–1471)

Pachacuti became the ruler of the Inca in 1438. His name means "reformer of the world." Under his leadership, the Inca began the conquest of their neighbors. Like the Romans, Pachacuti used both force of arms and alliances to enlarge his empire. He managed the new parts of the empire with a mix of local rulers and his own appointed officials. Later emperors followed his system of government.

Pachacuti used the wealth from his empire to beautify his capital. Huge stone palaces and temples replaced mud buildings. It is possible that he designed his grand capital himself.

Biography

the sun god. The lands for the sun god supported the priests who took care of the temples and conducted religious ceremonies.

Local rulers could remain in power as long as they were loyal to the emperor. The Inca did not demand tribute in gold or other goods from conquered people. Instead, the Inca required labor. Whole communities had to spend several weeks each year working on lands given to the Empire or to the sun god. They also had to work on building projects.

The Inca had several ways to ensure the loyalty of conquered people. Quechua (KEH•chuh•wuh), the language of the Inca, was taught to new people. The Inca sent Quechua-speaking colonists to live among a newly conquered group. Sometimes the Inca uprooted a new group. They were sent to live in an area where the people had been part of the Empire for a longer period of time. A road system kept Cuzco in touch with all parts of the Empire. Like the Roman system of roads, the Incan roads enabled the government to quickly send troops to troublespots. The Empire had 24,000 miles of criss-crossing roads.

Like the Aztec, the Inca believed that the sun was the chief deity. The Inca called their sun god Inti, and the Temple of

Role of Women in Mesoamerica

Empire	Role
Mayan	• take care of the home
	• take care of the children
Aztec	• could inherit property
	• could make legal contracts
	• take care of the home
	• take care of the children
Inca	• could inherit property
	• could own property
	• work the fields
	• take care of the home
	• take care of the children

The Inca produced intricate pieces of gold.

A 1609 Spanish print of an Incan and quipu.

the Sun in Cuzco was the center of Incan religion. Emperors were considered descendants of the sun god. They were mummified like Egyptian pharaohs and their mummies were worshiped.

Incan Society

The social and economic structure of the Inca Empire was similar to other early civilizations. The ruler and family were at the top. Below them were nobles and priests. Below them were merchants and craft workers. Most Inca were farmers who lived near their fields.

The Inca did not develop a writing system. Instead they used **quipu** (KEE•poo), knotted and colored strings to keep records. Special government officials were taught to use quipu. These officials could keep track of tax payments and similar information by knotting different strings. For example, the first string showed thousands. The second string showed hundreds. The third and fourth strings showed tens and ones. Suppose a farmer paid 1,200 bushels of grain in taxes. The official would tie one knot on the thousands string and two knots on the hundreds string. It is also possible that the quipu recorded dates and important events in Inca history.

Incan quipu

The Inca also developed a calendar and a way to farm in the mountains. Look at the photo of Machu Picchu at the beginning of this chapter. The sides of the mountain were **terraced**, or cut out like steps. The Inca farmed each level of the terrace. The Inca also developed an irrigation system to bring water to their fields high in the mountains.

Like the Aztec, the Inca Empire ended when the Spanish came. Incan swords were no match for Spanish guns and horses.

Putting It All Together

Imagine you are an Incan tax collector. Work with a partner to draw a picture of a quipu to record the following tax payments in bushels of grain: (a) 141, (b) 1,322 (c) 2,535.

LESSON 2

North American Cultures

Thinking on Your Own

What do you already know about Native North Americans? Make a list of at least five facts that you know about Native Americans. To refresh your memory, look through the lesson. Read the subheadings and the captions. Look at the illustrations. Then write your list.

Experts think that about 70 million people lived in the Americas when Christopher Columbus sailed west in 1492. Of these, about 5 million lived in what would become the United States. There were various cultural regions, each with many different groups. This lesson includes **representative groups** in three of the regions. Representative groups are ones that have many characteristics in common with other groups.

focus your reading

What happened to the ancestral Puebloan culture?

Describe how the coming of the Spanish affected the culture of Native Americans on the Plains?

Why is the Iroquois League considered important?

vocabulary

representative groups

plateau

hides

tepees

reservation

sachem

The Ancestral Puebloans of the Southwest

More than 800 rooms were part of the ancestral Puebloan dwellings at Pueblo Bonito.

The ancestral Puebloans (Anasazi) are just one of the groups that lived in the area of modern day Arizona, New Mexico, Colorado, and Utah. The ancestral Puebloans began to develop their unique way of life around A.D. 100. They turned from hunting and gathering to farming. The area is very hot and dry for much of the year. However, if

rains came in the spring and midsummer, they brought occasional flash flooding. The ancestral Puebloans figured out how to use the rain water to irrigate their fields.

Around 900, ancestral Puebloan settlements began to grow in size. To fit the increasing population, the ancestral Puebloans developed an apartment-building style of housing. One of the largest settlements was Pueblo Bonito in northwestern New Mexico. From its ruins, archaeologists can tell that its 800 rooms housed more than 1,000 people. In Mesa Verde, part of modern day Colorado, the ancestral Puebloans built their houses into the sides of cliffs. They farmed on the **plateau** on top of the mountain.

In the 1200s, the ancestral Puebloans began to abandon their stone buildings and move out of the area. No one knows for sure why. One possible reason is the drought that lasted from 1276 to 1299. At about the same time, Navajos and Apaches began moving into the area. They may have pushed out the ancestral Puebloans.

It was the descendants of the ancestral Puebloans that the Spanish met in the Southwest in the 1500s. The Spanish called them Pueblo Indians because they lived in villages. *Pueblo* means "village" in Spanish.

Plains Peoples

The earliest people on the Plains were hunters and gatherers. Some, like the Mandan along the Missouri River, became farmers and traders. But many of the descendants of the first Plains people continued to hunt bison and gather wild foods until the late 1800s—but with one big change. The change came about when the

Between 1000 B.C. and the A.D. 1200s, people known as Mound Builders lived in the area from the Great Lakes to the Gulf of Mexico. They are called Mound Builders because they built huge mounds of earth (top). Some mounds were tombs. Others, like the Great Serpent Mound (bottom), were shaped like animals. Most Mound Builders were farmers, but a few were traders. Trade goods from as far away as Mexico have been found in the mounds. Over time, cities developed. One of the largest was Cahokia, in what is today Illinois. When the Spanish came, they met Natchez Native Americans, who were descendants of the Mound Builders.

stop and think

Create a Venn diagram to compare and contrast the ancestral Puebloans and the Plains people. Work with a partner to list information in each part of the two circles.

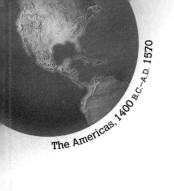

Animal hides were used to cover tepees.

Spanish brought horses to the Americas. Some horses escaped from the Spanish in Mexico and the U.S. Southwest. Other horses were stolen by Native Americans. Native Americans traded horses until they reached the Plains in the early 1700s.

Instead of hunting bison on foot, the Plains people began hunting on horseback. With horses they could kill more bison and go longer distances on the hunt. The bison was central to the Plains' way of life. It provided meat for food and **hides** for making clothes. The people also used hides to cover the sides of their cone-shaped homes called **tepees**. Because they moved often, Plains people sewed bags from bison hides to carry their belongings.

The Plains' way of life stayed much the same until the 1800s. Then settlers from the East Coast of the United States began to move onto the Plains. A series of Plains Wars in the

Cultural Regions of North America, 4000 B.C.—A.D. 1500

Inuit

ARCTIC
Inuit

GULF OF ALASKA

Hudson Bay

FAR NORTH

Haida

Peace R.

NORTHWEST COAST

Cree

PLATEAU

Chinook

Nez Perce

Saskatchewan R.

Chippewa

Missouri R.

PLAINS

Sioux

Algonquin

Yahi

Sauk
Fox
Kickapoo

Iroquois League

Cheyenne

Mound Builders

Pomo

Shoshone

Anasazi

Arapaho

EASTERN WOODLANDS
Miami

Miwok

GREAT BASIN

Pawnee

Powhatan Confederation

CALIFORNIA

Paiute

Colorado R.

Mesa Verde

Querechos

Cahokia Shawnee

Chumash

Navajos

Kiowas

Tuscarora

ATLANTIC OCEAN

Pima
Hopi

Pueblo

Cherokee

PACIFIC OCEAN

Pueblo Bonito

Comanches

Chickasaw
Creek

SOUTHEAST

Yuma SOUTHWEST

Choctaw

Apaches

Natchez

Rio Grande

NORTHERN MEXICO

GULF OF MEXICO

N
W E
S

CENTAL AMERICA

CARIBBEAN

Caribbean Sea

0   500 miles

mid-1800s killed many Native Americans. By 1890, those who were left were forced to live on **reservations**.

The Iroquois of the Eastern Woodlands

Before Europeans came to North America, about half of what is today the United States was forest. It is known as the Eastern Woodlands. In general, Native Americans in the region combined hunting and farming. They lived in villages and towns, sometimes surrounded by high walls made of logs. The walls were needed to keep out invaders.

The longhouse provided shelter for Eastern Woodland people.

The Iroquois lived in the Eastern Woodlands in parts of present-day New York, Pennsylvania, and Canada. Like other languages, Iroquois is a language family. There were several tribes, or groups, who spoke this language.

About 1570, Deganawida, an elder chief, tried to end the constant warfare among the Iroquois. Hiawatha, a **sachem**, or chief, of the Mohawk, joined him. Together, they enlisted the chiefs of five nations, or groups of people, in New York to form the Iroquois League. The five nations—Mohawk, Oneida, Onondaga, Cayuga, and Seneca—elected representatives to a Grand Council. The purpose of the council was to find solutions to problems and prevent warfare.

Women were very important in the government of the Iroquois nations. The women members of each clan in a nation chose a clan mother. The clan mothers then chose the 50 representatives to the Grand Council. A clan mother could remove a representative if she did not approve of his voting.

The Iroquois League was still in existence when the British began to settle the east coast. It did not help the five nations much in their dealings with the colonists. The Iroquois were caught in wars with the colonists and between the British and French for control of land.

Putting It All Together

Add to the list of facts you began writing at the start of this lesson. Compare your facts with a partner. Then use your facts to write a comparison and contrast paragraph about two of the Native-American groups you read about in this lesson.

Chapter Summary

- Experts think the first Americans came across a **land bridge** from Asia 12,000 to 15,000 years ago.
- The Mayan civilization developed in the **Yucatán Peninsula**. The Mayans developed **ceremonial centers**.
- **Overfarming** the land may have been one of the reasons the Mayans left their homes around A.D. 900.
- The Aztec built their capital, Tenochtitlán, on an island in Lake Texcoco because of a **prophecy**.
- The Aztec Empire was made up of conquered people. Most people were **commoners**.
- The Inca Empire began in the mountains of Peru.
- The Inca used **quipu** to record information. The Inca also developed a calendar and a system of farming that used **terracing** on mountainsides.
- The ancestral Puebloans, Plains people, and Iroquois are **representative groups** of North American cultures.
- The ancestral Puebloans farmed on a **plateau**.
- Plains people ate bison meat and used bison **hides** for clothing and **tepee** covers. By the end of the 1800s, Plains people were forced onto **reservations**.
- The chiefs, or **sachems**, of five Iroquois nations formed the Iroquois League.

Chapter Review

1 Make a table to compare and contrast information about the Mayans, Aztec, and Inca. For topics, use "Location," "Dates," "Government," "Religion," "Social and Economic Classes," "Roles of Men and Women," and "Achievements."

2 Imagine you are a farmer living outside a Mayan center. You have just come back from market day in the city. Write a description of the city. Use the information in Lesson 1 to give you ideas.

3 Choose a cultural region from Lesson 2. Describe life in this region prior to the arrival of Christopher Columbus in 1492.

Skill Builder

Drawing Conclusions

Suppose you come home from school to find a pillow torn apart on the living room floor. The stuffing has been pulled out, and small pieces of it are everywhere. As you set down your backpack, your dog runs up to you. She is covered with pieces of the pillow's stuffing. You know that you were the last person to leave that morning. No one has been at home since you left for school. You think about this information and conclude, based on the facts, that your dog shredded the pillow. This process is called drawing a conclusion.

You can also apply the skill of drawing conclusions to your schoolwork. Suppose you had to answer the following question: Why did early people migrate?

To draw a conclusion:

- Gather information about the topic. In this case, re-read the information about the Bantu in Chapter 10 and about the first Americans in this chapter.
- Write down any other facts you know about the topic.
- Draw a conclusion based on the information you gathered.

Early people migrated for different reasons. Hunters and gatherers followed herds wherever they went. Farmers moved when the land wore out. Others moved when there were too many people in a place and they could not get enough food.

Answer the following questions by drawing conclusions.

1 Why do you think so many different Native-American cultures developed in North America?

2 Tribute states in the Aztec Empire became allies of the Spanish. They helped overthrow the Aztec king. Why do you think the tribute states joined the Spanish?

Chapter 12

THE SPREAD OF CULTURES IN ASIA

(500–1650)

Getting Focused

Skim this chapter to predict what you will be learning.
- Read the lesson titles and subheadings.
- Look at the illustrations and read the captions.
- Examine the maps.
- Review the vocabulary words and terms.

This chapter discusses China, Japan, Korea, and India. Look through the chapter and choose one picture to describe from each lesson. In your descriptions, state what country the picture represents, what the picture shows, and why you chose this picture to write about. Be sure to use interesting words to describe what you see. Remember to add Japan and Korea to your world map.

New Dynasties in China

Thinking on Your Own

As you read this lesson, create a timeline in your notebook. Include dates and facts for the five dynasties discussed in this lesson.

In A.D. 581, the Sui Dynasty brought order to China. With the collapse of the Han Dynasty in 220, the Chinese people had endured more than 300 years of civil war. The Sui rulers reunified the Empire. Among their lasting contributions was the building of the Grand Canal, which made it easier to ship rice from the south of China to the north.

> **focus your reading**
>
> Explain why the Tang and Song Dynasties are called Golden Ages.
>
> How was the Yuan Dynasty similar to earlier dynasties?
>
> Summarize how Yong Le attempted to restore China's greatness.
>
> **vocabulary**
>
> corrupt   fleet
>
> monk   voyage

> **Time Box**
>
> 581–618
>   Sui (SWAY) Dynasty
>
> 618–907
>   Tang (TAHNG) Dynasty
>
> 960–1279
>   Song (SOHNG) Dynasty
>
> 1279–1368
>   Yuan (YOO•AHN) Dynasty
>
> 1368–1644
>   Ming (MING) Dynasty

The Tang and Song Dynasties

The Tang and Song Dynasties ruled during what are called Golden Ages in Chinese history. China was prosperous during these periods and extended its influence into new lands. These periods were also times of great cultural achievements.

The leaders of the Tang Dynasty expanded the area of Chinese rule and influence in Asia. The Tang Empire extended from the Pacific Ocean to

The Spread of Cultures in Asia, 500–1650

Tibet. Tang armies conquered the Tibetan people. Through trade, China's influence later spread east into Korea, Japan, and Southeast Asia.

Tang and Song emperors tried to end corruption in government. They restored the ancient civil service system to fill government posts. Office seekers had to pass a civil service exam based on Confucian teachings. That kept powerful officials from appointing their relatives to offices.

The Tang and Song Dynasties brought prosperity to China. They limited the power of the wealthy landowners, taking land from them to give to the peasants. The growing trade with other nations also created business for merchants and craftspeople. As a result, the population of China's cities grew rapidly.

The Tang and Song Dynasties were periods of cultural advances. Among the most important was the invention of printing. It began with woodblock printing on paper in Tang China, in

stop and think section

stop and think

The Tang and Song Dynasties were Golden Ages. What do you think this phrase means? Write a definition for *Golden Age*. Share your definition with a partner. Combine your ideas and write one definition for the phrase.

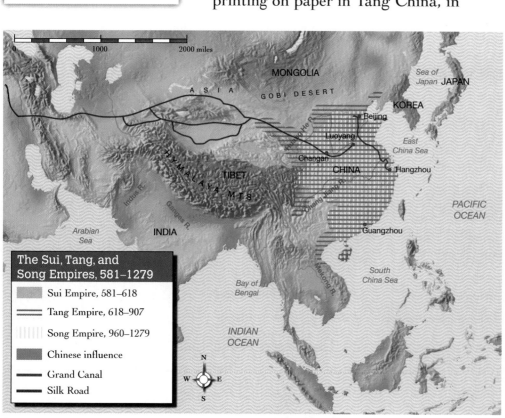

The Sui, Tang, and Song Empires, 581–1279

- Sui Empire, 581–618
- Tang Empire, 618–907
- Song Empire, 960–1279
- Chinese influence
- Grand Canal
- Silk Road

Chinese artists usually painted scenes of nature. If people were in a scene, they were usually small. What was important was the grandeur of nature. However, people, horses, camels, and other animals were often the subjects of statues by Tang and Song artists. Brightly colored statues offer a view of how people looked and what they did during the Tang and Song periods.

164 | Chapter 12

Chinese Inventions, 600s to 1200s

Dynasty	Invention	Importance
Tang	gunpowder	• first used in fireworks • used in guns and cannons by the 1200s
Tang	woodblock printing	• invented printing 700 years before the European printing press
Tang	porcelain	• improved the production method • became valuable trade good under the Ming
Tang	steel	• developed process 900 years before Europeans • used for swords and farm tools
Song	movable type	• improved woodblock printing

the early 700s. Each page was carved in wood. By about the year 1000, printers of Song China had created moveable type. This allowed a printer to use the same type to print many different books.

As in earlier dynasties, peasant unrest over taxes helped to weaken Tang power. In 907, rebels overthrew the emperor. A series of civil wars followed. By 960, a general of the Song

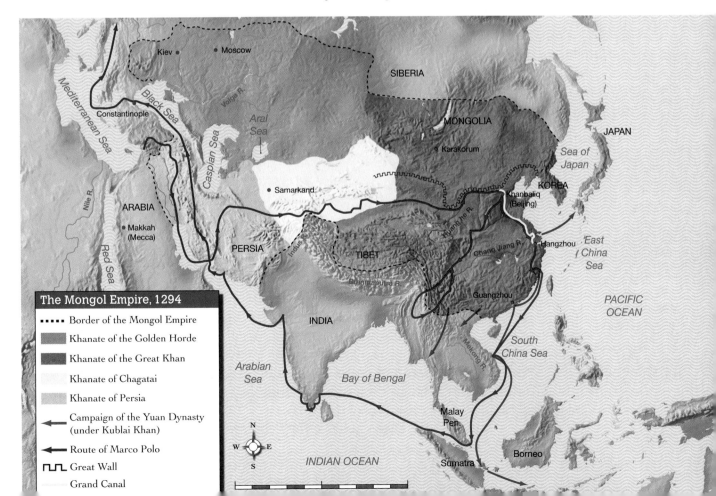

The Mongol Empire, 1294

- ▪▪▪▪ Border of the Mongol Empire
- Khanate of the Golden Horde
- Khanate of the Great Khan
- Khanate of Chagatai
- Khanate of Persia
- → Campaign of the Yuan Dynasty (under Kublai Khan)
- → Route of Marco Polo
- ⊓⊔ Great Wall
- Grand Canal

clan was strong enough to declare himself emperor.

The Song were unable to hold the Tang Empire together. Attacks by rebel groups within the Empire resulted in the loss of territory. In 1215, the Mongols began their conquest of China.

Mongols in battle

Mongol Invaders: The Yuan Dynasty

Under Genghis Khan (JEHN•GUHS KAHN), the Mongols roared into China in 1215 and conquered the northern section of the country. When Genghis Khan died in 1227, his empire was divided among his four sons into territories known as khanates. In 1279, Kublai Khan, one of his grandsons, overthrew the Song Dynasty. With the support of his army, Kublai Khan then declared himself ruler of China.

Kublai (KOO•BLUH) Khan took a Chinese name for his dynasty, Yuan (YOO•AHN). He followed a policy similar to

The Travels of Marco Polo

Marco Polo was a trader who found his way to Beijing. Polo spent 20 years in China and may have worked for Kublai Khan for part of that time. When Polo returned to Italy, he wrote about what he had seen in *The Travels of Marco Polo*.

reading for understanding

Why might a resident of Hangzhou think he or she was in paradise?

Marco Polo sometimes exaggerated what he saw, especially numbers. What in this excerpt might be exaggerated?

Why do you think Polo might have exaggerated what he saw?

❝There are within the city ten principal squares or market places, besides innumerable shops along the streets. Each side of these squares is half a mile in length, and in front of them is the main street, forty paces in width and running in a straight line from one end of the city to the other. It is crossed by many low and convenient bridges. These market squares are four miles from each other. Parallel to the main street, but on the opposite side of the square, runs a very large canal. On the nearer bank of this stand large stone warehouses provided for merchants who arrive from India and other parts with their goods and effects. They are thus situated conveniently close to the market squares. In each of these, three days in every week, from forty to fifty thousand persons come to the markets and supply them with every article that could be desired.❞

Read a Primary Source

Genghis Khan's. Both allowed the conquered Chinese bureaucrats to remain in place at the local level. Higher level jobs, however, were filled by Mongols. Separate laws governed Chinese and Mongols in the Empire. The Chinese were also required to pay tribute to their Mongol rulers. No Chinese could serve in the army.

Kublai Khan re-established law and order in China. He had roads built and revived trade along the Silk Road. Arabs, Russians, Italians, and other traders made their way to Chinese cities. China prospered under his rule.

However, Kublai Khan was not satisfied with the size of his empire. He sent troops into Southeast Asia and Japan. They were successful only in conquering Vietnam.

Later Yuan emperors could not keep peace and order. Like earlier emperors, later emperors were **corrupt** themselves, or allowed others to take bribes and misuse their power. Peasants were angered by heavy taxes that were used for military campaigns. In 1368, Zhu Yuanzhang, a Buddhist **monk**, or holy man, led an army of peasants against the Mongols. The peasants succeeded in toppling the Yuan Dynasty. Zhu changed his name to Ming Hong Wu and took the title Emperor of China. The Ming Dynasty was born.

The Ming Dynasty

Ming Hong Wu was succeeded as emperor by his son Yong Le in 1398. Yong Le set about restoring China's greatness. Since the days of Kublai Khan, China had lost control of Vietnam. Yong Le sent an army to retake it. He had the Great Wall strengthened. He also built the Imperial City. This is a walled city—which still stands—within the capital city of Beijing. Beautiful gardens, great courtyards, and flowing waterways fill the Imperial City. The emperor's palace and government offices were there. Yong Le built the Imperial City to send a message about the wealth and power of the emperor.

The Imperial City in Beijing represented the power and might of dynastic rule.

During Yong Le's rule, **fleets** of Chinese ships made

seven trips to explore Southeast Asia, India, and the Arabian Peninsula. Zheng He (JUNG HUH), a trusted official, led the expeditions. About 28,000 sailors, merchants, and soldiers sailed on 62 ships for the first **voyage**, or trip. The largest ship was 440 feet long. The average ship weighed 1,500 tons. One hundred years later, the average length of the first Portuguese ships to reach Asia was only 60 feet. Those ships averaged about 300 tons. Chinese naval technology was far more advanced than that of European nations at the time. The voyages ended after Yong Le's death. Historians are not sure why but offer some theories.

Confucianism was a strong influence on the Chinese. Confucianism honored tradition and the way that things had always been done. The voyages of exploration brought new goods and ideas back to China. These new ideas might upset tradition. As a result, government officials may have convinced the new emperor to end the voyages. It is also possible that the cost of the voyages was a factor. In time, the Ming limited how far Chinese ships could travel beyond China. The Chinese had decided that their ways were the best and everyone else's were inferior.

Like other Chinese dynasties, the Ming Dynasty slowly weakened. The final blow came in 1644 from a peasant revolt that overthrew it. The Manchus, who lived north of the Great Wall, saw an opportunity. They swept into China, conquered it, and set up the Qing (CHING) Dynasty.

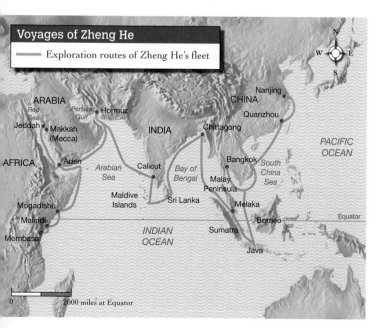

Voyages of Zheng He

—— Exploration routes of Zheng He's fleet

Putting It All Together

Complete your timeline of Chinese dynasties. Write down the names, dates, and three important facts about each dynasty. With a partner create a visual timeline like the ones that introduce each unit in this book. You will need to plan ahead to figure out how much space each dynasty will take on your sheet of paper.

The Spread of Cultures in Asia, 500–1650

LESSON 2

Japan and Korea

Thinking on Your Own

As you read this lesson, create an outline to help you study. Use the titles of the subheadings for the Roman numerals I, II, and III. Compare your outline with a partner. Fill in the information as you read.

Japan is an **archipelago**, or chain of many islands. Since early times, most Japanese have lived on the four largest islands. Examine the map on the next page to see where Japan is in relation to China and Korea.

Rule by Emperor and Powerful Families

People settled in Japan as early as 3000 B.C. By the first couple of centuries A.D., the Japanese were living in **clans**. Clans are small groups of related people. Most clan members were farmers. However, there was a small number of wealthy members, or **aristocrats**, in each clan. The leader, or chief, of each clan was an aristocrat.

By A.D. 500, one clan, the Yamato, had gained power over the other clans. The leader of the Yamato became emperor of Japan and also high priest of **Shinto**, their religion. The Yamato claimed that the emperor was descended from Amaterasu, the female god of the sun. From the Yamato until 1945, the Japanese emperor was worshiped as a god.

The emperor may have come from the Yamato clan, but other clans remained powerful. By the 700s, the Fujiwara family had

focus your reading

How did the Fujiwara gain power?

Discuss how the Japanese feudal system worked.

In what ways did the Chinese influence Korea?

vocabulary	
archipelago	daimyo
clan	samurai
aristocrat	ronin
Shinto	hostage system
imperial	
shogun	tenant farmers

become so powerful that the Yamato ruled in name only. The Fujiwara held the real power. Power was gained in two ways. They filled top government jobs with family members. In these positions, the Fujiwara could determine government policy. The Fujiwara also married into the **imperial** family. Family relationships made it easier to control the emperor.

Buddhism came to Japan in the 500s from Korea.

Eventually, the Yamato and the Fujiwara ignored what was happening in the provinces. Various emperors had tried to centralize the empire's government. However, wealthy families in the provinces worked against the reforms. They saw the reforms as ways to limit their power, and they were right. As a result, the families weakened centralization however they could. In time, these wealthy families became powerful enough to challenge the Fujiwara and each other. The result was civil war by the 1100s.

> ### ⧖ Time Box
>
> **1192–1333**
>   Kamakura Shogunate
> **1333–1477**
>   Ashikaga Shogunate
> **1467–1603**
>   Civil wars
> **1603–1868**
>   Tokugawa Shogunate

Rule by Shogunate

In 1192, Minamoto Yoritomo used alliances and force to end the civil war. He kept the emperor as a figurehead. However, Yoritomo took the title of **shogun**, meaning military commander. The new government structure was called a Shogunate. The real power lay with the shogun.

Yoritomo called his shogunate Kamakura, and it lasted for about 140 years. It ended after a Mongol invasion in 1281. The bloodshed and destruction that followed the invasion weakened the Kamakura. In 1333, it was toppled by the Ashikaga.

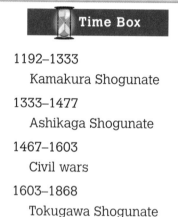

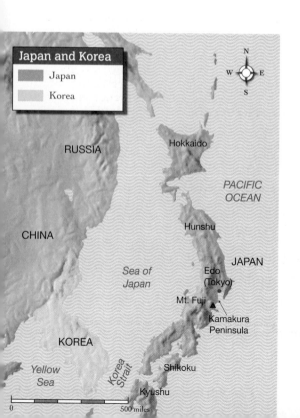

Japan and Korea
  Japan
  Korea

RUSSIA

Hokkaido

PACIFIC OCEAN

CHINA

Hunshu

Sea of Japan

JAPAN

Edo (Tokyo)

Mt. Fuji

Kamakura Peninsula

KOREA

Yellow Sea

Korea Strait

Shikoku

Kyushu

0   500 miles

Japanese Feudal Society

Emperor
- figurehead

Shogun
- held real power

Daimyo
- wealthy landowners
- vassals of the shogun

Samurai
- nobles and soldiers
- vassals of the shogun or daimyo

Ronin
- soldiers for hire

Peasants and Craftworkers
- most Japanese
- served higher classes

Merchants
- lowest class

Under the first two shogunates, Japan became a feudal society. The emperor was at the top. However, the real connection was between the shogun and the **daimyo** (DY•mee•OH). These were the heads of wealthy families. They owed the shogun loyalty and service in exchange for land. Under them were their vassals and **samurai**, or professional soldiers. Soldiers who would fight for any daimyo were called **ronin**. Next came peasants, farmers, and craftworkers. At the bottom of Japanese society were merchants. Making money by selling the work of others was looked down upon. Confucianism was the influence behind this idea.

In the mid-1400s, civil war broke out between rival daimyo. The Ashikaga Shogunate lost control of the country. It was not until 1603 that a daimyo was powerful enough to end the conflict. In that year, Tokugawa Ieyasu (tok•kuh•GAH•wah ee•YAH•soo) declared himself shogun and founded the Tokugawa Shogunate.

Minamoto Yoritomo founded the shogunate system.

Among the first acts of Ieyasu was limiting the power of the daimyo. The shogun used a **hostage system** to achieve this goal. He forced the daimyo and their families to live at the royal court, or palace, in Edo—present-day Tokyo. If a daimyo left Edo to visit his lands in the provinces, his family had to stay behind.

Another factor that changed the feudal system was the economy. Up to the time of the Tokugawa, Japan's economy was based on farming. Beginning in the 1600s, manufacturing and trade became more and more important. One reason was the coming of Europeans and the opening of trade with Europe.

The feudal system also changed because the Tokugawa

Samurai wore colorful armor made of steel strips. The strips were covered with silk to hold them together. Samurai were supposed to live by a code of behavior called *bushido*. The word means "way of the warrior." Loyalty, unquestioning obedience to one's lord, courage, and honor were valued. If a samurai did not follow the code, he was expected to kill himself with his sword.

Shogunate was a time of peace. People could concentrate on earning a living. As a result, there was little warfare for samurai. Instead of professional soldiers, they became government officials and security guards.

Only the peasant farmers continued to suffer. Many lost their land because they could not pay their taxes. They became **tenant farmers**, paying rent to wealthy landowners. During the 265 years of the Tokugawa Shogunate, there were almost 7,000 peasant revolts. None managed to topple the shogunate.

Korea and Chinese Influences

Korea developed on a peninsula that juts out from southeastern China. As a result of its closeness to China, Korea was strongly influenced by Chinese ideas.

The Han had seized control of northern Korea in 109 B.C. When the Han Dynasty collapsed in A.D. 220, Korea slipped from China's control. However, no single ruler rose up to unite the Koreans. Instead, three rival kingdoms fought for power until 668. By then the Tang Dynasty was in power in China and wanted to retake Korea. The Tang made an alliance with Silla, the smallest of the three kingdoms. China would help Silla defeat the other kingdoms. In exchange, Silla would agree to make Korea a tribute state of China.

The Silla Dynasty ruled Korea until 918. As in China, peasant revolts weakened the ruling dynasty. A new dynasty, the Koryo, was able to seize control. In 1231, the Mongols launched a successful invasion of Korea. They remained in Korea until the 1350s. It was around this time that their dynasty, the Yuan, collapsed in China.

In 1392, Yi Song-gye, a general, reunited Korea and founded the Yi Dynasty. Under the Yi, Korea remained an independent kingdom for almost 250 years. In the 1630s, the Ming ruler of China sent an army to subdue

> **stop and think**
>
> Imagine that you are a diamyo during the Tokugawa Shogunate. You have decided to make a gift of gold to a powerful person who can help you keep the land you hold. To which of the following would you make the gift: the emperor, the shogun, your favorite samurai, a peasant farmer, or a merchant? Write a paragraph to explain why you chose that person.

> Buddhism spread to Korea in the 300s.

Korea. Once again Korea became a tribute state of China. However, the Yi were allowed to remain in power. The Yi continued to rule until 1910.

During the Han occupation of Korea, Chinese colonists were sent to settle among the native people. These colonists were the first to bring Chinese ideas to Korea. Chinese influence increased when Chinese missionaries began traveling to Korea around 300. They came spreading the teachings of Buddha. Many Koreans converted to Buddhism. Around this time, the Chinese writing system was introduced into Korea.

When Korea became a tribute state of China, Korean officials, scholars, and merchants regularly visited China. They brought back news about everything from how the rich Chinese dressed to how they decorated their palaces. Scholars carried back Chinese paintings and books for Korean students. Confucianism was taught in Korean universities. When Yi became emperor, he based his government on Confucian principles.

Time Box

668–918
　Silla Dynasty

918–1392
　Koryo Dynasty

1231–1350s
　Mongol occupation

1392–1910
　Yi Dynasty

1630s–1895
　Tribute state of China

Because Korea was under Chinese authority, there was a continuing peace between China and Korea. As a result, merchants grew wealthy from trade between the two kingdoms. Korean merchants were able to buy and then sell at home goods such as Chinese silk. They were also able to sell Korean trade goods to Chinese merchants for resale to Chinese customers.

Koreans improved Chinese pottery-making techniques to create Celadon pottery.

The Koreans did not simply imitate what they got from the Chinese. They adapted it to their own needs and skills. For example, Koreans learned to make pottery from the Chinese. However, Korean craftworkers used what they learned to develop their own style of pottery.

Putting It All Together

Create a concept web to show China's influence on Korea. Label the central circle "China's Influence." Draw smaller circles for each way that China influenced Korea. Add details from the lesson and share your web with a partner.

A Series of Empires in India

Thinking on Your Own

As you read this lesson, keep a list of events in the order in which they occurred. If a date is given, write the date, too.

The Gupta Dynasty in India began to weaken in the 400s. Rival groups fought for power, as they had in China when dynasties fell. For about the next 700 years, India was divided among a number of local Hindu rulers.

Delhi Sultanate

In the early 1200s, things changed in India. An Arab army under the **sultan**, or ruler, of Ghur invaded India. Hindu warriors, known as **rajputs**, fought the invaders but were defeated. The sultan's army extended Islamic rule across the northern plain of India. In 1206, the sultan founded the **Sultanate** of Delhi, based in the city of Delhi. A sultanate is an area ruled by a Sultan. In the 1300s, the Sultanate added the Deccan Plateau to its territory.

Over time the Sultanate's hold on its territory weakened. By 1398, the Sultanate could not defend its Empire from an army of Mongols and Turks. Timur-i Lang (TEE•MOOR•YEE LAHNG), sometimes called Tamerlane, and his forces invaded India from the northwest. They robbed, burned, and killed as they moved across northern India. Even the city of Delhi came under their control. Delhi was left a smoking ruin. Supposedly

Time Box

1206–1526
    Sultanate of Delhi
1526–1757
    Mogul Empire

not even a bird stirred in the city for months.

Timur and his forces did not stay to set up an empire in India. They took their **loot** and rode west. The city of Delhi was rebuilt, but it was no longer the center of a prosperous empire. Local rulers carved up large parts of India for themselves.

Muslim Influences on Indian Society

Under the Delhi Sultanate, India became part of a vast network that stretched from Southeast Asia to Europe. The sultans, however, were not interested in understanding or adopting Indian customs and traditions. The sultans created a division between their Muslim subjects and their Hindu subjects. The Hindu were a conquered people. The Muslims meant to keep it that way.

But Muslim rulers also wanted to convert Hindus to Islam. Some early sultans persecuted Hindus and destroyed their temples. A heavy tax was placed on non-Muslims. This was an effort to get Hindus to convert. The Delhi Sultanate was strongest in northern India, and most converts were made there. Hindus converted for many reasons. One reason, of course, was that some people truly came to believe in Allah. Others converted because of the equality that Islam offered.

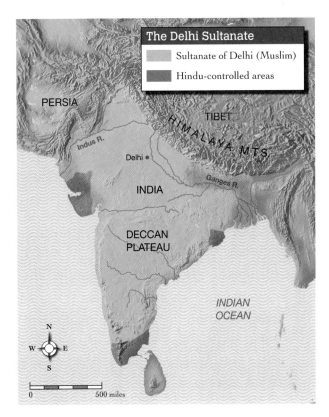

The Delhi Sultanate
- Sultanate of Delhi (Muslim)
- Hindu-controlled areas

PERSIA · TIBET · HIMALAYA MTS. · Indus R. · Delhi · Ganges R. · INDIA · DECCAN PLATEAU · INDIAN OCEAN

Hinduism and Islam	
Hinduism	**Islam**
• polytheistic, belief in many deities • many sacred books • caste system • priests • belief in cows as sacred animals • music as part of religious ceremonies	• monotheistic, belief in one God—Allah • one sacred book, the Quran • equality of all people • no priests • viewed cows as food • music in religious ceremonies was offensive to Allah

There was no caste system in Islam. Some Indian merchants probably converted so they could more easily tap into the Muslim trade network. Some Hindus converted in order to marry a Muslim. Some people, of course, converted so they would not have to pay the nonbelievers' tax.

There were a number of differences between Islam and Hinduism. The differences were not just in religious ideas. There were also cultural differences, such as the use of music.

Ultimately, the sultans relaxed their opposition to Hinduism. Hindus were free to worship their deities as long as they paid the nonbelievers' tax. A vast number of people remained Hindus.

The Mogul Empire

The Moguls and Turks returned to India in the 1500s. In 1526, Babur led a combined Turkish and Mogul force. They easily defeated what was left of the Delhi Sultanate and other small kingdoms. Babur set up the Mogul Empire.

The most famous emperor was Akbar, Babur's grandson, who ruled from 1556 to 1605. He expanded the empire and set up an efficient organization to run it. He made sure that the tax system that supported the government was fair. Akbar understood that the tension between

stop and think

Create a concept web to list the effects of the Delhi Sultanate. Label the large circle "Sultanate of Delhi." Draw a smaller circle for each effect that the Sultanate caused. Draw lines to connect the smaller circles to the large one.

A wedding feast in 1562

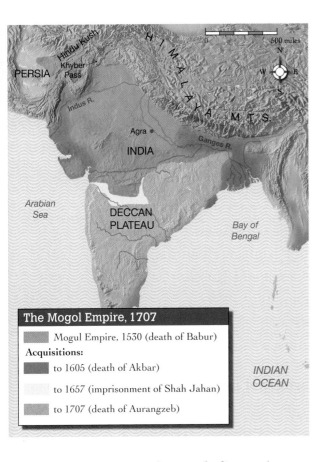

The Mogul Empire, 1707

Mogul Empire, 1530 (death of Babur)

Acquisitions:

to 1605 (death of Akbar)

to 1657 (imprisonment of Shah Jahan)

to 1707 (death of Aurangzeb)

Islam and Hinduism created problems in the Empire. He ordered a policy of religious **toleration**. He married a Hindu and appointed Hindus to lower-level government positions. Top-level positions went to Muslims. The tax on non-Muslims was ended.

Not all of Akbar's successors followed his policies. In 1658, Aurangzeb, Akbar's great-grandson, seized power from his father, Shah Jahan. Aurangzeb ended religious toleration and began the persecution of Hindus. The nonbelievers' tax was reinstated. No new Hindu temples could be built. **Suttee**, burning a widow with the body of her deceased husband, was forbidden. Gambling and drinking, both banned under Islam, were also forbidden.

These actions resulted in a number of rebellions against Mogul emperors. However, no revolt succeeded in overthrowing the Empire. The Mogul Empire lasted until 1757 when Great Britain seized power. The first British traders had arrived in India in the 1600s.

The Taj Mahal (above) was built by Shah Jahan, the fifth Mogul emperor, as a tribute to his wife Mumtaz Mahal. The complex took 22 years to build and was completed in 1648.

Emperor Akbar (below) symbolically passes his crown from his son, Shah Jahan, to his great-grandson who seized power in 1658.

Putting It All Together

Imagine that you are a Hindu living in Delhi in 1757 when the British gained control of India. Write a letter to the new British governor asking for better treatment of the Hindus. Explain how India's Muslim leaders have treated your family during the past two hundred years.

Chapter Summary

- The Tang and Song Dynasties are known as the Golden Ages in China.
- Mongols invaded China in 1215. Kublai Khan founded the Yuan Dynasty. Later emperors were **corrupt**.
- In 1368, a **monk** and his followers overthrew the Yuan and founded the Ming Dynasty. Yong Le built the **Imperial** City. A **fleet** of his ships made **voyages** to explore Southeast Asia, India, and the Arabian Peninsula.
- Japan is an **archipelago** close to China and Korea.
- The early Japanese lived in clans and most were farmers. There were a few **aristocrats**.
- The Yamato **clan** gained power and the Yamato leader declared himself emperor and high priest of **Shinto**.
- Japan became a feudal society. The real power was with the **shogun**. The highest vassals were the **daimyo**. They were followed by the **samurai** and **ronin**. Most Japanese were **tenant farmers**.
- Tokugawa used a **hostage system** to control the daimyo.
- The **Sultan** of Ghur invaded India and defeated **rajputs**. He founded the **Sultanate** of Delhi and introduced Islam into India. Timur later invaded India, **looted**, and left a badly weakened Delhi Sultanate.
- In 1526, Babur set up the Mogul Empire. His grandson Akbar adopted religious **toleration**. A later emperor, Aurangzeb, banned **suttee**.

Chapter Review

1 Work with a partner to decide on topics and headlines for four newspaper articles about people and events in Chapter 12. Then write an introductory paragraph for each that includes *who, what, when, where,* and *why.*

2 Play "Who am I?" with a partner. Choose five people discussed in this chapter. Write three or four sentences to describe each person. End your descriptions with the question "Who am I?" Take turns quizzing each other.

Skill Builder

Analyzing Sequence Using a Flowchart

Sequence is the order in which events happen. *Chronology* is another word for *sequence*. A timeline is one way to arrange the sequence of events. You can see that one thing happened before or after another from the location of events on the timeline. Making a timeline as you read can help you understand sequence more easily.

A writer does not always use dates to describe sequence. Sometimes a writer uses signal words. Some words that signal sequence are:

first, second, third . . .	first . . . last	before	after
now earlier	later	next	then

Sometimes you have to figure out sequence without any timeline or any signal words. A flowchart can help you. Start with the first event and fill in each event in the order in which it happened. A flowchart of the invasion of India by Timur looks like the following:

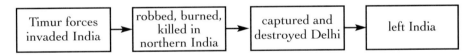

Timur forces invaded India → robbed, burned, killed in northern India → captured and destroyed Delhi → left India

The flowchart presents the main ideas. Details are left out. Making a flowchart can help you identify and remember the most important information.

Complete the following activities:

1   In Lesson 1 of this chapter you created a timeline. Use your timeline to create a flowchart of events. Share your flowchart with a partner. Quiz each other on when events happened in relation to each other. Use some of the signal words to ask your questions.

2   Create a flowchart to show the order of events under the Ming Dynasty.

3   Create a flowchart to show the chronology of events in India. Use your list of events from Lesson 3.

4
UNIT

THE GLOBAL AGE

The end of the Roman Empire in the West barely affected most people. They looked to their local landowners for protection and a way to earn a living. The Catholic Church remained a governing force in people's lives. But change was creeping across Western Europe.

By the 1500s, change came more rapidly—and not just to Western Europe. Europeans began to search out routes to rich trading nations in Asia. By accident, they bumped into the Americas. The race was on among European nations to establish colonies and gain riches.

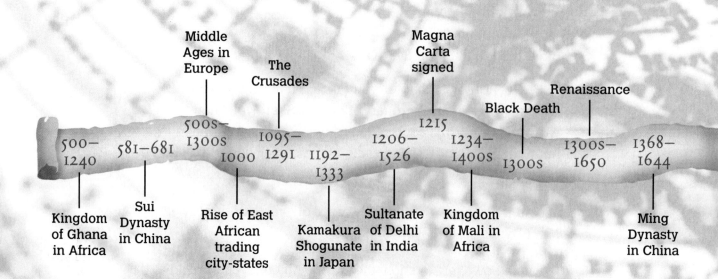

Middle Ages in Europe
500s–1300s

The Crusades
1095–1291

Magna Carta signed
1215

Renaissance
1300s–1650

Black Death
1300s

500–1240

581–681

1000

1192–1333

1206–1526

1234–1400s

1368–1644

Kingdom of Ghana in Africa

Sui Dynasty in China

Rise of East African trading city-states

Kamakura Shogunate in Japan

Sultanate of Delhi in India

Kingdom of Mali in Africa

Ming Dynasty in China

What was life like on the medieval manor?

Why is the Renaissance considered a turning point in world history?

How did European voyages of exploration and trade affect non-Europeans?

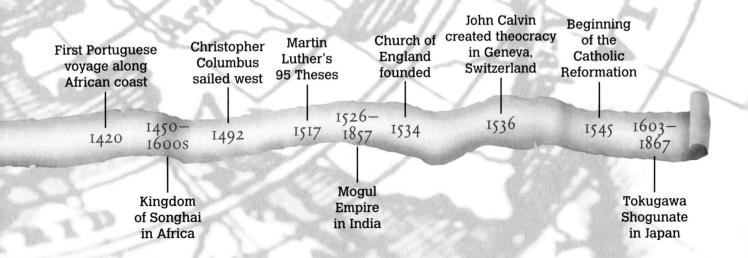

First Portuguese voyage along African coast — 1420

Kingdom of Songhai in Africa — 1450–1600s

Christopher Columbus sailed west — 1492

Martin Luther's 95 Theses — 1517

Mogul Empire in India — 1526–1857

Church of England founded — 1534

John Calvin created theocracy in Geneva, Switzerland — 1536

Beginning of the Catholic Reformation — 1545

Tokugawa Shogunate in Japan — 1603–1867

Chapter 13

MEDIEVAL EUROPE

(500–1300)

Getting Focused

Skim this chapter to predict what you will be learning.
- Read the lesson titles and subheadings.
- Look at the illustrations and read the captions.
- Examine the maps.
- Review the vocabulary words and terms.

In your notebook create a KWL Chart. Title the first column "What I Know." Title the second column "What I Want to Know," and the third column "What I Learned." Fill in the first two columns as you preview the chapter. Fill in the last column after you complete your reading.

Feudalism and Manorialism

Thinking on Your Own

Examine the pictures and captions in the lesson. Choose two pictures to write about. Describe how the people are dressed and what they are doing in each picture. Use words that will help your reader imagine the pictures. Also, use the vocabulary words.

In the early 700s, Muslims were on the march in Europe. When they invaded France, Charles Martel led an army of Franks against them. In 732, at the Battle of Tours, the Franks defeated the Muslim army. The Muslims were pushed back into Spain where they ruled until the late 1400s. By 800, Charles Martel's grandson Charlemagne had begun to put together an empire. His armies seized land in what are today France, Germany, and Italy. At the same time, Vikings were moving south from Norway and Sweden. They were threatening coastal cities in Britain and France.

Beginning in the 400s, Germanic invaders set up small kingdoms in England to take the place of Roman authority. In the 800s, a single Anglo-Saxon kingdom gained power over the others. In 1066, England fell to Norman invaders from France. Their leader, William the Conqueror, seized the throne.

focus your reading

How did European feudalism work?

Compare feudalism and manorialism.

Explain why the Roman Catholic Church was so important in the lives of Europeans.

vocabulary

fiefs	bishop
chivalry	archbishop
manor	cardinal
parish	pope

Charlemagne

Feudalism

During the Middle Ages—the period between the fall of the Roman Empire and the Renaissance—Europeans began to use the political system called feudalism. It provided protection for people and a new way to organize governments. Feudalism also developed in the Byzantine Empire in eastern Europe, in the Monomotapa Empire in Africa, and among the Japanese.

Feudal Society

Monarch

Higher Lords

Nobles

Lesser Lords

Knights

Serfs

At the top of the feudal system was the monarch, or chief lord. All of the land belonged to him. He gave land to nobles who were loyal to him. The land grants, or gifts of land, were called **fiefs**. The nobles were vassals of the monarch, but they were lords to those below them in society. In return for land, the nobles owed the monarch loyalty. In time of war, they had to raise an army of knights and soldiers to defend the monarch. The nobles also made a yearly payment to the monarch for the use of their land.

Below the nobles were knights. They, in turn, were vassals of the nobles. The knights received land from the nobles and owed them loyalty in return. The knights had to defend their lord and his lands against attack. They also owed their lords annual payments for the land.

A medieval king gives orders during a battle.

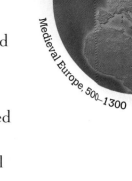

Serfs were the lowest class in European society. They owed both loyalty and labor to the nobles, their lords. In addition, serfs had to pay yearly rent to their lords.

Over time, a code of behavior known as **chivalry** developed among the nobles and knights. Knights were supposed to be loyal, brave, and honorable. They were to treat prisoners well and defend women, children, the sick, and the elderly. Women were given a special place of honor in chivalry, but they lacked many of the rights that men had.

Manorialism

Manorialism was Europe's economic system during the Middle Ages. Most Europeans in the early Middle Ages farmed and lived on **manors**. These were the estates, or large landholdings, of the nobles. The manors were the nobles' fiefs from the monarch.

Very wealthy nobles, like dukes, might live in a castle. At times, the knights who served the noble lived there, too. However, the typical noble and his family lived in a large house on their manor. Serfs lived in a village on the manor. The village included a church and a mill for grinding grain.

Nobles kept about one-third to one-half of their manor's land for themselves. In return for protection, the serfs worked the lord's land about three days out of every week. The serfs worked the rest of the land in return for an annual payment. Women as well as men worked in the fields.

Since few serfs had money, part of every crop was paid to the lord. Serfs also had to pay to use the manor's mill to grind their corn or wheat into flour. The fee would be several sacks of the flour.

> ### stop and think
>
> Feudalism was the political system of the Middle Ages. Manorialism was the economic system. Explain how these systems worked together in medieval society. Write down your ideas. Talk with a partner to test your ideas. Then write one or two paragraphs to explain how feudalism and manorialism were related.

An English manor house

The lord had absolute control over the serfs on his manor. This control maintained law and order. The noble held his own court to try serfs accused of crimes. He also sentenced those who were convicted and saw that the punishment was carried out. If a serf wanted to leave the manor for any reason, the lord had to give permission. If a lord lost his manor, the serfs as well as the land became the property of the new lord. The new lord could not throw serfs off their land. Unlike slaves, serfs could not be bought and sold.

Roman Catholic Church

In the early Middle Ages, the Roman Catholic Church contributed to the stability of Western European society. Nobles and monarchs came and went, but the Church remained. Except for Muslims in Spain and groups of Jews, everyone in Western Europe was a member of the Roman Catholic Church.

Religion and learning were important during the Middle Ages. Cathedrals such as Notre Dame in Paris were constructed (above left). Religious figures were often the subject of paintings (above right). Oxford University was a center for learning (bottom).

Church teachings helped people accept the hardships of their life on Earth. It also taught the common people to obey the rulers. The Church taught that the soul was more important than the body. People endured cruel lords, unjust laws, and poor living conditions. They believed that such hardships would earn them entry to heaven. As a result, the Middle Ages was not a time of rebellions and revolutions.

Since the days of the first Christians, the Church had grown in size and organization. At the local

China and cotton from India. Among the goods that they bought were wool cloth and crockery from Flanders—an area in modern Belgium and France—and furs from Russia.

Until the later Middle Ages, the **barter** system, or exchange, was used for business. The growth of trade networks and the specialization of trade made barter impractical. Merchants wanted gold or silver coins. This was the beginning of the **money economy**.

Increased trade brought about another change in the way people did business. Merchants began to borrow money to pay for trading voyages. Once they sold the goods their traders bought in Constantinople or Flanders, they could repay the loan. The banking business developed to finance these deals.

The growth of trade also fueled the growth of **capitalism**. This is an economic system based on the private ownership of production for the purpose of making a profit. Besides repaying the loan, a smart merchant could also make a profit.

The development of both the money economy and capitalism were unintended consequences of global trade. Another unintended effect was the spread of the **bubonic plague**, or Black Death. It was carried by infected fleas that lived on rats.

The plague, or Black Death, was carried by infected fleas that lived on rats.

The rats traveled on ships beween European ports and cities in Asia. People became ill after they were bitten by infected fleas. Between 1348 and 1353, some 38 million out of 75 million, or about half of all Europeans, died from the plague.

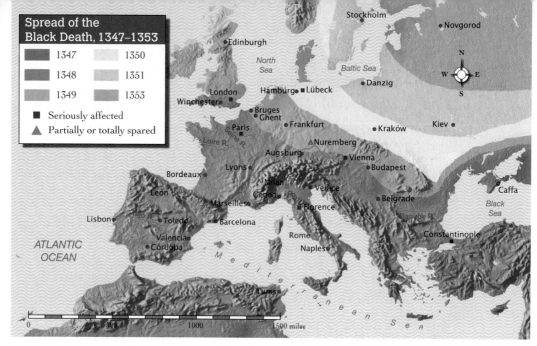

Spread of the Black Death, 1347–1353

1347	1350
1348	1351
1349	1353

■ Seriously affected
▲ Partially or totally spared

The Rise of Cities

Another outcome of the growth of trade was the growth of cities. These cities were often the sites of trade fairs. Sometimes a group of merchants built a new settlement. Often they chose a place near a castle. The merchants arranged with the lord of the castle to provide protection—for a fee. As the towns and cities grew, the population became more diverse.

Medieval towns and cities grew and prospered.

Often, lords found themselves in need of money. They found an unusual way to get it. They sold rights to the towns in their territory. In exchange for money, the towns received **charters** spelling out their rights.

Typical Rights of Towns

- Townspeople could elect leaders.
- Townspeople could manage the government of the town.
- Townspeople had their own law courts.
- Townspeople could buy and sell property.
- Townspeople were free from military service to the lord.
- If a runaway serf lived a year and a day in the town, the serf would be a free person.

Guilds

Craftworkers were drawn to the new towns because merchants needed goods to sell. Craftworkers set up shop and began to make products. Over time, craftworkers developed **guilds**. A guild was an organization of merchants or craftworkers who banded together to protect their economic interests. The purpose of the guilds was to set standards for the quality of work produced by its members. Guilds also set working hours and prices for goods.

The guilds trained young people to become masters, or highly skilled workers, in a craft. Women as well as men could become master craftworkers. The first step was to become an apprentice. At ten years of age, a boy or girl entered an apprenticeship with a master craftworker. The apprentice worked for the master for seven years without pay. While doing whatever work was needed in the shop, the young person learned the skills of the craft.

At the end of seven years, the apprentice became a **journeyman**. He or she was allowed to work for wages but was not yet a guild member. To become a member, the journeyman had to create a masterpiece. This was a piece of work that the journeyman considered his or her best. Guild members would then decide if the journeyman was good enough to become a master.

Fabric being weighed by a member of the Guild of Wool Merchants

Rise of the Middle Class

The rise of towns and cities was a major reason for the decline of manorialism and feudal society. Because lords needed money, they began to require money from their serfs instead of payments of crops. In this case, serfs became **tenant farmers**. Other nobles chose to keep all the land for themselves. They hired former serfs as laborers to work the land. By the 1300s, the manorial system had ended in Western Europe.

In feudal society, there were two classes: lords, or nobles, and serfs. Now there was a new social and economic class between nobles and farmers. The development of towns and cities resulted in the birth of a **middle class**. It was made up of merchants, traders, and craftworkers.

The nobles looked down on the middle class because they made their living by selling goods and services. Farmers looked up to the middle class because they wanted to be one of them. The middle class eventually grew in size, wealth, and power.

Merchants were often middle class members of their villages.

Putting It All Together

Review the list of important changes that you have made while reading this lesson. Compare your list with that of a partner and make a second list that you can both agree upon.

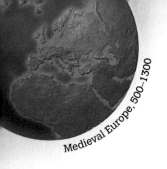

LESSON 3

The Beginning of Nation-States

Thinking on Your Own

Read the Focus Your Reading questions. As you read the lesson, take bulleted notes to help you answer the questions. When you have finished reading the lesson, review your notes with a partner. Check to make sure you listed all the important points in your notes.

The development of the **nation-state**, a large area of land ruled by a single government, did not happen at the same time in all of Europe. France and England developed as nation-states during the late Middle Ages. A single German nation did not exist until 1871.

The English Monarchy

William the Conqueror and his forces invaded England in 1066. They were from Normandy, a region in northern France. Their Viking ancestors had invaded France in the 900s and settled in the area that became known as Normandy.

William was the Duke of Normandy. His forces were made up of his Norman vassals and their knights and foot soldiers. Once he had conquered Anglo-Saxon England, William rewarded his Norman vassals with fiefs in England. He took the lands from the Anglo-Saxon lords he had defeated. In doing this, William was taking land from his enemies and

focus your reading

Explain why the Magna Carta is so important.

How did the English Parliament become so powerful?

Summarize how the Capetians gained and kept power.

vocabulary

nation-state

circuit courts

Magna Carta

rule of law

Parliament

representative government

King John signed the Magna Carta in June 1215.

putting it into the hands of his loyal followers.

But William and his successors were aware that these same Norman vassals were possible rivals. Future English monarchs set up a paid bureaucracy to run the government. The monarchs also set up a royal court system, called the **circuit courts**, and a single set of laws for everyone. Judges rode from place to place on a regular circuit, or route, to try cases. This made it possible for all subjects everywhere in the kingdom to use the courts. Cases were heard by a jury of peers, not simply by a judge.

As a result of these actions, the power of the nobles was weakened. In 1215, a group of nobles rebelled. They forced King John to sign the **Magna Carta**, or "Great Charter." Most of the

The Magna Carta, 1215

The Magna Carta set out the basic rights of the English people. The document influenced the development of the government of the United States and of other nations. The following are five of the 63 articles in the Magna Carta.

1. We have . . . granted to all the freemen of our Kingdom, for us and our heirs forever, all the underwritten Liberties, to be enjoyed and held by them and by their heirs, from us and from our heirs.

12. No tax . . . shall be imposed in our kingdom, unless by the common council of our kingdom. . . .

13. [T]he City of London shall have all its ancient liberties. . . . Furthermore, we will and grant that all other Cities, Burghs, and Towns, and Ports, should have all their liberties. . . .

39. No free-man shall be seized, or imprisoned, or dispossessed . . . nor shall we condemn him, nor shall we commit him to prison, excepting by the legal judgment of his peers, or by the laws of the land.

40. To none shall we sell, to none will we deny, to none will we delay right or justice.

reading for understanding

Which article guarantees the right to a trial?

Which article do you think was the basis of the American colonists' cry of "no taxation without representation"?

Explain in a paragraph what Article 1 means.

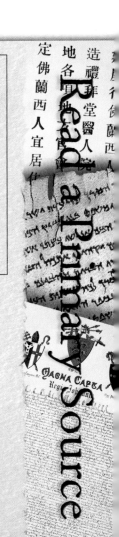

Read a Primary Source

articles of the Magna Carta applied only to the nobles. However, the rights and liberties began to be applied to all English citizens. The Magna Carta established the **rule of law**. England was to be governed according to laws. The document stated that the monarch was not above the law. Unlike the French monarch, the English ruler did not gain absolute power over his or her subjects.

King John's seal from the Magna Carta

British Parliament

The Power of Parliament

According to the Magna Carta, the English monarch was supposed to be advised by the Great Council of nobles and bishops. Beginning in the 1200s, the Council was replaced by a larger assembly, or group, called **Parliament**. Two knights from each county and two representatives from each town joined the nobles and clergy. This was the beginning of **representative government** in England. Later, Parliament gathered in two groups: the House of Lords and the House of Commons.

Parliament had two duties: to set taxes and to pass laws to govern England. According to the Magna Carta, the Great Council had to approve taxes. Parliament took over this power and began to use it against the monarchs. By threatening not to enact taxes, Parliament could force the English monarchs to agree to its demands.

> ### stop and think
>
> List the actions English monarchs took to limit the power of their nobles. Did these actions help ordinary English people—that is, everyone who was not a noble? Work with a partner to decide if these actions helped, hurt, or had no effect on ordinary English people.

The French Monarchy

Charlemagne founded the Frankish Empire in what today includes the countries of Germany, France, northern Spain, and most of Italy. After his death, his sons fought over the

Empire. In 843, his grandsons divided the Empire rather than fight over it. Modern France developed from the western part of the Empire.

The last of Charlemagne's descendants in the western kingdom died in 987. The feudal lords of the kingdom chose a new king from among themselves. The man they selected was Hugh Capet, the Count of Paris. He founded the Capetian Dynasty of French rulers. They remained in power until the late 1700s when the French Revolution ended the monarchy.

Hugh Capet did not have large landholdings, nor did he have a huge army of knights and foot soldiers. But he was smart and so were his descendants. First, Capet made the position of monarch hereditary. Instead of selecting a lord to be king, the crown would pass from father to son.

Second, the Capetians increased the amount of land under royal control. Loss of their land lessened the power of the nobles. Additional land increased the wealth of the monarchy. Third, taxes were collected from the people. Fourth, war between nobles was outlawed. Fifth, an army was organized and led by generals appointed by the king. Sixth, like the English monarchs, the French kings set up a large and efficient bureaucracy to run the country. The bureaucrats came from the middle class, not from the nobility. Their only loyalty was to the monarch.

Hugh Capet

Over the centuries, through actions such as these, the Capetians were able to strengthen their rule. By the late 1600s, the power of the French kings—for good or bad—had become absolute, or all-powerful.

Putting It All Together

France and England developed two different forms of government. In England, Parliament held a great deal of power. In France, the king held all the power. With a partner, create a Venn diagram to show the similarities and differences between the two governments.

Chapter Summary

- The monarch gave **fiefs** to the nobles.
- **Chivalry** developed to guide the behavior of knights.
- Nobles, knights, and serfs lived on **manors**.
- **Bishops, archbishops,** and **cardinals** all reported to the **pope.** Local communities were called **parishes.**
- European Christians went on eight **crusades** to the **Holy Land.** The crusades had many **unintended consequences.**
- In the early Middle Ages, business was done by **barter.** The increase in trade resulted in the development of the **money economy** and **capitalism.**
- **Bubonic plague** spread quickly throughout Europe.
- In exchange for a money payment to a local lord, a town received a **charter** guaranteeing certain rights.
- Craftworkers organized **guilds. Journeymen** were highly-skilled workers.
- By the 1300s, **tenant farmers** and hired farm laborers replaced serfs.
- By the end of the Middle Ages, a new **middle class** and **nation-states** had developed.
- Early English monarchs set up a paid bureaucracy, a **circuit court** system, and trial by jury. The **Magna Carta** established the **rule of law** in England.
- **Parliament** developed in the 1200s. It began **representative government** in England.

Chapter Review

1 Imagine it is time to become an apprentice and learn a craft. What would you like to learn to do? Write a letter to a master craftworker asking to become his or her apprentice. Explain why you want to learn that craft.

2 Write two-line headlines for the following: (a) the Crusades, (b) the bubonic plague, (c) a new town charter, (d) William, Duke of Normandy, being crowned the English king. Then write a lead paragraph for each headline.

Skill Builder

Synthesizing Information

To *synthesize* means "to bring together separate pieces or parts." Suppose you want to go to the movies. There are two movies playing and you cannot decide which one to see. You ask four friends who have seen one movie or the other. You think about all the information you have gathered. You then make your decision. You have synthesized the information you gathered.

Writing a research report requires you to synthesize information from different sources.

> To synthesize information, follow these steps:
>
> 1 Choose the sources you will need to use.
>
> 2 Find the main idea and supporting details for the information you find.
>
> 3 Look for links between the information.
>
> 4 Put the information together based on those links.

Complete the following activities.

1 Lesson 2 in Chapter 12 and Lesson 1 in this chapter discuss feudalism. Work through Steps 2 and 3 to compare feudalism in Europe to feudalism in Japan. To help you, create a table or Venn diagram comparing feudalism in Europe and Japan. Use information in the two lessons to fill in the table.

2 Use the table or Venn diagram to write a three- or four-paragraph essay about feudalism in Europe and Japan.

Chapter 14

RENAISSANCE AND REFORMATION

(1300–1650)

Getting Focused

Skim this chapter to predict what you will be learning.
- Read the lesson titles and subheadings.
- Look at the illustrations and read the captions.
- Examine the maps.
- Review the vocabulary words and terms.

The 1300s to around 1650 was a time of great change in western Europe. As you read this chapter, create a T-chart to keep track of the changes that occurred and the causes and effects of those changes. On the left side of the chart, list the cause of the change. List the effect, or result, of the change on the right side of the chart.

The Renaissance

Thinking on Your Own

Outline this lesson in your notebook. Use the subheadings for Roman numerals I, II, and III. Be sure to organize information on the outline in descending order of importance. The more important the detail, the higher it belongs on the outline.

The **Renaissance** began in Italian city-states around 1300. The word *renaissance* means rebirth. It describes the spirit of curiosity and adventure that developed after the Middle Ages. By the late 1400s, the Renaissance had expanded into northern Europe.

The Renaissance started in Italy for two reasons. First, the Roman Empire had begun on the Italian peninsula. A major feature of the Renaissance was an interest in ancient Roman culture. Second, Italian city-states were growing rich from trade. Wealthy Italian citizens could support the cultural developments of the Renaissance.

focus your reading

Discuss the three key characteristics of the Renaissance.

Why was the invention of the printing press so important?

How did the lives of European women change during the Renaissance?

vocabulary

Renaissance

monasteries

scholarship

humanism

patrons

vernacular language

nuclear families

The Spirit of the Renaissance

The Renaissance had three major characteristics. First was an interest in the ideas of the ancient Greeks and Romans. Many people from the north and east migrated into western Europe beginning in the 200s. Invasions helped cause the fall of the Roman Empire. Education suffered in the centuries after the end of the Empire. If it had not been for monks in **monasteries,**

the works of the ancient Greeks and Romans would have been lost. The monks copied the works to study and preserve them. Islamic scholars in Spain and elsewhere also recorded much of the early Greek and Roman **scholarship**.

In the early 1300s, Italians began to rediscover the works of ancient Greek and Roman authors. The ideas of these early thinkers began to influence Italian writers and artists. As a result, a new intellectual movement known as **humanism** developed. Scholars turned to the study of poetry, philosophy, and history rather than to spiritual matters. Instead of using religious themes, many artists began to paint everyday subjects. Some painted portraits of their **patrons**. These were wealthy people who supported artists with money.

Petrarch is known as the founder of humanism.

How people viewed life on Earth began to change as a result of humanism. Philosophers and writers began to stress the importance of life on Earth instead of a future life in heaven. This was a second major feature of the Renaissance. The teachings of the Roman Catholic Church promised people a better life in heaven. This promise helped the people of the Middle Ages to endure their terrible living conditions. Humanism prompted a change. Humanist thinkers called on the educated and the wealthy to take an active role in their communities. They had a duty to work for the good of the city and state.

The belief in individual achievement was a third major characteristic of the Renaissance. The Renaissance was a time of progress, or great change. As more things improved, people's belief in the ability of humans to make more changes and improve more things grew. Anything might change; anything might happen.

Architect Filippo Brunelleschi built Il Duomo in Florence. It is modeled after the dome of the Pantheon in Rome.

⏳ **Time Box**
1517
Martin Luther nails 95 theses to door of church in Witttenberg
1521
Pope excommunicates Luther
1534
Henry VIII and Parliament create Church of England
1536
John Calvin invited to make Geneva, Switzerland, a model city
1545
Council of Trent

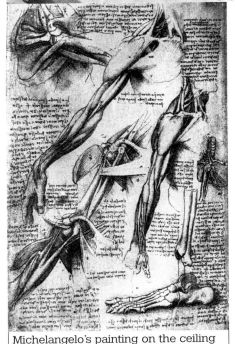

Michelangelo's painting on the ceiling of the Sistine Chapel (top left), Raphael's *Madonna and Child*, and DaVinci's drawings are examples of the great artists of the Renaissance.

The Printing Press

One of the most important inventions of the Renaissance was the printing press. The Chinese invented movable type during the Song Dynasty. Around 1455, Johann Gutenberg in Germany used movable type to print the first book in Europe. It was a copy of the Bible. Within 50 years, Europe had over one thousand printers. Almost 40,000 books were in print. Many were about religious topics. The writings of Martin Luther were quickly printed and widely shared. Without the printing press, his ideas would never have reached so many people.

The invention of the printing press made books more affordable. In addition, the printing press made copies of books available quickly. It took years for a monk to make one copy of the Bible by hand.

The printing press spread Protestant teachings and it also spread the use of the **vernacular language**. This is the language of ordinary people. At that time, highly educated people like scholars and lawyers wrote to one another in Latin. However, with the invention of the printing press, writers began to use the language spoken in their region, such as Italian or French.

Two of the most popular and important writers of the period were Dante, who wrote *Divine Comedy* in Italian, and Geoffrey

stop and think

List the three characteristics of the Renaissance. Write down ideas that you could use to explain each characteristic. Use your notes to explain the characteristics to a partner.

Johann Gutenberg produced the first printed book—the Bible—in 1455.

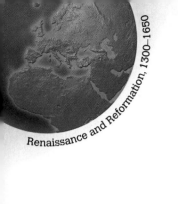
Chaucer, author of the *Canterbury Tales* in English. Dante's work takes readers on a journey through hell, purgatory, and heaven. Chaucer wrote about a collection of pilgrims on their way to a holy place in England.

Renaissance Society

The Renaissance brought about a number of changes in western European society. Towns and cities were growing in size and number. Serfdom was ending, and many farm workers were moving to the new urban centers. A new middle class of merchants and craftworkers was developing as well. However, as much as 30 to 40 percent of the urban population still lived in poverty.

Upper-class Renaissance women were often well-educated since they had servants to do their work.

As people moved to towns and cities, the organization of the family changed. Instead of living in extended families as people had on manors, townspeople began to live in **nuclear families**. A household contained only a father, a mother, and their children. The age when people married also increased. By the 1500s, Europeans did not marry until their late twenties.

Women's chief duties were to raise children and take care of the house. Farm women still worked in the fields at harvest time. Women in towns and cities were able to find work as servants for wealthy families. Women were also employed in crafts such as spinning and weaving.

Because reading the Bible was important in Protestantism, girls were taught to read. However, Protestantism reaffirmed the lesser place of women in the family. Women were to bear and raise Christian children while obeying their husbands in all things.

Putting It All Together

The invention of the printing press caused an increase in the number of books that were written and printed. Write a paragraph that explains the importance of printed books.

Martin Luther and the Protestant Reformation

Thinking on Your Own

As you read this lesson, create a cause-and-effect flowchart of Martin Luther's actions. Share your chart with a partner. Then create a flowchart for John Calvin's actions.

The Renaissance was not the only movement in Western Europe during this time period. The **Protestant Reformation** began as a way to protest against and reform practices of the Roman Catholic Church. Once begun, the Reformation had many unintended consequences.

Martin Luther and Lutheranism

Martin Luther was a Roman Catholic monk and professor in Wittenberg, Germany. He was disturbed by certain teachings of the Catholic Church, in particular the practice of selling **indulgences**. An indulgence frees a person from all or part of the punishment for sins. A monk in Wittenberg named Johann Tetzel was taking money in exchange for indulgences.

In 1517, Luther put together a list of 95 **theses**, or arguments, against the misuse of indulgences. He nailed the list to the front door of the church in Wittenberg. This act marks the

focus your reading

What ideas of the Roman Catholic Church did Martin Luther oppose?

What happened in German states as a result of Luther's teachings?

Explain how Calvinism became so important.

vocabulary

Protestant Reformation

indulgences

theses

salvation

excommunicated

Lutheranism

predestination

theocracy

Martin Luther

beginning of the Protestant Reformation. Luther's document was printed and was distributed throughout Germany. It won many supporters.

By 1520, Luther was calling on the German princes to break with the authority of the pope in Rome. Luther urged them to set up their own German church. This new church would be based on two teachings that Luther considered central.

First, faith in God alone is all that is needed for **salvation**, or entrance into heaven. The Roman Catholic Church teaches that people need to believe in God and do good works. Luther rejected good works as a way to earn salvation. He preached that humans cannot earn salvation. God alone grants salvation to a person who has faith. Luther's teaching became known as "justification by faith alone."

Second, the Bible is the only source of God's word and religious truth. Luther believed that the pope and other members of the church's hierarchy, such as bishops, were unnecessary. He stressed the need for people to read the Bible. This increased the demand for Bibles in vernacular languages.

Lutheran churches were simple in design.

Art, such as stained glass windows, are one item Protestants wanted removed from churches.

In 1521, the pope **excommunicated** Martin Luther. He was no longer a Roman Catholic. Luther continued to spread his teachings and to attract followers. His ideas became known as **Lutheranism**.

Political Consequences

Many German princes cared less about Luther's religious teachings than they did about their own power. Over the centuries, the Roman Catholic Church had gained a great deal of power across Europe. The German princes saw Luther's

stop and think

Germans were not the only people who were forced to practice a religion chosen by their ruler. In many nations for many centuries, rulers chose their people's religion. With a partner, make a list of at least three reasons to either support or oppose this practice. Then write two or three paragraphs to explain why you support or oppose the practice.

invitation as a way to do away with the pope's power over them. They also saw it as a way to do away with the Holy Roman Emperor.

For centuries, Germany had been divided into several hundred small states ruled by princes. Ruling over them was the Holy Roman Emperor. The present emperor, Charles V, tried to force the Lutheran princes to abandon Lutheranism and become Catholics again. In the 1530s and 1540s, a series of wars broke out between Catholic and Lutheran princes. Charles and his allies were not strong enough to defeat the Lutheran princes. In 1555, he had to agree to the Peace of Augsberg.

The peace treaty allowed the German princes to choose which religion they would practice. However, their subjects were not given the same choice. They had to accept whatever religion their ruler chose.

John Calvin and Calvinism

John Calvin was a Roman Catholic who was born and educated in France. As an intellectual, he was disturbed by certain practices of the Church. In 1536, Calvin published *Institutes of the Christian Religion*. This work set out his ideas about Protestantism.

Like Luther, Calvin believed in justification by faith alone. However, Calvin went further than Luther. John Calvin preached **predestination**. According to Calvin, God determines who will be saved and who will be damned to hell forever.

John Calvin in Geneva, Switzerland

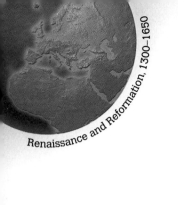

In 1536, leaders in Geneva, Switzerland, invited Calvin to help them make their city into a model Christian community. Calvin organized a **theocracy**—a government run by religious leaders. A group known as the Consistory enforced morality. Misbehavior like dancing, playing cards, and swearing resulted in punishment. Hard work, honesty, and thrift were highly valued. Over time, Calvinists came to view these virtues as the sign of being saved by God.

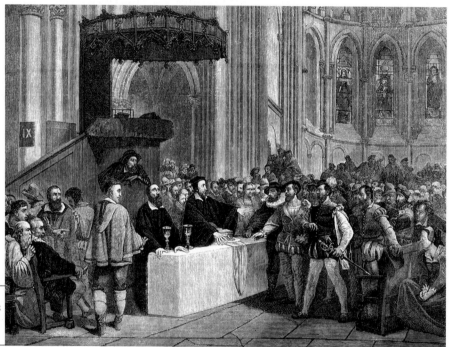

John Calvin in St. Peter's Cathedral, Geneva

Religious leaders from across Europe traveled to Geneva to see Calvinism in practice. They took Calvin's ideas back to their people. Calvinism soon spread to Germany, France, England, Scotland, and the Netherlands. Calvinism had greater influence in Europe than Lutheranism. Puritanism and Presbyterianism developed from Calvinism.

Putting It All Together

Imagine you are a member of the Consistory. You want to promote hard work, honesty, and thrift. Work with a partner to write three laws that would encourage these values and discourage their opposites: laziness, dishonesty, and foolish spending of money.

LESSON 3

The Influence of the Reformation

Thinking on Your Own

Examine the paintings in this lesson. Choose one to describe. Begin by writing a list of five words or phrases about the painting. Consider what is happening in the painting, who is in the painting, what colors are used, and how the painting makes you feel. Then use these words and phrases to write a one-paragraph description of the painting.

The Protestant Reformation began as an effort to reform practices of the Roman Catholic Church. Reform became mixed with political ambition in Germany. In England, politics was the major force that caused the end of the Roman Catholic Church and the creation of the Church of England.

focus your reading

Why was the Church of England created?

What were the results of the Catholic Reformation?

Explain why religious persecution increased during the Reformation.

vocabulary

annulled   Inquisition

doctrines   heretics

decrees   reconquista

Henry VIII and the Church of England

King Henry VIII had been a strong defender of the Catholic Church when the Reformation began. He even wrote a book defending the Church. However, by the 1530s, Henry had a problem of his own to solve. To ensure that the English throne would stay in his family, he needed a male heir. His wife, Catherine of Aragon, had produced a daughter, Mary, but no son. Henry wished to have his marriage **annulled** in order to marry Anne Boleyn. An annulment would mean that the marriage had never taken place as far as the Church was concerned. There was no divorce in the Roman Catholic faith.

Henry VIII

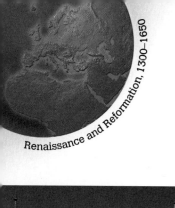
The pope refused to grant an annulment. Henry then asked the Archbishop of Canterbury, the highest Church official in England, for an annulment. The archbishop, Thomas Cranmer, granted it in 1533. Anne and Henry were married and Anne produced a child—a girl, Elizabeth. When Henry tired of Anne, he took another wife, Jane Seymour. They had a son, Edward. In all, Henry had six wives.

In addition to marrying Anne Boleyn, Henry set up a new church. In 1534, he asked Parliament for and was granted the Act of Supremacy. This law created the Church of England with the monarch as head. The Church of England is also know as the Anglican Church. Henry closed all monasteries and took away all the land and buildings of the Roman Catholic Church. He kept some for himself and sold others to loyal followers among the nobility and wealthy middle class.

Many riches from Canterbury Cathedral were taken by Henry VIII.

Biography

Elizabeth I (1558–1603)

Elizabeth took the throne after the deaths of her half-brother Edward and half-sister Mary. Edward was only ten when he became king. His advisors attempted to tighten Protestant control of the nation. When Mary became queen, she attempted to return England to Roman Catholicism. Her harsh policies turned many English against her and in favor of Protestantism.

Elizabeth ruled for 45 years. Her primary goal was to make England a rich and powerful nation. She also set about making England a Protestant nation. She cared less about religious doctrine than she did about power. She saw Protestantism as a way to unify the nation and strengthen her power. Anyone who opposed her—Catholic or Protestant—was persecuted.

The religious wars that raged on the European continent did not affect England. Elizabeth was able to keep her subjects from fighting one another over religious differences. By the time she died, England was the most powerful nation in Europe. Her subjects mourned her as "Good Queen Bess."

stop and think

What characteristic did Henry and Elizabeth share? Discuss the question with a partner. When you come to an agreement, write a sentence that states the characteristic. Then make a bulleted list of the facts that support your conclusion.

However, Henry made little change in religious **doctrines**, or teachings. With the exception of the authority of the pope, religious teachings were much the same in the Church of England as they were in the Roman Catholic Church. It was Henry's daughter Elizabeth who changed religious doctrines. Among other changes, priests were allowed to marry. The Church of England adopted the Calvinist doctrine of predestination. English replaced Latin in church services.

The Catholic Reformation

By the 1600s, the number of people who followed the teachings of Protestantism had increased dramatically. The Roman Catholic Church did not ignore what was happening. Many Church leaders recognized the truth in some of the complaints about Church practices. The Church had clearly strayed from the simple spiritual message of Jesus.

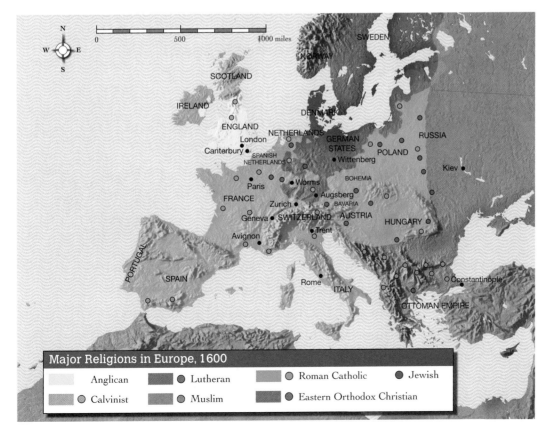

Major Religions in Europe, 1600

Anglican · Lutheran · Roman Catholic · Jewish
Calvinist · Muslim · Eastern Orthodox Christian

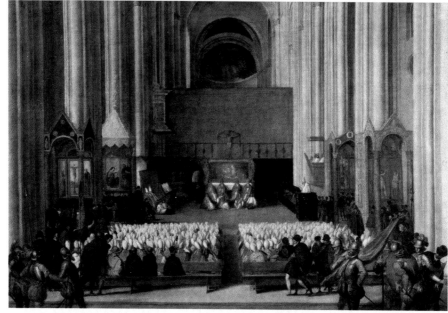

Council of Trent

The Catholic Reformation set about renewing the spirit of the Church and returning it to its mission. In 1545, Pope Paul III called the Council of Trent. This committee of Church leaders met until 1563 and issued a number of **decrees**, or orders, to clarify Church teachings and reform its practices. Four of the decrees were:

- Luther's doctrine of faith without good works was rejected.
- Calvin's doctrine of predestination was rejected.
- The selling of indulgences was forbidden.
- The authority of the pope was reaffirmed.

After the Council of Trent, popes played less of a role in political affairs. At times, earlier popes had competed with monarchs and emperors for wealth and power. Later popes focused on their role as the spiritual leaders of Catholics.

Persecution and Inquisition

In the Middle Ages, the Catholic Church had set up a tribunal called the **Inquisition** to find **heretics**. These are people who believe in religious ideas that are not approved by the Church. The goal of the Inquisition was to bring people back to Catholicism. Anyone who refused to give up his or her wrong beliefs was punished by a fine, a prison sentence, and usually the loss of his or her property. Later, torture was added

Judgment scene during the Spanish Inquisition

to the questioning process. If a person refused to confess, he or she could be tortured. Execution became the final punishment. In the 1540s, the Inquisition was used to find Protestants in Italy.

Perhaps the most brutal use of the Inquisition was in Spain. In the 700s, Muslims had conquered large parts of Spain. They allowed Jews and Catholics to practice their religions in peace. Beginning in the 800s, Spanish nobles fought the Muslims and slowly forced them out of Spain. This was known as the **reconquista**.

By 1492, the armies of Spain's King Ferdinand and Queen Isabella had defeated the last of the Muslim strongholds in Spain. The monarchs were determined to unify their new nation. They ordered all Jews and Muslims to convert to Catholicism or leave. Forcing everyone to practice one religion was one way to unify the nation. The monarchs set up an Inquisition to make sure that everyone obeyed. It investigated Jews and Muslims who had converted to Catholicism but were suspected of practicing their old religions in private.

Putting It All Together

"Religion may be used as a cover for political actions." Find three examples in this lesson that support this statement. List them in your notebook. Share them with a partner and discuss how each political act was done in the name of religion but really disguised a grab for power.

Chapter Summary

- The **Renaissance** began in Italy in the 1300s.
- The Renaissance had three major characteristics: ancient Greek and Roman ideas, which gave rise to **humanism;** the importance of life on Earth rather than on a future life in heaven; and a belief in individual achievement.
- Monks in **monasteries** helped preserve early **scholarship**.
- **Patrons** supported artists who painted everyday objects.
- The invention of the printing press spread Protestant teachings and the use of **vernacular languages**.
- People lived as **nuclear families**.
- The **Protestant Reformation** was a way to protest and reform practices of the Catholic Church, such as selling **indulgences**. Martin Luther's 95 **theses** marked the beginning of the Reformation.
- Luther taught that faith alone is all that is necessary for **salvation**. This **doctrine** is known as "justification by faith alone." Luther was **excommunicated**. His new ideas were called **Lutheranism**.
- John Calvin adopted Luther's teachings and added **predestination**. He set up a **theocracy** in Geneva.
- Henry VIII wanted his marriage **annulled**. The pope refused, so Parliament created the Church of England.
- Council of Trent **decrees** clarified Church teachings.
- The **Inquisition** found **heretics** in the Catholic Church. A **reconquista** gained Spanish lands back from Muslim rulers.

Chapter Review

1 Write two-line headlines for each of the following: (a) invention of the printing press, (b) Protestant Reformation, (c) Council of Trent, (d) Inquisition.

2 The invention of the printing press was as revolutionary in the 1400s as the invention of the computer was in the 1900s. With a partner think of all the ways that the printing press could have changed life in the 1400s. Write a bulleted list of the changes.

Skill Builder

Fact and Opinion

The following sentence is a fact. It states specific information that could be proved to be true or false through additional research.

In the 700s, Muslims had conquered large parts of Spain.

The following sentence is an opinion. It represents the author's personal belief about the Spanish Inquisition. The author provides no evidence to support this statement.

Perhaps the most brutal use of the Inquisition was in Spain.

A fact is a statement

- of specific information
- that can be proved true or false

An opinion

- is what a person thinks or feels
- cannot be proved true or false

Signal words and phrases can help you decide if a statement is a fact or an opinion.

Signals for statements of fact include

- the use of specific people, places, events, and dates

Signals for statements of opinion include

- words such as *none, no one, every, always, never, perhaps, probably, maybe, excellent, greatest, best, worst, bad, good, poor*
- phrases such as *I think, I believe, in my opinion, in my judgment, as far as I am concerned*

Decide whether each of the following is a statement of fact or of opinion. Explain how you decided.

1 Luther nailed his 95 theses to the church door in 1517.

2 The Renaissance had the greatest artists that ever lived.

3 Wealthy Italians supported the artists of the Renaissance.

4 All the wealthiest people in Europe lived in Italy.

5 The 1300s began a period of great change in Europe.

Chapter 15

AGE OF EUROPEAN EXPLORATIONS

(1415–1800)

Getting Focused

Skim this chapter to predict what you will be learning.
• Read the lesson titles and subheadings.
• Look at the illustrations and read the captions.
• Examine the maps.
• Review the vocabulary words and terms.

Every continent in the world except Antarctica is discussed in this chapter. You have been making a world map. By now some part of every continent should be colored in. Make a list of each region that you have added to the map. Next to each region on your list add the name of the earliest human civilization in that region and its dates. With a partner, quiz each other on where the civilizations began and how long ago each one existed.

New European Trade Routes

Thinking on Your Own

Turn each subheading in this lesson into a question. Write them in your notebook. As you study each section of the lesson, write the answers to the questions.

The Renaissance was marked by a spirit of adventure and curiosity. This spirit was the result of a number of influences. In turn, it created an outcome of huge importance: the beginning of the **global age**. During the 1400s, for the first time, Europeans had direct contact with Africans, Asians, and by the end of the century, Americans.

> ### focus your reading
>
> Discuss what prompted Europeans to explore the world.
>
> What successes did the Portuguese have in their voyages of exploration?
>
> What European nations set up trading routes in Asia?
>
> ### vocabulary
>
> global age   astrolabe
>
> compass   cargo

The Time Is Right

A number of developments took place that made the 1400s the right time for the global age to begin. The first development, or influence, was the Crusades. Large numbers of Europeans went to the Holy Land to fight the Muslims. Their travels showed them the marvels of other places. When they returned home, they told stories of what they had seen. The ships that returned from the Holy Land carried luxury goods like spices and silks. These goods were sold in European markets. Marco Polo's journal also told Europeans about life outside Europe.

But it was more than excitement about new lands that moved Europeans. For many, it was riches. Merchants in northern and western Europe wanted to sell goods like silks and spices without having to pay Arab and Italian merchants. Goods from Asia

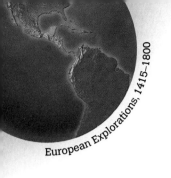

traveled through either Southwest Asia or the Ottoman Empire. In both regions, they were sold to Arab merchants, who moved the goods along the trade routes to Europe. Merchants in the Italian city-states usually bought them. It took a long time for goods to reach merchants in northern and western Europe.

Each time the goods changed hands, the price went up. Each merchant took a share of the profits. If merchants in Portugal, England, or the Netherlands could buy goods direct from merchants in India, China, or Southeast Asia, the prices would be cheaper. The Europeans could then make more money. But to get to Asia, the merchants had to sail around Africa. No one had ever done that before.

Even if Europeans had wanted to explore beyond Europe by sea before the 1400s, they would not have been able to get very far. The technology that would allow them to make long sea voyages had not been invented in Europe. Four innovations made European exploration possible: accurate maps, the **compass**, the **astrolabe**, and a new type of triangular sail called the lateen sail. This new sail design allowed ships to sail into the wind.

The fourth reason that caused Europeans to want to explore new lands was to bring religion to nonbelievers. Specifically, Europeans wanted to bring and expand the influence of Christianity. Spreading Christianity became an important factor in exploration in most regions around the world.

Europeans learned the use of the compass (above) and astrolabe from the Arab traders.

Europeans also learned a new design of triangular sails from Arabs that resulted in the development of the caravel, a small, more easily maneuverable ship that could hold cannon and more cargo. The sails made it possible to sail farther out to sea.

Prince Henry and Portuguese Explorers

Beginning in 1420, the first Europeans to explore along Africa's west coast were the Portuguese. Prince Henry, the son of Portugal's king, encouraged Portuguese sea captains to make these voyages. He wanted Portugal to become rich from the spice trade. Prince Henry, known as Henry the Navigator, even set up a school that taught skills related to sailing.

The first trips were short voyages along the west coast of Africa. The captains were trying to determine the size of the African continent. Wherever they stopped, the captains

Time Box

1488
Dias rounds tip of South Africa

1487
da Gama sails to India

1492
Columbus sails to the Americas

1564
first permanent Spanish settlement in North America at St. Augustine

1607
first permanent English settlement in North American at Jamestown

1608
first permanent French settlement in North America at Quebec

established trading posts. This was the beginning of Portugal's trading empire in Africa. One of the goods they traded for was gold. They tapped into the existing gold network in West Africa. The Portuguese also began to take enslaved Africans back to Portugal to use as servants.

Portuguese sea captains continued their explorations long after Prince Henry's death. In 1488, Bartholomeu Dias finally rounded the southern tip of Africa. The Portuguese named the area the Cape of Good Hope. The wealth of the spice trade was almost in their hands.

Vasco da Gama in Calicut, India

In 1497, Vasco da Gama set out to become the first Portuguese explorer to actually make the trip to India. He sailed south around the Cape of Good Hope and then across the Indian Ocean to southern India. He filled his ship with spices and set sail for Portugal. The round-trip took two years. His **cargo** of spices sold for 60 times the cost of his trip.

stop and think

Why did European nations send out voyages of exploration in the 1400s? Check your ideas with a partner. Then write a paragraph to explain your reasoning.

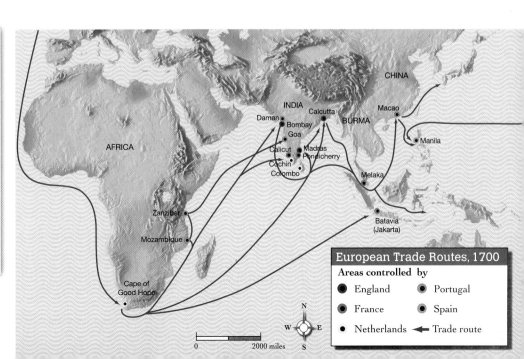

European Trade Routes, 1700

Trading in India, Southeast Asia, and China

Europeans were able to reach India to purchase spices, but India was not the source of the spices. Muslim merchants in India bought them from other merchants farther to the east. Many of the spices came from the Melaka islands in the East Indies. Europeans called these islands the "Spice Islands."

Afonso de Albuquerque, governor and commander of the Portuguese empire in Asia, gained control of Melaka, on the Malay Peninsula, in 1511.

The Portuguese set out to gain control of the spice trade. First, they destroyed Muslim and Indian shipping along the coast of India. Then the Portuguese moved farther east and seized the Strait of Melaka in what is today Malaysia. By controlling this waterway, they could keep other Europeans out of the area. Finally, the Portuguese forced the ruler of the Spice Islands to sell them all its spices. In their dealings with the people of Asia, the Portuguese set the model for how Europeans dealt with non-Europeans. They used guns and cannon to get what they wanted.

In the meantime, the Portuguese tried to expand their trade with China. However, in 1535 China limited European traders to two ports. The Portuguese and other Europeans also failed in Japan. The Japanese, like the Chinese, thought the Europeans were uncivilized. Their trade goods had little appeal to either the Chinese or Japanese people. The rulers of China and Japan feared that the Europeans would use their weapons to seize land. Also, the missionaries who came with the traders raised suspicion among the rulers.

In time, more powerful European nations seized Portugal's trading empire in Asia. In 1595, the Netherlands began a campaign to capture Portuguese trading posts in the East Indies. The Dutch were able to end Portuguese control and also to keep France and England out of the East Indies.

Putting It All Together

Choose two events described in this lesson and write a paragraph about each event. Exchange your paragraphs with a partner. Review each other's paragraphs to see if you can make them more interesting by adding action words.

LESSON 2

Sailing West to Go East

Thinking on Your Own

Write the name *Christopher Columbus* in your notebook. List at least five facts that you know about him. Discuss these with a partner. As you read this lesson, add five new facts to your list.

While the Portuguese were exploring the African coast, the Spanish were busy fighting Muslims. The armies of King Ferdinand and Queen Isabella drove the last Muslim invaders out of Spain in 1492. When Christopher Columbus came to them asking for help, the time was right. The Spanish were ready to think about an **overseas** empire.

focus your reading

Explain why Columbus wanted to sail west to find Asia.

How did the Spanish conquer the Aztec Empire?

Summarize how the Spanish conquered the Inca Empire.

vocabulary

overseas

Line of Demarcation

conquistadores

Columbus and the Spanish Monarchs

Columbus' plan was to sail west to go east. He believed that he could reach Asia and the East Indies by sailing west. For many centuries, common people believed the earth was flat. If a ship sailed too far, it would fall off the edge. By the 1400s, educated people knew that this was not true. However, they could only estimate the true size of the earth. They did not know how far west the East Indies were located.

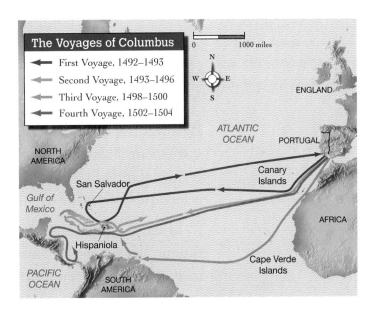

The Voyages of Columbus

0   1000 miles

← First Voyage, 1492–1493
← Second Voyage, 1493–1496
← Third Voyage, 1498–1500
← Fourth Voyage, 1502–1504

ENGLAND
ATLANTIC OCEAN
PORTUGAL
NORTH AMERICA
Canary Islands
San Salvador
Gulf of Mexico
AFRICA
Hispaniola
Cape Verde Islands
PACIFIC OCEAN
SOUTH AMERICA

For years, Columbus tried to persuade the rulers of Portugal and then Spain to finance his plan. When he tried again in 1492, Queen Isabella agreed. He persuaded her by telling her of the riches that would come to Spain. Perhaps more important to her, however, were the non-Europeans that could be converted to Catholicism.

Columbus and 90 sailors set sail in three caravels on August 3, 1492. They found land slightly more than two months later, on October 12. However, the land they found was not Asia; it was the islands of Hispaniola and Cuba. Columbus returned three more times to the Caribbean looking for the Asian mainland. Because he thought he had reached the East Indies, he called the people he met *Indios*, or Indians.

Ferdinand and Isabella of Spain funded the voyages of Columbus in 1492.

It did not take long for Spain and other nations to realize Columbus' mistake. He had not found Asia. He had found two unknown continents that Europeans called the *New World*. The Spanish and the Portuguese, who had discovered what is now Brazil, decided that the wealth and people of these continents belonged to them. To prevent disputes between the two nations, Pope Alexander VI divided the New World in 1494. The Treaty of Tordesillas established the **Line of Demarcation** at 38° west longitude. It separated Spanish lands from Portuguese lands. Everything west of the line belonged to Spain; everything east of the line belonged to Portugal.

stop and think

The phrase "for God, glory, and gold" is sometimes used to describe why Europeans set out to find new lands. What information in this lesson supports the reasons given in this phrase? Check your ideas with a partner. Then write a three-paragraph essay to explain the phrase.

Overthrowing the Aztec Empire

By 1515, the Spanish controlled most of the islands in the Caribbean. From their base in Cuba, they set out to explore the mainland of Central America. One of the first conquerors, or **conquistadores**, was Hernán Cortés.

In 1519, Cortés, 500 soldiers, some horses, and a few cannon landed on the Yucatán Peninsula. They began a march inland. Early on their journey, they met Malinche, an Aztec

This illustration, from an Aztec codex, shows native leaders meeting to discuss the arrival of Cortés.

who had been captured by Mayans. Cortés took Malinche along as interpreter.

While Cortés continued his march to the city of Tenochtitlán, the Aztec ruler, Montezuma, waited. He had learned that the Spanish were on their way, and he was fearful. According to an ancient prophecy, a white god, Quetzalcoatl, had once lived among the Aztec. He had returned home, but would one day come back. When he did, the Aztec Empire would end.

Montezuma decided to welcome the Spanish. He showered them with food and riches. He gave them a palace where they could live. In a short time, however, Cortés tricked Montezuma into becoming his prisoner. Cortés and the Spanish were then in control of the city. In 1520, the Aztec rebelled against the Spanish. Montezuma died in the fighting. The Spanish fled Tenochtitlán.

A Spanish Attack

Most records of the Aztecs and Incas were destroyed by the Spanish. A few survived. The following excerpt is from an Aztec description of a battle to capture Tenochtitlán.

"On one occasion, four Spanish cavalrymen entered the market place. They rode through it in a great circle, stabbing and killing many of our warriors and trampling everything under their horses' hooves. This was the first time the Spaniards had entered the market place, and our warriors were taken by surprise. . . .

"It was at this time that the Spaniards set fire to the temple and burned it to the ground. The flames and smoke leaped high into the air with a terrible roar. The people wept when they saw their temple on fire. . . .

"The battle lasted for many hours and extended to almost every corner of the market place."

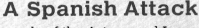

reading for understanding

Why were the Aztecs taken by surprise?

Why do you think the Spanish burned the temple?

Discuss why fighting on horseback was an advantage to the Spanish.

The following year Cortés returned with more soldiers. Reinforcements had been sent from Cuba. The new Spanish force, fully equipped with horses and guns, defeated the Aztec. They destroyed Tenochtitlán and built Mexico City in its place. The Aztecs' temple was replaced by a Catholic Church.

Overthrowing the Inca Empire

During the 1520s, the Spanish moved throughout Central America. They took land and began building settlements. Native Americans were considered subjects of Spain but had no rights. As the Spanish moved farther south, they heard stories of a rich kingdom somewhere in the Andes Mountains. This was the Empire of the Inca.

Atahualpa

Francisco Pizarro, another conquistador, set out to find the Inca. In 1531, he reached the Incan capital of Cuzco. He had only 180 soldiers with him, but they were enough. The Empire was torn by civil war. Rival forces of Atahualpa and Huascar, half-brothers, were fighting for power over the Empire.

Atahualpa asked Pizarro for help in defeating Huascar. Instead, Pizarro made Atahualpa his prisoner. To save himself, Atahualpa arranged for enough gold and silver to fill two rooms to be given to Pizarro. Atahualpa also had to arrange for the murder of Huascar. Rather than set Atahualpa free, Pizarro seized the ransom. He then had Atahualpa tried, convicted, and executed for Huascar's death.

The Inca were leaderless. Without a ruler, the Empire began to fall apart. Pizarro seized much of the territory and its vast wealth of gold and silver for Spain.

Putting It All Together

What did the Spanish overthrow of the Aztec and Inca Empires have in common? Create a Venn diagram to decide whether the Spanish tactics were the same or different against the two empires. Work with a partner to complete the diagram. Then write a paragraph that explains the tactics of the Spanish.

Colonizing Central and South America

Thinking on Your Own

What do you know about the Spanish in the Americas? Create a T-chart. Label one side "Spanish Government." Label the other side "Spanish Society." List at least three facts on each side of your chart. As you read the lesson, add to your chart.

The Spanish quickly expanded their territory in the Americas. By the mid-1500s, they claimed Mexico and much of Central and South America. They were also moving north into what would become the United States. How would the Spanish control this vast new territory? How would they govern it?

focus your reading

How did Spain govern its colonies in the Americas?

Explain how the encomienda affected Native Americans and Africans.

How was Spanish society organized in the colonies?

vocabulary

viceroyalties	creoles
encomienda	mestizos
immunity	mulattos
peninsulares	

Governing Spanish America

The Spanish decided to set up colonies. The Spanish monarchs encouraged their citizens to sail to the Americas and build settlements. The more wealth the colonies created, the wealthier the monarchs became. Part of every shipment of gold, silver, and other goods from the colonies went to the monarchs.

To govern Spanish America, Spain set up **viceroyalties**. Each viceroyalty was an area governed by a viceroy—or a governor who represented the monarch. By 1535, there were two viceroyalties: the Viceroyalty of New Spain and the Viceroyalty of Peru. In the 1700s, the latter was split into three units.

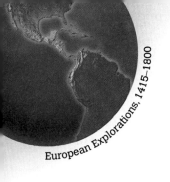

Converting Native Americans to Christianity, however, remained an important goal. Missionaries came with the colonists to Christianize Native Americans. They burned native books and tore down native temples and statues. Their mission was to turn Native Americans into Spaniards. Native Americans were to give up their native dress, customs, language, and religion.

Slaves working on a sugar plantation on the island of Hispaniola

Enslaving Native Americans and Africans

When colonists began settling the islands in the Caribbean, Queen Isabella granted them **encomienda**. This was the right to demand labor from Native Americans living on the land. The queen had intended to protect Native Americans. However, the colonists used the encomienda to enslave them. When the Spanish discovered gold and silver in Peru and Mexico, the Spanish forced Native Americans to work in their mines.

The Spanish worked hundreds of thousands of Native Americans to death. Hundreds of thousands more starved to death. European diseases caused even more deaths. Native Americans had no **immunity** to diseases such as smallpox and measles. The island of Hispaniola is an example. Experts believe that 250,000 Native Americans lived on the island when Christopher Columbus landed there in 1492. By 1538, only 500 Native Americans remained. Experts estimate that between 1519 and 1630, some 24 million Native Americans died in Central Mexico alone.

In an effort to save Native Americans, Bartolomé de Las Casas, a priest, urged using Africans as workers. As early as 1518, a few Africans had been shipped to the Caribbean. The Spanish replaced Native American

stop and think

"Two wrongs don't make a right" is an old saying. Write an essay of two or three paragraphs to support the idea of the saying. Use the enslaving of Africans to save Native Americans as your example. Ask a partner to read your essay and suggest ways to make it stronger and clearer.

laborers on sugar plantations. After 1542, the Spanish were forbidden to enslave Native Americans. As a result, the trans-Atlantic trade in enslaved Africans became big business for the Spanish—and later for the English. It is estimated that at least 10 million Africans came to the Americas in chains. Perhaps twice that many died on the journey.

Society in Spanish America

The most important posts in colonial government were held by **peninsulares**. These were native-born Spanish who were sent from Spain, which was a peninsula, to run the colonies. They consisted of a very small number of people, but they made up the highest social class.

The next social class were **creoles**. Their ancestors had been the original Spanish colonists. Creoles usually owned plantations, mines, and trading businesses. They had little power in the colonies.

Mestizos were descended from Spanish and Native Americans. **Mulattos** had ancestors who were Spanish and African. The two groups made up the lowest social classes. Native Americans and enslaved Africans were below the social system.

The big cities of Spanish America such as Mexico City and Lima, Peru, were designed like European cities. They had wide avenues and huge churches and government buildings. The homes of the wealthy were decorated with beautiful furniture and paintings. Universities were built to educate young men of the upper classes. Wealthy young women were educated at home or by Catholic nuns at local convents. Spanish influence could be seen in all aspects of daily life.

Gold was used to praise God in La Compania Church in Quito, Ecuador.

The adobe mission in Picuria Pueblo, New Mexico, shows the blending of Spanish and Native American cultures.

Putting It All Together

Create a diagram to illustrate the social system in Spanish America. Work with a partner to decide on the shape of the diagram. Include the details about government and society from the T-chart you created.

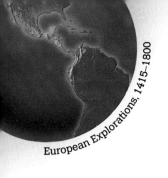

LESSON 4

Colonizing North America

Thinking on Your Own

Create a concept web to help you remember information about the colonization of North America. Label the large circle "Colonizing North America." Add a circle for each European nation that built colonies in North America. Add smaller circles for the most important information about the colonies.

By the 1500s, European nations were competing for land and power in Europe. As their explorers found "new" lands, European monarchs often transferred their rivalry to these parts of the globe. For example, Queen Elizabeth I made Francis Drake a knight for sailing around the world. He and the crew of his ship *Golden Hind* chased down Spanish treasure ships on their way back to Spain from the Americas. The English seized the Spanish cargoes of gold and silver. To the English, Drake was a hero. To the Spanish, he was a pirate.

focus your reading

Describe the Spanish settlements in what is today the United States.

How did people make their living in New France?

How did Sweden and the Netherlands lose their colonies in North America?

Explain why people came to the English colonies.

vocabulary

mission

joint-stock company

proprietary colonies

royal colonies

This rivalry among European nations was behind the desire to claim territory and set up colonies in the Americas. It was not only the Spanish and Portuguese who wanted to build empires. The French, English, Dutch, and Swedes also claimed land in North America.

Map of St. Augustine from 1588

New Spain

By 1513, Spanish explorers were moving into what is today the United States. In that year, Juan Ponce de Leon explored Florida. The first permanent Spanish settlement was built in Florida in 1564. St. Augustine was settled to keep the French out of the area. In 1598, Spanish colonists moved into what is today the Southwest United States. In 1682, the Spanish built two **missions** and forts in Texas. By the mid-1700s, the Spanish also had settlements in modern day California, Arizona, and New Mexico.

Spanish priests, soldiers, and farmers played an important part in settling the Southwest. Many settlements were forts or missions. The missions housed a priest and Native Americans who had been converted to Catholicism. Spanish farmers in New Mexico settled next to Pueblo villages. At first, they fought for control. In time, they became good neighbors. Both had to protect their homes from raids by unfriendly Native American warriors from the Great Plains.

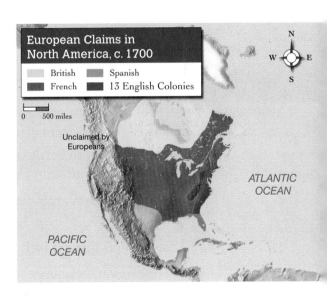

European Claims in North America, c. 1700

British
French
Spanish
13 English Colonies

0   500 miles

Unclaimed by Europeans

ATLANTIC OCEAN

PACIFIC OCEAN

Trappers, Traders, and New France

Quebec during the 17th century was a small, but growing, frontier town.

The French attempted to build forts and claim territory all along the Atlantic coast. However, the Spanish drove them out.

In 1608, Samuel de Champlain founded Quebec in what is today Canada. By the late 1600s, the French had a line of trading settlements in New France from Canada all the way to the Gulf of Mexico. Most of the settlers were fur trappers and traders. They hunted animals like beaver for their fur or

Age of European Explorations   229

traded with Native Americans for animal skins. The furs and skins were shipped to France where they sold for high prices.

New Netherlands and New Sweden

The Netherlands was a rich and powerful nation in Europe. They financed the exploration of North America. As a result, the Netherlands claimed a large part of what is today New York, Connecticut, New Jersey, and Delaware.

New Amsterdam during the 1600s

The Dutch founded trading posts along the Hudson River. They tried to take the Native American fur trade away from New France. The Dutch did not have a powerful army in the colony. In 1664, the English sailed several ships into the New Amsterdam harbor, what is now New York Harbor. They demanded that the Dutch surrender. With no way to defend itself, the colony gave up.

Sweden had also grown wealthy from trade. It sent colonists to settle along the Delaware River in what is today southern New Jersey. The Dutch seized the settlements in 1655. They, too, became English territory in 1664.

English Colonies

England's first permanent colony in North America was Jamestown, settled in 1607. A group of merchants set up a **joint-stock company** to pay for the voyage and the settlement. In return, they expected to make a fortune on the gold the colonists would find. However, there was no gold and many of the early colonists starved to death.

In 1620, a religious group known as Pilgrims settled Plymouth Colony. They fled religious persecution in England. Ten years later, another group of English Protestants, the Puritans, settled nearby. They came voluntarily to set up a community based on their Puritan religious views. They founded the Massachusetts Bay Colony, which was a church-state. Like the Pilgrims and Puritans, Quakers, Catholics, and Jews came to the colonies for religious freedom.

stop and think

The Spanish, French, Dutch, and English settlers in North America were not alike in how they treated the Native Americans. How and why were they different? With a partner, look for information to answer this question. Write a one-paragraph answer.

People came to the English colonies to make a better life for themselves. They looked for economic opportunities as farmers, fishers, and crafts people. Many people in the New England and Middle Colonies were the owners of small farms. However, a plantation system developed in the Southern Colonies. The climate and soil were well suited to growing crops like rice and indigo. Eventually, tobacco became a major crop. To work their plantations, owners began to import enslaved Africans. As a result, the colonies became part of the trans-Atlantic slave trade.

As more colonists immigrated, they wanted more land. The only way to get land was to push the Native Americans off. This resulted in a number of wars between colonists and Native Americans. By the 1700s, most Native Americans had been killed or forced west.

While taking away the freedom of Africans and killing Native Americans, the colonists were working to keep and enlarge their own rights. About half the colonies were **proprietary colonies**. They were owned by individuals or private companies. The other colonies were **royal colonies**. They belonged to the English monarch.

Putting It All Together

Play "Ten Questions" with a partner. Write ten questions and answers about the information in this lesson. Then take turns asking and answering the questions.

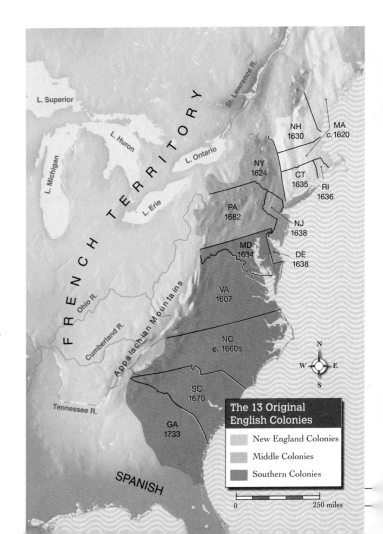

The 13 Original English Colonies

New England Colonies
Middle Colonies
Southern Colonies

LESSON 5

The Effects of the First Global Age

Thinking on Your Own

Look at the vocabulary words. Write them in your notebook. Write a definition for the words that you think you know. Then check the meaning as you read and rewrite your definitions.

The first global age began with Christopher Columbus' voyage in 1492. By the late 1700s, the interactions of Europeans with Asians, Africans, and Americans greatly changed the world. Four of the most important changes occurred between 1492 and 1800. These four changes affected all parts of the world.

Columbian Exchange

The **Columbian Exchange** is named for Christopher Columbus who began all the changes. It refers to the sharing of goods and ideas that

focus your reading

What was the Columbian Exchange?

Explain how mercantilism affected European colonies.

What effects did European colonization have on Native Americans?

Summarize how the trans-Atlantic slave trade affected both African nations and individual Africans.

vocabulary

Columbian Exchange

mercantilism

favorable balance of trade

exports

imports

ethnocentric

began with Columbus' first voyage. The diagram on this page shows just some of the foods and animals that Europeans carried from region to region as they moved around the world. They also introduced their own ideas about religion, government, the arts, and language. The Spanish, for example, forced Native

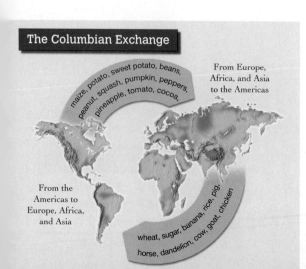

The Columbian Exchange

From the Americas to Europe, Africa, and Asia

maize, potato, sweet potato, beans, peanut, squash, pumpkin, peppers, pineapple, tomato, cocoa,

From Europe, Africa, and Asia to the Americas

wheat, sugar, banana, rice, pig, horse, dandelion, cow, goat, chicken

Americans to convert to Catholicism and learn Spanish. Native Americans had to give up their own religions and languages.

The exchange was not all one-sided, however. Europeans taught Native Americans how to make iron and copper. Native Americans taught Europeans how to farm unfamiliar land in unfamiliar climates. They also introduced Europeans to corn and tobacco. The early colonists would have starved without corn. It became the major part of their diets. Tobacco became the chief crop in Virginia Colony. Its farmers grew wealthy growing and selling tobacco to European markets.

Mercantilism

European governments encouraged global trade for their own reasons. Across Europe, governments adopted the policy of **mercantilism**. According to mercantilism, the wealth of a nation depends on how much gold and silver it has. One way to keep gold and silver in a country is to keep a **favorable balance of trade**. This occurs when the value of the goods that a nation **exports**, or sells to other nations, is greater than the value of the goods that it **imports**, or buys from other nations.

Dutch fur traders along the Hudson River

Colonies played an important role in mercantilism. Colonies provided their home countries with raw materials to be used for manufacturing. In return, colonies were markets for finished goods from their home countries. Home countries passed laws to keep their colonists from buying goods from other nations.

stop and think

With a partner, read the diagram about the Columbian Exchange. Choose two items from the diagram. Discuss how life in the United States would be different if these two items were not exchanged. Make notes as you discuss your ideas. Then write two paragraphs, one for each item, to explain how life would be different without it.

Native American Defeats

Interactions between Native Americans and Europeans resulted in the deaths of millions of Native Americans. Some experts estimate that 70 million Native Americans lived in the Americas when Christopher Columbus landed on Hispaniola in 1492. About 5 million lived in what is today the United States. Less than 400 years later, there were only 340,000 Native Americans in the United States.

King Philip's War was fought between the Wampanoag and New England colonists in the 1670s.

European colonists throughout the Americas murdered, worked to death, and starved to death Native Americans. What European guns did not do, their diseases did. Europeans wanted Native-American labor, wealth, and lands. After the end of the encomienda, Spanish colonists could no longer enslave Native Americans. In various parts of Spanish America, Native Americans were forced to live at missions.

English colonists had less concern for Christianizing Native Americans. They wanted Native American land and fought deadly wars to gain it. After the American Revolution, the new United States continued the policy of taking Native American land—usually at gunpoint.

The African Slave Trade

Many Europeans did not think that there was anything wrong in enslaving Africans. Slaves had been used by the ancient Egyptians, Greeks, Romans, and Gauls. Europeans thought of themselves as far superior to everyone else in the world. Africans' languages and customs were very different from European ways. Therefore, Africans must be greatly inferior to Europeans. This **ethnocentric** view developed because of the slave trade. It also made the slave trade possible. Otherwise, it would not be possible to enslave another person.

In addition to this attitude toward Africans, the slave trade had many other effects. First, slave raiders kidnapped the

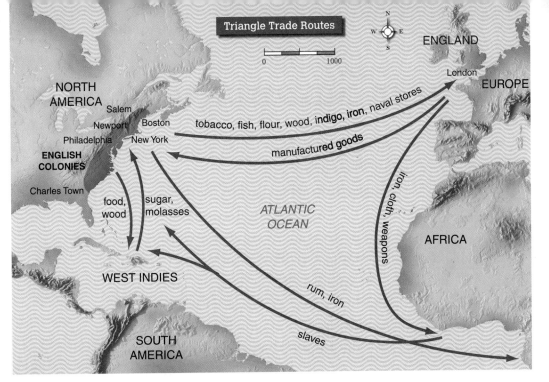

Triangle Trade Routes

NORTH AMERICA

Salem
Newport · Boston
Philadelphia · New York
ENGLISH COLONIES

Charles Town

London
ENGLAND
EUROPE

tobacco, fish, flour, wood, indigo, iron, naval stores

manufactured goods

iron, cloth, weapons

ATLANTIC OCEAN

AFRICA

food, wood

sugar, molasses

WEST INDIES

rum, iron

slaves

SOUTH AMERICA

European Explorations, 1415–1800

youngest and healthiest Africans. This meant that large areas of West Africa were left without young people to have families.

Second, the empires of West Africa became less important. New kingdoms, closer to the coast, rose in importance. These kingdoms were based on trading people in exchange for guns.

Third, the more wealth a ruler had, the more he wanted. A cycle of warfare to gain captives to sell to slavers developed among many African kingdoms. People lived in a state of constant warfare and fear.

A tunnel led slaves to ships at the House of Slaves on Goree Island off the coast of Dakar.

Putting It All Together

Imagine you have to teach about European actions either toward Native Americans or toward Africans. Choose one of the two. Make notes to help you explain what happened and why. Review Lessons 2, 3, and 4 if necessary. Present your ideas to a partner as though you were teaching. Ask if your presentation was clear and how you might make it clearer.

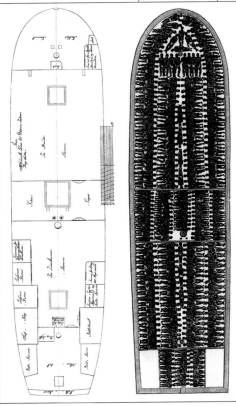

A diagram of the cargo hold in a slave ship.

Chapter Summary

- The first **global age** began with Christopher Columbus' voyage of exploration in 1492.
- Four factors caused Europeans to begin **overseas** exploration in the 1400s: the Crusades; the desire for riches from trade with Asia; inventions including better maps, the **compass**, the **astrolabe**, and a new type of sail; and the desire to expand Christianity.
- China and Japan limited **cargo** trade with Europeans.
- The Portuguese and Spanish divided the New World between them by the **Line of Demarcation**.
- **Conquistadores** set out to explore and conquer the Americas for Spain.
- Spain divided its territory into **viceroyalties** to govern.
- The **encomienda** gave Spanish landholders the right to the labor of Native Americans. Millions died from a lack of **immunity** to European diseases.
- Society in the Spanish colonies was made up of **peninsulares**, **creoles**, **mestizos**, and **mulattos**.
- The Spanish forced Native Americans to live at **missions** and convert to Spanish ways.
- **Joint-stock companies** paid the expenses to set up some **proprietary colonies**. Other colonies were **royal colonies**.
- The effects of the first global age included the **Columbian Exchange** and **mercantilism**. Mercantilism required a **favorable balance of trade** between **exports** and **imports**.
- The slave trade supported **ethnocentrism**.

Chapter Review

1 Imagine you are a Native American. Write two-line headlines for the following events: (a) Columbus lands in the Caribbean, (b) Cortés lands in Mexico, (c) Pizarro marches toward Cuzco.

2 Now write headlines for these events as though you were writing for a Spanish newspaper.

Skill Builder

Analyzing a Line Graph

A line graph shows information about a topic over a period of time. Usually, the quantity, or amount, is listed along the left side, or vertical axis, of the graph. Time is shown along the bottom, or horizontal axis. A line on the graph shows the ups and downs of the amounts. Sometimes, a graph will have several lines. Each line stands for a separate item.

By reading a line graph, you can see a trend, or pattern, over time. Understanding a trend can help you decide if something is important. For example, a line graph shows increasing shipments of tobacco from Virginia to England between 1650 and 1700. You can decide that tobacco was becoming more and more important to the economy of Virginia.

To read a line graph:

- Read the title of the graph to see what it is about.
- Examine the vertical axis to determine the quantity.
- Examine the horizontal axis to determine the time period.
- Read the key for the graph.
- Examine the lines on the graph.

1 What is the title of the graph?

2 What do the lines represent?

3 When do imports become greater than exports?

4 What trends do the two lines show?

5 What conclusions can be drawn based on the information on the graph?

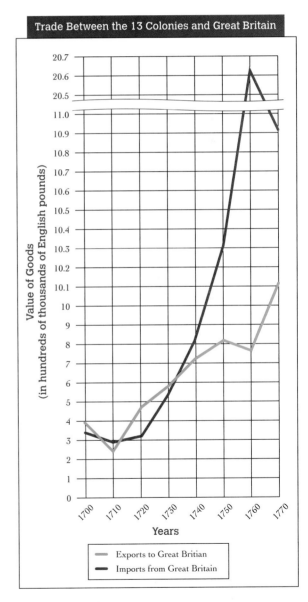

Trade Between the 13 Colonies and Great Britain

Value of Goods (in hundreds of thousands of English pounds)

Years

— Exports to Great Britian
— Imports from Great Britain

5
UNIT

MONARCHIES AND REVOLUTIONS

The 1600s to the mid-1800s were a time of revolution. Some of the revolutions involved political change. For example, the French overthrew their king and set up a republic. The English replaced one king with another. At the same time, the English greatly limited the power of the monarchy. Across Spanish America, descendants of Spanish settlers fought Spanish armies in order to gain their independence.

The Agricultural and the Industrial revolutions were peaceful. However, their effects were dramatic and far-reaching. The two revolutions began in Europe and spread around the globe. The way people earned their living, and where and how they lived, would never be the same.

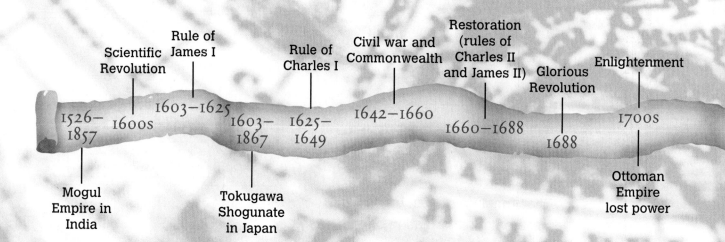

Mogul Empire in India
1526–1857

Scientific Revolution
1600s

Rule of James I
1603–1625

Tokugawa Shogunate in Japan
1603–1867

Rule of Charles I
1625–1649

Civil war and Commonwealth
1642–1660

Restoration (rules of Charles II and James II)
1660–1688

Glorious Revolution
1688

Enlightenment
1700s

Ottoman Empire lost power

Why did the French overthrow the monarchy?

What changes did the Industrial Revolution bring about?

How did the English safeguard their rights?

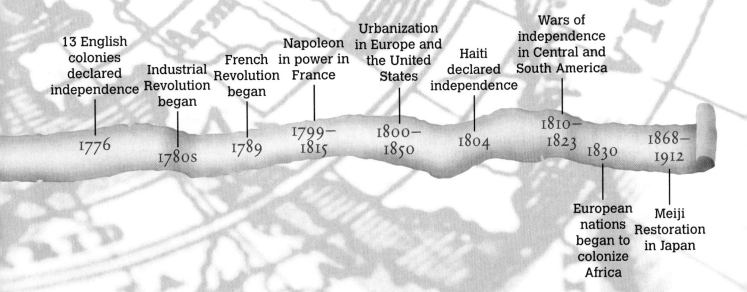

13 English colonies declared independence
1776

Industrial Revolution began
1780s

French Revolution began
1789

Napoleon in power in France
1799– 1815

Urbanization in Europe and the United States
1800– 1850

Haiti declared independence
1804

Wars of independence in Central and South America
1810– 1823

European nations began to colonize Africa
1830

Meiji Restoration in Japan
1868– 1912

Chapter 16

POLITICAL REVOLUTIONS

(1600–1815)

Getting Focused

Skim this chapter to predict what you will be learning.
• Read the lesson titles and subheadings.
• Look at the illustrations and read the captions.
• Examine the maps.
• Review the vocabulary words and terms.

The following actions are described in this chapter:
1) Oliver Cromwell's supporters tried King Charles I, convicted him of being a traitor, and had him beheaded.
2) Colonists in Boston rebelled against unfair taxes.
3) Radical Jacobins in Paris arrested and executed thousands of their opponents. Could you defend any of these actions if you believed they advanced freedom and liberty? Discuss this question with a partner. Then write a short paragraph that explains your position.

The Importance of the English Parliament

Thinking on Your Own

This lesson is about how the English gained additional rights. As you read about each event, create a time box. Include important dates and events.

The English people gained certain rights under the Magna Carta. Over the centuries, English monarchs did not give up or take away any more rights.

Monarchs versus Parliament

James I succeeded Elizabeth I on the throne of England. Many monarchs in Europe at that time, such as in France, believed that they ruled by **divine right**. Their right to rule came directly from God. The English monarchs had not adopted this idea until James I. He and his successor, Charles I, believed that the king's power to rule came from God and, therefore, was absolute. No one could question his decisions.

Parliament was used to exercising its rights in the name of the English people. The king and Parliament soon clashed. James I lived a life of luxury. He needed more money than existing taxes provided. Parliament refused to pass new taxes. When James wanted to go to war, he also needed new taxes. He called Parliament into session and asked for more money. In order to get it, James I had to agree that the monarch

> **focus your reading**
>
> Why did James I and Charles I quarrel with Parliament?
>
> Discuss the causes of the English civil war.
>
> Why is the Glorious Revolution considered so important in English history?
>
> **vocabulary**
>
> divine right
>
> traitor
>
> commonwealth
>
> military dictatorship
>
> constitutional monarchy
>
> Restoration
>
> Glorious Revolution

could not make laws without the approval of Parliament.

In 1625, Charles I succeeded his father. By 1628, Charles I was badly in need of money and called Parliament into session. Before it would agree to new taxes, Parliament forced him to agree to the Petition of Right. This document added to the basic rights of the English people. Parliament alone had the right to impose taxes. Charles I got the money and promptly dismissed Parliament.

Parliament in the 1600s

The English Civil War

The troubles of James I, and especially of Charles I, were not just economic. The two kings also made enemies of the Puritans. They believed that the Church of England was still too much like the Roman Catholic Church.

Since Henry VIII, many large landowners and wealthy merchants had become Puritans. They were elected to the House of Commons and opposed James I and Charles I. Although Protestant, the two kings strongly supported the Church of England as it was. Both kings persecuted the Puritans.

In 1640, Charles called Parliament into session. He needed money for a war against Scotland. The Puritans were now in control of Parliament. Before giving Charles I the money, Parliament passed a law that the monarch could not dismiss Parliament unless it agreed. Charles I agreed. Once he got the money, he marched into Parliament with a unit of soldiers to arrest the Puritan leaders, but they escaped. The fight between Charles I and the Puritans exploded into civil warfare in 1642.

Oliver Cromwell

The leader of the Puritans was Oliver Cromwell. He pulled together an army of supporters known as Roundheads. Charles' supporters were known as Cavaliers. In 1646, Cromwell's forces defeated Charles' Cavaliers. Charles I surrendered and was tried, convicted, and beheaded as a **traitor** in 1649.

Cromwell seized control of the government. The House of Commons was allowed to remain. The House of Lords was abolished. The new Parliament ended the monarchy and declared England a republic, or **commonwealth**. A Council of State governed in place of the monarch. The members of the Council were chosen from the House of Commons. By 1653, Cromwell could not control his new Parliament. He dismissed it and the Council. In their place, he set up a **military dictatorship**. He ruled alone with support from the army.

Cromwell tried to turn England into a strict Puritan nation. However, most English people were satisfied with the Church of England. Most English people also did not want a republic. They wanted a **constitutional monarchy**. Under this system of government, the power of the monarch is limited by law.

Men in the 1600s wore long hair. The Roundheads cut off their hair to distinguish them from Charles' supporters.

stop and think

Write a summary of one section in this lesson. Share your summary with a partner. Ask your partner to make sure that you included all the most important ideas.

The Glorious Revolution

The Commonwealth quickly fell apart after Cromwell's death in 1658. By 1660, Parliament had asked Charles' son to return as King Charles II. The period between 1660 and 1688 is known as the **Restoration** because the monarchy was brought back.

The Church of England was also restored as the nation's official religion. At the same time, Parliament passed laws limiting the rights of Catholics and Puritans. Charles II was a Protestant—at least in name. Charles also cancelled the laws against Catholics and Puritans.

When Charles died, his brother James II became king. He was a Catholic. In 1687, he granted freedom of worship to Catholics and Puritans. Some members of Parliament thought that James II meant to return England to Catholicism and also limit Parliament's power. These wealthy nobles, landowners, and merchants plotted against James.

Charles' supporters were Cavaliers.

Charles II returned to London from exile in 1660.

William and Mary accepted Parliament's request for the English Bill of Rights.

They negotiated with Mary, James' oldest daughter, and her husband, William, the Duke of Orange, to become king and queen. In 1688, William led 14,000 soldiers in an invasion of England. James II fled to France.

Before William and Mary could be crowned, however, Parliament forced them to sign the English Bill of Rights. The monarch now ruled by the power of Parliament, not God. This event became known as the **Glorious Revolution**.

English Bill of Rights

Parliament:
- alone had the right to make laws
- alone had the right to impose taxes
- had to agree to the suspension of any laws—the monarch could not act alone
- had to agree to maintain an army during peacetime
- was to meet yearly
- was guaranteed free elections

Citizens' rights that were confirmed included:
- the forbidding of large bail and fines
- the forbidding of cruel and unusual punishment
- the right to a jury trial

Putting It All Together

Create a sequence flowchart to help you remember when events happened in this lesson. Add a date to each event to turn it into a timeline. Share your flowchart/timeline with a partner. Take turns quizzing each other about time periods between events.

Scientific Revolution and Enlightenment

Thinking on Your Own

Progress was an important concept to people during the Enlightenment. They believed that the Scientific Revolution and Enlightenment thinking would bring progress to humankind. Write a list of five events from your lifetime or earlier in history that you think show progress. After you have written your list, write a sentence to explain why each event shows progress. As you read, add to your list of events and sentences.

In the 1600s, people began to question old ideas about the world around them. They used reason, or rational thinking, to look for new answers. This questioning spirit led to the Scientific Revolution and the Age of Reason, or the **Enlightenment**.

focus your reading

Summarize the controversy over the work of Copernicus, Kepler, and Galileo.

Why were the philosophes important?

Explain how Adam Smith affected economic thinking.

vocabulary

Enlightenment

scientific method

natural law

Scientific Revolution

natural rights

social contract

laissez-faire economics

philosophes

The Scientific Revolution

The modern study of science began in Europe in the 1600s. The systematic process for gathering and analyzing evidence is called the **scientific method**. Francis Bacon developed the idea.

Bacon called for scientists to develop theories, or hypotheses, and then test them in carefully designed experiments. The scientists would observe what happened during the experiments.

Isaac Newton's telescope, c. 1670

The results would either prove or disprove the theory. Through experimentation and observations, scientists would learn how things in nature such as the planets, weather, and plants worked. From their observations, scientists would be able to figure out the laws of nature, or **natural law**.

Using experiments and observation gave rise to the **Scientific Revolution**. Scientists were making so many discoveries and overturning so many ideas that it seemed like a revolution. Not everyone was happy with the changes.

Galileo demonstrates using a telescope in this fresco.

Perhaps most alarming to many Europeans were the ideas of Nicholas Copernicus, Johannes Kepler, and Galileo Galilei. Each man's work built on the ideas of the other. They all investigated the relation between Earth and the other planets.

Ptolemy, a Greek astronomer in the A.D. 200s, developed the idea that the planets revolved around the earth. In 1543, Copernicus published a book disagreeing with this theory. He stated that all the planets, including the earth, revolve around the sun. The Catholic Church decided to accept Ptolemy's theory and taught that the earth was the center of the universe.

In the early 1600s, Kepler further developed Copernicus's theory. Around the same time, Galileo used the telescope to observe the sky. What he saw confirmed that the earth moved around the sun. He also developed some theories of his own. His work attracted the attention of many Europeans—including the Catholic Church. Galileo was tried and convicted of heresy by the Inquisition. He had to recant, or take back, his theory or be burned alive. He agreed to recant. However, as he left the court, he supposedly said under his breath, "The earth does move." Copernicus, Kepler, and Galileo, however, were correct. Their theories have been proved to be true.

Nicholas Copernicus developed theories about the universe.

European Contributions to Science

Andreas Vesalius (1514–1564)	described the structures and organs of the human body
William Harvey (1578–1657)	described the heart and blood circulation system in humans
Anton van Leeuwenhoek (1632–1723)	discovered cells in living matter using a simple microscope
Isaac Newton (1642–1727)	developed the Universal Law of Gravitation; explained why planets orbit the sun
Joseph Priestly (1733–1804)	discovered oxygen
Antoine Lavoisier (1743–1794)	developed a system for naming chemical elements; considered the founder of modern chemistry
Edward Jenner (1749–1823)	discovered a vaccine for smallpox

Political Revolutions, 1600–1815

Enlightenment Thinkers

The Scientific Revolution influenced European philosophers as well as scientists. Philosophers tried to apply principles of rational thought to the study of human life. By using the scientific method and reason, they hoped to figure out ways to improve conditions for people.

One of the most important English philosophers was John Locke. He believed that people have certain **natural rights** that belong to them as human beings. Among these rights are life, liberty, and property, or belongings. Locke also believed that government is necessary to ensure that people keep those rights. However, the powers of government should be limited. According to Locke, a **social contract** exists between people and their government. If a government does not govern justly, the people have the right to overthrow that government.

Adam Smith

Another important British thinker was Adam Smith. He developed the idea of **laissez-faire economics**. He believed that when it came to the economy, governments should do nothing. The natural forces in the economy, such as supply and demand, should be allowed freedom to work. That means the role of government is greatly limited. For example, Smith believed that government should protect its citizens from invasion by an enemy, but not from poverty.

stop and think

Examine the table "European Contributions to Science." How do you think these contributed to human progress? With a partner, choose two ideas. Discuss how each discovery or invention has made a difference to people over the centuries. Write two or three paragraphs to explain your ideas for each discovery or invention.

The Philosophes

A group of French philosophers, *philosophes* in French, also attempted to use reason for the good of society. Three **philosophes** stand out for their contributions.

Charles-Louis de Secondat, the Baron de Montesquieu, studied a number of European governments. In 1748, he published his findings. He greatly admired the English government. The English had created a separation of powers by having three branches of government: executive, legislative, and judicial. Each branch was to limit the power of the others through a system of checks and balances. Although Parliament was fast becoming the dominant branch of government, Montesquieu helped make the idea of a separation of powers popular. This idea influenced the future leaders of the United States of America.

French salons were a meeting place for the philosophes.

Another important philosophe was François-Marie Arouet, or Voltaire. He was a poet, novelist, and playwright as well as a philosophe. Some of his themes were the need for religious toleration, justice for all, free speech, and an end to the slave trade. He attacked corruption in government as well as in the Catholic Church. His enemies had him arrested and sent into exile where he continued to write.

Denis Diderot published the 28-volume *Encyclopedia*, or *Classified Dictionary of the Sciences, Arts, and Trades*. It took from 1751 to 1772 to complete and contains articles by important philosophes. It found customers among the French middle class, including doctors, lawyers, and teachers. The *Encyclopedia* was also translated into other languages and spread the ideas of the Enlightenment as far as the Americas.

Putting It All Together

Play "Who Am I?" with a partner. First, choose five people from this lesson. Then write two or three sentences to describe, or identify, each person. End each identification with the question "Who am I?" Take turns asking and answering the questions with a partner.

The 13 English Colonies Rebel

Thinking on Your Own

What do you already know about the American Revolution? Write a bulleted list of 10 facts in your notebook. As you read this lesson, add new facts to your list.

The rivalry among European nations spilled over into their colonies around the world. In the 1750s, France and Great Britain were at war against each other in India and North America. When the French and Indian War was over, Great Britain controlled its 13 colonies in North America. It also controlled Canada and all French territory west of the Mississippi River. Great Britain also had won control of a large part of India from the French.

> ### focus your reading
>
> What were the causes of the American Revolution?
>
> Explain how the British lost the American War for Independence.
>
> The new United States government was based on what ideas?
>
> ### vocabulary
>
> possessions
>
> mercantilism
>
> revenue tax
>
> federal system
>
> ratify

The war and its new **possessions** put an economic strain on the British Empire. The need for money became a major problem between Britain and its 13 North American colonies.

Causes of the American Revolution

European countries operated under the policy of **mercantilism**. Colonies existed to make the home country rich. One way to do this was to make sure that trade with the colonies was regulated, or managed, to the home country's benefit. Before the Stamp Act, this was the purpose of taxes imposed on the colonies. The Stamp Tax was a different kind of tax. Its purpose was not to regulate trade, but to raise money. It was a **revenue tax**.

Under this law, colonists had to pay a tax for all kinds of printed materials ranging from newspapers, playing cards, and wills to marriage licenses. An official stamp on the document proved that the tax had been paid.

The colonists reacted swiftly with loud cries of "No taxation without representation." Colonists claimed that only their own colonial legislatures could impose taxes on them. Parliament and the king rejected this idea. They claimed that Parliament represented all citizens including those in the colonies. Therefore, Parliament could impose taxes on the colonists.

Colonists reacted violently to the Stamp Tax. Parliament repealed the Stamp Act in 1766. However, it refused to agree with the colonists' view of taxation.

The disagreement flared again and again throughout the 1760s and early 1770s. By 1775, colonists were stockpiling weapons. The first shots of the American Revolution were fired at Lexington, Massachusetts, early on the morning of April 18. By summer, the Second Continental Congress had organized an army. The following summer, on July 4, 1776, the Congress adopted the Declaration of Independence. In writing this document, Thomas Jefferson used many ideas from John Locke about the social contract.

British uniforms were impractical for fighting the North American colonists.

The War of American Independence

The Americans had many disadvantages in their battle for independence from Great Britain. They faced the largest and strongest professional army and navy in the world. The American army was made up of untrained recruits who served for only short periods of time. Their navy never had more than a handful of ships.

The Americans also had advantages. The first and possibly greatest advantage was their leadership—men like George Washington,

Members of the Second Continental Congress sign the Declaration of Independence.

The Battle of Saratoga was the turning point of the war.

Thomas Jefferson, Benjamin Franklin, and John Adams. Washington put together an army, chose good officers, and inspired his men to fight.

Benjamin Franklin negotiated with France to enter the war on the side of the United States. Spain and the Dutch Republic also joined against their old enemy, Great Britain. France sent soldiers and ships as well as money and supplies. With the help of the French navy, Washington was able to block Lord Cornwallis' retreat at Yorktown, Virginia. Cornwallis surrendered in October 1781. The war was over and a new nation emerged.

Setting Up the New Nation

The first written plan of government for the new nation was the Articles of Confederation. The states deliberately adopted a plan that did not create a strong central government. By 1787, however, it was clear that the Articles did not cover the many issues that came before the new government.

That summer, state delegates met in Philadelphia. Rather than revise the Articles, they wrote a new plan. The United States Constitution set up a **federal system**. Power was shared between a national, or central, government and the state governments. Among the powers given to the national government were the powers to establish an army, regulate trade, impose taxes, and create a national system of money.

The central government was divided into executive, legislative, and judicial branches. A system of checks and balances was developed so that no one branch of government could gain too much power over the others. The writers of the Constitution borrowed both ideas from Montesquieu, the French philosopher. Before the Constitution could go into effect, nine of the thirteen states had to **ratify**, or approve, the document. A number of Americans did not think that the Constitution went far enough. They wanted certain rights

From the Independent Chronicle and Universal Advertiser, Boston, Thursday June 26, 1788.

This political cartoon depicts the first nine states to ratify the U.S. Constitution and the two states that soon followed.

guaranteed by the Constitution. The battle over ratification was fierce in some states. Finally, an agreement was reached. If the Constitution was ratified, one of the first acts of the new Congress would be to add a Bill of Rights.

The Constitution was ratified in 1788 and the Bill of Rights was added. These first 10 amendments to the Constitution guarantee freedoms of religion, speech, press, assembly, and petition; the right to bear arms; freedom from housing soldiers against one's will; freedom from unlawful search and seizure; the right to a fair and speedy trial and to a trial by jury; and freedom from excessive bail, fines, and punishment.

Many of these rights are the same as Americans had as English colonists. These rights are also similar to the natural rights identified by philosophers of the Enlightenment. To many people in the 1700s, the American Revolution was the fulfillment of Enlightenment ideals.

Putting It All Together

Write an explanation of how the separation of powers and system of checks and balances works. Share your explanation with a partner. Then incorporate your notes with the bulleted notes you wrote at the start of this lesson to create a short essay about the outcomes of the American Revolution.

stop and think

Write two-line headlines for the following events: (a) passage of the Stamp Act, (b) Battle of Lexington, (c) Declaration of Independence, (d) Washington is made general of the army, (e) France becomes an ally, (f) Cornwallis surrenders. Share your headlines with a partner. Ask your partner to suggest words that could make your headlines more interesting or exciting.

LESSON 4

Napoleon and the French Revolution

Thinking on Your Own

As you read this lesson, create a cause-and-effect flowchart for each event. Remember that a cause may have more than one effect, or result. A result may have more than one cause. Then write a paragraph about one cause-and-effect event.

Through the centuries, French monarchs kept a tight hold on their power. The one thing they did not control was their expenses. By 1789, France was on the verge of bankruptcy.

To raise taxes, King Louis XVI needed the agreement of the Estates-General — France's legislature. It was made up of three **Estates**, or groups. The First Estate was the **clergy**. The Second Estate was the nobility, who owned about a third of the nation's land and held all the high government posts. Everyone else was a commoner and made up the Third Estate. The First and Second Estates paid no taxes. France's entire tax burden fell on the poor Third Estate.

> ### focus your reading
>
> Explain what the National Assembly accomplished.
>
> What was the sequence of events during the National Convention?
>
> Why did Napoleon rule France for so short a time?
>
> ### vocabulary
>
> Estates   nationalism
>
> clergy
>
> Napoleonic Code

National Assembly

On May 5, 1789, the Estates-General met for the first time in 175 years. Each Estate met by itself and had one vote. Members of the Third Estate feared what would happen if this practice continued. Their attempts at reform would fail.

The Third Estate wanted the Estates-General to meet and count each member's vote individually. Because some members of the

Women march on the Palace of Versailles on October 5, 1789.

First and Second Estates had agreed on the need for reforms, all three Estates could force Louis XVI to agree to the changes. Only then would he get his money.

Louis refused to allow the three Estates to vote together. The Third Estate renamed itself the National Assembly and began work on a constitution. Louis locked the Assembly out of its meeting hall. Members simply moved to the palace tennis court. They took what is called the Tennis Court Oath. They swore they would not disband until they had written a new constitution.

Declaration of the Rights of Man
• all men equal before the law
• right to liberty and property
• right to hold public office and to elect others to public office
• taxes based on ability to pay
• religions to be tolerated

Louis began secretly bringing in troops to drive out the Third Estate. They were saved when the people of Paris took to the streets in rebellion. On July 14, 1789, a mob destroyed the Bastille, a hated Paris prison. This day marks the beginning of the French Revolution.

The National Assembly eliminated privileges of the First and Second Estates. The Assembly approved the Declaration of the Rights of Man. Like the American Declaration of Independence, it stated the reasons for the Revolution.

In 1791, the National Assembly adopted a constitution for France. The powers of the monarchy were limited. The government was divided into three branches—executive, legislative, and judicial. Church property was taken by the government and sold. The government controlled the Catholic Church in France and paid the salaries of priests. The National Assembly disbanded and a new Legislative Assembly was elected.

National Convention

Fearing the French Revolution would spread to their nations, Prussia and Austria attacked France. They wanted to defeat France and restore

Time Box

1789
French Revolution began
Declaration of the Rights of Man

1791
Constitution adopted
Prussia and Austria attacked France

1792–1795
National Convention governed France
French Republic declared

1793
Louis XVI executed

1795–1799
Directory governed France

1799
Directory overthrown; Napoleon seized power

1804
Napoleon crowned himself emperor

Marie Antoinette, wife of Louis XVI, was beheaded at the guillotine in 1793.

Louis to absolute power. Mobs again took to the streets of Paris.

Radicals who wanted a republic opposed more moderate members of the Legislative Assembly. The radicals took advantage of the chaos in Paris and called for a National Convention to write a new constitution. The National Convention governed from 1792 to 1795. During this time, the monarchy was abolished. Louis was tried, convicted, and beheaded for treason.

The Jacobins, the most radical members of the Convention, seized power in 1793. They began what is called the Reign of Terror. Anyone suspected of opposing the Jacobins faced arrest and execution. The Terror lasted only one year, but thousands died.

In 1795, a new constitution established a legislature with two houses and an executive branch of five directors. The Directory governed France from 1795 to 1799. While the nation was living through political chaos, a young military officer, Napoleon Bonaparte, was winning victories on the battlefield. In 1799, he and a group of officers overthrew the Directory. Napoleon became the new ruler of France.

Rise and Fall of Napoleon

Napoleon soon agreed to a peace treaty to end the wars against France. France had already won control of a large part of North America. France also controlled the island of Haiti.

In 1803, France was once again at war with Great Britain. To raise money, Napoleon agreed to sell the Louisiana Territory to the United States for $15 million. At home, Napoleon restored order and the economy improved. Napoleon set up a centralized government managed by a professional bureaucracy.

One of Napoleon's most important reforms was the **Napoleonic Code**. This was actually seven law codes that replaced the many systems of law in France. At the same time, Napoleon took more and more power for himself. He ignored the freedom of the press guaranteed by the Revolution and shut down newspapers

Once emperor, Napoleon crowned his empress, Josephine.

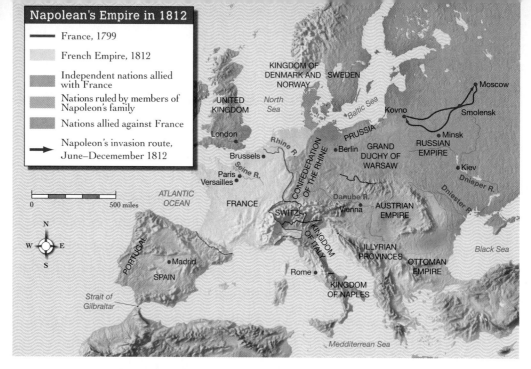

Napolean's Empire in 1812

— France, 1799

French Empire, 1812

Independent nations allied with France

Nations ruled by members of Napoleon's family

Nations allied against France

→ Napoleon's invasion route, June–Decemember 1812

0   500 miles

ATLANTIC OCEAN

N W E S

KINGDOM OF DENMARK AND NORWAY   SWEDEN

UNITED KINGDOM

North Sea

Baltic Sea

Moscow

Smolensk

London

Rhine R.

PRUSSIA

Kovno

Minsk

Brussels

Berlin

GRAND DUCHY OF WARSAW

RUSSIAN EMPIRE

Kiev

Paris

Seine R.

CONFEDERATION OF THE RHINE

Dnieper R.

Versailles

FRANCE

Danube R.

Dniester R.

SWITZ.

KINGDOM OF ITALY

Vienna

AUSTRIAN EMPIRE

PORTUGAL

Madrid

SPAIN

Rome

ILLYRIAN PROVINCES

OTTOMAN EMPIRE

Black Sea

KINGDOM OF NAPLES

Strait of Gilbraltar

Medditerrean Sea

that opposed him. Napoleon was determined to create an empire in Europe. In 1804, Napoleon declared himself emperor. From 1805 until 1813, he led France into one war after another, including an invasion of Russia.

Europe's rulers joined forces against Napoleon. After more defeats, he was forced to step down in 1813 and was sent to the island of Elba in the Mediterranean. He escaped in 1815 and took command of another French army. Three months later, they fought a coalition of European armies at the Battle of Waterloo. Again, Napoleon was defeated. This time he was sent to Saint Helena Island in the South Atlantic where he died in 1821.

Napoleon wanted to spread the ideas of the French Revolution. In the nations that he conquered, he set up governments based on legal equality, economic opportunity, and religious toleration. He also stripped the clergy and nobility of their special privileges. Other nations may have welcomed the changes, but they did not like French rule. This resulted in a growing spirit of **nationalism** across Europe. Nationalism is a strong feeling of loyalty for one's own culture.

Putting It All Together

Create a bulleted list of events that relate to Napoleon becoming emperor. Compare your list with a partner's and make needed corrections.

stop and think

Choose two events from the Time Box. Write an explanation of each event. Be sure to include any causes and effects. Share your explanation with a partner. Ask for suggestions about how to make it clearer.

Latin American Revolutions

Thinking on Your Own

As you read, create a table to keep track of the Latin American nations that won their independence. Your table should have three columns. The first column should list the name of the nation. Column 2 should list the date it became independent. Column 3 should briefly explain how it became independent.

The American Revolution was influenced by the ideas of the Enlightenment. The French Revolution was influenced by the American Revolution and the Enlightenment. All three influenced revolutions in Latin America in the early 1800s.

Society in Spanish America was divided among **peninsulares**, creoles, and mestizos. As the creole population grew in numbers and wealth, they wanted a say in government. However, a council in Spain made all the laws for the colonies. The council sent officials from Spain—the peninsulares—to see that the laws were carried out. The ideas of the Enlightenment and the success of the American and French revolutions inspired the creoles to act. However, the first uprising in Latin America did not take place among the Spanish.

> ### focus your reading
>
> How did Haiti gain its independence from France?
>
> How was the Mexican revolution different from other revolts in Spanish America?
>
> What was the sequence of events that led to the liberation of Spanish South America?
>
> ### vocabulary
>
> peninsulares
>
> L'Ouverture

Uprising in Haiti

The French Revolution sparked a rebellion in the French colony of Saint Domingue in the Caribbean. The island colony had a population of about 500,000 enslaved people of color, about

Toussaint L'Ouverture and soldiers fight the French at the Ravine aux Couleuvres.

32,000 French colonists, and another 24,000 free people of color. After learning of the "Declaration of the Rights of Man," the free people of color demanded citizenship. The wealthy French colonists resisted. The result was rebellion.

In 1794, the National Convention ended slavery in France's colonies. At the time, the French were fighting Spain and Great Britain to keep control of Saint Domingue. The rebels, under the control of François-Dominique Toussaint L'Ouverture, were allied with Spain. They switched sides and joined forces with the French. Together, they defeated France's enemies. As a reward, the French government made Toussaint governor-general for life of the colony.

Biography

François-Dominique Toussaint L'Ouverture (c. 1743–1803)

François-Dominique Toussaint was the son of enslaved plantation workers in the French colony of Saint Domingue. The plantation owner allowed Toussaint to learn to read. From books, he learned about the Enlightenment.

Toussaint joined the Haitian rebellion that broke out in 1791. His skills soon made him the rebel leader. He was given the name **L'Ouverture** because of his bravery in battle. The word *l'ouverture* means "opening." He once broke through an enemy line, allowing his forces to overwhelm the enemy.

After the rebellion, the French appointed him governor-general of the colony for life. When Napoleon attempted to restore slavery, Toussaint once again took to the battlefield. The French captured him. As he was taken to prison in France, he supposedly said:

"In overthrowing me, you have cut down in Haiti only the trunk of the tree of liberty. It will spring up again by the roots, for they are numerous and deep."

On January 1, 1804, Toussaint was proved right. On that day, Haiti declared its independence from France.

Napoleon seized control of France in 1799. One of his goals was to create an American empire. His plan was to restore slavery and put French officials in control of Saint Domingue. Napoleon sent troops to invade the island and take control. The invasion failed. However, Toussaint was captured, shipped to France, and died there in prison. One of his former generals, Jean-Jacques Dessalines declared Saint Domingue independent on January 1, 1804. The new nation took the name Haiti, meaning "a higher place."

Mexican Independence

The Enlightenment and the French Revolution also influenced Mexico's fight for independence from Spain. Father Miguel Hidalgo, a creole, began the fight. The Enlightenment ideas of liberty and equality inspired him. On September 16, 1810, he rang the bell of his church and called on his people to rebel against the Spanish. Known as "El Grito de Dolores!" (the Cry of Dolores), his call to rebellion marks the beginning of the Mexican revolution.

Hidalgo's army numbered some 60,000 mestizos and Native Americans. Armed with clubs and knives, they marched toward Mexico City. The rebel army captured several provinces and set up a government. Land was returned to Native Americans, and slavery was ended.

Miguel Hidalgo

Unfortunately, Hidalgo was not much of a general. In addition, the peninsulares and creoles were frightened of Hidalgo's policies. They did not want to give up their wealth and power to mestizos and Native Americans. The creoles and peninsulares wanted an end to the revolution and supported the Spanish government. Hidalgo's army was no match for well-trained and well-armed Spanish troops. In the fighting, Hidalgo was caught. He was later tried and executed.

But El Grito de Dolores did not die. Another priest, José Maria Morelos, a mestizo, took over the fight. By 1821, peninsulares and creoles decided to act for themselves. With their support, Agustín de Iturbide, a creole, came to power. He had the backing of rebels as well as the wealthy. His forces defeated the Spanish, and Mexico declared its independence. The following year, Iturbide proclaimed himself emperor.

The New Nations of Central and South America

- European colonies
- Gran Colombia
- Independent nations with date of independence
- United Provinces of Central America

He was overthrown in 1823, and Mexico became a republic with a government headed by a president.

Freeing Spanish South America

Simón Bolívar and José de San Martín were major figures in the fight for independence in Spanish South America. Both men were creoles and were sent by their families to study in Europe. While there, they read the works of the Enlightenment. They became convinced that the colonies must free themselves from Spanish rule.

Bolívar returned to his native Venezuela and spent 11 years fighting to free it. He finally succeeded in 1821. He was hailed as the "Liberator" and made president of the new republic of Gran Colombia.

San Martín and his army crossing the Andes

In 1812, San Martín returned from Europe to what is today Argentina. Part of the area had already declared its independence from Spain. But Spanish forces remained in what are today Chile and Peru. San Martín believed that freedom was not safe as long as Spanish forces remained anywhere in South America. In January 1817, he put together an army of volunteers and marched them over the Andes. His strategy worked. He caught the Spanish by surprise and defeated a large Spanish force.

In 1821, San Martín set out to capture Lima, the capital of the Viceroyalty of Peru, and end Spanish control in South America. His forces took Lima, but the Spanish army retreated into the mountains. Bolívar and his army joined San Martín. The two men could not agree on tactics and San Martín withdrew. Bolívar's forces liberated the rest of Peru. By 1825, all that was left of the Spanish empire in the Americas were the islands of Cuba and Puerto Rico.

stop and think

What similarities and differences can you find between the fights for independence in Haiti and Mexico? Work with a partner to create a Venn diagram to show how they were alike and different. When you are finished, use the information to write three or four paragraphs explaining the differences and similarities.

Putting It All Together

With a partner examine a map of Central and South America. Chose one of the countries indicated. Use the library or the Internet to find out more about the struggle for independence. Create a concept web using the information from your research. Then write a short essay about the country's independence movement.

Chapter Summary

- James I and Charles I introduced rule by **divine right**.
- Charles I was executed as a **traitor**. Oliver Cromwell set up a **commonwealth** and later a **military dictatorship**.
- The **Restoration** placed Charles II on the English throne. Concern over his Catholic faith resulted in the **Glorious Revolution**. The Bill of Rights set up a **constitutional monarchy**.
- The **Scientific Revolution** and the **Enlightenment** began during the 1600s. Philosophers used the **scientific method** to determine **natural law** and people's **natural rights**.
- John Locke wrote about the **social contract** between government and the governed. Adam Smith developed the theory of **laissez-faire economics**.
- Montesquieu, a **philosophe**, wrote about the separation of powers and checks and balances.
- England passed tax laws for their colonial **possessions**.
- European **mercantilism** relied on taxes. The 13 English colonies objected to **revenue taxes**.
- The **ratified** U.S. Constitution set up a **federal system**.
- The French Revolution began when the three **Estates** met and ended special privileges for the **clergy** and nobles.
- In 1799, Napoleon Bonaparte introduced the **Napoleonic Code**. Nations under his rule developed **nationalism**.
- Spanish **peninsulares** tried to maintain laws in Central and South America.
- Toussaint **L'Ouverture** led the rebellion in Haiti. Mexico rebelled against being a Spanish possession. San Martín and Bolívar became the liberators of Spanish Central and South America.

Chapter Summary

1 Create a concept map to show how many nations were influenced by the ideas of the Enlightenment.

2 Create a concept web for one of the revolutions described in this chapter. Use your web to write a short essay about the revolution.

Skill Builder

Analyzing Paintings and Photographs

Paintings and photographs can be valuable tools in studying the past. Some show us historical events such as Napoleon crowning his empress, Josephine. Such visual images show us who was there and what they were doing.

Paintings and photographs can also show us how people dressed and what they did for a living. Look through this textbook and find examples of these kinds of visual images.

Like all historical sources, visual images can be biased. A painter or photographer may arrange the subject of the picture in such a way as to favor his or her interpretation, or point of view. For example, the painter of the picture on page 243 included commoners and soldiers to emphasize the support of the English people for Charles II's return.

To analyze paintings and photographs:

1. Identify what is happening in the image.
2. Examine the details. Look at what is happening in the background and in the foreground. Look at the clothing or furniture. Look at the choice of colors an artist uses.
3. Identify the emotions or attitude the artist or photographer is trying to show.
4. Read the caption.
5. Identify the purpose in making the image.
6. Identify any bias in the image. Who is the artist or photographer? Do you know anything about him or her? What can you tell about the person's point of view?

Complete the following activities.

1 Examine the images on pages 244 and 255. Use the six steps listed above to analyze the images.

2 Choose one illustration from Chapter 16 and follow steps 1 through 6. Then write three paragraphs analyzing your choice.

Chapter 17 SOCIAL REVOLUTIONS

(1750–1910)

Getting Focused

Skim this chapter to predict what you will be learning.
• Read the lesson titles and subheadings.
• Look at the illustrations and read the captions.
• Examine the maps.
• Review the vocabulary words and terms.

Before the Industrial Revolution, most people in Russia, China, India, Europe, and the United States lived in rural areas. Most made their living by farming. The development of factories changed where people lived and what they did for a living.

Imagine that you are a farmer living on a small plot of land in England or Europe about the year 1800. You see more opportunity in the cities for yourself and your family. But you know life will be very different. Make a list of what you would expect to find in an industrial city.

The Industrial Revolution

Thinking on Your Own

You have read about a number of revolutions in this book: Neolithic, American, Scientific, and French. Now you will read about the Industrial Revolution. Look at the illustrations in this lesson and the subheadings. Then write a definition of "Industrial Revolution." Share your definition with a partner. As you read this lesson, add to or change your definition as needed.

Until 1800, most people in Western Europe and the United States lived on farms. The economies of these nations were based on farming, the making of goods by hand, and trading. During the **Industrial Revolution**, machines replaced hand tools in the manufacturing of goods. More and more people left their farms to work in factories. Within 100 years, many nations had become industrial giants.

focus your reading

Why did industrialization begin in Great Britain?

How was the factory system different from earlier ways of producing goods?

Explain how industrialization spread.

vocabulary

Industrial Revolution

natural resources

capital

textile

cottage industry

entrepreneur

Industrial Great Britain

The Industrial Revolution began in the 1780s in Great Britain. There were a number of reasons why it began there. Britain at that time had all the factors of production that were needed to succeed in changing from an agricultural to an industrial society. The country had the people needed to work in manufacturing. Britain also had valuable **natural resources**. It had the iron and coal needed to make machines and run steam engines. In addition, Britain had money to invest in railroads and

factories, as well as the markets where it could sell the manufactured goods.

By the 1780s, Britain had a surplus of food. That is, it had more food than was needed to feed the population. Farmers had learned ways to grow new crops, such as potatoes, and better ways to farm. Fewer farmers produced more food than ever before. This forced many farm laborers off the land. They were available to work in factories.

With more food to eat, people lived longer. They also had more children. Discoveries about what causes diseases and how they are spread were also important. Better sanitation and medical care were available. More people were able to avoid and survive disease. A large population meant there was a large number of workers available. All of these factors contributed to the development of the Industrial Revolution.

Great Britain had a large number of very wealthy people. Economic stability meant that people had the **capital**, or money, to invest in manufacturing. Investing in new businesses like factories was one way they could make huge profits on their money.

Children haul a coal wagon in Lancashire, England.

Manufacturing depended on natural resources. Great Britain had large amounts of two of the most important resources: coal and iron ore. It also had a colonial empire to supply other needed materials. India, for example, sent tons of raw cotton to England's new **textile**, or cloth-making, mills.

Factory owners needed markets for their products. Britain had a growing market at home and markets in its overseas colonies. In addition to supplying raw materials, Britain's colonies could buy the finished goods from Britain's factories.

Finally, Britain was the center of a revolution in technology. Inventors created new machines that made goods faster and cheaper than goods made by hand. The invention of the steam

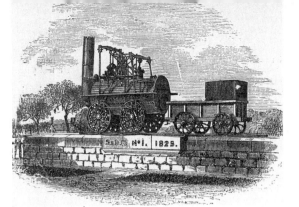

An 1825 steam engine in Darlington, England

engine created a new source of energy and a revolution in transportation.

Inventions in transportation helped move raw materials and finished products more quickly. In 1807, Robert Fulton launched the first successful steamboat in the United States. Soon ships could sail around the world without waiting for the wind. Another American, Peter Cooper, took James Watt's steam engine and made the first successful steam locomotive.

The Factory System

Before people worked in factories, they worked in their own homes or in workshops. Cloth was made in steps by different workers in their homes, or cottages. This was known as the **cottage industry** system. Raw cotton was delivered to the homes of spinners. They used a spinning wheel operated by a foot pedal to spin it into thread. The thread was then taken to weavers. Weavers worked on small, hand-operated looms to weave cloth. A merchant collected and sold the finished cloth and paid the workers.

A series of inventions in the late 1700s changed the textile industry. John Kay invented a flying shuttle that speeded up the weaving of cloth. To speed up the production of thread, James Hargreaves, in 1764, invented a new spinning machine. This spinning jenny spun several threads at the same time. Richard Arkwright invented a water-powered spinning frame that produced thread still more quickly and cheaply.

stop and think

Create a table showing the reasons that industrialization began in Great Britain. Label the left side "Industrialization in Great Britain." In that column, list the various factors that you read about that led to industrialization. Label the right side "Examples." In that column, provide examples and details for each factor in the left column.

Factors of Production

Any industry or service must have some form of the factors of production in order to succeed.

- Land—includes natural resources
- Labor—people to do the work
- Capital—money to invest
- Enterprise—ability to combine the other three factors and create a business or service

Eli Whitney invented the cotton gin in 1793. This machine greatly improved the cleaning of raw cotton. This led to an increase in cotton production.

Children work in a English brickyard.

In 1782, James Watt figured out how to use the steam engine to power machines. The next step was adding steam power to spinning and weaving machines. The steam engines used coal for fuel. In time, water-powered and steam-powered looms replaced the weavers' hand looms.

Machines powered by water and steam led to the factory system of production. Few old-time spinners could afford to buy these new machines. Building the dozens of spinning frames that could be run by a single water wheel or steam engine involved a large investment of money. This required a wealthy person or a group of investors. They also had to build the factory to provide a central location for the machines. As most of the early spinning factories used water as their power source, they were located along a stream or canal.

Factory owners hired workers to run the machines. They did not need skilled spinners or weavers. Workers with few skills could be trained in a short time to operate the machines. Because the machines were so large, they needed many workers to operate them. The owners even hired children to do the work. Now large numbers of workers were brought together in the factories. There, the workers ran endlessly whirring machines, turning out cotton cloth for world markets.

The Spread of Industrialization

By the mid-1800s, Great Britain was the leading industrial nation in the world. Its mines and factories turned out half the world's coal and manufactured goods. British technology spread to continental Europe and the United States.

The first nations in Europe to shift to the factory system of

Robert Owen's textile mill in Tewkesbury, England

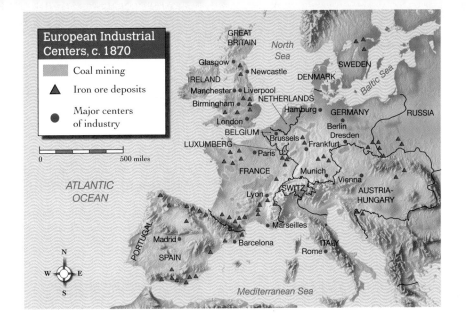

European Industrial Centers, c. 1870

Coal mining

▲ Iron ore deposits

● Major centers of industry

0   500 miles

GREAT BRITAIN
North Sea
Glasgow
Newcastle
SWEDEN
DENMARK
IRELAND
Manchester • Liverpool
Birmingham
Hamburg
NETHERLANDS
GERMANY
RUSSIA
London
BELGIUM
Berlin
Dresden
LUXUMBERG
Brussels
Frankfurt
Paris
Munich
FRANCE
Vienna
SWITZ
AUSTRIA-HUNGARY
ATLANTIC OCEAN
Lyon
Marseilles
PORTUGAL
Madrid
Barcelona
ITALY
SPAIN
Rome
Baltic Sea
Mediterranean Sea

N W E S

production were Belgium, Germany, and France. Germany and France, in particular, became highly industrialized nations in the 1800s. Japan also became industrialized. Russia, on the other hand, remained a rural country where most goods were made by hand.

The technology needed to start a textile industry reached the United States in the early 1800s. **Entrepreneurs** in New England invested in the first textile factories. Entrepreneurs are people who organize, operate, and assume the risk for a new business. Improvements in technology similar to what happened in the textile industry caused changes in other industries.

European nations were not interested in industrializing their colonies in Asia and Africa. The home countries wanted to keep their colonies as sources of raw materials and as markets for manufactured goods. Wealthy planters and mine owners in newly independent Latin American countries were happy to make their money selling raw materials to European businesses. Why risk money by building factories and starting new businesses?

Iron played a crucial role in the development of new machines.

Putting It All Together

Create a diagram to show how spinning and weaving went from a cottage industry to factory work. Work with a partner to figure out what to show on the diagram. Then decide how to illustrate your diagram.

Growth of Cities

Thinking on Your Own

Examine the illustrations in this lesson. From what you observe, what do you think life was like for people during this time? Write two paragraphs to describe life for the working class and the middle class.

Between 1800 and 1850, the population of cities in Europe and the United States grew rapidly. Workers needed to live close to factories and mills. At the same time, changes in farming meant that fewer farm workers were needed. People were being pushed out of rural areas. Some countries also suffered years of poor harvests, which drove even more farmers off the land. As a result, more people moved from rural areas to industrial cities.

focus your reading

Explain what the first industrial cities were like.

What was life like for the working class?

Describe the new middle class.

vocabulary

urbanization

slums

tenements

middle class

Industrial Cities

Between 1800 and 1850 there was a significant increase in the number and size of cities in Europe and the United States. This is called **urbanization**. For example, London's population grew from 1 million people in 1800 to 2.5 million in 1850.

Living conditions in cities were terrible for workers. They gathered in neighborhoods near their work. These very poor, crowded neighborhoods became known as **slums**. People lived in five- and six-story wooden apartment buildings called **tenements**. Whole families crowded into tiny, two-room

The Krupp Steelworks in Essen, Germany

Tenement life was crowded and dirty.

apartments. People got their water from hand-operated pumps. There was no organized fire or police protection. Cities also had no garbage collection or sewer systems. Waste piled up in streets and alleys. Diseases spread quickly through these urban areas. It was not until the late 1800s that nations began to clean up their cities and pass laws that regulated tenements.

stop and think

Imagine you are living in a new industrial city. Plan a letter to the editor demanding that living conditions be improved for the working poor. Discuss your ideas with a partner. Then write a three- or four-paragraph letter stating what you think should be done and why.

The Working Class

Cities may have offered work, but the work paid poorly. The work day was long and hard. Working conditions in the new factories and mills were dangerous.

Factories could be boiling hot in summer and freezing cold in winter. They lacked large windows to let in fresh air and furnaces to heat the rooms in winter. Dust in the air in textile factories sickened workers.

Men and women worked 12- to 16-hour days. However, women were typically paid 50 percent of what men were paid. Children, too, worked because their families needed the money. Most countries did not require all children to attend school in the early 1800s. After 1833 in Great Britain, children from ages 9 to 13 could work only 9-hour workdays. Children over the age of 13 could work 12 hours a day.

Tired workers were sometimes careless. Accidents could cost workers a finger, a hand, an eye, or even their life. There was no medical insurance to pay for medical care for injured workers. Until the late 1800s, there were no labor unions to demand shorter working hours and safe and healthful working conditions.

 Time Box

1780s
Industrial Revolution began in Great Britain

1800s (early)
Industrial Revolution spread to United States

1850s
Industrial Revolution spread to Germany, Belgium, and France

1920s
Industrial Revolution spread to Russia

The New Middle Class

Since the Middle Ages, there had been a **middle class** of craftworkers, merchants, shop owners, and professionals such as lawyers and doctors. The Industrial Revolution created new members of the middle class. These new members were the men who provided the money to build the new factories and the men who managed the new businesses.

Middle-class families lived around the central city of working-class neighborhoods. They had large, well-built, single-family homes with yards. Often, they had a servant or two. The wives did not work outside the home. Their job was to manage the servants, raise the children, and make a pleasant home for their husbands when they came home for work.

Putting It All Together

Imagine you are a member of a union in a textile mill. Work with a partner to design a sign to carry in a protest for better working conditions.

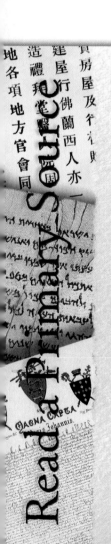

Read a Primary Source

Factory Conditions

The following excerpt is from testimony by Elizabeth Bentley. She appeared in 1815 before a commission of the British Parliament that was looking into factory conditions.

What time did you begin work at the factory?
When I was six years old.

What were the usual hours of labour?
From six in the morning till seven at night.

What time was allowed for meals?
Forty minutes at noon.

Had you any time to get your breakfast or drinking?
No, we had to get it as we could.

Suppose you flagged a little, or were late, what would they do?
Strap us.

And they are in the habit of strapping?
Yes.

reading for understanding

How long was Elizabeth's workday?

What happened if a worker was slow at his or her job?

Using the information in this reading, write a bulleted list of facts about child labor.

Is the strap used so as to hurt you excessively?
Yes, it is. . . . I have seen the overlooker go to the top end of the room, where the little girls [work]; he has taken a strap, and a whistle in his mouth, and sometimes he has got a chain and chained them, and strapped them all down the room.

LESSON 3

Changes in Society

Thinking on Your Own

Look at the vocabulary words for this lesson. Write them in your notebook. Work with a partner to develop definitions. As you read, change the definitions if they are not correct.

The way people lived changed greatly during the Industrial Revolution. For the working classes, life became harder. For the wealthy and well-educated, it was a time for discovery. Discovery and invention often led to a better life for all classes.

New Philosophies

New philosophies of life developed during the Industrial Revolution. Some people wanted to find ways to make conditions better for workers. Others thought that the poor were responsible for their own troubles.

focus your reading

Discuss the social philosophies that developed during the Industrial Revolution.

What did labor unions want to achieve?

Explain how some of the inventions of the nineteenth century changed the way people lived.

vocabulary

socialism

proletariat

Social Darwinism

labor union

strike

realism

invention

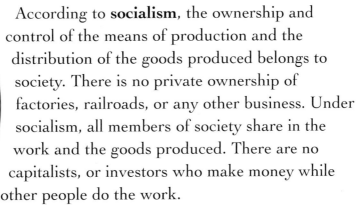

Karl Marx

According to **socialism**, the ownership and control of the means of production and the distribution of the goods produced belongs to society. There is no private ownership of factories, railroads, or any other business. Under socialism, all members of society share in the work and the goods produced. There are no capitalists, or investors who make money while other people do the work.

The most famous socialist was Karl Marx. In 1848, he published his ideas and beliefs in *The Communist Manifesto*. He predicted that the **proletariat**, or workers, would overthrow the capitalists. His philosophy gave rise to communism and the Russian Revolution in the 20th century.

Social Darwinism was a philosophy based on the ideas of Charles Darwin. Darwin's theory was that only the strongest and best adapted animals survived. In 1842, he wrote an essay called *Natural Selection.* In 1859, he wrote *On The Origin of Species by Means of Natural Selection.* Darwin, however, studied animals, not humans. Others took his work and adapted his ideas to humans. Social Darwinists said that, like animals, only the fittest—or the strongest and smartest—people grew wealthy. The poor were poor because they were stupid and lazy. Wealthy business owners used this argument to explain their rise to wealth and power. It also gave them a reason not to improve conditions for their workers.

Charles Darwin

Goals of United States Labor Unions 1850–1910

Knights of Labor
- eight-hour workday
- equal wages for women
- end child labor

American Federation of Labor
- eight-hour workday
- higher wages for working men
- safer working conditions
- benefits for injured workers

Women's Trade Union League
- eight-hour workday
- minimum wage
- end child labor

Rise of Labor Unions

The horrible working conditions in factories in the 1800s led to the development of **labor unions**. Groups of workers formed organizations to protest the conditions. They also wanted reforms like shorter working hours, age limits for working children, and safety measures.

The unions used **strikes**, or work stoppages, to pressure employers. They organized protests and marches to make their issues known. Unions won the right to strike in Great Britain in 1870. By 1900, trade unions in the rest of Western Europe and the United States had made progress.

Science and Literature

Realism, or the philosophy of seeing the world as it really is, influenced science, politics, literature, and the arts after 1850. A number of scientific discoveries and inventions took place. Writers such as Charles Dickens described the life of the urban poor in such novels as *Oliver Twist* and *David Copperfield*.

The rise of industrialism and **inventions** to make work easier and faster led to other discoveries. With leisure time created by machines doing work, people had more opportunity to read, think, and experiment. Inventors in the United States changed the way the world lived with their inventions. Alexander Graham Bell invented the telephone in 1876, which allowed people to talk with each other over distances. In 1879, Thomas Edison invented the incandescent light bulb. This was one of more than one thousand items he worked on.

In 1885, Louis Pasteur, a French scientist, developed a vaccine against rabies. Marie Curie, also a French scientist, working with her husband, Pierre, announced the discovery of new chemical elements in 1898. Working together, they had isolated polonium and radium.

Many more inventors around the world made machines and discoveries that changed the way of life of millions.

Putting It All Together

Make a concept web with "Scientific Discoveries" in the center. Draw lines to circles with inventions in them. Then write how each invention affected daily life in the new urban cities.

Alexander Graham Bell (1847–1922)

Thomas Edison (1847–1931)

Louis Pasteur (1822–1895)

Marie (1867–1934) and Pierre (1859–1906) Curie

Chapter Summary

- The **Industrial Revolution** began in the 1780s in Great Britain. It was made possible by the growth in population, the number of people with **capital** to invest, large supplies of **natural resources**, large markets for finished goods, and improvements in technology.
- Before the Industrial Revolution, **textiles** were made by a **cottage industry**.
- Belgium, Germany, and France soon industrialized. **Entrepreneurs** in New England invested in building textile factories.
- To find work, people moved to cities. The result was rapid **urbanization** of industrial nations.
- Workers lived in **slums** in five- and six-story **tenements**.
- A new group of business owners and managers developed in the **middle class** as a result of the Industrial Revolution.
- **Socialism** calls for the ownership and control of the means of production and distribution of goods to belong to society. Karl Marx believed that the **proletariat** in time would overthrow capitalists.
- The philosophy of **Social Darwinism** states that only the strongest and smartest people succeed.
- **Realism** describes life the way it really is.
- Working conditions for the working class were very hard, unsafe, and unhealthful.
- Workers organized **labor unions** and **strikes** to protest their problems.
- **Inventions** such as the light bulb and telephone changed peoples' lives.

Chapter Review

1 Imagine that you are a skilled textile spinner in the late 1780s. Write a letter to a friend about the changes taking place in your village as a result of the factory system. Is your life better or worse? Why?

2 Do you think the Social Darwinists were right or wrong? Write a paragraph or two defending your position. Use information from this chapter to support your argument.

Skill Builder

Analyzing a Bar Graph

In Chapter 15, you learned that a line graph is a good way to show changes in statistics over time. A bar graph also shows data. It shows information for several nations or companies at a particular time.

Usually, the quantity, or amount, is listed along the left side, or vertical axis. The subjects are shown along the bottom, or horizontal axis. The time period is given in the title.

To read a bar graph, follow these steps:

1. Read the title of the graph to learn what it is about.
2. Examine the vertical axis to learn the quantity.
3. Examine the horizontal axis to learn the subjects.
4. Examine the bars to learn about the relationship between the subjects.

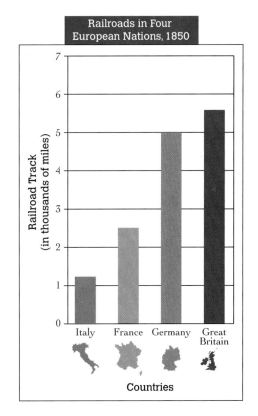

Use the graph to answer these questions.

1. What is the title of the graph?

2. What do the bars represent?

3. Which nation had the most railroad track in 1850?

4. Which nation had about 2,500 miles of track?

5. What can you infer about industrialization in these four countries?

6. How might the amount of railroad track influence a country's ability to industrialize?

6 UNIT

A NEW AGE

The late 1800s was another time of important changes. In Europe, German and Italian nationalists were fighting to unify their countries. Their success had far-reaching results in the 20th century.

Europeans also brought dramatic changes to other parts of the world. European nations competed with one another to increase their power in Asia, Africa, and Latin America. Their goals were the same. They wanted more raw materials for their growing industries at home and more overseas markets for their goods. The results were tragic for Asians, Africans, and Latin Americans.

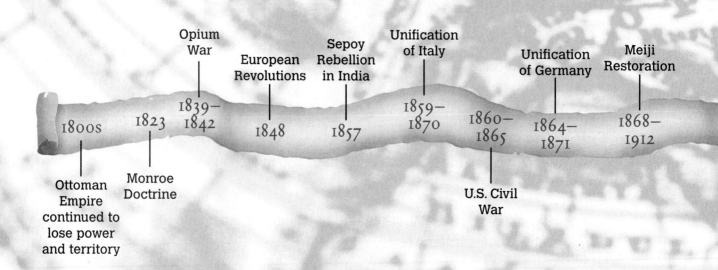

Opium War
1839–1842

European Revolutions
1848

Sepoy Rebellion in India
1857

Unification of Italy
1859–1870

Unification of Germany
1864–1871

Meiji Restoration
1868–1912

1800s

1823

1860–1865

Ottoman Empire continued to lose power and territory

Monroe Doctrine

U.S. Civil War

Who joined Garibaldi's Red Shirts to create an Italian nation?

What did Japanese officials hope to gain by modernizing their nation?

How did Great Britain win control of India?

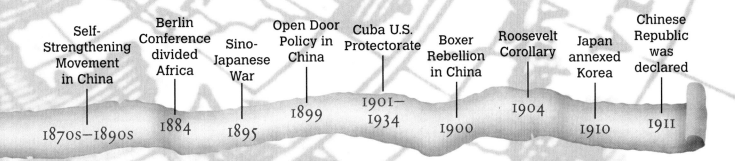

Self-Strengthening Movement in China
1870s–1890s

Berlin Conference divided Africa
1884

Sino-Japanese War
1895

Open Door Policy in China
1899

Cuba U.S. Protectorate
1901–1934

Boxer Rebellion in China
1900

Roosevelt Corollary
1904

Japan annexed Korea
1910

Chinese Republic was declared
1911

Chapter 18

NATIONALISM IN EUROPE

(1815–1914)

Getting Focused

Skim this chapter to predict what you will be learning.
- Read the lesson titles and subheadings.
- Look at the illustrations and read the captions.
- Examine the maps.
- Review the vocabulary words and terms.

Until the late 1800s, Germany and Italy were not their own nations. Parts of each were ruled by princes, dukes, or other nobles. What would make people want to join together and become part of a large nation? Work with a partner to think of economic, geographic, political, religious, technological, societal, and cultural reasons.

LESSON 1

Conservatives in Control

Thinking on Your Own

Read the subheads in this lesson. As you read the lesson, create a sequence flowchart. Use the subheads to help remember the order in which events happened. Use as many vocabulary words as possible in your flowchart.

After defeating Napoleon I at Waterloo, the rulers of Europe wanted peace and stability. They hoped to prevent future wars, revolutions, and democratic change. At the Congress of Vienna, held in Vienna, Austria, in 1815, they agreed to restore power to Europe's royal families. These **conservatives** believed that the monarchy was the best form of government. They also wanted to maintain a **balance of power** between Europe's strongest nations. That is, they wanted Russia, the Austrian Empire, Prussia, France, and Great Britain to keep one another in check.

> ### focus your reading
>
> What caused the revolutions of 1848?
>
> What part did Camillo di Cavour play in the unification of Italy?
>
> Why was Giuseppe Garibaldi successful in helping to unify Italy?
>
> ### vocabulary
>
> conservatives
>
> balance of power
>
> liberals
>
> nationalists
>
> ethnic groups
>
> appease
>
> depose

Preventing Change

The leader of the conservatives was Prince Klemens Von Metternich of Austria. He wanted to keep **liberals** and **nationalists** from gaining power. Liberals wanted to protect people's civil liberties, including freedom of speech, press, and assembly. They believed that governments elected by the people

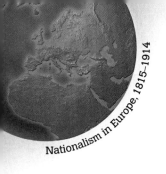

were best able to do this. Nationalists insisted that people owed loyalty to the nation, not to a king or royal family. They thought that each **ethnic group**, or nationality, should have its own government. Both liberals and nationalists were a threat to the existing order.

The Vienna uprising of 1848

Revolutions in Europe, 1848–1849

⬟ Uprisings

▬ The German Confederation, 1815

For several years, Metternich and the leaders of Europe managed to prevent change. In 1823, liberals in Spain tried to overthrow the monarchy. A French army crushed the uprising. Revolts also broke out in France, Belgium, and Italy. These, too, were put down by military force.

Many ethnic groups in the Austrian Empire wanted nations of their own. These groups included Croats, Czechs, Germans, Hungarians, Italians, Poles, Serbians, Slovaks, Slovenes, and Romanians. They were a serious problem to Metternich.

The year 1848 saw liberal and nationalist uprisings across Europe. In France, liberals overthrew the monarchy and set up the Second Republic. But the French soon replaced it with a Second Empire under Emperor Napoleon III—sometimes referred to as Louis-Napoleon. He was the nephew of Napoleon Bonaparte.

Leaders of France, Prussia, and Austria tried to sweep away the revolutionaries in 1848.

In Austria, Hungarian and Italian nationalists tried to set up new nations of their own. The Austrian government tried to **appease** the rebels by removing Metternich from his position as foreign minister. When that did not work, Austrian armies put down both uprisings.

Unifying Italy

While nothing happened in the 1848 uprising, Italian nationalists did not give up their desire for a nation. Austria controlled a large section of what is now northern Italy in 1848. The rest of the peninsula was made up of small kingdoms. Here, conservatives finally met their match.

One of those kingdoms, Piedmont, was ruled by a king, Victor Emmanuel II. In 1852, he chose Camillo di Cavour as his prime minister. Cavour set about freeing Italian territory from Austrian control and uniting the peninsula.

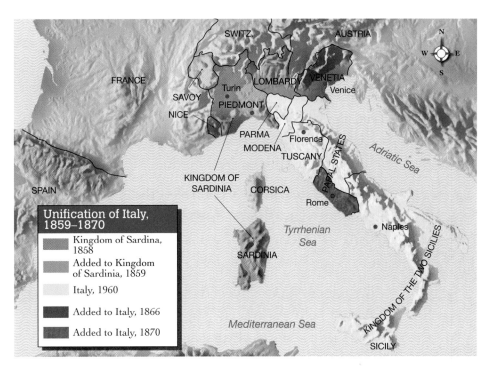

Cavour joined Emperor Napoleon III in a military alliance. In 1859, the armies of France and Piedmont went to war against Austria. The allies won the war. Examine the map of the unification of Italy from 1859 to 1870. Locate the territory that was added to the Kingdom of Piedmont after the war in 1859. In exchange for France's help, Cavour agreed to let France take the regions of Nice and Savoy.

Austria supported the governments of several northern Italian states. Nationalists in these states were inspired by Piedmont's success. They **deposed**, or overthrew, their rulers and joined their states with Piedmont.

Emperor Louis-Napoleon was Napoleon Bonaparte's nephew and the first president of the short-lived Second Republic.

Garibaldi and His Red Shirts

Victor Emmanuel and Cavour had united most of northern Italy. In the south, Giuseppe Garibaldi was building support for a single Italy. Garibaldi was a strong nationalist. Unlike Cavour, he did not want to see Italy become a monarchy. He wanted an Italian republic.

By 1860, Garibaldi had pulled together a volunteer army of 1,000 patriots. They wore red shirts as their uniforms. As a result, they were known as Red Shirts. Garibaldi and his army aided a revolt on the island of Sicily. It was part of the Kingdom of the Two Sicilies, made up of Sicily and Naples. When they had freed the island, the Red Shirts took the fight back to the mainland. Within two months, they controlled the entire kingdom.

Garibaldi meeting Victor Emmanuel

Garibaldi turned over control of the kingdom to Victor Emmanuel. In exchange, the king and Cavour agreed to a constitutional monarchy to govern the new nation.

The regions of Venetia and the Papal States were not yet part of Italy. Austria gave up Venetia in 1866 after Austria lost the Austro-Prussian War. Italy had been an ally of Prussia in the war.

Italian forces invaded the Papal States in 1870. Emperor Napoleon III defended the states. After he removed his troops to fight Prussia in the Franco-Prussian War, the citizens of the Papal States voted to join the new nation of Italy. Rome became its capital.

King Victor Emmanuel III

Putting It All Together

Create a concept map to show how Italy became a nation. Label the large center circle "Unifying Italy." Then draw smaller circles for the different steps in the process. Work with a partner and be sure to include details from the lesson.

stop and think

Imagine you are Cavour. What would you say to Napoleon III to get his help in adding territory to Piedmont? List as many ideas as you can think of that would convince Napoleon III to help. Then use those ideas to write a persuasive letter to the emperor asking for France's support against Austria. Share your letter with a partner. Ask a partner for ideas to make your letter more persuasive.

The New Nation of Germany

Thinking on Your Own

As you read the lesson, take bulleted notes about Bismarck and his policies. Include information from his biography. Use the vocabulary words in your notes. After you have finished reading the lesson, think about the kind of man Bismarck must have been. Write one sentence that describes Bismarck's character. Use information from your notes to support your opinion.

In 1860, there was no single German nation. People who considered themselves German lived in Prussia, the Austrian Empire, and 39 small states ruled by princes, dukes, and kings. German nationalists were inspired by the success of Cavour in Italy. They began to look for ways to unify the many German states. The best choice to lead them seemed to be Prussia.

focus your reading

How did Otto von Bismarck enlarge the Prussian army?

How did William I become kaiser of a united Germany?

What policies did Bismarck adopt for governing the new German nation?

vocabulary

industrialize

kaiser

militarism

authoritarian

domination

Prussia and Bismarck

Prussia in the early 1860s was large, wealthy, and rapidly **industrializing**—or developing a strong manufacturing sector. Prussia already had a leadership role among the other German states. It had put together a trade association that negotiated trade policies between the German states and other nations.

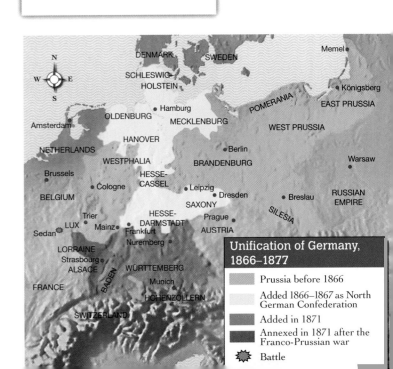

Unification of Germany, 1866–1877

Prussia before 1866

Added 1866–1867 as North German Confederation

Added in 1871

Annexed in 1871 after the Franco-Prussian war

Battle

The Prussian army was well-disciplined, tough, and well-equipped.

What Prussia needed was someone to make unification happen. That person was Count Otto von Bismarck. In 1862, Bismarck was appointed prime minister by King William I of Prussia. Both men strongly believed in **militarism**. They supported having a strong military force.

The king had asked Parliament to raise taxes to increase the size of the army. The Prussian Parliament refused to go along with the king's proposal. Bismarck ignored the legislature. He moved forward with the king's plan to enlarge the Prussian army. If it would not vote him new taxes, he would use money from current taxes. Bismarck bled the national tax revenues to build up the army.

William I being crowned emperor

The Siege of Paris, 1870

Building the German Empire

Bismarck then set about using the army. He wanted to gain the regions of Schleswig and Holstein from Denmark. He also wanted to drive the Austrians from German territory. By 1866, the Prussian army had succeeded in achieving both goals. The following year, Schleswig and Holstein combined to form the North German Confederation. The new confederation was under Prussia's **domination**—or control. New areas were added to Prussia between 1864 and 1867.

At the same time the four southern German states entered into military alliances with Prussia. These states bordered France. Bismarck convinced them that France would try to take them over. Becoming allies of Prussia, he argued, would protect them.

There was some truth to Bismarck's claim about France. Or so he believed. He was convinced that France did not want a strong Germany as its neighbor. In 1870, Bismarck pushed France into declaring war on Prussia. The Franco-Prussian War lasted less than six months. The Prussian army invaded France and quickly captured the French army and Napoleon III. The citizens of Paris held out until January 1871, but they finally surrendered.

The German states celebrated their victory over France. In appreciation, they asked William I of Prussia to become **kaiser,**

stop and think

With a partner, create a flowchart to track the causes and effects that resulted in a united Germany. Include all key events, people, and dates from the lesson.

or emperor, of a new German Empire. The coronation took place in the palace of Versailles, not far from Paris. German nationalists had achieved their dream. Led by Bismarck, they had created a single nation.

Building German Power at Home

The government of the new Germany had a constitution and a legislature with two houses. The upper house was appointed by the rulers of the German states. The lower house was elected by male citizens. The real power, however, lay with the kaiser—and with Bismarck.

When the constitution was written, Bismarck made sure that the legislature had little power. The heads of all government departments reported to the president of the upper house. The president was appointed by the kaiser. For nearly 20 years, William I and then William II appointed Bismarck to this post. The military and government bureaucracy reported to the kaiser, not to the legislature. In addition, foreign policy was controlled

Biography

Otto von Bismarck (1815–1898)

Otto von Bismarck is known in history as the "Iron Chancellor." This title comes from his first speech as prime minister to the Prussian Parliament. He said, "The great issues of the day will not be decided by speeches and the resolutions of the majorities . . . but by iron and blood."

Bismarck used the iron of weapons and the blood of soldiers to build the German state. He was not educated to be a soldier. His university studies prepared him for work as a civil servant. He did not like the work and resigned. He returned home to manage his father's estate, but he was not content to remain in the country. Bismarck eventually joined the diplomatic service in the late 1840s and served Prussia until 1862.

In that year, Bismarck was called to Berlin to meet with William I. His views evidently pleased the king who named Bismarck prime minister and later foreign minister. As reward for putting together the German Empire, he was appointed chancellor in 1871.

Once the German Empire was created, Bismarck kept the new nation out of war. He spent Germany's resources on building up the nation. His views clashed with the new kaiser, William II. The kaiser wanted Germany to play a larger role in world politics. Bismarck was forced to step down in 1890.

by the kaiser. The result was an **authoritarian** government. All power was in the hands of the ruler.

Although a nationalist, Bismarck became a strong conservative. He believed that people would not demand political rights if their basic needs were met. As a result, once Germany was united, Bismarck focused on the economy. Among Bismarck's actions was raising tariffs to protect German manufacturing. The banking system was also strengthened. A few laws were passed to aid workers. Workers who were too sick or injured to work were paid for six months. An old-age pension was set up for retired workers aged 70 and older. Bismarck's motive for these laws was to prevent workers from joining a new socialist political party.

By the end of the 1870s, Germany was the greatest industrial power in Europe. By 1910, it had surpassed Great Britain.

Germany, like Great Britain, had coal and iron resources to fuel industrialization. It also had a large population, so there were plenty of workers for the growing factories. Like Bismarck, wealthy business owners were conservatives. They supported strong government and militarism. By 1910, all these factors combined to make Germany the largest industrial nation in Europe.

Putting It All Together

Each paragraph under the subheading "Building German Power at Home" has a different topic. Draw four columns in your notebook. Label each column with the topic of one of the four paragraphs. Then list additional information about each topic in the correct column. Share your chart with a partner to make sure you have included all the important details about each topic.

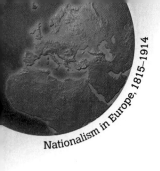

Chapter Summary

- In 1848, a series of revolutions broke out in Europe. The first was in France. It resulted in Louis-Napoleon becoming emperor of the Second Republic.

- Major uprisings also took place in the Austrian Empire. To **appease** revolutionaries, the emperor made some changes.

- The 1800s saw disagreements between **conservatives** and **liberals** over the proper role of government. Conservatives tried to keep a **balance of power**.

- A spirit of nationalism inspired **ethnic groups** within the Austrian Empire to fight to have their own nations.

- In 1859, Camillo di Cavour was allied with France. Together, they defeated the Austrian Empire.

- **Nationalists** in other northern states on the Italian peninsula **deposed** their governments and united with the Kingdom of Piedmont.

- Giuseppe Garibaldi and his Red Shirts defeated the Kingdom of the Two Sicilies in southern Italy.

- Otto von Bismarck was a strong supporter of **militarism**.

- Bismarck set out to **dominate** territory from Denmark and to break Austria's control over German territory. He created a North German Confederation.

- The Franco-Prussian War lasted six months. William I was asked to become **kaiser**.

- The government of the new Germany was **authoritarian**. Its economy was based on **industrialization**. Germany soon became the largest industrial nation in Europe.

Chapter Review

1 Review your list of reasons why people would want to become part of a large nation. Choose three reasons and write a short essay explaining the reasons.

2 Write two-line headlines for each of the following: (a) 1848 revolutions, (b) alliance between Cavour and Napoleon III, (c) Garibaldi and the Red Shirts, (d) Franco-Prussian War, (e) crowning of William I, (f) firing of Bismarck.

Skill Builder

Analyzing a Political Cartoon

Political cartoonists use the current events of their time as topics for their cartoons. As a result, political cartoons, like photographs and paintings, can be valuable tools to study history.

The goal of a political cartoonist is to make people think about an issue. However, a political cartoonist has a point of view. He or she may be for or against the issue and may want readers to agree with that point of view. The bias is usually easy to detect.

Political cartoonists use symbols and caricature to make their point. A symbol is a person or object that stands for something else. For example, a crown may represent Louis XVI in an 18th-century cartoon about the abuses of the French monarchy.

To analyze political cartoons:

1. Identify the characters and other images used in the cartoon.
2. Identify the topic of the cartoon. Determine what is happening and read all labels and writing.
3. Identify the opinion, or point of view, of the cartoonist.

Complete the following activities. You may need to review the biography of Bismarck.

1 (a) Who is the man putting on his hat? (b) Who is the man wearing the crown?

2 Why is the man leaving?

3 Who is the woman watching what is happening?

4 (a) What object is the man with the crown holding? (b) Why do you think the political cartoonist used this symbol?

5 (a) What is the man with the crown sitting on? (b) Why do you think the political cartoonist used this symbol?

IMPERIALISM AND MODERNIZATION

(1800–1914)

Getting Focused

Skim this chapter to predict what you will be learning.
• Read the lesson titles and subheadings.
• Look at the illustrations and read the captions.
• Examine the maps.
• Review the vocabulary words and terms.

Suppose you are the leader of a kingdom in Africa or Asia. A European government has sent troops to take over your country and officials to tell you how to run your government. You are angry and decide to write a letter to the European government explaining your position. What would you say? Work with a partner to create a list of reasons why the Europeans should leave. Use the list to write your letter.

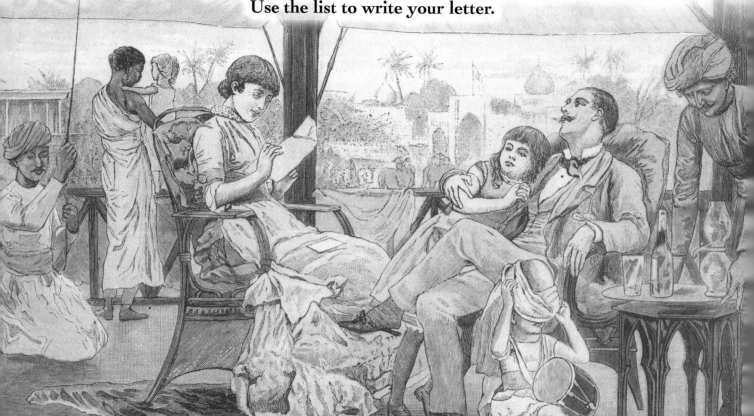

British Rule in India

Thinking on Your Own

Draw two columns in your notebook. Label the left column "Causes of Imperialism" and the right column "Facts and Examples." As you read, fill in the chart with causes. Then add facts and examples found in the lesson to explain each cause.

The Industrial Revolution speeded up the economic development of Europe and the United States. It also established the way industrial nations viewed their colonies. They began to see the colonies as markets for goods as well as sources of raw materials. The result was a new stage of **imperialism**. This activity took place in Africa, Asia, and Latin America.

For the first time, the United States began looking overseas for areas to colonize. At the same time, the U.S. wanted to keep Europeans out of the Americas. U.S. presidents in the late 1800s reminded Europeans of the Monroe Doctrine. This document was written in 1823 by President James Monroe. It declared the Western Hemisphere closed to further colonization by European nations. In reality, the U.S. used the Monroe Doctrine to control the Americas.

focus your reading

What factors caused imperialism in the 19th century?

Explain how the British gained control of India.

How did the British rule India?

Summarize the Indian Nationalist Movement.

vocabulary

imperialism	racism
markets	sepoys
humanitarian	Westernize

Causes of the New Imperialism

The major reason for European interest in imperialism was economic. The factories and mills of the Industrial Revolution required vast amounts of raw materials, like cotton. Regions in Africa, Asia, and Latin America had raw materials in abundance.

Once goods, such as cloth, were produced, European and U.S. business owners needed **markets**—people to whom they could sell the finished goods. European and U.S. business owners could sell their goods to their home countries. However, Africa, Asia, and Latin America represented huge new markets.

Setting up colonies ensured that the flow of raw materials to the home country continued. It also ensured that the home country controlled the sale of goods in the colonies.

The colonies provided raw materials for businesses in Europe and the United States.

In addition to economic reasons, a spirit of nationalism motivated imperialists. European nations were still competing with one another for power and wealth. This competition started the beginning of the global age. Setting up colonies was one way to show how one nation was more powerful and wealthy than another. The United States began to build an overseas empire for this reason.

Humanitarian reasons also moved some people to support imperialism. Humanitarians often thought that native people should be more like Europeans. Sometimes, humanitarians were helpful, like when medicine and education were provided. However, they often caused more harm than good. The main force behind humanitarianism was Social Darwinism. Social Darwinists believed that Western civilization—European and U.S.—was far superior to all other civilizations. As a result, they believed that whites had a responsibility to convert and educate native peoples. They thought that helping colonized people was the "white man's burden." This belief in Western superiority is a type of **racism**—the belief that one race is superior to another.

The East India Company and the Sepoy Rebellion

European nations first competed for colonies in India. In the 1600s, the British East India Company began trading in India and elsewhere in Asia. France also established trading posts in India. War broke out between the two nations in India in the 1750s. The British, under the command of Robert Clive, were victorious. The French were limited to a few small areas in southeastern India.

Clive was the head of the East India Company in India. His job was to increase the Company's wealth. To gain more trading rights, he fought the Indians as well as the French. In 1757, Clive's forces defeated a Mogul army at the Battle of Plassey. The East India Company slowly extended its rule across the Indian subcontinent.

By the 1850s, more than 60 percent of India was under the control of the East India Company. The Company did make life better, in some ways, for some Indians. It set up schools, improved roads, and built railroads. It also kept peace between rival local leaders. At the same time, the Company grew more and more powerful and wealthy. Many of the officials of the

Indian workers and British officials at the British East India Company.

Company, as well as other British merchants who went to India, made fortunes from Indian resources and labor.

The Company had its own army and forts to protect its property and British citizens. It also hired Indian soldiers known as **sepoys**. In 1857, the Company gave these soldiers new rifles. To load them, the soldiers had to bite off the end of the powder cartridges with their teeth. The cartridges were greased with fat either from cows, which were sacred to Hindus, or pigs, which Muslims were forbidden to eat.

When the sepoys refused to put the cartridges in their mouths, they were sent home without pay. They rebelled against this unfair treatment. British men, women, and children were slaughtered. It took a year for the British to

The Sepoy Rebellion was known as the First War of Independence by Indians.

regain control of the rebellious regions. The British, in turn, burned villages and slaughtered Indians. The British Parliament acted quickly. It ended the East India Company's control of India. Beginning in 1858, India was ruled directly by Parliament. It sent more British troops to India.

British Rule

Parliament appointed a viceroy to govern India. A civil service was set up with British officials in top positions. British officers also commanded the army. However, lower government posts were filled by Indians. Most soldiers were also Indians. Upper-class Indian families sent their sons to Great Britain for their education.

The effect of British rule on India was disastrous for most Indians. First, British manufacturers sent British-made cloth to India for sale. This destroyed the Indian textile industry because the imported cloth was cheaper. Second, the British collected taxes from Indians to keep the British army in India.

stop and think

The Indians call the uprising in 1857 the First War of Independence. The British call it the Sepoy Rebellion. These names represent opposite opinions about the same event. Write a paragraph from the viewpoint of a British citizen to justify the term *Sepoy Rebellion*. Then write a paragraph from the viewpoint of an Indian to justify the term *First War of Independence*. Share your writings with a partner. Discuss how you could make your arguments stronger.

Colonial British often lived luxurious lives in India.

Trade increased between India and Europe when the Suez Canal opened in 1869.

This bankrupted some Indian farmers. Third, the British need for cotton moved many Indian farmers to grow cotton instead of food. As a result, famines in the late 1800s caused millions of deaths among India's poor.

The Indian Nationalist Movement

By the late 1800s, a small group of upper-class Indians was working to end imperial rule. They had learned about such Western ideas as democracy and freedom in their British schools. In 1885, they set up the Indian National Congress, or Congress Party. They expected a gradual end to British rule. They agreed with British ideas about modernizing—or **Westernizing**—the Indian economy and society. They also wanted a greater say in governing.

In 1906, Muslim nationalists broke away from the Congress Party. They set up their own All-India Muslim League. They were already talking about a separate Muslim nation once the British left.

Representatives at an early Indian National Congress meeting

Putting It All Together

Create a T-chart. On one side write "Benefits to Indians from British Rule." On the other side write "Costs to Indians." With a partner discuss whether the Indians were better off or worse off under the British.

LESSON 2

The Scramble for Africa

Thinking on Your Own

Continue to fill in the "Causes of Imperialism" and "Facts and Examples" chart that you began in Lesson 1. Use as many vocabulary words as you can in your chart.

"The scramble for Africa" refers to the race among European nations to seize parts of the continent. In 1850, there were only a few small European colonies along the coasts of Africa. By 1914, Europeans had carved up the entire continent. Only Ethiopia and Liberia remained independent nations.

European nations viewed Africa much as they did other less-developed parts of the world. It was a source of ivory, copper, and other raw materials. They also saw Africa as a market for European goods. Europeans also wanted to stamp out the slave trade and bring Christianity to Africa. By 1850, most European nations had outlawed the African slave trade. But Arab and African traders still bought and sold slaves.

> **focus your reading**
>
> How was the African continent divided among European nations?
>
> What were the different ways that Europeans ruled their colonies?
>
> Describe how Africans resisted colonial rule.
>
> **vocabulary**
>
> partition   assimilate
>
> indirect rule   elite
>
> direct rule

Partitioning Africa

The first Europeans to move into the interior were explorers who mapped Africa's rivers, mountains, and plains. European missionaries soon followed. The goal of missionaries was to convert the native people to Christianity and to abolish slavery. As in India, local civilizations were considered inferior to Western culture. European merchants and settlers also moved into the African interior.

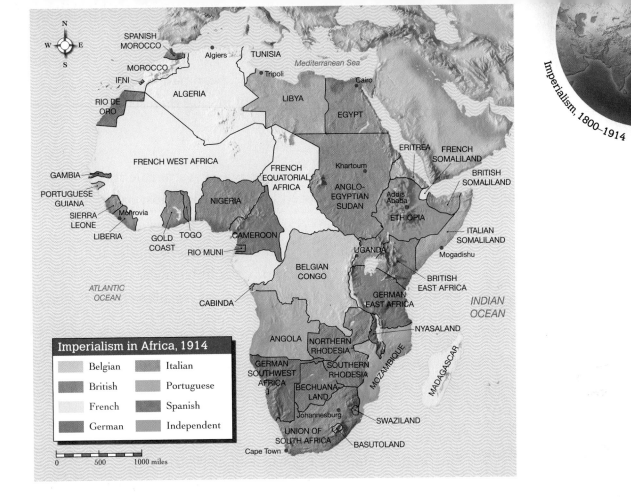

Imperialism, 1800–1914

Imperialism in Africa, 1914

Belgian	Italian
British	Portuguese
French	Spanish
German	Independent

0   500   1000 miles

stop and think

Write four statements about the information shown on the map on this page. Then turn your statements into questions. Take turns asking and answering questions with a partner.

Africans often resisted these groups. The Europeans then asked their home countries for military protection. Their governments sent troops with instructions to end the problem and build permanent forts. Once in Africa, the military was there to stay.

By the early 1880s, European nations were quarrelling among themselves over territory in Africa. In 1884, German Chancellor Otto von Bismarck called a conference in Berlin to **partition**—or divide up—the continent by formal treaty. Fourteen European nations and the United States were represented. Not one African nation or person was invited.

Germany and Great Britain agreed on the division of East Africa. King Leopold of Belgium personally took control of Central Africa. Portugal's claim to territory was also recognized. Some earlier claims of nations, such as those of France, were also

This cartoon from the late 1800s portrays European countries "carving up the African pie."

recognized. Between 1885 and 1914, European nations continued to divide the African continent among themselves.

Colonial Rule

European nations mainly chose one of two ways to rule their new colonies. The British favored **indirect rule**. Most other nations used **direct rule**.

The Belgian Congo was the most brutal of all colonial administrations.

The British ruled through existing rulers and local officials. The British believed it would be easier to maintain law and order if the people were allowed to keep some of their traditions and customs. This included their political system. British officials, however, made all the decisions. Local African officials simply carried them out.

The French used direct rule. The government in France appointed a governor for each colony. Below him were a number of government officials. The highest levels were filled with men sent from France. Lower levels, down to the local villages, were filled by native Africans.

Biography

Menelik II (1844–1913)

Ethiopia remained independent while other African kingdoms were seized by Europeans. Why? The answer is Emperor Menelik II. He came to the throne of Ethiopia in 1889. By that time, France and Italy had set up colonies on Ethiopia's borders. He knew that to stay free, his kingdom would need to modernize—and quickly.

Menelik began with education. He used European teachers to modernize the curriculum. He upgraded the Ethiopian army. He played Italy off against France to buy new weapons from both. He also strengthened ties with local leaders of different groups across Ethiopia.

In 1895, Italy went to war against Ethiopia. At the Battle of Adowa in 1896, the Ethiopians overwhelmingly defeated the invading Italians. Menelik led an army of 90,000 soldiers against a badly outnumbered Italian army. Italy was forced to sign a peace treaty recognizing Ethiopia's independence. Europe was shocked that an African nation had defeated a European power.

The French wanted to **assimilate** their African subjects. The French government set out to introduce French culture, including its political system, to its colonies. The goal was to have Africans think and act like French men and women. As in India, the British and French encouraged the ruling **elite**—the upper class—to send their sons to school in Europe. These young men provided educated rulers and officials in later years. Most Africans, however, were little affected by assimilation.

Muhammad Ahmad al-Mahdi attacks British General Gordon in Khartoum.

African Resistance

The educated elite saw both the good and bad side of Westernization—the acceptance of Western culture. They learned about Western ideas like freedom and democracy. Yet, they saw how Western democracies refused to extend these rights to their colonies. By the early 1900s, groups of nationalists in many colonies were working for independence from imperialist rule.

In some areas, local groups fought European rule. In 1885, Muhammad Ahmad al-Mahdi and his followers crushed British forces led by General Charles Gordon at Khartoum in Sudan. The British ended the uprising 13 years later.

The Asante fought the British in West Africa and lost. Britain annexed the region in 1901. In East Africa, the Maji-Maji rebelled against the Germans in 1905 but were defeated. Each time, the superior weapons of the Europeans ended African defiance.

Putting It All Together

Why were Europeans able to carve up Africa so quickly? Make a bulleted list of reasons and share them with a partner. Then write an essay of two or three paragraphs to explain your reasons.

LESSON 3

Modernizing Japan

Thinking on Your Own

What do you think *modernizing* means? Examine the subheadings and illustrations in this lesson. Then write a three- or four-sentence definition of the word *modernizing*. Use examples from the subheads and illustrations to support your definition.

One Asian nation that was able to stay free of European control was Japan. It took the West as a model and modernized quickly. It learned Western ways so well that it became an imperialist power.

focus your reading

Explain how Japan was opened to outsiders in the 1850s.

What changes did the Meiji Restoration make in Japan?

Why did Japan become an imperialist power?

vocabulary

isolation

fleet

Meiji Restoration

subsidy

Opening to Western Influences

The Tokugawa Shogunate came to power in Japan in 1603. By the mid-1600s, it had closed off Japan to outsiders. It maintained diplomatic relations only with Korea. In the mid-1800s, however, the United States decided to force an end to Japan's **isolation**. The goal was to open trade with the island nation.

In 1853, Commodore Matthew Perry and a **fleet** of four U.S. warships sailed into Tokyo Bay. Perry presented a letter from President Millard Fillmore to the emperor. The letter demanded that Japan open diplomatic and trading relations with the United States. Perry and his fleet sailed out of the bay with a promise to return. Japanese officials debated the issue for six months. They determined that Japan could not win against the cannon power on Perry's warships.

Emperor Mutsuhito

Commodore Perry arriving in Tokyo Bay in 1853

At the end of the six months, Perry sailed back with a larger fleet of warships. The Japanese government reluctantly agreed to a treaty with the United States. Japan also was forced to sign similar treaties with the major European nations.

Meiji Restoration

Not all Japanese were pleased with the new agreements. But they came to realize that Japan could not defeat the westerners. In 1867, rival leaders forced the end of the Tokugawa Shogunate. They said they "restored" power to the emperor. The emperor, however, did not govern. As under the shoguns, the men who kept the emperor in power controlled the government.

The period from 1868 to 1912 is called the **Meiji Restoration**. The word Meiji means "enlightened rule." During this period, Japanese officials modernized and Westernized the nation. They made a careful and systematic study of Western technology and science, as well as political and economic ideas. They put an end to feudalism and made Japan an industrial nation.

The Meiji adopted a constitution modeled after Germany's. An executive branch was set up with a prime minister and cabinet who supposedly reported to the emperor. Real power, however, remained in the hands of a small group of

Traditional Japanese values (top) were influenced by Western ideas (bottom) during the Meiji Restoration.

Meiji officials. They selected the prime minister and cabinet. The constitution also established a legislature of two houses. The upper house was appointed by the emperor. The lower house was elected by male voters.

Japanese factories made silk cloth in the late 1800s.

The legislature had little power. Japan also adopted a legal system modeled after the French system.

Industrialization was an important part of the Meiji's plans for Japan. They realized that a farming economy would not make Japan a rich country and a strong state. To aid industrial growth, the government created a **subsidy** program. A subsidy is a payment by a government to nongovernment entities. The Japanese government provided money to help start new industries. By 1900, Japan was becoming a leading producer of silk cloth, steel, ships, and weapons.

To aid modernization, the Meiji used British expertise to build the first Japanese railroad and a telegraph system. Western-style banking and postal systems were also organized. Harbors and roads were improved. The Meiji also set up a modern army and navy. All men had to serve in the army for three years.

Modernization also included changes in society. The public education system was modeled on the U.S. system. All boys and girls were required to attend school for six years. Many of the subjects were the same as those studied by students in other countries. The schools also taught traditional Japanese values.

stop and think

Create a concept web to show the changes that occurred in Japan as a result of the Meiji Restoration. Draw a large circle and label it "Meiji Restoration." Draw and label a smaller circle for each change caused by the Meiji. Connect the smaller circles to the large circle with lines.

Japanese Imperialism

As an island nation, Japan faced many problems in trying to become an industrial power. Japan lacked many of the natural resources, such as coal, that were needed for industry. Gaining colonies would provide sources of raw materials. Colonies would also provide larger markets for Japanese goods.

There was one additional roadblock. Although there are thousands of islands in the Japanese island chain, almost all the population lived on four islands. As Japan industrialized, the population grew. This meant more workers, but also a lack of living space. Moving some of the population to colonies would ease the strain of overpopulation.

In 1874, the Meiji made the decision to build an empire overseas. They seized the Ryukyu Islands off the coast of China. In 1895, Japan defeated China in the Sino-Japanese War and added Taiwan to its territory. In 1905, Japan and Russia went to war. Western nations were shocked at Japan's easy victory over Russia. No Asian nation had defeated a Western power before. Each time, Japan added territory to its empire.

In 1910, Japan was bold enough to make Korea part of its nation. It attempted to do in Korea what Western nations were doing in other parts of the world. Japan took most of Korea's wealth for itself. It imposed the Japanese language on Koreans and tried to stamp out their culture. The result was the development of a nationalist movement similar to those growing in other colonies.

Japanese Expansion, 1870–1918

- Japanese Empire, 1870
- Japanese acquisitions to 1910

PACIFIC OCEAN · South Sakhalin (1905) · Kuril Islands · Hokkaido · RUSSIA · MANCHURIA · MONGOLIA · Vladivostok · Honshu · Sea of Japan · JAPAN · Beijing · Port Arthur · KOREA (1910) · Kyoto · Osaka · Shimonoseki · Tokyo (Edo) · Yellow Sea · Tsushima Strait · Shikoku · Kyushu · Nagasaki · Shanghai · East China Sea · Ryukyu Islands (1874) · CHINA · TAIWAN (1895) · 0–600 miles

Putting It All Together

List the reasons why Japan became an imperial power. Share your list with a partner to make sure you included everything. Then write a short essay explaining the reasons and outcomes of Japanese imperialism.

Soldiers in the Russo-Japanese war, 1905

LESSON 4

European Powers and the Chinese Revolution

Thinking on Your Own

This lesson describes foreign pressures on China and its political changes over more than 80 years. As you read, create one timeline that shows both series of events.

The first Qing (CHING) emperor came to power in 1644. After ruling more than 200 years, the Dynasty might have collapsed without outside help. The Qing was so corrupt that in time, people would have overthrown it. However, the demands of foreign nations added to the problems of the Chinese government and weakened it even more.

The Empress Dowager Ci Xi ruled in the name of her son and nephew for almost 50 years and added to the problems of the Qing and China.

focus your reading

How did foreign nations gain spheres of influence?

Discuss the causes of the fall of the Qing Dynasty.

Describe the role Sun Yat-sen played in the founding of the Chinese Republic.

vocabulary

extraterritoriality

concessions

spheres of influence

self-strengthening

Foreign Pressures

By the early 1800s, British merchants were importing opium from India into China. The Chinese government demanded that the British government halt the opium trade. Opium is an addictive drug. The Chinese appealed to the morality of the British. However, the British government refused to stop the British East India Company. When the Chinese attempted to end the trade themselves in 1839, the British attacked several cities. This was the beginning of the three-year Opium War. The Chinese were not equipped to fight the modern British army and navy. In the end, the Chinese government backed down and signed the Treaty of Nanjing. The British opium trade continued.

Chinese and French forces fought for control of Nam-Dinh, in northern Vietnam, on July 19, 1883.

China agreed to

- repay Great Britain for its costs in the war
- open five treaty port cities to foreign trade
- allow Westerners to live in their own sections under their own laws in these treaty ports.
  This is known as **extraterritoriality**.
- give Great Britain the island of Hong Kong

The Opium War was only the beginning of foreign pressure on the Chinese government. Over the next 50 years, foreign nations won more **concessions** from China, usually by force. China fought and lost five wars between 1842 and 1895. As a result of unequal treaties, foreign nations were able to carve out **spheres of influence** for themselves. A sphere of influence was an area where only the foreign power had the right to trade with the Chinese. By 1912, foreign nations controlled more than 50 treaty ports and the areas around them.

The United States did not have its own sphere of influence. In 1899, John Hay, the U.S. secretary of state, played the foreign powers in China off against one another. He forced them to accept an Open Door Policy. All nations would have equal rights to trade in China. This made it easier for U.S. companies to do business in China.

Hong Kong was returned to the People's Republic in 1997.

Internal Pressures

At the same time the Chinese government was dealing with foreign nations, it was trying to deal with internal problems. China was suffering from a population explosion and food shortages. Officials in the bureaucracy could be easily bribed. The government could not collect enough tax revenue to cover its costs. Peasants and urban workers made up the majority of the population. They lived in terrible poverty.

Imperialism, 1800–1914

The anger of the lower class erupted into open rebellion in 1850. The Tai Ping Rebellion lasted until 1864 when the Chinese government crushed it with foreign help. By that time, some 20 million Chinese had died in the uprising. Its leader was Hong Xiuquan (HOONG shee•OH•chew•an), who had converted to Christianity. He called for land reforms and equal treatment for women.

stop and think

As you read, make a list of the external and internal problems that China faced during the 1800s. At the end of this lesson, compare your list with that of a partner.

Qing officials realized that something had to be done to regain their power. By 1870, local warlords were challenging the central government. The Qing began a period of reform known as **self-strengthening**. The most radical reformers wanted to introduce democracy. However, they lost to Qing officials who wanted to keep the Confucian system of governing.

These officials accepted the need to introduce Western technology and science but nothing else. As a result, China began industrializing. Railroads, shipyards, weapons factories, and other types of factories were built. The army was modernized. However, the government continued to be based on Confucian values and the civil service system.

The final blow to the Qing Dynasty was the Boxer Rebellion. The Boxers were a secret society whose members swore to

The Boxer Rebellion

destroy foreigners. In 1900, they began killing foreigners across China, especially Christian missionaries. They trapped foreign residents in Beijing, China's capital. France, Germany, Great Britain, Japan, Russia, and the United States sent troops to rescue them. This ended the rebellion. Once again, China had to give up more treaty ports. It also had to make another huge payment to the foreign nations for their losses during the rebellion.

The Founding of the Chinese Republic

The Boxer Rebellion frightened the Qing officials into action. The civil service examination system was ended. A new public school system was adopted in its place. Women were allowed to attend school. A new national assembly was set up but had no law-making powers. Its role was to advise Qing officials. None of these changes, however, reached the peasants or urban workers.

One result of China's growing Westernization was the development of a middle class. Often the sons of these families were sent to study in the United States or Europe. They came back wanting to replace the emperor with a government based on Western principles. One of these young men was Sun Yat-sen. He called for a new government that adapted Western ideas to Chinese needs. He called his policy *Three Principles of the People*. His principles were nationalism, democracy, and livelihood — or economic well-being for everyone.

Sun Yat-sen speaking at a gathering

Throughout the early 1900s, various groups began uprisings but nothing came of them. Then in 1911, one uprising succeeded. Within months, the rebels held most of southern China. Sun, who had been in the United States, rushed back to China. A republic was declared, and Sun was elected president by his followers.

However, Sun's Nationalist party was not strong enough to seize control of China from local warlords. In 1912, Sun resigned in favor of Yuan Shigai (YOO•AHN SHUR•GIE). Yuan was himself a powerful warlord from northern China who promised to rule democratically. However, once in power, he had no interest in creating a democratic China. He wanted to set up his own dynasty and rule as emperor. Yuan was overthrown in 1916. Civil war and foreign invasions marked China's history until 1949. In that year, Mao Zedong finally unified China under a Communist government.

Putting It All Together

Create a chart with the following four columns: "Opium War," "Boxer Rebellion," "Treaty of Nanjing," and "Sun Yat-sen." Under each, list one or two ways imperialism influenced each topic. Then use your chart to write a paragraph explaining how imperialism influenced China.

LESSON **5**

Imperialism in Latin America

Thinking on Your Own

As you read this lesson, make an outline of the important points. Use Roman numerals I, II, and III for your subheadings. Include details under each Roman numeral in their order of importance, from most important to least important.

The independence movements in the 1800s ended Spanish and Portuguese rule in Central and South America. However, independence brought little political or social change to Latin Americans. A huge gap still existed between the rich upper class and the generally poor mestizos, mulattos, and blacks. The majority of wealth in the new nations remained in the hands of large landowners. These landowners were also the most politically powerful people in the new nations. They ran the national governments and saw that government policies favored their interests.

> **focus your reading**
>
> Explain how Latin American nations became economically dependent on the United States and European nations.
>
> In what ways did the United States use force to gain territory in Latin America?
>
> How was the Roosevelt Corollary used to intervene in Latin America?
>
> **vocabulary**
>
> economic imperialism
>
> cash crops
>
> protectorate
>
> annex

Economic Imperialism

Once free of Spain and Portugal, the new nations adopted free-trade policies. Their major trading partners became Great Britain and the United States. British and U.S. investors also bought large amounts of farmland in some countries and ran plantations and ranches. During the Industrial Revolution, foreign investors also built factories to produce goods for local and overseas sale.

Workers on a United Fruit plantation around 1900

However, Latin American nations did not become industrialized like the United States and European nations. They remained farming nations.

It was in the economic interests of the United States and European nations to keep Latin Americans dependent on them for manufactured goods. If Latin American nations industrialized, their trading partners would lose their markets. This Latin American dependence on the United States and European nations was a form of imperialism. It was **economic imperialism**. The buyers set the prices because Latin American producers had nowhere else to sell their crops and raw materials. As a result, foreign companies and investors made fortunes from Latin American resources and labor. Local landowners and business owners also grew rich from trade.

Latin American nations exported raw materials such as tobacco, wool, rubber, and silver. They also exported **cash crops** such as wheat, sugar, cotton, bananas, and coffee. Cash crops are crops grown to be sold to others rather than to be used by the farmer. In exchange, companies in Britain, the United States, and other European nations sold Latin Americans finished goods, such as cloth and machinery.

stop and think

To help you remember the information about economic imperialism, write a summary of this section. Share your summary with a partner. Ask your partner to make sure that you have included all the major points.

United States Intervention

The United States issued the Monroe Doctrine in 1823. Its purpose was to close the Americas to any future European colonization. Some European nations were considering sending troops to restore Spanish power over its former colonies. European nations did not think the new United States could stop them. However, Great Britain supported the goal of the Monroe Doctrine. The British navy was the strongest navy in the world, and no nation wanted to engage it in battle. As a result, nothing came of the idea of European intervention.

As it turned out, the United States took territory from a former Spanish colony. As a result of the Mexican War from 1846 to 1848, the United States gained what are the present

states of California, Nevada, Utah, and parts of Arizona, New Mexico, Colorado, and Wyoming. Texas, which had declared its independence from Mexico earlier, asked to join the United States. This had begun the war.

The United States gained more territory as a result of the Spanish-American War in 1898. The United States came to the aid of Cuban patriots trying to free their island from Spain. After the war, the United States made Cuba a **protectorate**. The United States set up a government for the island and declared that Cuba was under its protection. Cuba did not gain independence until 1934. The United States also **annexed** Puerto Rico after the war. Unlike Cuba, Puerto Rico became a territory of the United States. U.S. territories are directly governed by the United States. In 1917, U.S. citizenship was given to Puerto Ricans. In 1952, Puerto Rico became a commonwealth with its own governor and legislature. However, it continues a voluntary association with the United States.

By 1900, the United States also had political and economic interests in the Pacific. For example, it had recently annexed Hawaii and taken control of the Philippine Islands in the Pacific. The U.S. needed to be able to move its warships and merchant ships quickly from one coast to the other. The only way to do this was to build a canal through Central America. The best place seemed to be Panama, which was then part of Colombia. A French company had already started a canal there in 1881.

When there seemed no other way to gain control of the area, the United States aided a rebellion in Panama in 1903. President Theodore Roosevelt

Benito Juarez, the son of Native-American peasants, served as president of Mexico from 1861–1865 and again from 1867–1872. He initiated many social reforms, including separation of Church and state, distribution of land to the poor, and universal public education.

Workers digging the Panama Canal

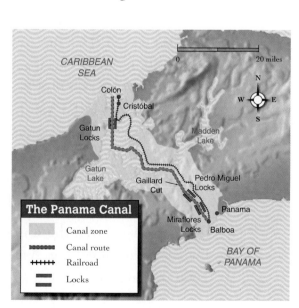

CARIBBEAN SEA

Colón
Cristóbal
Gatun Locks
Gatun Lake
Madden Lake
Gaillard Cut
Pedro Miguel Locks
Panama
Miraflores Locks
Balboa
BAY OF PANAMA

0   20 miles

The Panama Canal

Canal zone
Canal route
Railroad
Locks

sent warships to threaten Colombia. Colombia had little choice and allowed the rebels to declare independence. The Panamanians gave the United States control of what became the Panama Canal Zone. The canal opened in 1914.

The Roosevelt Corollary

In 1904, Venezuelans could not repay debts to German and British businesses and investors. It looked as though these foreign governments might send troops to collect payment. President Roosevelt acted first. He announced in 1904 that the United States would police the Western Hemisphere. It would keep order and prevent wrongdoing. Great Britain, Germany, and Venezuela negotiated a settlement. President Roosevelt's policy is known as the Roosevelt Corollary to the Monroe Doctrine.

The Roosevelt Corollary is often referred to as the "Big Stick" policy.

The United States used its self-appointed police powers the following year. Several European nations appeared ready to invade the Dominican Republic to collect its citizens' debts. Instead, Roosevelt insisted that the president of the Dominican Republic ask the United States to collect taxes. U.S. officials used the tax money to repay the foreign businesses and took a fee for the United States. The United States remained in the Dominican Republic until 1941.

Eventually, the U.S. government sent military forces into Cuba, Mexico, Guatemala, Honduras, Nicaragua, Panama, Colombia, and Haiti to protect U.S. interests. Sometimes they stayed for years. Besides the Dominican Republic, for example, U.S. forces remained in Haiti from 1915 to 1934. This action often gave rise to hard feelings against the United States.

Putting It All Together

Create a concept map of U.S. intervention in Latin America. Include the use of the Roosevelt Corollary. Draw a large circle and label it "U.S. Intervention." Then draw smaller circles for each example. Draw lines to connect them to the large circle.

Imperialism and Modernization 313

Chapter Summary

- Four factors contributed to **imperialism**: economics, nationalism, **humanitarianism**, and Social Darwinism. Social Darwinism led to **racism**.
- The British East India Company governed and attempted to **Westernize** India until the **Sepoy** Rebellion.
- European nations **partitioned** Africa in the 1880s.
- Imperialist powers used two methods to govern their colonies: **indirect rule** and **direct rule**. The British used indirect rule and the local ruling **elite**. The French used direct rule and attempted to **assimilate** their colonists.
- Japan's **isolation** ended when a **fleet** of U.S. warships arrived in 1853.
- The **Meiji Restoration** tried to Westernize and industrialize Japan by providing **subsidies**.
- Nations carved out **spheres of influence**. China also had to agree to **extraterritoriality** for foreign citizens. Foreign nations continued to demand **concessions** to Chinese **markets**.
- The **self-strengthening** movement resulted in some reforms in China in the late 1800s.
- **Economic imperialism** in Latin America led to exported raw materials and **cash crops** in exchange for manufactured goods.
- After the Spanish-American War, the United States made Cuba a **protectorate** and **annexed** Puerto Rico.
- The Roosevelt Corollary enhanced the Monroe Doctrine.

Chapter Review

1 Imagine you are going to a protest against European imperialism in your nation. Design a sign to carry.

2 Imagine you are founding a nationalist organization in an African nation. List the goals for your organization. Then write a newspaper article supporting your position.

3 Write a letter to the editor either for or against U.S. policy in Latin America in the early 1900s.

Skill Builder

Creating and Analyzing Tables

Tables are good tools to use to sort information. They provide a way to focus on just the important information about a subject. There are a number of tables in this textbook. You have also been asked to make tables as study aids. The following are some general steps for making tables.

How to Make a Table

Step	Process
1	Decide on the categories you need to use to sort the information.
2	Create the form for your table. You will need a column for each category and a row for each topic you want to include under each category. Suppose you want to create a table about the nations of Central America. The categories you want to include are "Nations," "Population," "Type of Government," "Exports," and "Imports." That means you will need five columns. Your topics are the seven nations in Central America. Your table will need seven rows.
3	Find the information to complete your table. Sometimes, you might not find information for every box in every row. A blank box is just as important as one with information. A blank box tells you that the topic is missing something that others in the same category have. For example, suppose one of the categories on your table was "Oil." If one of the nations did not have that box filled in, you would know that it lacked a major export that would bring it money.
4	Write a title for your table.

Complete the following activities to practice using tables.

1 Create a table about the development of independence in Africa. You will need information from the lesson on pages 298–301. Your table will need three columns. Make 10 rows and select 10 independent nations in modern Africa. The labels for your columns are "Modern Nation," "Colonial Name," "Imperial Power." Some modern nations may have been part of more than one colony. Check your table with a partner to make sure that you listed every modern nation.

2 Discuss the information on the table with a partner. For example, count the number of modern nations that were once French colonies. Name the nations that were once British colonies.

7 UNIT

THE WORLD AT WAR

For much of the 20th century, the world was at war. World War I began in 1914 and ended in 1919. World War II began 20 years later and ended in 1945. During the period between the wars, the Russians overthrew the czar. A worldwide depression occurred. Dictators came to power in Italy, Germany, and the Soviet Union. Japan continued its pursuit of an empire through military force.

The end of World War II laid the basis for the Cold War. It was a war of nerves and words between the United States and the Soviet Union. However, the Soviet Union supported Communist takeovers in Eastern Europe. In other world regions, the two superpowers took opposite sides in civil wars.

Word War I
1914–1919

Russian Revolution; Lenin in control
1917

Hitler in control of Nazi Party
1921

Mussolini prime minister of Italy; Stalin in power in Soviet Union
1922

Stalin in control of Soviet Union
1928

Hitler named German chancellor
1933

Nazi Holocaust began
1938

What decisions made during World War II set the stage for the Cold War?

Why were Mussolini, Hitler, and Stalin able to come to power in the 1920s and 1930s?

How was World War I fought differently from earlier wars?

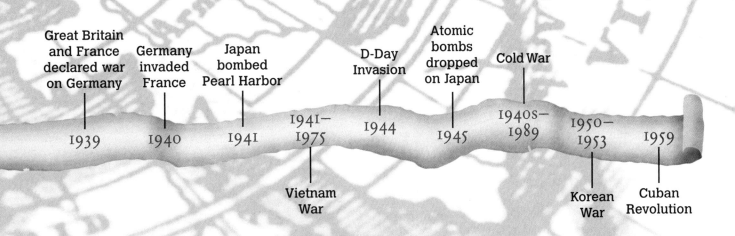

Great Britain and France declared war on Germany

1939

Germany invaded France

1940

Japan bombed Pearl Harbor

1941

1941–1975

Vietnam War

D-Day Invasion

1944

Atomic bombs dropped on Japan

1945

Cold War

1940s–1989

1950–1953

Korean War

1959

Cuban Revolution

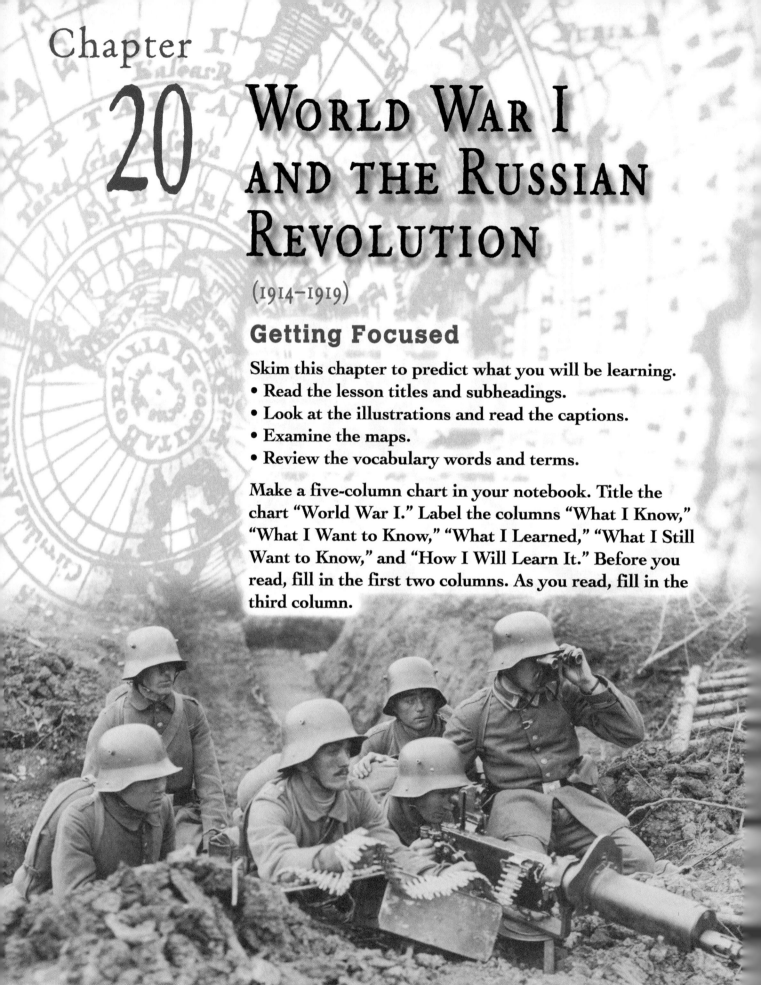

Chapter 20

WORLD WAR I AND THE RUSSIAN REVOLUTION

(1914–1919)

Getting Focused

Skim this chapter to predict what you will be learning.
- Read the lesson titles and subheadings.
- Look at the illustrations and read the captions.
- Examine the maps.
- Review the vocabulary words and terms.

Make a five-column chart in your notebook. Title the chart "World War I." Label the columns "What I Know," "What I Want to Know," "What I Learned," "What I Still Want to Know," and "How I Will Learn It." Before you read, fill in the first two columns. As you read, fill in the third column.

LESSON 1

War Breaks Out in Europe

Thinking on Your Own

Kaiser William II, of Germany, believed that the way to end disagreements between nations was by war. Do you agree or disagree with him? Think of three reasons to support your opinion. Read this lesson and then review your position. Revise your ideas if you have changed your mind or have found stronger reasons.

European nations competed for territory and economic gain in Asia and Africa in the late 1800s. Tensions between European nations grew. Eventually, these tensions affected Europe.

World War I

In the early 1900s, the situation in Europe was extremely tense. Its industrial nations competed for trade, markets, and colonies. Rivalry between these great powers was fueled by intense feelings of nationalism.

Suspicious of one another, the nations of Europe formed defensive alliances. In 1882, Germany, Austria-Hungary, and Italy organized the **Triple Alliance**. In 1907, France, Great Britain, and Russia formed the **Triple Entente**. In the spirit of militarism, most alliance members built up large navies

---

focus your reading

Discuss the causes of World War I.

Explain how new weapons of war changed the fighting.

What events led to the U.S. joining the war?

vocabulary

Triple Alliance

Triple Entente

trench warfare

stalemate

neutral

armistice

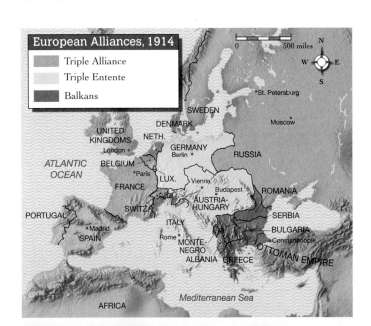

European Alliances, 1914

Triple Alliance
Triple Entente
Balkans

0   500 miles

ATLANTIC OCEAN

UNITED KINGDOMS
London
NETH.
DENMARK
SWEDEN
St. Petersburg
Moscow
GERMANY
Berlin
RUSSIA
BELGIUM
Paris
LUX.
FRANCE
Vienna
AUSTRIA-HUNGARY
Budapest
ROMANIA
PORTUGAL
SWITZ.
ITALY
Rome
SERBIA
BULGARIA
Constantinople
SPAIN
Madrid
MONTE-NEGRO
ALBANIA
GREECE
OTTOMAN EMPIRE
AFRICA
Mediterranean Sea

and well-equipped armies. They also made war plans that could be put into effect on short notice. Europe was becoming a region waiting to explode.

Ethnic nationalism in Austria-Hungary provided the spark. Many ethnic groups lived in larger nations, especially in Austria-Hungary and the Ottoman Empire. Once Italy and Germany were unified, these groups also wanted their own nations. The result was a series of uprisings. Russia supported the new nation of Serbia against Austria-Hungary. This added to tensions between the European alliances. Serbia was part of an area known as the Balkans. The area was now known as the "powder keg of Europe" because the situation there was so tense.

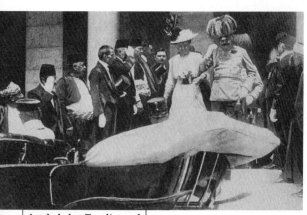

Archduke Ferdinand and his wife leave the Sarajevo Senate on June 28, 1914, minutes before their assassination.

The immediate cause of World War I was the assassination of Archduke Francis Ferdinand of Austria-Hungary and his wife, Sophia. They were shot by Gavrilo Princip, a young Serbian nationalist. He was a member of a group called the Black Hand. The organization wanted Bosnia to become part of the new kingdom of Serbia. Bosnia was part of Austria-Hungary at the time.

A Global War

During July and August, 1914, peace in Europe quickly fell apart. Austria blamed the Serbs for trying to break up its empire. It declared war against Serbia. Serbia's ally, Russia, then prepared its army for war. Fearing that Russia would attack it as well as Austria, Germany declared war on Russia. Russia was France's ally. When France offered to help Russia, Germany declared war against France. To attack France, Germany invaded neighboring Belgium. Belgium's ally, Britain, then declared war against Germany. Soon all of Europe was at war. As the war began, the Triple Alliance became known as the Central Powers. The Triple Entente became the Allies.

stop and think

Create a T-chart for the causes of World War I. Label the left column "Causes of World War I," and the right column "Details." As you read, add specific information about the causes. Share your T-chart with a partner.

World War I, 1914–1919

Trench warfare was a factor in the length of WWI.

Europe's leaders hoped the war would be over by Christmas, but it dragged on for four years. **Trench warfare** is one explanation. Each side dug trenches, or ditches, deep enough for a soldier to stand in. Both sides dug a line of trenches from the English Channel to Switzerland. The Western Front, or combat area in Western Europe, turned into a **stalemate**. Neither side was able to budge more than a few miles from this line for four years.

World War I Combatants
The Allies (Triple Entente)
Australia, Belgium, Brazil, Britain, Canada, China, Costa Rica, Cuba, France, Greece, Guatemala, Haiti, Honduras, India, Italy, Japan, Liberia, Montenegro, New Zealand, Nicaragua, Panama, Portugal, Romania, Russia, San Marino, Serbia, Siam, South Africa, United States

The Central Powers (Triple Alliance)
Austria-Hungary, Bulgaria, Germany, Ottoman Empire

On the Eastern Front, Germany and Austria-Hungary were more successful. Early in the war, they defeated Russia in several battles. The Russian army was poorly equipped. The Russians began retreating eastward in 1915. A revolution in 1917 ended Russia's role in the war.

In 1915, Italy left the Triple Alliance to join the war on the side of the Allies. An Italian army began an attack on Austro-Hungarian forces. Like Russia, Italy was badly defeated. Only the help of British and French troops saved Italy from being overrun.

Great Britain soon took the war to the Middle East. In 1916, the British aided a revolt by Arabs against the Ottoman Empire. Within two years, the empire of the Ottoman Turks had been greatly reduced. To fight its battles in the Middle East, Great Britain used colonial troops from India, Australia, and New Zealand. France used troops from its colony of Morocco in North Africa.

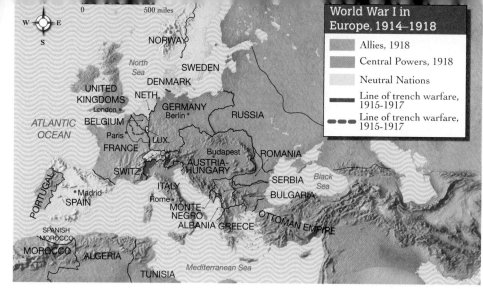

World War I in Europe, 1914–1918

	Allies, 1918
	Central Powers, 1918
	Neutral Nations
——	Line of trench warfare, 1915-1917
---	Line of trench warfare, 1915-1917

In Asia, Japan used the war to further its own imperial interests. It seized German islands in the Pacific. These islands included the Marshalls, the Marianas, and Carolines. It also took control of German areas in China, including Kiaochow, on China's Shantung Peninsula.

But the war in Europe dragged on until 1917. A revolution in Russia caused that nation to leave the war. There was no longer any danger to Germany on its eastern border. Germany could send all its forces against the Western Front. They hoped to end the stalemate and seize all of France.

A New Kind of War

Several inventions changed the way World War I was fought.

- Airplanes were used first for observation and later for bombing enemy targets.
- Machine guns fired large numbers of bullets rapidly at advancing soldiers. They helped to create trench warfare.
- Poison gas sickened and killed thousands. Gas masks were the only protection.
- Submarines, known as German U-boats, crippled Allied shipping.

The End of the European Stalemate

When the war broke out, President Woodrow Wilson asked Congress to declare the United States a **neutral** nation. It would take neither side in the war. However, events in Europe pushed the United States to enter the war in 1917. Those events included unrestricted submarine warfare and the Zimmermann telegram.

A cannon workshop in Germany in the Krupp factory

German U-boats torpedoed and sank both merchant and passenger ships. The United States had protested the policy in 1916 and Germany had stopped. However, in an effort to starve the British, the Germans restored the policy in 1917. President Wilson was furious. At the same time, the Zimmermann telegram became public. In it, Germany asked Mexico to enter the war on its side. In return, it promised that Mexico would receive Texas and the other territories it had lost to the United States in the 1800s.

In April 1917, the United States declared war on Germany. Within a year more than 1 million U.S. troops had arrived in Europe. They were in time to fight the final German advance. It began near Paris in April and lasted until September 1918.

By then it was clear that Germany could not win. It asked for peace. The Allies refused as long as the kaiser and his government remained in power. Uprisings began across Germany. The German people were tired of the misery of war. Without support, the kaiser stepped down. The Social Democrats, a political party, set up a German republic. The Allies agreed to an **armistice**, or cease fire. It was signed on November 11, 1918.

The sale of war bonds helped morale on the home front and kept soldiers supplied.

Putting It All Together

Create a timeline to track the sequence of events that led to the war, fighting the war, and the war's end. Review your timeline with a partner. Ask your partner if you have included all the important dates and events.

Making the Peace

Thinking on Your Own

As you read, create an outline of this lesson. Use the subheadings for Roman numerals I, II, and III. Be sure to include information in your outline in order of most important to least important. Use the vocabulary words in your outline.

B y the end of the war, Austria-Hungary no longer existed. Like Germany, the people rebelled. Ethnic groups took advantage of the war to claim nationhood. The Austro-Hungarian Empire was divided into the Kingdom of Yugoslavia and the republics of Austria, Hungary, and Czechoslovakia. Other ethnic groups in Eastern Europe also demanded independence. Would they get it? The Ottoman Empire was no longer strong and powerful. What would the Allies do with it? What would happen to Germany's colonies in Africa?

The war had been costly. Some 8.5 million people died. More than 17 million had been wounded. The regions where battles had been fought lay in ruins. National war debts had mounted into the millions. Who was going to pay for the rebuilding? Who was going to repay the war debts?

---

focus your reading

Describe the goals of the Big Three at the Paris Peace Conference.

How did the Treaty of Versailles change the map of Europe?

Summarize how the Treaty of Versailles dealt with the Middle East and Africa.

vocabulary

League of Nations

reparations

demilitarized zone

mandate system

Prime Minister Bethlen of Hungary addresses the crowd during elections.

Government officials draft the Treaty of Versailles in the Hall of Mirrors.

Treaty of Versailles

The Paris Peace Conference that began in 1919 tried to answer these questions. Great Britain, France, and the United States were the major decision makers at the conference. They were called the Big Three. Germany was not allowed to take part in the negotiations. German representatives were called in at the end to sign the final treaty, called the Treaty of Versailles.

The Big Three disagreed about what the peace settlement should contain. David Lloyd George, prime minister of Great Britain, wanted to punish Germany. He wanted Germany to pay the entire cost of the war. Georges Clemenceau, premier of France, shared this goal. He also wanted to make sure that Germany could never threaten France again. Germany had to be disarmed.

Woodrow Wilson, the U.S. President, had a very different goal for the Paris Peace Conference. He proposed setting up an international peacekeeping organization to settle disagreements between nations. He called his idea the **League of Nations**. It was one of Fourteen Points that he wanted included in the peace treaty. These included such worthwhile goals as the end to secret treaties, freedom of the seas, and the right of self-determination—or the right of all people to govern themselves.

In the end, Wilson gave up a number of his Fourteen Points. However, he held firm to his idea of a League of Nations. The Allies finally accepted it. However, the U.S. Senate refused to ratify the Treaty of Versailles. Senators

World War I, 1914–1919

Thousands attend a demonstration to protest the loss of the Alsace-Lorraine region in Germany.

worried that membership in the League meant the United States was giving up its ability to act in its own interests. Without the United States, little came of Wilson's grand idea of a global peacekeeping organization.

The final Treaty of Versailles included the following:

1. Germany and Austria-Hungary had to admit guilt for starting the war.
2. Germany had to pay $30 million in **reparations**—or damages—to the Allies for their costs in the war.
3. The German army and navy were reduced in size. Its air force was disbanded.
4. An area between Germany and France was set up as a **demilitarized zone**. No weapons or fortifications, like trenches, were allowed in the area.
5. Germany had to return territory to France that it had taken in the Franco-Prussian War. It also lost land to the new nation of Poland.
6. German colonies in Africa and Asia were taken.

Europe After World War I

New nations

Changes in Europe

The negotiators at the peace conference redrew the map of Eastern Europe. They took land from Germany, Austria-Hungary, and Russia. The redrawn map included the new, independent nations of Finland, Latvia, Estonia, Lithuania, Poland, Czechoslovakia, Austria, Hungary, and Yugoslavia.

Poland had once been an independent nation. However, 100 years before, Russia, Prussia, and Austria had divided it after a series of wars. Bosnian nationalists who started World War I got their wish. They were joined with Serbia and four other areas to become the nation of Yugoslavia. Yugoslavia also included large numbers of Croatians and Slovenes.

The Fourteen Points

On January 8, 1918, President Woodrow Wilson delivered a speech to a joint session of Congress. In it, he discussed Fourteen Points for reconstructing Europe at the end of World War I. Several of the points address broad topics such as abolishing secret treaties (Point I), freedom of the seas (Point II), arms reduction (Point IV), and the creation of a League of Nations (Point XIV).

I. Open covenants of peace, openly arrived at, after which there shall be no private international understanding of any kind but diplomacy shall proceed always frankly and in the public view.

II. Absolute freedom of navigation upon the seas, outside territorial waters, alike in peace and in war, except as the seas may be closed in whole or in part by international action for the enforcement of international covenants.

reading for understanding

Explain why a government may not support Point I.

How do countries today work to achieve the same goals listed in the Points?

What is the modern outcome of Point XIV?

IV. Adequate guarantees given and taken that national armaments will be reduced to the lowest point consistent with domestic safety.

XIV. A general association of nations must be formed under specific covenants for the purpose of affording mutual guarantees of political independence and territorial integrity to great and small states alike.

Read a Primary Source

This combining of different ethnic groups in a single nation had long-term consequences. Over centuries, different ethnic groups in Eastern Europe had migrated throughout the area. When the negotiators at the peace conference set new borders, they included ethnic minorities in most of the new nations. There was little the negotiators could do about it. Forcing these different groups to live within the same boundaries, however, would create problems in the future.

Middle East after World War I
New nations

The Mandate System

World War I ended the Ottoman Empire. During the war, Great Britain had helped Arabs in the Middle East fight the Ottoman Turks. The Arabs had been promised independence if they supported the Allies.

After the war, the Allies went back on their promises. Instead of granting independence, they created the **mandate system**. Under the mandate system, members of the League of Nations were responsible for setting up governments in former German territories. The Ottoman Empire was broken up and divided between France and Great Britain. Supposedly, Great Britain and France were to help the mandates modernize. When the mandates were considered ready, they were to become independent nations. This did not happen. The mandates were supposed to be governed under the authority of the League of Nations. However, Great Britain and France treated them like their other colonies.

The system was also applied to former German colonies in Africa. Great Britain, France, and Belgium were given authority over Lebanon, Syria, Iraq, and Palestine.

Putting It All Together

Review the outline notes you took as you read this lesson. Work with a partner to make sure you included all the main ideas and key information. Use your notes to write a three paragraph essay about the Treaty of Versailles, changes in Europe, or the mandate system.

Russian Revolution and Communism

World War I, 1914–1919

Thinking on Your Own

As you read, create a cause-and-effect flowchart to show the causes of the Russian Revolution and its effects. List all the causes that led to the Russian Revolution. Then list all the events that happened as a result of the revolution.

Russia's entry into World War I drew attention to the nation's problems. Because of its lack of factories, soldiers went into battle without guns and supplies. Two million soldiers died and perhaps as many as six million more were wounded or captured. People on the **home front**—those not in the military—suffered from shortages of food and other goods.

focus your reading

Describe the sequence of events that brought about the Russian Revolution.

How did Lenin gain power?

Explain how Lenin turned Russia into a communist nation.

vocabulary

home front

serfs

emancipated

provisional

soviets

war communism

New Economic Policy

The Beginning of Revolution

Russia did not industrialize quickly, as many European nations did. By 1890, the Russian economy was still based on farming. However, in the 1890s the government began to work with foreign investors and Russian businessmen. New industries were started and industrial production began to grow. The need for workers caused people to begin moving from farms to cities.

Until 1861, Russian peasants, called **serfs**, could not become factory workers. They were the property of their landowners and could not move from one estate to another or to a town. This system of feudalism had ended in Western Europe in the Middle

Ages. The czar finally **emancipated**, or freed, Russia's serfs in 1861. Most serfs continued to work on farms. Some of these former serfs, however, became the new urban working class in the 1890s. Just as in Western Europe and the United States, these workers lived and worked under terrible conditions. They were paid poorly, worked in unsafe factories, and lived in slums.

Women demonstrate in Petrograd in April 1917.

The Russian Revolution began among these workers in March 1917. Women workers in Petrograd—now St. Petersburg—began a protest. Some 10,000 women marched with shouts of "Peace and Bread." They and other workers called for a general strike on March 10. All factories in the city shut down. Czar Nicholas II ordered the army to fire their guns at the demonstrators. Many of the soldiers refused. The soldiers turned on the government and joined the demonstrators.

The Duma, or Russian legislature, met on March 12. It set up a **provisional**, or temporary, government and called for the czar to resign. Nicholas II had little choice and resigned. His abdication ended three centuries of Romanov rule. The former royal family was executed in July, 1918, by the Bolsheviks.

Once the czar was removed from power in 1917, the Duma began writing a constitution to create a Russian republic. It also continued Russian participation in World War I. The peasants and urban workers were angered by this decision. After three years, they wanted an end to the war.

In the meantime, socialists were organizing **soviets**. These were councils made up of workers, peasants, and soldiers. The soviets soon came under the influence of Vladimir I. Lenin and the Bolshevik Party.

stop and think

Why do you think the soldiers joined the marchers in March of 1917? Make a list of possible reasons. Discuss your list with a partner. Add to it or cross off ideas. Then use these ideas to create a concept web of ideas that answer the question.

The Rise of Lenin and the Bolsheviks

As a young man, Vladimir I. Lenin read the writings of Karl Marx. By 1895, Lenin was trying to stir up revolution in Russia. The government arrested him and sent him to prison. On his release, he left the country. When the czar stepped down, Lenin returned to Russia.

The provisional government was losing control of the country. Russians were still dying on the battlefields. Shortages of food and other goods were worsening. Workers were rioting in the streets. The Bolsheviks promised to take Russia out of the war. They would seize land from large landowners and give it to the peasants. Capitalists would lose their factories. The workers would run them. The provisional government would be overthrown and the soviets would take control of the government.

Vladimir Lenin addresses a Moscow crowd in 1920.

In the November Revolution of 1917, Lenin and the Bolsheviks seized power. On November 6, they took over the building that housed the provisional government. Officials put up little resistance. On November 8, Lenin turned over the government to the All-Russian Congress of Soviets. A small group of officials called the Council of People's Commissars actually ran the government. Lenin was the leader of this group.

The Bolsheviks changed their name to the Communist Party. They withdrew from World War I and made peace with Germany. They also determined to turn Russia into a communist state. However, not everyone agreed. A civil war broke out in 1918 and lasted until 1921.

Lenin's Red Army was opposed by the White Army, which supported the czar and landowners. Ethnic groups in areas ruled by Russia also opposed the communists. These groups were fighting for the freedom to set up independent nations. The Allies sent troops and supplies to aid the White Army. However, the communist forces defeated the White Army and the nationalist groups.

Comparison of Revolutions

Criteria	American Revolution	French Revolution	Russian Revolution
Was it a short-term success?	Yes. It freed the 13 English colonies from Great Britain. Yes. It set up a government based on democratic ideas.	Yes. It ended the French monarchy Yes. It set up principles of democracy.	Yes. It ended the monarchy No. It did not give Russians political, social, or religious freedoms.
Was it a long-term success?	Yes. Its ideas are still the basis of the U.S. government in the 21st century.	No. Several times during the 1800s, France returned to being a monarchy. Yes. Since the late 1800s France has been a republic.	No. The communist system in Russia collapsed in the late 1980s and early 1990s.
Did it have influence?	Yes. It influenced the French revolution and the revolutions in Latin America. Yes. It continues to influence the government of nations in the 21st century.	Yes. It influenced the revolutions in Latin America.	Yes. It provided a model of communist government for in Eastern European nations and other parts of the world. No. Eastern European nations rejected communism in the 1980s also.

Beginning of Communist Government

By the end of the civil war, Russia had a new centralized government and a single political party, the Communist Party. During the war, Lenin developed what he called **war communism**. In order to supply the Red Army, the government took over banks, mines, factories, railroads, and the food supply.

Workers on a Ukrainian collective farm have dinner in the fields.

However, war communism was not an effective way to govern. Two years of famine caused great hardship and millions of deaths. Industrial production slowed dramatically. Workers may have owned the factories according to communist theory, but in practice they worked for very low wages. Life in general had not improved under communism.

In order to turn the economy around, Lenin introduced his **New Economic Policy** (NEP) in 1921. Some private ownership was allowed. Peasants could keep some of what they raised and grew. They could use it themselves or sell it. Small factories were returned to private ownership. Small stores could also be privately owned. Wages were increased for factory workers.

Lenin died in 1924. Various Communist Party leaders fought among themselves for power. By 1928, Joseph Stalin was firmly in control of the Soviet Union, Russia's new name.

Putting It All Together

"Private ownership of farms, factories, and stores is good for a nation's economy." Discuss this statement with a partner and make a bulleted list of reasons that either support or argue against the statement. Then use your flowchart, concept web, and bulleted list to develop an outline for an essay about the Russian Revolution.

Chapter Summary

- Long-term causes of World War I were rivalry among European nations, a system of alliances, ethnic nationalism, and militarism.
- The **Triple Alliance** included Germany, Austria-Hungary, and Italy. The **Triple Entente** included Great Britain, France, and Russia.
- The immediate cause of World War I was the assassination of Archduke Francis Ferdinand.
- The United States remained **neutral** at the start of the war because of pressure on the **home front**.
- **Trench warfare** resulted in a **stalemate**. An **armistice** ended the war in 1918.
- President Wilson's Fourteen Points included a **League of Nations**. In the end, Germany had to pay large **reparations**. A **demilitarized zone** was set up between France and Germany.
- The Treaty of Versailles established a **mandate system** in the Middle East.
- In 1861, Russian **serfs** were **emancipated**.
- The Russian Revolution began in March 1917. The czar was forced out and the Duma set up a **provisional** government. A socialist government used the **soviets** and seized power in November 1917.
- Lenin developed **war communism** to take control of Russia's means of production during the civil war.
- After the war, Lenin announced his **New Economic Policy** (NEP) to increase economic development.

Chapter Review

1   With a partner, play a question-and-answer game. First, write ten answers with a question for each answer. Take turns giving answers and responding with questions.

2   Complete the last two columns of the chart you began at the start of the chapter. Select three topics from column four—topics that you still want to learn more about. After researching the topics, write a five-paragraph essay about your topics.

Skill Builder

Analyzing Propaganda

Propaganda is the spreading of information, beliefs, and ideas to influence people for or against an issue or person. Propaganda does not always tell the whole truth and is usually biased. Bias is a strong feeling for or against a person or issue without facts to support that feeling.

Advertising is a form of propaganda. Advertisers want you to buy their products instead of their competitors' products.

To analyze propaganda:

1. Identify the topic of the cartoon, poster, ad, or writing.
2. Identify who is responsible for the piece—for example, a political candidate, a company, or the government.
3. Determine the message of the piece.
   Ask yourself: Does it present only one side?
   Does the picture or text exaggerate?

Nations also use propaganda to sell the public on an idea. For example, governments want to inspire their people to make sacrifices during wartime. They sometimes use propaganda against the enemy to do this. Posters were used by the U.S. government to raise money during World War I. Notice how the Germans are portrayed as blood thirsty, vicious Huns in the 1918 war bond poster. They have blood on their hands and bayonets as they seize control of Europe.

Complete the following activities.

1 What emotions is this poster designed to evoke? What impression does the looming figure provide to the viewer? In a time before television and the internet, why do you think the government relied on posters such as this?

2 With a partner, think of a TV commercial about one of your favorite products. List three ways it uses propaganda.

Chapter 21

BETWEEN THE WARS

(1919–1939)

Getting Focused

Skim this chapter to predict what you will be learning.
• Read the lesson titles and subheadings.
• Look at the illustrations and read the captions.
• Examine the maps.
• Review the vocabulary words and terms.

A totalitarian government is one that attempts to control the politics, economy, society, and culture of a nation. People's freedoms are limited. Between 1919 and 1939, three totalitarian governments emerged in Europe: Italy, the Soviet Union, and Germany.

What freedoms would people lose under a totalitarian government? How would a government make people obey laws that take away their freedoms? Work with a partner to make a list of your ideas. As you read this chapter, check your list against what these governments actually did.

LESSON **1**

Totalitarianism in Italy

Thinking on Your Own

Make a list of the vocabulary words in your notebook. Then skim the chapter for more words that you do not know. Work with a partner to define each of the words on your list. Once you agree on a definition, write a sentence that shows the word's meaning. Then write a synonym for each of the words.

After World War I, people in Europe and the United States were tired of war. They were horrified at its costs in lives and damage. The League of Nations was created to ensure that a global war would never happen again. However, the League was doomed to fail. Its 40-member nations could not agree on policies, including how to stop aggressive nations. In addition, the United States never joined the League.

focus your reading

Explain how Mussolini gained power.

What is fascism?

How was the government set up under Mussolini?

vocabulary

depression	fascism
inflation	censor
Blackshirts	corporate state
dictator	

A major problem that nations also faced in the 1920s was a worldwide **depression**. A depression is a period of rising unemployment and low economic activity. It began in the early 1920s in Europe and spread around the world. By the early 1930s, the economy of the United States had also collapsed. The depression caused great hardship everywhere. Leaders in several countries promised to end the suffering by setting up totalitarian governments.

 **Time Box**

1919
  Fascist Party founded

1922
  Mussolini named prime minister

1926
  Mussolini declared himself *Il Duce*

The Rise of Mussolini

The first person to set up a totalitarian government was Benito Mussolini in Italy. He used the Treaty of Versailles and Italy's economic problems to gain power.

Benito Mussolini in the early 1920s

During World War I, Italy fought on the side of the Allies. At the end of the war, Italy wanted to annex land to its east along the Adriatic Sea. Instead, the Big Three—the United States, Great Britain, and France—gave the land to the new nation of Yugoslavia. This angered Italian nationalists. Mussolini appealed to them by promising to create a new Italian empire.

Like much of Europe, economic troubles began in Italy right after World War I. **Inflation** became a problem. Inflation is a rapid increase in the prices of goods. Prices rose but workers' wages did not. Workers called strikes to demand higher pay. Socialists preached an end to capitalism. Middle-class owners of businesses and large landowners feared socialism. They were worried about a Communist takeover of Italy. At that time, Communists were calling themselves Socialists.

Fascist "March on Rome," 1922

Mussolini used the fears of the middle class. In 1919, he founded the Fascist Party. In the early 1920s, groups of his supporters known as **Blackshirts** broke up strikes and attacked Socialists' meetings and offices. By 1922, Mussolini had the support of a large portion of the middle class. In that year, Mussolini and his followers marched on Rome. Mussolini boldly demanded power from King Victor Emmanuel III. The king saw no choice and made him prime minister.

By 1925, Mussolini had set up a dictatorship. Under a dictatorship, a single person, the **dictator**, has complete

stop and think

As you read, create a cause-and-effect flowchart that illustrates how Mussolini came to power.

control of the government. Italy was still called a constitutional monarchy. Victor Emmanuel III was still king. However, Mussolini had taken control of the government for himself. He had elections fixed so that only his supporters were elected to office. He removed opponents from government jobs. By 1926, he was calling himself Il Duce, the leader. The king was only a figurehead.

Fascism

Mussolini's dictatorship was called **fascism**. The name came from his political party. Fascism is a totalitarian government that is not Communist. Fascists in the 1920s and 1930s were strong anti-Communists and anti-Socialists.

According to fascism, the state is more important than individuals. As a result, a Fascist nation has a strong central government. There is a single leader who is a dictator. The government controls the economy. Individuals and companies may own businesses and land. However, the government controls how the owners run them. Individuals have limited freedoms.

In a Fascist state, rival political parties are banned. The mass media—newspapers, radio, and movies—is **censored**. In this context, to censor means to forbid the communication of views that oppose the government. Police spies and terror are used to enforce government policies. Propaganda is another important tool in a Fascist state. It is used to brainwash people into believing what the government says. The way Mussolini governed Italy shows how a Fascist state works.

Mussolini in Power

As prime minister, Mussolini banned all political parties except the Fascist Party. The press, radio, and movies were

Benito Mussolini speaking to followers in 1930

censored. Nothing could be printed or said that opposed Mussolini's rule.

Terror became a weapon of the government. In 1926, Mussolini set up a secret police force to spy on people and create fear. Opponents were arrested and tortured. Some were sent into exile and others were killed.

To gain support, Mussolini used propaganda. The message was obedience to the government and dedication to the nation. One slogan was "Believe! Obey! Fight!" Another was "Mussolini Is Always Right." Propaganda urged women to stay at home and raise children. Men were told to be ready to fight for Italy. Children were enrolled in youth groups to learn Fascist philosophy. These youth groups were based on military principles. Children practiced marching like soldiers and learned discipline and obedience to their leaders.

A Fascist youth group on parade

Under Mussolini, the government controlled Italy's economy. He set up a **corporate state** in which workers were grouped by occupations. These groups were called *corporations*, and Mussolini headed them. He did not end capitalism as a Socialist would have. Rather, he used capitalism. The corporations, along with the Fascist Party, controlled how businesses and farms were run. The economy improved, but workers lost out. They could not strike and their wages remained low.

Mussolini was building a nation based on military discipline. He expected to use it to build a new Italian empire.

Putting It All Together

Create a T-chart. In the left column, list the characteristics of a Fascist nation. Then write examples from Mussolini's government for each characteristic. Work with a partner and compare your charts.

Stalin and the Soviet Union

Thinking on Your Own

Italy under Mussolini and the Soviet Union under Stalin were totalitarian states, or nations. As you read this lesson, make a list of the characteristics of a totalitarian communist society.

Joseph Stalin came to power in the Soviet Union in the late 1920s. He survived a struggle with other Communist Party leaders after Lenin's death. Part of the struggle had been over how quickly to industrialize the nation. Lenin's New Economic Policy had improved the economy after the war. However, Stalin and his supporters wanted more improvements—and quickly. They wanted the Soviet Union to become a major industrial nation.

focus your reading

Discuss how the Five-Year Plans affected the Soviet economy.

At whom were Stalin's purges aimed?

Describe what life was like in the Soviet Union under communism.

vocabulary

Five-Year Plans	kulaks
collectives	purges
quotas	

Stalin's Five-Year Plans

Once Stalin had defeated his rivals, he pushed through a series of **Five-Year Plans**. The Plans began in 1928. They were aimed at increasing industrial and agricultural production.

Industry was to focus on making steel, machines, weapons, and farm and transportation equipment. The transportation system was improved and expanded. New power plants were built. More money was put into mining and oil drilling.

To increase farm production, Stalin ended private ownership of farms. Farms were turned into **collectives**.

The Soviet symbol of the hammer and sickle. The hammer represented industrial workers, and the sickle, farm workers.

Workers on a collective farm in the early 1930s

These huge farms were made by combining the small farms of many peasant families. The collectives were to be run by groups of peasants. The peasants could keep their homes and a small plot of land on which to grow their own food. However, all farm animals, tools, and supplies belonged to the collective. The peasants were to manage and work the farms together. They would not be paid wages, but they would share in any profits. However, the government set prices and **quotas** for production. A quota is a set amount. Quotas regulated the amount of crops that each collective could produce.

The peasants, especially those who had owned their own farms, rebelled. They burned their fields or hid their crops after the harvest. They killed their farm animals and broke the new tractors and other tools the government had given them.

Stalin used force to end the resistance. He sent the **kulaks** to labor camps in Siberia, the coldest, farthest part of the Soviet Union. Kulaks were the farm owners who resisted collectivization. Stalin's policies and the resistance of peasants had a cost. Terrible famines occurred across the Soviet Union in 1932 and 1933. As many as 10 million peasants may have died.

Stalin's Purges

The persecution of the kulaks was just one of Stalin's **purges**. A purge is an attempt to get rid of political opponents. The period from 1934 to 1936 is called the Great Purge.

Stalin used his secret police to spy on and arrest those who disagreed with him. The accused were tried and sentenced to death or to a labor camp in Siberia. Perhaps 8 million people died because of the Great Purge.

Like Mussolini, Stalin used terror to make Soviets obey the government. He also used the Great Purge to

stop and think

Make a Venn diagram. Label the circles "Italian Fascism" and "Soviet Communism." Fill in the diagram with information about how the two governments were similar and different.

remove anyone from the Communist Party who might challenge his power.

Russian workers meet to approve the first Purge.

Those jobs were filled by young Communists who were grateful to Stalin and, therefore, loyal to him.

Life in Soviet Society

Stalin put few resources into producing consumer goods such as refrigerators, furniture, and cars. As a result, there were few luxuries for workers to buy. Additionally, they had little money to spend on anything except food and housing. Wages were low. Like that of earlier European and U.S. factory workers, housing was crowded. Living conditions were bad. Families often shared two- or three-room apartments. Food in the cities was in short supply. Women stood in long lines daily to buy food.

Stalin had achieved his goal of increasing food production. However, much of the food was exported. Stalin needed to sell huge amounts of food to other nations in order to buy goods needed for industry and the military. Like Mussolini and Hitler, Stalin was building a strong military.

Also like Mussolini and Hitler, Stalin used propaganda to promote his goals. Everywhere, Soviets saw and heard messages glorifying the Soviet Union. They were encouraged to work harder and to produce more. Stalin also encouraged nationalism and suspicion of Western nations. Religion was banned because it distracted people from loyalty to the government.

Time Box

1922
Stalin elected leader of Communist Party

1928
Five-Year Plans

1934
Great Purge began

Putting It All Together

Why is the Soviet Union called a totalitarian nation? Review the list that you made as you read this lesson. Use it to write an essay of three or four paragraphs to answer the question. Ask a partner to review your essay. Ask for suggestions on how to make it clearer and more interesting.

The shortage of food that began during the 1930s remained an issue for Soviet citizens into the 1980s.

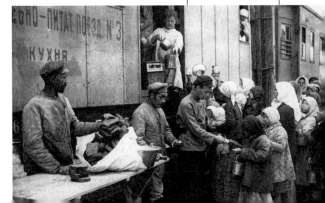

LESSON 3

Hitler and Nazi Germany

Thinking on Your Own

As you read this lesson, take bulleted notes on the ways that Hitler gained and kept power. Title your notes "Hitler's Policies." When you finish the lesson, compare your notes with that of a partner. Add any new concepts to your list.

The conditions that helped Adolf Hitler take over Germany were similar to those that helped Mussolini. Germans were angered at their treatment by the Allies at the Paris Peace Conference. German nationalists wanted the land that was taken from them under the Treaty of Versailles. Germany was also suffering from the worldwide depression. However, the Allies insisted that Germany continue to pay the huge reparations called for by the treaty.

focus your reading

Describe how Hitler gained absolute power in Germany.

Explain the policies of the Nazi government.

List examples of the ways in which Hitler persecuted the Jews.

vocabulary

Nazi Party

concentration camp

anti-Semite

genocide

Inflation was so severe in Germany that money was used to light a stove.

Hitler's Rise to Power

After the war, many nationalist political parties were developing in Germany. Adolf Hitler joined one of them, the small National Socialist German Workers' Party. The name was eventually changed to the **Nazi Party**. By 1921, he headed the party. Two years later the party tried to overthrow the German government. Nothing came of the uprising, and Hitler was sent to jail.

After his prison term, Hitler set out to make the Nazis the most powerful political party in Germany. By 1929,

Adolph Hitler preparing to address a crowd

its membership had expanded from 27,000 to 178,000. Like Mussolini, Hitler appealed to nationalists. If Germans followed him, he promised to stop the payment of reparations. He would rebuild the German military. Germany would create a new empire. Like Mussolini, Hitler also appealed to business leaders and large landowners. He promised security from a Communist takeover and an end to the depression.

At the beginning of 1933, the president of the German Republic was forced to make Hitler chancellor. The Nazis had

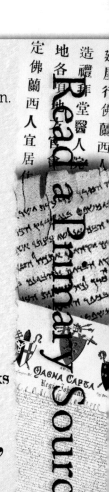

Inflation in Germany

U.S. writer Ernest Hemingway and his wife Hadley spent September 19, 1922, in Kehl, Germany. In this excerpt, Hemingway describes how high prices were because of inflation.

❝[W]e changed some French money in the railway station at Kehl. For 10 francs I received 670 marks. Ten francs amounted to about 90 cents . . . The 90 cents lasted . . . for a day of heavy spending and . . . we had 120 marks left!

"We picked out five very good-looking apples and gave the woman a 50 mark note. . . . A very nice-looking, white-bearded old gentleman saw us . . . and raised his hat.

"'Pardon me . . . how much were the apples?'

"I . . . told him 12 marks.

"He . . . shook his head, 'I can't pay it. It is too much.'

"With marks at 800 to a dollar, or 8 to a cent, . . . [p]eas were 18 marks a pound, beans 16 marks. . . . Kehl's best hotel . . . served a five-course . . . meal for 120 marks, which amounts to 15 cents in our money.❞

reading for understanding

How many marks did Hemingway receive for 10 francs?

Why wasn't the man able to buy apples?

How do you think Germans felt about not being able to buy basics like food?

Read a Primary Source

won a majority of seats in the German Parliament. Hitler acted quickly to cement his power. He had Parliament suspend the constitution. Hitler no longer needed the legislature to make laws. The law was whatever Hitler decided it was. With the support of the Nazi Party, Hitler created a dictatorship. Germans began calling him Der Fuhrer, or the leader.

stop and think

Create a sequence flowchart to track how Hitler came to power. Share your flowchart with a partner. Ask your partner to check it to make sure it has all the events in order. Discuss which events caused other events.

The Nazi Government

By 1934, there was no one who could challenge Hitler. The only political party allowed in Germany was the Nazi Party. Labor unions were banned. Hitler used terror and propaganda to maintain control and achieve his policies. The Gestapo, his secret police, spied on possible enemies. Anyone who opposed Hitler's ideas could be sent to a **concentration camp**—a type of prison camp. This was the beginning of the persecution of Jews, homosexuals, gypsies, Roman Catholics, and others.

SS troops in 1933

Hitler had promised to end the depression. Unlike Stalin, Hitler did not do away with private industry. But like Mussolini, he did control business and labor. The government set up massive public works projects to employ people. It also provided funding to private industry to create jobs. Hitler also stopped World War I reparation payments and set about re-arming Germany. Thousands of jobs were created to help build and equip the military.

A constant chorus of propaganda urged Germans to support the Third Reich. This was Hitler's name for the new German empire. Youth groups trained young men in military discipline and values. Like Mussolini, Hitler discouraged women from working outside the home.

A Nazi youth group

Jews were forced to wear a Star of David.

Between the Wars, 1919–1939

Anti-Semitism

Hitler was a fanatical **anti-Semite**. He hated Jews. Hitler had developed a theory that Germans were descended from a pure Aryan race. To Hitler, this was the master race, superior to all other races. Jews in Germany endangered the purity of the race. He also blamed the Jews for most of Germany's problems. In the beginning, Hitler wanted to drive all Jews from the country. Later, he turned to **genocide**, which is the murder of all members of an ethnic group.

In 1935, the Nuremberg Laws stripped German Jews of their German citizenship. Germans Jews could no longer marry non-Jewish Germans. German Jews were also forced to wear a yellow Star of David on their clothes to mark them as Jews.

The night of November 9, 1938, is known as Kristallnacht, the Night of Broken Glass. In Paris two days before, a young Jew had shot a German diplomat. He was taking revenge for violence against his parents in Germany. The Nazis used this as an excuse to attack Jews. Jewish businesses, homes, and synagogues were destroyed. Jews were beaten in the streets, and more than 100 Jews were murdered. After the violence, some 30,000 German-Jewish men were sent to concentration camps.

More persecution followed. German Jews could not ride public transportation. They could not attend or teach in German schools. They could not work in stores or in hospitals.

Time Box

1921
Hitler took over Nazi Party

1933
Hitler named chancellor of Germany

1935
Nuremberg Laws

1938
Kristallnacht

The aftermath of Kristallnacht

Putting It All Together

You have now read about three totalitarian dictators. With a partner create a table to compare and contrast them. Use the following categories or topics: "Country," "Date Came to Power," "Official Title," "Political Party," "Type of Government," and "Ways to Control the Nation."

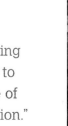

Chapter Summary

- Benito Mussolini in Italy, Joseph Stalin in the Soviet Union, and Adolf Hitler in Germany set up totalitarian governments. The worldwide **depression** and soaring **inflation** aided their rise to power.

- Mussolini used the **Blackshirts** to terrorize Socialists. He promised nationalists that he would create a new Italian empire. He established a **corporate state**.

- Mussolini set up a totalitarian government with himself as **dictator**. He governed Italy according to **fascism**. Newspapers, radio, and the movies were **censored**.

- Joseph Stalin replaced Lenin's NEP with a series of **Five-Year Plans**. The government set **quotas** for industrial and farm production. Peasants rebelled at the **collectivization** of their farms. To end their resistance, Stalin had **kulaks** sent to labor camps in Siberia.

- In the Great **Purge**, Stalin used the secret police to arrest those who disagreed with him or who might challenge him.

- Adolph Hitler led the **Nazi Party** to power in Germany.

- Once in power, Hitler banned labor unions and all political parties except the Nazi Party. Those who opposed him were sent to **concentration camps**.

- Hitler was a fanatical **anti-Semite**. He adopted a policy of **genocide** toward Jews. The Nuremberg Laws and Kristallnacht are two examples of his anti-Semitism.

Chapter Review

1 Review the table you created at the end of Lesson 3. Use the information to write an essay comparing and contrasting two of the following leaders: Mussolini, Stalin, and Hitler.

2 What could German non-Jews have done about the treatment of Jews? Discuss the question with a partner. Write your ideas in a paragraph.

3 Write a five-paragraph essay discussing the formation of governments under Mussolini, Stalin, and Hitler.

Skill Builder

Identifying Point of View

A person's point of view is shaped by his or her family, religion, education, friends, and experiences. The time period in which a person lives is also important in determining what a person thinks about an event or another person.

For example, although British, French and Germans all fought in World War I, their experiences after the war led to different points of view. Many Germans believed that the Treaty of Versailles was unfair. Most British and French thought Germany should be punished.

To help in identifying a point of view, follow these steps:

1. Identify the author or the speaker's background.
2. Identify the argument, issue, or main idea.
3. Identify the facts and other information used to support the argument. Distinguish facts from opinions.
4. Examine the kinds of words and phrases that the author or speaker uses. Do they favor one side of the issue?
5. State the person's viewpoint in your own words.

Read and answer the questions about the excerpt below.

Bahithat al-Badiya lived from 1886 to 1918. She was an educated, upper-class woman who lived in Cairo, Egypt.

"Men say when we become educated we shall push them out of work. . . . But isn't it rather men who have pushed women out of work? Before, women used to spin and to weave cloth . . . but men invented machines for spinning and weaving. . . . I am not urging women to neglect their home and children to go out and become lawyers or judges or railway engineers. But if any of us wish to work in such professions our personal freedom should be not be infringed."

1 What do you know about the writer?

2 What point or argument is she making?

3 What information does she use?

4 Write a sentence stating the writer's point of view.

Chapter 22
World War II and the Cold War

(1931–1955)

Getting Focused

Skim this chapter to predict what you will be learning.
• Read the lesson titles and subheadings.
• Look at the illustrations and read the captions.
• Examine the maps.
• Review the vocabulary words.

Make a World War II K-W-L chart with three columns in your notebook. Label the columns: "What I Know," "What I Want to Know," and "What I Learned." After skimming the chapter, make a list of what you know about World War II in the first column. In the second column, list questions you have about World War II.

LESSON 1

The Road to War

Thinking on Your Own

Take outline notes on the important information in this lesson. Use the dates on the timeline as the basis for your notes. Write down the date and the information from the timeline. Then list details from the text to help you remember why each event was important.

During the 1930s, Germany, Japan, and Italy prepared for war. Hitler and Mussolini were firmly in control of their nations. The emperor ruled Japan, but military leaders made most of the decisions. In each nation, these dictators wanted to build great empires. They were ready to use their armies and navies to do this.

Japan and Italy on the March

Japan faced serious economic problems in the early 1930s. Like other industrial nations, it suffered from the Great Depression. But Japan had its own special problems. A small island nation, it lacked iron ore, oil, rubber, and other resources. It also needed markets beyond Japan for the goods it produced. The Japanese government decided to expand into Asia to get control of resources and to sell its goods.

focus your reading

Explain why Italy and Japan seized territory in the 1930s.

Describe how Germany took control of neighboring nations in the 1930s.

Why did Great Britain and France finally act to stop Hitler?

vocabulary

appeasement

Anschluss

blitzkrieg

isolationist

Hitler salutes tanks in 1936 during the re-arming of Germany.

Japanese troops in Nanjing, China, in 1937

In 1931, Japanese troops took control of Manchuria, a region in northeastern China. The Japanese claimed that Chinese troops had attacked their railroad in that region. The Japanese had actually staged the attack themselves. They dressed up in Chinese army uniforms and raided their own railroad.

Chiang Kai-shek, the head of China's government, tried to limit the spread of Japanese power in China. He agreed to let Japan govern parts of northern China. However, by 1937, China and Japan were fighting a full-scale war.

In 1940, Japan moved farther south to the French colony of Indochina. The United States warned the Japanese that it would stop selling them oil and scrap iron if they did not retreat. Japan did not retreat.

The League of Nations had objected to each of Japan's invasions and seizures of territory. However, it had no power to force Japan to give up the territory. This also was true when Italy invaded Ethiopia in 1935.

Ethiopia had resisted European domination longer

Map: Japanese Expansion, 1933–1941

SOVIET UNION
KARAFUTO
MONGOLIA
MANCHUKUO (Manchuria)
JAPAN
Beijing
KOREA
Yan-an
CHINA
Nanjing
Hankow
Shanghai
Chongqing
Sichuan province
Formosa
Guangzhou
Hong Kong
FRENCH INDOCHINA

Japanese Expansion, 1933–1941
Japanese territory, 1933
Japanese acquisitions to November 1941

0   1000 miles

stop and think

Pretend that you an American citizen living in 1937. Write a letter to the League of Nations pointing out how the actions of Germany, Italy, and Japan are a threat to world peace. What would you ask the League to do to preserve the peace?

than any other African nation. But in 1936, the nation fell to Italy. Mussolini had finally conquered the kingdom that defeated Italy in 1898.

Germany on the March

In Germany, Adolph Hitler also decided to ignore the Treaty of Versailles and defy the League of Nations. By the terms of the treaty, Germany's air force was abolished and its army reduced in size. In 1935, Hitler began to create an air force and expand the army. The League of Nations did nothing to stop him.

The treaty also created a zone along Germany's border with France that the German army could not enter. This area along the Rhine River belonged to Germany, but it was demilitarized to help protect France. In 1936, Hitler sent a German army into the Rhineland. Again, the League did nothing.

France and Great Britain protested Hitler's re-arming of the Rhineland. France would have fought to force Germany to remove its soldiers but needed Great Britain's help. The British, however, would not fight. This was the beginning of Britain's policy of **appeasement**. Appeasement is giving in to the demands of a hostile person or group in order to keep peace.

German Expansion, 1935–1939

- Germany
- Rearmed territory
- German annexation, 1938
- German annexation, 1939

Hitler was now convinced that Great Britain and France would not fight. His next goal was **Anschluss**, or union of Austria with Germany. Austria was a nation that Hitler wanted to control, in part because he had been born there. By 1938, the Nazis had become an important political party in Austria. Hitler warned the chancellor of Austria to appoint Nazis to government positions of power or Germany would invade Austria. The chancellor agreed to Hitler's demand. Later, when Hitler made further demands, the chancellor refused. Hitler sent troops and proclaimed Austria part of Germany.

Next on Hitler's list was Czechoslovakia. Czechoslovakia was created by the Treaty of Versailles. It had a number of ethnic groups within its borders. One large group was German. Many lived in a region called the Sudetenland. In 1938, Hitler demanded the return of the Sudetenland to Germany.

In 1938, British and French officials met with Hitler in Munich. At the Munich Conference, these officials again gave in to Hitler. They agreed that Hitler could take control of the Sudetenland. In return, Hitler promised that Germany would not take control of additional regions of Czechoslovakia. British Prime Minister Neville Chamberlain said the settlement had achieved "peace in our time." The following spring, Hitler seized the rest of Czechoslovakia.

WAR!

Hitler and Mussolini established an alliance between Germany and Italy in 1936. That same year, Germany and Japan signed a defense pact, or agreement. This set up the Rome-Berlin-Tokyo Axis. These three nations became known as the Axis Powers. Hitler signed his final alliance in August 1939 with Joseph Stalin. They agreed to the Nazi-Soviet Non-Aggression Pact. The pact stated that the two nations would not fight one another. In addition, the Soviet Union was promised part of Poland if conquered by Germany.

German panzer division rolling into Poland on Sept. 1, 1939

The Non-Aggression Pact left Hitler free to invade Poland. He had feared that Stalin would join with western European nations to resist an invasion of Poland. On September 1, 1939, Hitler launched his **blitzkrieg**, or lightning war, against Poland. The blitzkrieg included armored columns, known as panzer divisions, each containing about 300 tanks. They were accompanied by airplanes and support troops. The speed and efficiency of the blitzkrieg stunned Polish forces, who surrendered after only four weeks of fighting.

On September 3, 1939, Great Britain and France, which were Poland's allies, declared war on Germany. However, it was too late to help Poland. Hitler's modern army quickly overran the western section of the country. Stalin's forces attacked from the east. Within one month, Stalin and Hitler had divided Poland.

In the meantime, the United States decided not to join the fighting. **Isolationists** in the United States believed that the country should stay out of European problems. They defended their argument by pointing out the number of deaths and money spent during World War I. President Franklin Roosevelt, however, was determined to help the Allies — the British and French. British and French leaders had hoped to avoid war by agreeing to Hitler's demands. Instead, appeasement allowed Hitler to buy time. He used that time to build a mighty war machine.

Putting It All Together

With a partner, create a timeline of the steps Hitler took that ignored the Treaty of Versailles. Then write a brief paragraph in your notebook to explain what Britain, France, and the League of Nations might have done to stop Hitler.

⧗ Time Box

1931
Japan seized Manchuria

1936
Germany seized the Rhineland

Italy conquered Ethiopia

Italy and Germany created the Rome-Berlin Axis

Germany and Japan signed the Anti-Comintern Pact

1937
Japan seized much of eastern China

1938
Germany annexed Austria

Germany took over the Sudetenland from Czechoslovakia

Munich Conference

1939
Germany seized the rest of Czechoslovakia

Hitler and Stalin signed the Nazi-Soviet Non-Aggression Pact

Germany seized Poland

Great Britain and France declared war on Germany

Fighting the War

Thinking on Your Own

As you read this lesson, create an outline. Use Roman numerals I, II, III, IV, and V for the subheadings. Under each Roman numeral entry, include information from the most important to the least important.

Germany's invasion of Poland plunged Europe into war. The devastation of the new war would be far worse than World War I. By the time World War II ended, 17 million men and women had died in battle. More than 20 million civilians had been killed. The world had also seen the terrible damage that an atomic bomb could produce.

focus your reading

Summarize the event that caused the United States to enter the war.

What was Hitler's "final solution"?

What was the Allied strategy in the Pacific?

Describe how World War II finally ended in the Pacific.

vocabulary

Battle of Britain   war crimes

D-Day   atrocities

Holocaust

The War, 1939–1941

Hitler and Stalin did not stop after invading Poland. During the winter of 1939–1940, Soviet troops seized Estonia, Latvia, Lithuania, and part of Finland. In the spring of 1940, German forces quickly overran Norway, Denmark, the Netherlands, and Belgium.

In May 1940, the German army invaded France. By then, Britain had sent an army to help protect France. In hard fighting, the Germans advanced, pushing the British army and many French troops west. The Allied forces found themselves at Dunkirk, France, on the English Channel. The British navy launched a huge rescue effort. Fishing boats and other private boats joined Royal Navy ships in carrying some 338,000 Allied soldiers to Great Britain. The French government surrendered to Germany on June 22, 1940.

The Axis powers dropped huge numbers of bombs on British cities.

Great Britain was now alone in the fight against Germany. The English Channel had protected England from invasion since 1066. In 1940, the British had an air force to help protect the country. Hitler decided he must defeat the air force in order to conquer England. He ordered a massive air war against Britain. This came to be known as the **Battle of Britain**. German planes bombed air fields, naval bases, shipyards, and war factories. Hitler also directed his air force to bomb British cities. However, the British sent their fighter planes against the German bombers. Realizing that he could not destroy the British air force, Hitler decided against invading Britain in 1940.

By 1941, Hitler had added the nations of the Balkans to his German empire. He then turned against Stalin and invaded the Soviet Union. At first the German army made great progress in its push east. However, the severe Russian winter again stopped an invading army, as it had Napoleon's army in 1812.

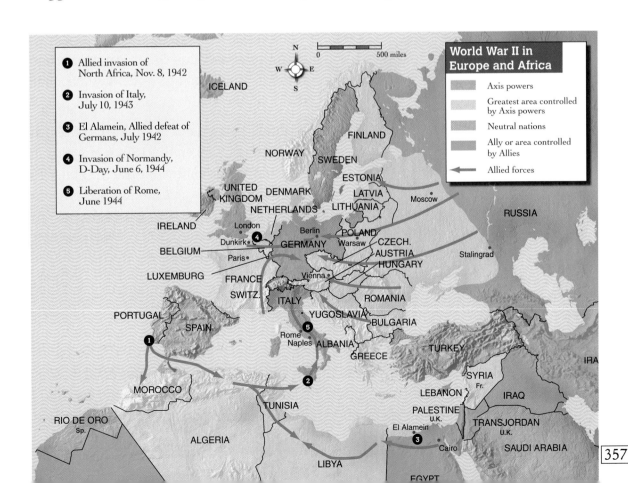

1 Allied invasion of North Africa, Nov. 8, 1942

2 Invasion of Italy, July 10, 1943

3 El Alamein, Allied defeat of Germans, July 1942

4 Invasion of Normandy, D-Day, June 6, 1944

5 Liberation of Rome, June 1944

World War II in Europe and Africa

Axis powers

Greatest area controlled by Axis powers

Neutral nations

Ally or area controlled by Allies

→ Allied forces

0   500 miles

The War, 1942–1945

The siege of Stalingrad, 1942

Japan was expanding its control in Asia in 1940. It wanted the European colonies and the Philippines, which the United States governed. To gain this new territory, Japan sought to destroy U.S. naval power in the Pacific and seize the colonies. On December 7, 1941, Japanese planes bombed the U.S. naval base at Pearl Harbor, Hawaii. The day after Pearl Harbor, the United States declared war on Japan. Germany then declared war on the United States. Italy, the third Axis power, also declared war.

The nations fighting the Axis powers called themselves the Grand Alliance, or the Allies. The main Allies included the United States, Great Britain, Free France (officials and officers who had escaped France),

stop and think

Make a timeline of the war in Europe from 1939 to 1945. Include where each major event took place and find that place on the map on page 357.

Biography

Sir Winston Churchill (1874–1965)

Winston Churchill became Great Britain's prime minister on May 10, 1940. This was the same day that Hitler launched his attack on the Netherlands, Belgium, and France.

Churchill spent most of his life in public service. He was a British soldier in the 1890s in Africa. In 1900, he was elected to Parliament for the first time. He held a number of important government positions between 1911 and 1929. Throughout the 1930s, Churchill opposed appeasement. His view was unpopular, and he was not appointed to any government jobs.

However, by mid-1939, the government realized that war was coming. A stronger leader than Neville Chamberlain was needed to direct the nation against the Nazi menace. Churchill was noted for his determination and inspiring speeches. He promised, "We shall never surrender." Churchill kept Britain's morale up until the United States joined the war at the end of 1941. Churchill then made sure that Great Britain remained an equal partner in the war and in post-war negotiations. He is considered one of history's greatest wartime leaders.

Pearl Harbor, December 7, 1941

China, and the Soviet Union. They agreed to defeat Hitler first and then Japan. The Allies invaded North Africa in November of 1942. By May 1943, they had defeated German forces there. Then they invaded Sicily and mainland Italy. Hitler sent German troops to save Mussolini and keep the Allies from taking Italy. Fierce fighting continued until May 1945 when Italy surrendered. By then, Italian resistance fighters had killed Mussolini.

On June 6, 1944, Allied armies crossed the English Channel from Britain to land on the beaches of France. This is known as the **D-Day** invasion. General Dwight D. Eisenhower commanded the Allied troops that came ashore. They broke the German lines and pushed the Germans steadily eastward.

Allied marines march ashore during the D-Day invasion of Normandy.

By April 1945, the remaining German armies were being squeezed between the Allied armies in the west and the Soviets in the east. The Soviets had started moving across Eastern Europe in 1943. They pushed the Germans out and occupied the areas themselves. Hitler committed suicide on April 30, 1945. Germany surrendered on May 7, 1945. The war in Europe was over.

The Holocaust and War Crimes

Adolf Hitler's hatred toward Jews began many years before World War II. By 1942, Hitler had decided on a "final solution" for ridding Germany and Europe of Jewish people. He would kill them all. The result was the **Holocaust**, the killing of millions of Jews. The Holocaust also included Slavs, Gypsies, and those with mental illness or mental disabilities — anyone Hitler considered undesirable.

Governments in nations conquered by Germany helped carry out the Holocaust. Like the Germans, they arrested Jews

Allied troops found railroad cars filled with corpses as they liberated Nazi concentration camps across Eastern Europe.

and jammed them into railroad freight cars. The cars took these people to concentration camps in Eastern Europe, such as Auschwitz in Poland. Many died during the trip from lack of air and food.

When the prisoners arrived at the camps, the ill and weak were marched directly to the gas chambers to be put to death. The healthy were marched to barracks. German guards required them to work in war factories or on farms. Most died from starvation and exhaustion. Between 9 million and 12 million people died in the Holocaust. About 6 million were Jews. More than half came from just four countries: Germany, Austria, Czechoslovakia, and Poland.

As the Allies pushed into Germany and Poland, they found the concentration camps. Half-dead, human skeletons greeted them through barbed wire fences. Their German guards had fled.

German defendants at the Nuremberg Nazi Trial in 1946

After the war, the Allies held **war crimes** trials in Nuremberg, Germany. They tried German and Austrian leaders for the **atrocities** of the Third Reich, as Germany was known. Japanese and Italian wartime leaders also were tried for war crimes. The message was clear. Government officials and military officers were responsible for their actions. They were not above international law.

War in the Pacific

By early 1942, the Japanese had captured European colonies in Southeast Asia and the islands in the western Pacific. Although the Allies decided to defeat Hitler first, they did not give up fighting in the Pacific. They planned a two-pronged strategy to fight the Japanese. One prong, or branch, was made up of land forces under the command of General Douglas MacArthur. His orders were to attack the Solomon Islands, New Guinea, and then the Philippines.

By October 1944, the land forces had seized control of the Solomon Islands and New Guinea. On October 20, they invaded the Philippines. By March 1945, they had captured Manila, the capital of the Philippines. However, fighting in the Philippines continued until the end of the war.

The second prong consisted of naval forces led by Admiral Chester A. Nimitz. They were to fight their way through the Central Pacific to the Japanese home islands. In May 1942, Allied naval forces won a major victory at the Battle of the Coral Sea. The next month they defeated a Japanese fleet near Midway Island. This was a turning point in the war in the Pacific. The Allies had stopped the Japanese advance.

The Allies then began pushing the Japanese back. For the next two years, they fought their way north through the Central Pacific. By April 1945, they were only 800 miles from Tokyo, Japan's capital. Allied planes were bombing Japanese cities daily. The war in Europe was over. Japan's civilian leaders and Emperor Hirohito were willing to end the war. However, Japan's military leaders refused to surrender.

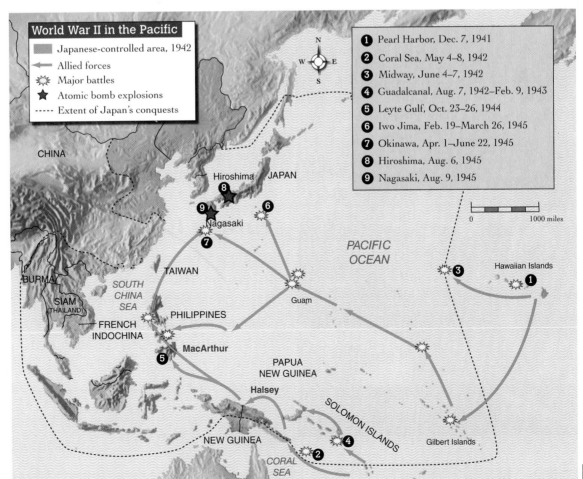

World War II in the Pacific

- Japanese-controlled area, 1942
- → Allied forces
- ✵ Major battles
- ★ Atomic bomb explosions
- ----- Extent of Japan's conquests

❶ Pearl Harbor, Dec. 7, 1941
❷ Coral Sea, May 4–8, 1942
❸ Midway, June 4–7, 1942
❹ Guadalcanal, Aug. 7, 1942–Feb. 9, 1943
❺ Leyte Gulf, Oct. 23–26, 1944
❻ Iwo Jima, Feb. 19–March 26, 1945
❼ Okinawa, Apr. 1–June 22, 1945
❽ Hiroshima, Aug. 6, 1945
❾ Nagasaki, Aug. 9, 1945

0   1000 miles

CHINA
Hiroshima   JAPAN
Nagasaki
BURMA
SIAM (THAILAND)
FRENCH INDOCHINA
TAIWAN
SOUTH CHINA SEA
PHILIPPINES
MacArthur
Guam
PACIFIC OCEAN
Hawaiian Islands
PAPUA NEW GUINEA
Halsey
NEW GUINEA
SOLOMON ISLANDS
Gilbert Islands
CORAL SEA

Dropping the Atomic Bomb

President Franklin Roosevelt died suddenly on April 12, 1945. Vice President Harry Truman was immediately sworn in as president. It was then that Truman learned about the atomic bomb. President Roosevelt had established a top-secret project in 1941 to develop an atomic bomb. It was called the Manhattan Project. Top scientists and more than 600,000 people worked to develop the atomic bomb. Physicist J. Robert Oppenheimer directed construction of the bomb in Los Alamos, New Mexico. The damage from such a bomb would be horrendous.

Truman asked for advice from his military advisors. They estimated that an invasion of the Japanese home islands would be costly. It would take months, and hundreds of thousands of U.S. soldiers and Japanese civilians would be killed.

During the summer of 1945, the Allies again offered Japan a chance to surrender. Its military leaders again refused. On August 6, a U.S. plane, the *Enola Gay*, dropped an atomic bomb on the city of Hiroshima. Between 80,000 and 120,000 people were killed. Thousands more died from burns and radiation poisoning. The Japanese government still did not surrender. A second bomb was dropped on the city of Nagasaki on August 9. Another 35,000 to 75,000 Japanese died. Japan finally surrendered on August 14, 1945.

The mushroom cloud over Hiroshima

Putting It All Together

Create a flowchart of the events in the Pacific that led to President Truman's decision to use the atomic bomb. Compare your flowchart with a partner's to make sure you included all the important information. Then write a short paragraph that summarizes the major events of World War II in the Pacific.

LESSON 3

The Cold War

Thinking on Your Own

Turn each subheading into a question. Write your questions in your notebook. As you read each subheading, write an answer to your question.

During World War II, Roosevelt, Churchill, and Stalin met several times. The purpose was to plan wartime **strategy** and the postwar peace. However, Stalin did not share the same goals for peace as Roosevelt and Churchill. He wanted to create a zone of Communist nations between the Soviet Union and the rest of Europe. This became clear soon after the war ended.

focus your reading

Explain how Communist governments came to power in Eastern Europe.

Describe how the United States dealt with communism during the Cold War.

vocabulary

strategy   Cold War

iron curtain   proliferation

containment

Losing Eastern Europe to Communism

During their wartime conferences, Roosevelt, Churchill, and Stalin made a number of agreements about what would happen after the war. Some of the most important were made at the Yalta Conference in 1945.

The three leaders agreed that Germany would be divided into four military zones. The United States, Britain, the Soviet Union, and France would each govern a zone. Roosevelt and Churchill insisted that Stalin hold free elections in the Soviet-occupied nations of Eastern Europe. Stalin agreed, but broke his promise. Instead, he imposed Communist governments on East Germany, Poland, Czechoslovakia, Hungary, and the Balkan nations. He also helped the Communist side in a civil war in Greece and tried to take territory from Turkey.

Europe After World War II

Area of Soviet influence
Area of Western influence

The alliance that won World War II quickly split apart. The nations of the West were on one side. On the other side were the Soviet Union and the nations of Eastern Europe that it controlled. The Soviet army cut off these nations from any contact with the West. This separated Europe into two blocks of nations divided by what Winston Churchill called an **"iron curtain."** He also warned that Stalin would not be satisfied with controlling Eastern Europe. He feared that Stalin wanted a Communist world.

America's Response to Stalin's Policies

The Free World looked to the United States for leadership. The British people were exhausted after the war. Many of their cities, factories, and shipyards had been badly damaged by German bombing raids. Much of France also lay in ruins. China was already fighting Communists in a civil war. The only nation that had the energy and resources to fight the Soviets was the United States.

In 1947, President Truman promised to aid nations struggling to remain free. In his message to Congress, he asked for $400 million for Turkey and Greece. The aid helped Turkey refuse Soviet demands. It also kept Greek Communists from winning the civil war. This new policy was called the Truman Doctrine.

President Truman also supported the European Recovery Act, known as the Marshall Plan. U.S. Secretary of State George Marshall proposed the plan to help Europe rebuild. Aid was offered to Stalin for the Soviet Union, but he rejected it. Between 1948 and

stop and think

If you were an American citizen in 1947, what advice would you have given to President Truman about dealing with the Soviets? Discuss this with a partner. Then write a letter to the president in your notebook.

U.S. aid being delivered to Europe under the Marshall Plan

1951, the plan provided $13 billion to western European nations. They used the money to build new housing, rebuild factories and cities, and get their economies growing again.

The goal of the Truman Doctrine and the Marshall Plan was **containment**. President Truman adopted this policy as a way to block further Communist expansion. The United States would provide money, equipment, weapons, and military support to nations threatened by communism. In addition to European nations, the United States provided aid to Chinese nationalists in the late 1940s. They were fighting Communists in a civil war.

The United States's policy of containment stopped the expansion of Soviet power in Europe. It also kept the United States and the Soviet Union—and later the United States and Communist China—from fighting each other during the **Cold War**. However, these great powers continued to support their democratic or Communist allies. Containment led to an uneasy peace.

However, containment could not stop a new arms race. By 1949, Soviet scientists had built an atomic bomb. Both the United States and the Soviet Union began a race to see who could build more nuclear bombs and the missiles to carry them. By the 1950s, other nations were developing their own nuclear weapons. One of the major problems in the world today continues to be the **proliferation**, or spread, of nuclear weapons and the nations that have them.

The Berlin Airlift provided food and supplies for more than 10 months, ending in May, 1949, after Soviet forces surrounded and cut off the city.

Putting It All Together

Think about appeasement and containment. Were they different or the same? Discuss this question with a partner. Write your ideas in your notebook. Then write a paragraph comparing appeasement and containment.

Chapter Summary

- In 1936, Italy invaded and conquered Ethiopia.
- In the mid-1930s, Hitler rebuilt the German military and sent troops into the Rhineland.
- Great Britain adopted a policy of **appeasement** toward Hitler, who took control of Austria to achieve **Anschluss**.
- On September 1, 1939, Hitler launched his **blitzkrieg** against Poland. Within two days, Great Britain and France declared war on Germany.
- **Isolationists** initially kept the United States out of the war.
- Hitler's forces conquered most of Northern Europe and launched an air war over Great Britain known as the **Battle of Britain**.
- The United States entered the war after the Japanese bombed Pearl Harbor on December 7, 1941.
- On June 6, 1944, known as **D-Day**, the Allies landed in Normandy, France.
- In May 1945, the German government surrendered.
- As the Allies pushed into German-held territory, they found concentration camps. Survivors told of the **atrocities** of the **Holocaust**. German, Austrian, Japanese, and Italian leaders were tried for **war crimes**.
- During the war, Roosevelt, Churchill, and Stalin met to plan wartime **strategy** and postwar peace.
- President Truman adopted a policy of **containment** toward the Soviet Union and communism. This policy continued throughout the **Cold War**.
- The arms race led to the **proliferation** of nuclear weapons on each side of the **iron curtain**.

Chapter Review

1 Draw a concept map to show the causes of World War II. Label the large circle in the center "Causes of World War II." Then draw a smaller circle for each cause. Add more circles to the small ones, including details about the causes.

2 Complete the K-W-L chart you began at the start of this chapter. Research three topics you want to know more about. Present your findings in a short essay.

Skill Builder

Comparing Points of View

It is often useful when studying history to compare different points of view. Understanding how different people think and feel about historic events makes what happened more understandable. Comparing points of view is also useful during elections. It can help voters decide which candidate to vote for in an election.

Winston Churchill and Neville Chamberlain, an earlier British prime minister, had different points of view about British appeasement of Hitler. Churchill's biography in Lesson 2 states that he opposed appeasement.

Read the following excerpts and then answer the questions.

Source A

"I make an earnest appeal to those who hold responsible positions . . . in this country . . . to weigh their words very carefully before they utter them . . . bearing in mind the consequences that may flow from some rash or thoughtless phrase. By exercising caution and patience and self-restraint we may yet be able to save the peace of Europe."

Source B

"Is it the new policy to come to terms with the totalitarian Powers in the hope that by great and far-reaching acts of submission . . . peace may be preserved.

"A firm stand by France and Britain, under the authority of the League of Nations, would have been followed by an immediate evacuation of the Rhineland without the shedding of a drop of blood; and the effects . . . might have enabled the . . . German army to gain their proper positions, and would not have given the political head of Germany the enormous ascendancy which has enabled him to move forward."

1 Between Chamberlain and Churchill, who do you think was Source A? Source B?

2 What words and phrases helped you determine the speaker?

3 In one sentence each, summarize the points of view of Source A and Source B.

8
UNIT

THE WORLD TODAY

The last 50 years of the 20th century and the beginning of the 21st century have seen huge changes in the world. After World War II, Asians and Africans gained their independence from colonial powers. In many cases they had to fight for years to win nationhood. Latin Americans nations were making progress in becoming more industrialized.

By the 1990s, the Cold War was over. The Soviet Union and Communist governments in Eastern Europe had collapsed. Chinese leaders had relaxed some Communist practices and were welcoming foreign business.

But new problems replaced the old ones. Supporters of a radical branch of Islam began a world-wide war of terror. Many nations were still poor. Women and children remained the primary victims of poverty. Industrialization eased poverty but created problems for the environment.

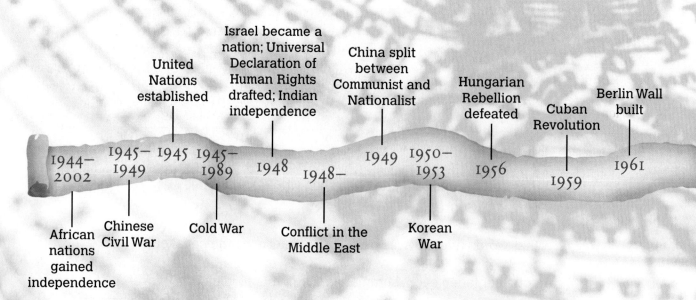

United Nations established — 1945

Israel became a nation; Universal Declaration of Human Rights drafted; Indian independence

China split between Communist and Nationalist — 1949

Hungarian Rebellion defeated — 1956

Cuban Revolution — 1959

Berlin Wall built — 1961

1944–2002

1945–1949

1945–1989

1948

1948–

1950–1953

African nations gained independence

Chinese Civil War

Cold War

Conflict in the Middle East

Korean War

What economic issues faced nations after World War II and continue to be important today?

Why is deforestation an important world issue today?

Why did Africans and Asians want independence after World War II?

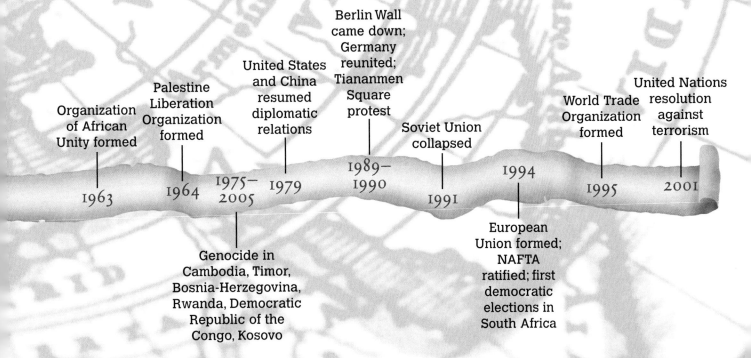

Organization of African Unity formed
1963

Palestine Liberation Organization formed
1964

1975–2005

United States and China resumed diplomatic relations
1979

Berlin Wall came down; Germany reunited; Tiananmen Square protest
1989–1990

Soviet Union collapsed
1991

1994

World Trade Organization formed
1995

United Nations resolution against terrorism
2001

Genocide in Cambodia, Timor, Bosnia-Herzegovina, Rwanda, Democratic Republic of the Congo, Kosovo

European Union formed; NAFTA ratified; first democratic elections in South Africa

Chapter 23

THE WORLD ENTERS THE 21ST CENTURY

(1945–)

Getting Focused

Skim this chapter to predict what you will be learning.
- Read the lesson titles and subheadings.
- Look at the illustrations and read the captions.
- Examine the maps.
- Review the vocabulary words and terms.

Look through the chapter at the photographs until you find one that captures your imagination. What questions does it raise in your mind? Write down three of the questions in your notebook. Share your questions with a partner. Remember to add the newest countries of the world to your world map.

European Economic Recovery

Thinking on Your Own

Look at the Focus your Reading questions. Note the countries or regions that are mentioned. Make a three-column chart with the headings "Germany," "Soviet Union," and "Eastern Europe." As you read the lesson, take bulleted notes on the changes that took place in each nation or region.

During World War II, President Franklin Roosevelt proposed a new global organization. It would replace the League of Nations. The new United Nations (UN) would negotiate disagreements among member nations. It would also be able to use force against aggressor nations.

The United Nations began in 1945 with high hopes for preventing another global war. Although wars have continued, none has been on the scale of the two world wars of the twentieth century. Many new nations have emerged and joined the United Nations. Today, the UN has many roles. Among its duties are peacekeeping and aiding the world's poor and sick.

Redrawing the Map of Eastern Europe

When World War II ended, Europe was divided into free and Communist-controlled states. The Soviet Union had freed most of Eastern Europe from Germany's power. As a result, the

Soviets imposed **totalitarian** governments in those nations. In 1949, the United States and 11 European nations formed a new military alliance. Known as the North Atlantic Treaty Organization (NATO), it was designed to stop Soviet expansion in Europe. Officials in the United States called it an "antidote to fear."

Despite earlier agreements, free elections were not allowed in Poland, Romania, Czechoslovakia, Bulgaria, or Hungary. East Germany and East Berlin were also under Communist control. These countries were known as **satellite nations**. That is, they were controlled by the Soviet Union, just as space satellites are held in place by the planet they circle.

Freedom fighters in Hungary and Czechoslovakia tried to free their nations from Soviet control. Soviet troops put down both rebellions. They quashed rebellions in Hungary in 1956 and in Czechoslovakia in 1968.

"Prague Spring," a move for democracy, ended with Soviet tanks entering the Czech capital.

Communists wanted to stop people who were leaving East Germany. East Germans were using West Berlin as an escape route to freedom. In 1961, the Soviets built a 12-foot wall made of barbed wire and several layers of concrete between East and West Berlin. The wall split the city into two sections, separating families and friends. It had searchlights, mines, and guards who shot anyone attempting to cross its border.

Mikhail Gorbachev, the Soviet leader who came to power in 1985, began to allow greater freedom. He changed the Soviet policy by refusing to intervene militarily in the affairs of satellite nations. This led to a greater freedom of movement for people living in Communist-controlled nations. People began moving out of Hungary and into Austria. Soon, a new government had been established in East Germany.

The Berlin Wall came down in 1989 after U.S. President Ronald Reagan challenged the Soviet leader, "Mr. Gorbachev, tear down this wall!" East and West Germans joined in

People tore down the Berlin Wall in 1989 without waiting for the government to do it.

tearing down the hated wall and formed one Germany in 1990. Gorbachev also announced that Eastern European nations would be responsible for their own lands without help from the Soviet Union.

Poland became the first satellite nation to hold democratic elections. Its citizens elected Lech Walesa president. Walesa had led the protest movement in Poland known as Solidarity. He was the leader of the shipyard workers' union. Bulgaria and Hungary followed. In free elections during 1989 and 1990, Communists lost power and democracy spread. In Czechoslovakia, this change was known as the "Velvet Revolution," because it was not accomplished through war.

Polish Solidarity leader Lech Walesa had been imprisoned for his fight for democracy.

Yugoslavia was a Communist country but not a Soviet satellite. Joseph Tito, the powerful leader after World War II, held its two provinces and six republics together. When he died in 1980, Yugoslavia joined other Eastern European nations in the quest for freedom.

Fighting for independence began in the republics of Slovenia, Croatia, and Bosnia-Herzegovina in 1990. These republics included Serbian minorities from the Republic of Serbia. The Serbian army went against Croatia after that nation and Slovenia declared independence from Yugoslavia. The fighting was fierce and moved into Bosnia-Herzegovina.

Many of the Bosnians were Muslim. Following the example of Nazi Germany, the Serbian army practiced **ethnic cleansing**. About a quarter of a million Bosnians had been killed by 1995. Two million people were homeless and living in refugee camps. Finally, after NATO intervened with bombing strikes, Serbs

and Bosnians signed a peace treaty. It split Bosnia into a Muslim-Croat federation and a Serb republic.

War broke out again in 1998 over Kosovo, a self-governing province in Yugoslavia. The people of Kosovo were mostly Albanians. They had kept their own customs and language. They wanted to remove the Serbs from power. The Serbs began killing ethnic Albanians. Once again, NATO tried to find a solution. Albanians were freed within Serbia in 1999. Three years later, Serbia and Montenegro created a loose union and dropped the name Yugoslavia.

Former Yugoslavia, 1991–1999

— Boundary of former Yugoslavia, 1991

▒ Yugoslavia, 1991

--- Dayton Peace Agreement boundary that ended the war in Bosnia, 1995

— Boundary of Bosnia and Herzegovina

Time Box

1961
Berlin Wall divided capital of Germany into East and West sections

1989
Berlin Wall came down; Poland gained freedom

1991
Soviet Union collapsed

1994
European Union began

The End of the Soviet Union

The Soviet Union had been facing economic troubles for several decades. Mikhail Gorbachev called for **perestroika**, or restructuring. At first, he intended only economic reform, wanting limited capitalism. However, he also saw the need for political reform.

The Soviet Union was a huge nation with 92 different nationalities, 112 languages, and 12 time zones. The reforms encouraged the republics to break away. Ukraine voted to become independent in 1991. Leaders of Ukraine, Russia, and Belarus soon announced that the Soviet Union no longer existed.

Out of the old Soviet empire emerged the Commonwealth of Independent States—a loose alliance of former Soviet republics. Each country was independent, but would work with the others in trade. Not all has been peaceful since then. In 1991, the Republic of Chechnya declared that it wanted to separate from Russia. Continued outbreaks of violence have hurt both countries.

Breakup of the Soviet Union, 1991
- Extent of former Soviet Union
- New boundaries
- ★ Capitals

A New Economic Power

Since World War II, the nations of Western Europe have learned to work together. In 1950, six nations created the European Economic Community (EEC), better known as the Common Market. It was a free-trade area that included France, West Germany, Belgium, the Netherlands, Luxemburg, and Italy. These nations agreed to not charge tariffs, or fees, on goods imported from each other. Free trade reduced prices and led to economic growth.

Economic cooperation led to closer political ties. In 1994, the Common Market nations formed the European Union (EU). While the nations remained independent, they agreed to enforce certain rules and regulations. For example, the EU nations have set standards for protecting the environment. In 1999, the EU also issued a common currency, called the euro. By 2004, twenty-five nations had joined the EU.

Putting It All Together

Make a concept web about the move to freedom in Eastern Europe. Write "Freedom" in the center of the web. Add each country that became free. Then add details.

> **stop and think**
>
> How would forming a commonwealth help the new nations that emerged from the Soviet Union? Make a list of three ideas and share them with a partner.

Economic Issues in Latin America

Thinking on Your Own

Look at the vocabulary terms for this lesson. As you read, write a sentence for each of the terms. Check with a partner to be sure you have used the words correctly. Then use a synonym for each word in a new sentence.

L atin America faced great challenges during the last half of the twentieth century. Most nations in Central and South America lacked modern economies. For income, they depended on exports to the United States of fruit, coffee, and farm products. Political turmoil also created problems in the region.

focus your reading

Explain why Fidel Castro took over the Cuban government.

Why did the world fear a nuclear war?

Summarize what NAFTA has done for the Mexican economy.

In what Central American conflicts did the United States intervene?

vocabulary

embargo	inflation
maquiladora	austerity
amnesty	

The Cuban Revolution

In the 1950s, the island nation of Cuba faced huge problems. Its economy was based on sugar plantations, owned mostly by companies in the United States. American support helped keep Fulgencio Batista, a harsh dictator, in power. The Cuban people were generally poor, many lived in shacks, and most lacked health care.

In 1959, a young lawyer named Fidel Castro led a revolt that overthrew Batista. The Peoples' Revolution was successful. Castro set up a Communist government

Fidel Castro and Che Guevara wanted to bring communism to Cuba and other Latin American nations.

and made radical changes in the economy. The government took over the sugar plantations and thousands of private businesses. Their Cuban and American owners fled the country.

The United States saw Communist Cuba as a major threat. It placed a trade and travel **embargo** on Cuba. This nearly wrecked the island's economy, as the United States controlled 70 percent of its trade.

The United States government also helped train an invasion force that landed at the Bay of Pigs in 1961. These Cuban exiles, who were trained by the CIA, hoped to lead a revolt against Castro. Instead, the people remained loyal to Castro and the invasion failed.

By then, Castro had turned to the Soviet Union for economic and military help. In 1961, the Soviets built missile sites in Cuba to help "protect" Castro from any future American attack. President John Kennedy blockaded the ships that were delivering missiles and supplies to Cuba. He also demanded that the Soviets turn back the ships bringing the missiles. The Cuban Missile Crisis could have led to a nuclear war. After six tense days, the Soviets backed down.

Castro's revolution was not a democratic revolution. His government controlled the newspapers and jailed its critics. Still, it did provide better medical care for the poor. It also nearly wiped out illiteracy.

The collapse of the Soviet Union in 1991 caused another crisis for Cuba. The Soviet Union was Cuba's major trading partner, buying most of its sugar crop. The result was a sharp economic downturn. In response, Castro allowed some private businesses to open. He also encouraged tourists to visit Cuba. Tourism now brings in more than $2 billion each year. About half of Cuba's workers have service jobs.

Mexico's Economic Boom

In an attempt to grow the economy during the mid-1960s, Mexico set aside a strip of land 12.5 miles (20 km) wide along the United States border. Within this area, any foreign nation can set up a factory, called a

In July 2003, the U.S. Coast Guard stopped this "boat" made of a 1951 Chevy truck. The people trying to come to the U.S. were forced to return to Cuba.

maquiladora. Because these workers are paid less than factory workers in other countries, goods can be produced more cheaply. Still, the workers in the maquiladoras generally earn more than twice the wage of the average Mexican worker.

Mexico and the United States joined with Canada in 1994 to ratify the North American Free Trade Agreement (NAFTA). The United States could see from the success of the European Union that regional trade groups offered an advantage. The second largest free-trade zone in the world, NAFTA nations hope to expand to other nations in the Western Hemisphere, except Cuba. NAFTA has helped Mexico's economy; in 2000, its gross domestic product grew a healthy seven percent. It is the United States's second largest trading partner, replacing Japan. In addition, Mexico has signed trade agreements with other countries in Central and South America, as well as European nations and Israel.

On January 1, 1994, the same day that NAFTA took effect, a revolt in the southern part of Mexico occurred. In the state of Chiapas, Indians and peasants protested the loss of land rights and the way that the economy was being developed. The revolutionaries wanted land, teachers and schools, health care, and roads. The first phase of the rebellion lasted 10 days. Uprisings broke out again in 1997 and continues to be a concern for Mexico's government.

By 2000, the government of Mexico had been controlled by the same political party for 70 years. Leaders were corrupt and debt was rising. In 2000, Mexicans elected Vicente Fox, a businessman from an opposing party—the National Action Party (PAN).

Vicente Fox changed "politics as usual" in Mexico.

One of the largest issues facing Mexico has been the status of its workers in the United States. As many as 3 million Mexicans work in the United States as undocumented immigrants. They do jobs that people born in the U.S. don't want. These jobs offer low pay and, in some cases, are dangerous. Still, Mexican workers send about $9 billion each year back to family members in Mexico. The issue between the two countries is still not resolved. Many undocumented immigrants support **amnesty**— or a general pardon for political offenses, including illegally entering a country.

Conflicts in Central America

The nations of Central America had their own challenges. Rich landowners and factory owners controlled most of the wealth. The majority of the people were very poor. In El Salvador, Nicaragua, and elsewhere, inequality of wealth led to political upheavals.

The economy of El Salvador grew rapidly after World War II. Wealthy land owners got richer by investing in factories. The factories paid low wages. Poor farmers and factory workers sank deeper into poverty.

In the 1970s, workers, farmers, and some leaders of the Catholic Church protested. Poor farmers organized armed guerrilla bands. The army, which ran the government in El Salvador, cracked down. It sent out death squads that killed protest leaders, including Catholic Archbishop Oscar Romero.

The result was a civil war. The United States supported the government, afraid the rebels would make El Salvador a Communist nation. It sent more than $4 million in aid, which only prolonged the war. The two sides finally made peace in 1992, after 75,000 people had been killed.

The economy of Nicaragua also boomed after the war, but workers and farmers felt left out. They organized protest movements. The dictator of Nicaragua, President Anastasio Somoza, sent out his army and police force to kill protestors. Joined by university students, the rebels formed the Sandinista National Liberation Front. In 1979, the Sandinistas overthrew Somoza and took control.

As in El Salvador, the United States opposed the rebels. After they seized power, President Ronald Reagan ordered a trade embargo against Nicaragua. His administration also provided

Time Box

1959
   Castro came to power in Cuba

1980s
   U.S. supported Nicaraguan rebels against Sandinistas

1994
   North American Free Trade Agreement

1999
   Panama Canal returned to Panamanian control

2000
   Vincente Fox elected president of Mexico

over $1 billion and trained a group called the contras, who tried to overthrow the government. Economic hard times in the mid-1980s finally defeated the Sandinistas. They lost the 1990 election to a more conservative candidate, Violeta Chamorro.

The challenges faced by El Salvador and Nicaragua were typical of the problems faced by Central American nations. So, too, was the United States's willingness to get involved in the region. In 1989, the United States sent troops to Panama to arrest its military dictator. They captured and arrested

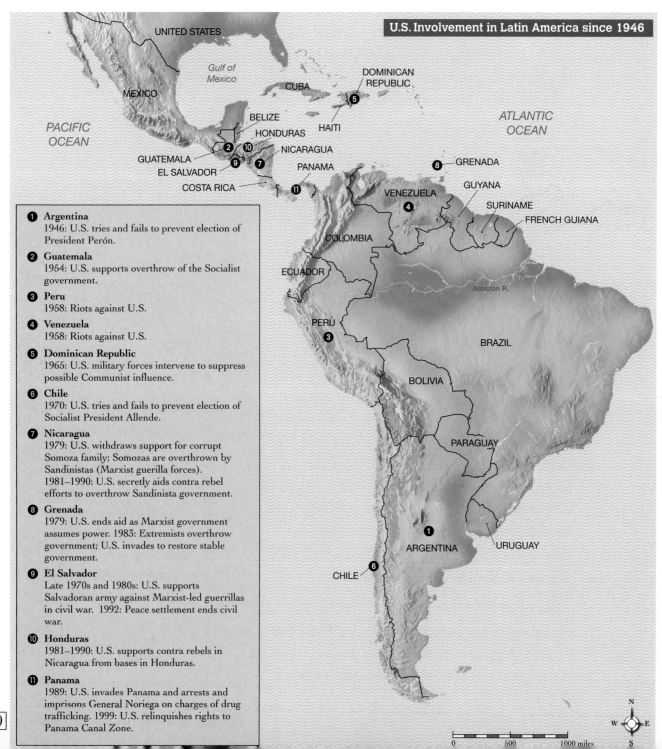

U.S. Involvement in Latin America since 1946

❶ **Argentina**
1946: U.S. tries and fails to prevent election of President Perón.

❷ **Guatemala**
1954: U.S. supports overthrow of the Socialist government.

❸ **Peru**
1958: Riots against U.S.

❹ **Venezuela**
1958: Riots against U.S.

❺ **Dominican Republic**
1965: U.S. military forces intervene to suppress possible Communist influence.

❻ **Chile**
1970: U.S. tries and fails to prevent election of Socialist President Allende.

❼ **Nicaragua**
1979: U.S. withdraws support for corrupt Somoza family; Somozas are overthrown by Sandinistas (Marxist guerilla forces).
1981–1990: U.S. secretly aids contra rebel efforts to overthrow Sandinista government.

❽ **Grenada**
1979: U.S. ends aid as Marxist government assumes power. 1983: Extremists overthrow government; U.S. invades to restore stable government.

❾ **El Salvador**
Late 1970s and 1980s: U.S. supports Salvadoran army against Marxist-led guerrillas in civil war. 1992: Peace settlement ends civil war.

❿ **Honduras**
1981–1990: U.S. supports contra rebels in Nicaragua from bases in Honduras.

⓫ **Panama**
1989: U.S. invades Panama and arrests and imprisons General Noriega on charges of drug trafficking. 1999: U.S. relinquishes rights to Panama Canal Zone.

Violeta Barrios de Chamorro, leader of the anti-Sandinista coalition, was elected president of Nicaragua in 1990.

General Manuel Noriega on charges of trafficking in drugs. They brought him to the United States to stand trial, where he was convicted and sentenced to prison.

Many countries in Latin America are trying to grow their economies. Traditionally, these countries have focused on agriculture. Many countries grow one major crop such as bananas or coffee. These countries are attempting to industrialize and to repay national debt. Military rulers often do not know how to deal with their economic problems. As a result, many Latin American nations have turned to democracy.

Argentina

Argentina is one example of a South American economy in danger. Although it once had one of the strongest economies in Latin America, Argentina came to the edge of financial collapse as the twenty-first century began.

During the 1930s, Argentina had a strong economy based on its exports of beef. After World War II, the nation set out to modernize. Dictatorships and military rule hurt the country. By the end of the 1980s, the rate of **inflation** was 200 percent a month. When neighboring Brazil's economy suffered in 1999, Argentina was harmed as well, because Brazil was a major trading partner.

Like Brazil, Argentina was being supported through loans from the International Monetary Fund (IMF) and other international lenders. By 2001, the nation's debt was $141 billion. Repayment of these loans drained Argentina's economy. The **austerity** measures that the government imposed led to riots and strikes. Austerity measures are designed to control a nation's economy. Many people were unemployed. Foreign companies were unwilling to invest in a nation with an uncertain economy. Argentina is working to recover from this financial disaster.

Putting It All Together

Make a T-chart labeled "Event" and "Importance." List at least five events from the lesson and explain why they were important.

LESSON 3

Asia: Conflict and Economic Growth

Thinking on Your Own

Since 1945, the United States has been deeply involved in Asia. It has fought two wars there. With a partner, list the possible reasons why the United States cares about Asia. Write this list in your notebook.

The late twentieth century brought changes to many countries in Southeast Asia. Both political and economic, these changes affected relationships with Western nations as well as with the people in Asia.

Revolution in China

China began a civil war in 1945. The People's Liberation Army, under the command of Mao Zedong, was strongest in northern China. The Nationalists were strong in central and southern China. They were led by Chiang Kai-shek and supported by the United States. By 1949, Mao's Communist group had defeated the Nationalists. They fled to Taiwan, an island off the southern tip of China. China and Taiwan still disagree over the political status of Taiwan.

Mainland China would like to have a unified country under Communist control, but Taiwan's leaders favor continuing independence. Still, they are tied economically. Hundreds of thousands of Taiwanese people work on the mainland. Trade between China and Taiwan rose more than 34 percent between 2003 and 2004, to $70 billion.

> **focus your reading**
>
> Why did China split into two nations?
>
> Summarize Mao's goals for China.
>
> How did the United States become involved in Korea and Vietnam?
>
> How did Japan improve its economy after World War II?
>
> Explain the four "Little Tigers" and why they were called that.
>
> **vocabulary**
>
> socialist market economy
>
> decolonization
>
> tsunami

stop and think

What do you think would happen to a country if all its ideas, cultures, habits, and customs were taken away? How would the citizens react? Write a bulleted list of five ideas and share them with a partner.

Under Mao, China began various attempts to strengthen the economy and practice communism. Land reform began in 1955, with poor peasants receiving land from rich landowners. Three years later, Mao began the Great Leap Forward, creating farm communes. The peasants did not agree with the system and the weather did not favor the crops. Nearly 15 million people starved before the communes were broken up.

Mao's next move was the Great Proletariat Cultural Revolution. The Red Guards, a group of revolutionary young people, were sent to destroy the "Four Olds." Old ideas, old cultures, old habits, and old customs all had to go.

After Mao died in 1976, a group of reformers ended the Cultural Revolution. These reformers were more moderate, seeking to modernize China. They concentrated on four areas—agriculture, technology, industry, and national defense. By the late 1970s, China had opened trade with other nations. In 1992, the nation began a **socialist market economy**. The government would no longer plan the economic system. Instead it would allow the demand for goods and services to determine pricing and production. China became a major exporter, benefiting from its huge domestic markets and its pool of cheap labor. It joined the World Trade Organization in 2001.

Despite movement into the larger world economically, China's leaders remained closed to democracy. In 1989, the government sent tanks to disperse demonstrators who were calling for

A single demonstrator faces tanks during the Tiananmen Square protest.

reform. Between 500 and 2,000 protesters were killed in Beijing's Tiananmen Square, the site of the protests.

Korean War

Leaders of the Soviet Union and the United States divided Korea into two parts after World War II. The split became permanent in 1948. North Korea was communist, while South Korea was democratic. North Korean troops surged into the south and captured the capital in 1950. The United Nations agreed that South Korea should receive help. The goal was to prevent it from becoming a Communist state.

The Demilitarized Zone in Korea

When troops from the United States and the United Nations pushed into North Korea, the Chinese sent troops. They pushed the U.N. troops back across the thirty-eighth parallel, the boundary between the two nations. This region became known as the Demilitarized Zone (DMZ). The war continued until a 1953 cease-fire, with neither side a clear winner. Tension between the two Koreas continues. A treaty ending the war has never been signed.

War in Vietnam

The period after World War II was marked by **decolonization**. Country after country became determined to be free of European control. One of the longest struggles took place in Vietnam, which had been under French control and was known as French Indochina.

Ho Chi Minh led Communist forces against France in 1946, taking control of most of Vietnam. France, refusing to recognize the new government based in Hanoi, took control of the southern part of the nation.

The French finally withdrew from Vietnam. In 1954, the Vietminh forced the French to surrender at Dien Bien Phu. The two sides agreed to divide Vietnam temporarily until an election could be held to decide on a new government. The election never took place.

Instead, President Dwight D. Eisenhower and President John F. Kennedy supported the anti-Communists who controlled South Vietnam. In 1965, President Lyndon B. Johnson sent American troops to Vietnam, the first of about 2.7 million who would serve there. The United States finally withdrew from Vietnam in 1973, after more than 58,000 soldiers were killed and 300,000 were wounded. In 1975, North Vietnam took over South Vietnam, creating one Communist nation.

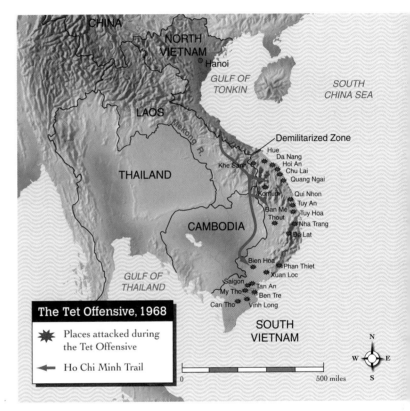

Economic Growth in the Pacific

After World War II ended, the United States tried to help Japan restore economic productivity. By 1949, only four years after its surrender, Japan was working at its prewar levels. Japan had few natural resources and a large population. It had also lost its overseas empire. Nevertheless, the nation focused on exporting goods. The low wages which Japanese workers received offset the cost of importing raw materials. Japanese products were competitively priced in the world market.

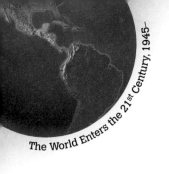

During the 1970s, Japanese industry began to focus on producing technology-related equipment. Although a recession slowed growth during the 1990s, the example Japan set was an encouragement to other Asian nations.

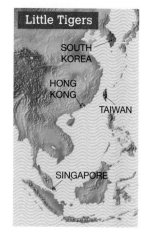

Little Tigers

SOUTH KOREA

HONG KONG

TAIWAN

SINGAPORE

Singapore, South Korea, Hong Kong, and Taiwan followed Japan's example. These Pacific Rim countries became known as the "Little Tigers." Like Japan, each of them had many people and little capital or natural resources. They also became export-driven and became Japan's competitors during the 1990s. Indonesia, Thailand, and Malaysia soon joined the original group of four.

India has also experienced unparalleled economic growth. After achieving independence from Britain in 1948, the country began to modernize. Many corporations in the United States moved part of their operations to India. These companies took advantage of the large labor force and low wages.

Asian nations experienced huge climate upheavals, as well as economic changes. In December 2004, a **tsunami** struck. This underground, oceanic earthquake began on the west coast of Sumatra, an island in the Pacific. Trillions of tons of water moved as the Earth shifted. The tsunami's effects reached more than 3,000 miles away to East Africa. Hundreds of thousands died, and the economies of several nations were severely affected.

Putting It All Together

Make a timeline showing the progress and challenges of Asian nations after World War II. Compare your timeline with that of a partner. Add details as you review the lesson.

Time Box

1949
Nationalist Army defeated, moved to Taiwan

1950
North Korea invaded South Korea

1952
Japan's independence restored

1958
The Great Leap Forward began in China

1965
U.S. troops sent to Vietnam

1979
The United States and China resumed diplomatic relations

1989
Protests in Tiananmen Square

1997
Hong Kong returned to China's control

Independence Movements in Africa

Thinking on Your Own

What are some of the first things a new government must deal with? Develop a concept web to answer this question. Then write a paragraph about the important issues. Share your paragraph with a partner to compare your ideas.

Some people refer to 1960 as "the year of Africa." It was a turning point for African nations wanting freedom from European colonial rule. Thirteen countries gained their independence from France that year, setting an example for the rest of Africa.

focus your reading

Discuss why 1960 was called "the year of Africa"?

Explain apartheid.

Why is Nelson Mandela important to South Africa?

What was Pan-Africanism?

vocabulary

apartheid   Pan-Africanism

sanctions

New Nations Form

By the beginning of the twentieth century, European rulers enacted laws that took away the land of the native people and forced them to work in mines or on farms. Many native people were little more than slaves. They had no rights and no support.

After decades of this treatment, Africans wanted to regain their independence. This process was called decolonization. It was complicated by the many divisions within the African societies. Many language groups, religions, and ethnic differences existed, and many different solutions were set forth.

This was also the era of the Cold War. Free European governments delayed granting independence. They assumed that Africans were not ready for self-government and feared that Communist ideas would grow. Harsh laws were passed, supposedly to prevent communism.

France was determined to keep its colony Algeria, in North Africa. While fighting there, the French allowed other colonies to be free. The conflict in Algeria lasted from 1954 until 1962, when France at last agreed to independence.

The Sub-Saharan nations of Central and Southern Africa slowly gained independence as well. Many changed their names, which had reflected the white colonization. For example, Rhodesia had been named for Cecil Rhodes, a British administrator. At independence, the nation became Zimbabwe, honoring one of the great African kingdoms of the past.

South African Independence

One of the most amazing examples of decolonization occurred in South Africa. Originally the Dutch settled the region, which later passed to British control. In 1948, the British enacted strict laws separating blacks and whites, a policy known as **apartheid**.

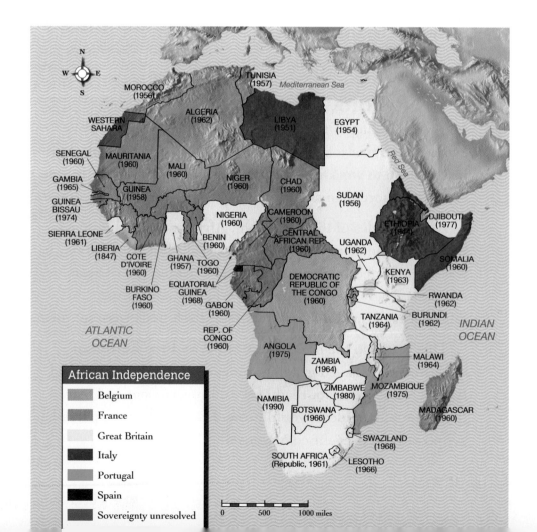

Blacks, who made up the majority of the population, struggled against the unjust rules. Apartheid governed every part of life: where a person could live, what entrance to the train he or she could use, how or if he or she would be educated. Many blacks were killed or jailed as a result of uprisings. Nelson Mandela, a black leader, was arrested in 1962 for resisting apartheid and sentenced to life in prison. For 27 years he remained a prisoner who believed in the cause of freedom.

Long lines of people waited to vote in the historic 1994 South African election.

Sanctions were passed against South Africa. Many nations, including the United States, refused to trade with the country because of its human rights violations. In

Nelson Mandela

addition, violent protests within the nation were heightened in 1984. Indians and "colored" people, who were of mixed race, gained some civil rights while blacks were still excluded. Finally, the white rulers determined that all non-whites should be allowed to vote. Nelson Mandela was freed from Robbin Island Prison in 1990. Four years later, when the first democratic elections were held, Mandela became the first democratically elected president.

The Quest for African Unity

Some of the new leaders throughout Africa believed in **Pan-Africanism**. This idea meant that all Africans would join together to meet common goals. Community is a strong African tradition. Pan-Africanism wanted to use that tradition to benefit all Africans.

stop and think

What are some of the problems that African nations could work together to solve? Make a list of concerns for that continent. Then choose one and, in a short paragraph, explain why it is a problem for all of Africa.

In 1963, leaders of 32 African nations created the Organization of African Unity (OAU). It became the African Union in 2002, with 53 members. The goals of the group include economic growth and democracy.

Many African nations are among the very poorest countries in the world. To modernize, educate, and care for the sick, they have borrowed from Western industrialized nations. At a meeting in 2005, the largest of these nations, known as the G7—or Group of Seven—worked to solve the problems caused by huge indebtedness. The Sub-Saharan African nations, for example, owe about $70 billion to large lenders such as the International Monetary Fund and the World Bank. The G7 have set a goal of ridding Africa of poverty by 2015.

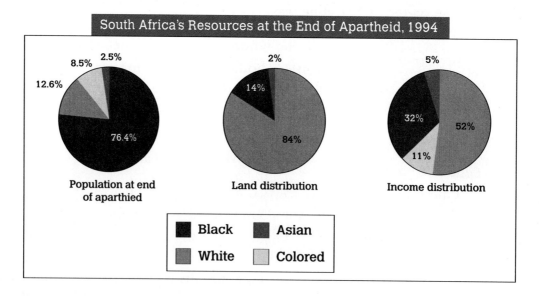

South Africa's Resources at the End of Apartheid, 1994

8.5%	2.5%
12.6%	
76.4%	

Population at end of aparthied

14% / 2% / 84%

Land distribution

32% / 5% / 52% / 11%

Income distribution

Black / Asian / White / Colored

Time Box

1951
Libya gained independence from Italy

1960
Thirteen French colonies gained independence

1963
Organization of African Unity (OAU) formed

1994
First democratic elections in South Africa

2002
African Union replaced OAU

Putting It All Together

Make a Venn diagram comparing and contrasting the experiences of freedom in Algeria and South Africa. Conduct additional research if needed.

Conflict in the Middle East

Thinking on Your Own

What do you already know about the nations in the Middle East? What would you like to know more about? Make a K-W-L chart and write the answers as you read the lesson. Then write a brief paragraph explaining one of the things you learned.

The Middle East has been a scene of political turmoil through the centuries. During the post-World War II era, conflict erupted many times.

The Nation of Israel

The region of Palestine was under British control between the two world wars. In the early twentieth century, groups of Jewish people had argued for the creation of an Israeli state. They wanted it located in the land known as Palestine, which they regarded as theirs since biblical times. Since being driven from the land by the Romans in A.D. 70, the Jewish people had been longing for a homeland.

Sympathy for the Jews increased as people learned of the deaths of millions in Hitler's Holocaust. However, Palestine was primarily an Arab Muslim region, and old hatreds between the groups were strong.

focus your reading

Why was there greater sympathy toward the idea of a Jewish state after World War II?

What is OPEC?

Describe Pan-Arabism.

What happened in Iran after the monarchy was overthrown?

vocabulary

intifada

Pan-Arabism

pre-emptive strike

Jewish children who survived the Holocaust arrived in Palestine looking for a home

In 1948, the United Nations divided Palestine into Arab and Jewish portions despite the objections of Arab nations. As soon as Israel was declared a nation, these old enemies attacked. Israel defeated them in 1948 and again in land disputes during 1967.

Israel

	Israel after UN partition of Palestine, 1947
	Israel after War of 1948–1949
	Occupied by Israel after Six-Day War, 1967
	Occupied by Israel after October War, 1973
	Returned to Egypt, 1978–1982

0   500 miles

SYRIA
Beirut • LEBANON
Damascus • Golan Heights
Haifa •
West Bank
Tel Aviv • Amman •
Jerusalem •
Gaza • Gaza Strip   JORDAN
Cairo •   ISRAEL   SAUDI ARABIA
Suez
EGYPT
IRAQ

The Palestine Liberation Organization was an Egyptian initiative. Founded in 1964, it has used terrorism to bring about a Palestinian state. In the early 1980s and in 2000, the PLO declared an **intifada**—or uprising—to achieve the goal of a Palestinian homeland.

Tensions with Israel began to ease with the death of longtime PLO leader Yasser Arafat in 2004. Discussion over peace and land issues continued with Jerusalem's West Bank being a major focus.

Egypt's leaders also favored **Pan-Arabism**, the unity of all Arabs. A union between Egypt and Syria did not last; however, several Arab states did join to form the Organization of Petroleum Exporting Countries (OPEC). This group controls oil prices and thus affects the world's economy.

In 1993, U.S. President Bill Clinton watches as Yitzhak Rabin, Israel's prime minister, and PLO leader Yasser Arafat shake hands after agreeing to a Declaration of Principles for peace.

Wars in the Persian Gulf Region

In addition to the conflicts between Israel and its Arab neighbors, the Persian Gulf region has been unstable. The nation of Iran ended the monarchy with a coup in 1979. Under fundamentalist Muslim clergy, the nation moved to a conservative interpretation of Islamic law.

stop and think

What do you think might have happened if Pan-Arabism had worked? Share your ideas with a partner. Then write a short paragraph explaining what the Middle East could have become.

Time Box

1948
Israel became a nation

1960
OPEC formed

1979
Shah of Iran overthrown

2001
Taliban driven from power in Afghanistan

2005
Democratic elections in Iraq

Also in 1979, Saddam Hussein came to power in neighboring Iraq. From 1980 until 1988, Iraq and Iran were at war. Victory bounced back and forth between the nations until the cease-fire. In 1990, Iraq invaded Kuwait, prompting the United Nations and U.S. forces to attack Iraq. Kuwait was restored as its own nation.

In 2003, the United States launched a **pre-emptive strike** against Iraq, declaring war in the mistaken belief that the Iraqis were developing weapons of mass destruction. Saddam Hussein and many of Iraq's key government officials were captured although insurgent fighting continued.

In early 2005, free elections were held in Iraq for the first time in 50 years. The Shiite Muslim majority regained control of the Iraqi government. Many Sunni Muslims, who had held power under Hussein, boycotted the election. Nevertheless, about 58 percent of eligible voters cast ballots. A 275-member National Assembly wrote the constitution for the new democracy.

The 2005 Iraqi elections

The United States also intervened in Afghanistan. In 1989, it helped remove the Soviets, who had been fighting there for a decade. An Islamic fundamentalist group, the Taliban, gained control of the nation in 1996. In 2001, American bombers and rebel forces defeated the Taliban regime as part of a response to the September 11 terrorist attacks.

Putting It All Together

Choose an important event in the Middle East and write a news story about it.

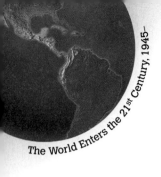

Chapter Summary

- **Totalitarian** governments existed in Eastern Europe.
- The Soviet Union controlled many Eastern European countries, known as **satellite nations**.
- When Mikhail Gorbachev came to power, he favored **perestroika**, or restructuring of the government.
- Several attempts at **ethnic cleansing** in the nations of Bosnia and Albania left thousands dead.
- The Mexican government would like **amnesty** for illegal Mexican workers in the United States.
- After World War II, the Mexican government allowed the U.S. to build factories, known as **maquiladoras**, near the border the two countries share.
- The United States placed an **embargo** on Cuba after Castro nationalized its industries.
- **Inflation** brought Argentina to the edge of collapse.
- Argentina enacted economic **austerity** measures.
- After the death of Mao Zedong, China favored a limited **socialist market economy**.
- A **tsunami** struck Southeast Asia at the end of 2004.
- The **decolonization** of Africa started in the 1960s.
- The **apartheid** policies in South Africa brought **sanctions** from the rest of the world.
- Some leaders favored **Pan-Africanism** as a way to address problems across the continent.
- Arabs declared an **intifada** to protest Israeli actions.
- **Pan-Arabism** attempted to join Arab nations of the Middle East.
- The U.S. moved to a **pre-emptive strike** against Iraq.

Chapter Review

1 Select one region of the world covered in this chapter. Write a five-paragraph essay explaining how it has or has not moved toward greater freedom since World War II ended.

2 Create a Venn diagram to compare and contrast two regions discussed in this chapter. Then write a comparison and contrast paragraph about the two regions.

Skill Builder

Problem Solving and Decision Making

Identifying a problem and deciding what to do about it are two skills that everyone can use — from students to business executives to government officials. For example, you would like to go to the movies once a week. However, you never seem to have any money. What do you do? Say "Well, that's life" and never go to the movies? Or, do you figure out how you spend your money and make a decision how to save some for movies?

Identifying the Problem

You have identified the problem: You never have enough money.

To determine how you spend your money, you should gather information about your spending habits for a week. Make a list of what you buy and how much you spend for each thing. After a week, you should know how you spend your money.

Some things you have to buy. You cannot stop paying for subway passes to school and for lunch. But do you need a new CD every week? How about that snack of a soda and slice of pizza a couple of days a week?

Making the Decision

You have figured out how you spend your money. Some things are necessities like lunch. Other things are "luxuries" like new CDs.

Which do you want more:
- to go to the movies or to eat pizza?
- to go to the movies or to have the latest CD?

To help you decide, look at the advantages of each thing and the disadvantages of giving it up. For example, what do you gain by buying the latest CD? If you did not buy the latest CD, what would you lose?

Skill Builder

Now ask yourself the same questions about going to the movies and eating pizza.

Look at your answers. Which choice offers you the most advantages and the least disadvantages? Choose the one that makes the most sense to you and follow it.

Evaluating the Solution/Decision

After a few weeks, review your decision. Evaluate how well it is working. Does it still make the most sense? Maybe going to the movies every week is not as much as fun as you thought it would be. Maybe having pizza is more fun. You could change your decision.

To help you identify problems and make decisions, follow these steps:

1. Identify the problem.
2. Gather information about the problem.
3. List as many solutions as you can think of.
4. Review the advantages and disadvantages of each solution.
5. Decide on your solution.
6. Put your solution/decision into practice.
7. Review and evaluate your decision after a period of time.

Complete the following activities.

1   Think of a problem that you have. It could be a real problem or a made-up one. Go through Steps 1 to 5 to reach a possible solution. Then think of how you would evaluate whether your solution is working.

2   Discuss with a partner two problems that the national government is facing. Talk about how the government might work through Steps 2 to 7 for each problem.

Chapter 24

THE WORLD: OPPORTUNITIES AND CHALLENGES

Getting Focused

The study of history is the study of connections. Historians look to the past for the causes of later events and the effects of those events on later happenings. There is an old saying that "history repeats itself." It does not have to. People can change tomorrow by learning from yesterday and today. The goal of this special chapter is to show you that change can happen. Each case study provides an overview of an important issue that people face today. Each case study also presents some ways that people are tackling these issues.

Businesses and governments go through problem-solving and decision-making processes. Suppose a business is considering building a factory in China. It must identify possible problems and look for solutions. Only after the company has done that, can it decide whether it makes business sense to build the factory.

Suppose a nation is trying to reduce pollution from factories. The government gathers information about how factories are polluting the air. Then it investigates ways to stop the pollution. All this work has to be done before the government can write laws to stop or reduce pollution.

How would you solve the problems presented in this chapter?

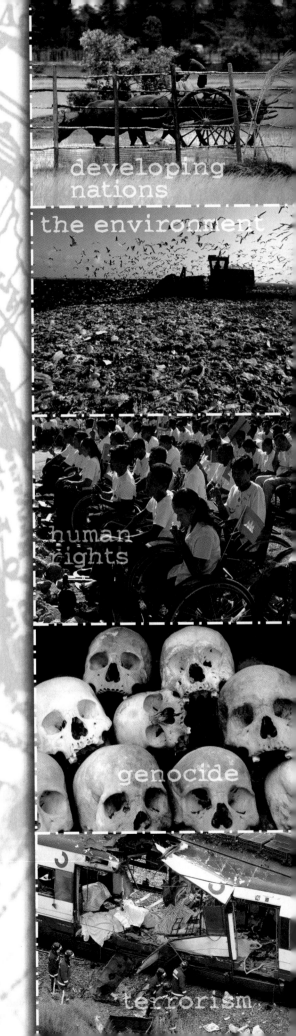

developing nations

the environment

human rights

genocide

terrorism

Case Study 1:
Developing Nations

▶ **What are the problems in developing nations?**

▶ **What are some possible solutions?**

In economic terms, the world is divided into rich nations and poor nations. The poor nations are called developing nations. Their economies are based on agriculture and the export of natural resources, and the standard of living is low. Developed nations have industrialized economies and a high standard of living. An industrialized economy is one in which the majority of people do not earn their living by farming. Instead, most people work in offices, stores, and factories.

Another way to look at developing and developed nations is by geographic location. Examine the map on this page. The rich, or developed, nations tend to be in the Northern Hemisphere, with the exception of Australia and

New Zealand. The poor, or developing, nations are generally in the Southern Hemisphere. Think back to your study of the European colonization of Central and South America, Southeast Asia, and Africa. European efforts to keep their colonies economically dependent help to explain the lag in development of these nations.

Economists and sociologists talk about the standard of living of a nation. Standard of living measures the quality of life of a nation's people. It evaluates how much people are able to buy of certain goods and services. Among these are food, housing, clothing, education, medical care, and recreation. Examine the table on the next page to learn more about the differences between developing and developed nations.

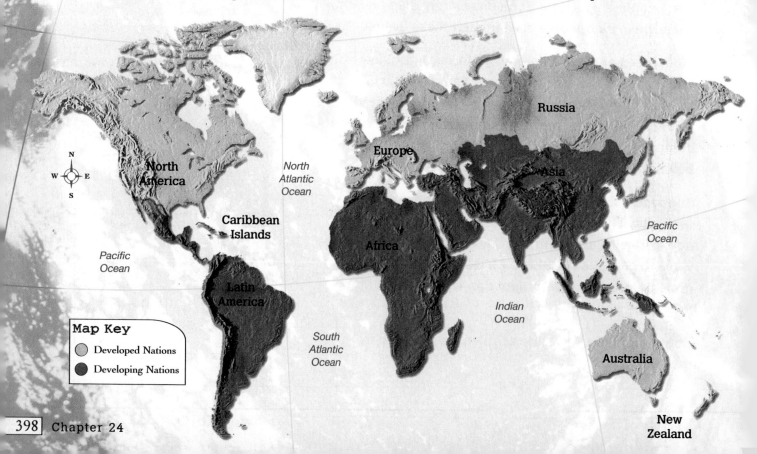

Map Key
- ○ Developed Nations
- ● Developing Nations

Selected Statistics of Developing and Developed Nations

Nation	Per Capita Income*	Infant Mortality Rate (deaths per 1,000 births)	Total Fertility Rate (births per woman)	Motor Vehicles (per 1,000 people)	Telephones*** (per 100 people)	Televisions (per 1,000 people)
Angola	$1,900	118	7	5	1	13
Bangladesh	$1,700	67	4	2	n/a♦	6
Cambodia	$2,000	73	5	1	n/a	9
China	$5,000	37	2**	10	9	321
Peru	$5,200	37	3	44	6	126
Germany	$27,000	5	1	554 (1991 est.)	59	567
Italy	$26,800	5	1	617	46	528
USA	$32,778	7	2	798	67	806

* Per capita income is the average income. All numbers are given in U.S. dollars.

** China has an official policy to discourage population growth.

*** The statistics for telephones do not include cell phones.

♦ n/a means not available.

Problems of Developing Nations

Many people in developing nations live in rural areas and make their living from agriculture.

Because they have limited money, developing nations have limited health care systems. As a result, the infant mortality, or death rate for children under one year of age, is high in these countries. Examine the table to see the contrast in infant mortality rates between developing and developed nations.

Even if children survive infancy in developing nations, many will die before they reach adulthood. Two million children die each year from diseases, such as measles, which can be prevented with vaccinations. Their parents are too poor to pay for the shots. In some cases, their nations are too poor to import the vaccines and distribute them through free clinics.

The world's population is now more than 6 billion people. Almost 800 million people suffer from malnutrition. They do not get enough to eat each day to meet their minimum energy needs. In certain areas of the world, such as sub-Saharan Africa, people live on less than $US2 per day. Over 200 million children under the age of five are malnourished.

As nations become more developed, infant mortality rates decline. Birth rates have also declined. There are several reasons for this. First, couples no longer need to have so many children to be sure that some will live. Second, raising children has become more expensive. Third, as a nation becomes wealthier, education becomes more available to women. Having an education and fewer children frees women to work outside the home.

World Food Day
October 16

World Food Day is organized by the Food and Agriculture Organization of the United Nations. Its goal is to educate people about world hunger and the need to end the problem. More than 150 nations, including the United States, participate in the event each year.

Foreign Aid

A major problem for developing nations is debt repayment. While they were colonies, developing nations exported raw materials and imported manufactured goods. After independence, the new nations had to borrow large sums of money to modernize and industrialize. These nations continue to borrow millions of dollars a year. In some countries, a large part of the borrowed money does not go to infrastructure—to buy machines and build roads. It goes to buy such basics as food and medical care and to pay the interest on the loans. Interest payments are a heavy burden on the borrowing nations.

In 2005, a group of 28 developed nations agreed to give grants of money to the very poorest nations rather than loans. In addition, the loans that these poor nations already had were forgiven. They do not have to repay them.

The money grants are part of what is called foreign aid. Foreign aid is economic and military assistance given by one nation to another. The Marshall Plan, after World War II, was one of the first U.S. foreign aid programs. Since then, the United States has contributed more than $460 billion in foreign aid. About $160 billion was for military help. Today, the United States is the second largest contributor of foreign aid in the world. Japan ranks first.

Zimbabweans wait in line for USA food aid.

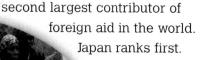

VIEWPOINT

Don't Just Throw Money at the World's Poor

"Poor countries face high tariffs, quotas, or subsidized competition from rich nations in industries such as food processing, textiles, and agriculture. The World Bank estimates that . . . dismantling of these barriers could be worth $350 billion to the developing world in the next decade and could lift 144 million people out of poverty. Reducing trade barriers would also help consumers in the industrialized nations."

—*Jeffrey E. Garten,* BusinessWeek, *March 7, 2005*

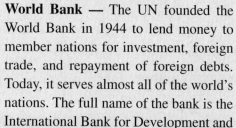

NAMES IN THE NEWS

The following international organizations work with developing nations on economic growth:

World Bank — The UN founded the World Bank in 1944 to lend money to member nations for investment, foreign trade, and repayment of foreign debts. Today, it serves almost all of the world's nations. The full name of the bank is the International Bank for Development and Reconstruction. Through contributions from member nations, the World Bank provides about 10 percent of the world's foreign aid.

International Monetary Fund (IMF) — The IMF, founded in 1945, is an agency of the UN. Its purpose is to promote economic cooperation among its 184 member nations. It works with nations to set exchange rates for their money and to expand foreign trade.

World Trade Organization (WTO) — The WTO was created in 1995. It oversees compliance with international trade agreements and rules on violations by member nations. It has more than 148 members, including all the major nations of the world.

Making a Difference: Microloans

Microloans are used throughout Indonesia.

A microloan is a loan of money in a small amount, such as $40. That may not seem like much, but in Bangladesh it could establish a woman in business making and selling bamboo stools. That is how microlending began.

In 1974, Muhammad Yunus was visiting a village in Bangladesh and met a woman making stools from bamboo. She earned very little because of an arrangement she had with a supplier. He gave her the bamboo and she had to sell him her finished stools. The supplier paid her what he wanted and then sold the stools for much more.

Dr. Yunus was a professor of economics and he began to think about the woman's problem. She had no capital, or money, to buy the bamboo. If she could actually buy bamboo, she could sell her stools herself and make a profit. Instead, the bamboo supplier was making a profit. Dr. Yunus studied the village. In all, he found 42 villagers who could start their own businesses if they had some money to invest. How much money did they need? Twenty-seven dollars—just $27 for all 42 villagers.

Dr. Yunus started the Grameen Bank to lend people like these villagers small amounts of money so they could start their own businesses. *Grameen* means "village." The Grameen Bank is not a charity. It charges interest on its loans just like any other bank and has branches throughout Bangladesh. About 90 percent of its loans are made to women starting their own businesses.

Today, the Grameen Bank is international. By the early 2000s, the bank had made 3.7 million loans around the world. Women make up 96 percent of the borrowers.

Other people have learned from Dr. Yunus' idea. For example, in Kazakhstan, the Asian Credit Fund makes similar microloans. The XacBank helps small borrowers get businesses started in Mongolia.

The Green Revolution

The Green Revolution was a program to increase crop yields—or the amount of food grown per acre. In the 1940s, scientists created new kinds of wheat that produced more grain. The new plants were also more resistant to disease. India, Pakistan, and nations in Latin America began growing the new wheat. New types of corn and rice were also developed.

The new plants more than doubled grain harvests worldwide between 1950 and 1990. However, the new plants required irrigation systems and chemical fertilizers and pesticides. Peasant farmers could not afford these and lost their land to larger farm owners with more money. The use of chemicals and large amounts of water for irrigation created environmental problems. Despite these problems, the Green Revolution improved living standards for millions of people.

investigative reporting

With a partner, research and prepare a presentation about one of the following programs that works with developing nations:

- Bill and Melinda Gates Foundation
- Grameen Bank
- Green Revolution
- Food and Agriculture Organization (FAO)
- World Food Day

Case Study 2:
The Environment

▶ **What are some of the issues affecting the environment?**

▶ **What specific environmental issues face developing nations?**

▶ **Explain five things you can do to help the environment.**

When people talk about the environment, they mean all the things around us in nature—our natural resources. The environment includes both renewable and nonrenewable natural resources.

Renewable resources are water, air, soil, and plant and animal life. They renew or replace themselves over time. For example, when trees die in a forest fire, new trees will grow in the same forest over time. When topsoil wears out and blows away, new topsoil will form—one inch every 200 years.

Nonrenewable resources are those that cannot be replaced. Once they are used up, they are gone. Fossil fuels and minerals such as iron and copper are nonrenewable resources. Fossil fuels are coal, natural gas, and petroleum, or oil.

The Industrial Revolution greatly changed how people affected the environment. In early farming economies, there was little need to use nonrenewable resources. Horses or oxen pulled plows, and water power moved the wheels that ground wheat. Women cooked over an open fire and sewed clothes by candlelight.

However, as nations began to industrialize, they needed more and more renewable and nonrenewable resources. Coal and petroleum became important sources of energy. The smoke from factories burning coal began to

THE LAST GLOBAL WARMING NON-BELIEVER

ALASKA'S GLACIERS MELTING FAST

www.caglecartoons.com

pollute the air in industrial cities. Wastes from factories and cities flowed into rivers and polluted them.

Earlier farmers used to let some fields lie fallow—or unused—each year to allow the soil to replace nutrients. As populations increased, farmers had to plant more and more fields every year to grow enough to feed the increasing population. As a result, soil began to wear out from overfarming. Forests were cut down faster than new trees could grow. The lumber was needed to build houses and factories as well as ships to carry all the new manufactured goods.

One way to understand this rapid use of resources is to look at the production of iron in Great Britain. In 1757, Great Britain produced 18,000 tons of iron. In 1850, it produced 2.25 million tons of iron. This jump in production increased not only the iron sold, but also the amount of iron ore and coal used. Coal was needed to power the huge furnaces that made iron from iron ore.

Today, even the use of resources is sharply divided between developed and developing nations. About 20 percent of the world's population lives in developed nations. However, they use 86 percent of the world's natural non-energy resources and 70 percent of its energy resources.

The Dilemma of Developing Nations

Environmentalism is the movement to conserve, or save, and improve the environment. Environmentalists want to save the world's natural resources and improve our quality of life. For example, if air pollution is reduced, the health of an area's residents will improve. There will be fewer cases of asthma and other respiratory diseases.

When it comes to the environment, developing nations face a dilemma, or difficult problem. Many developing nations still rely on selling raw materials or cash crops for export. Nations like the Philippines are cutting down their forests with little effort to replace them. Other nations like South Africa and Nigeria are selling their mineral resources and petroleum reserves. They need the money that their resources will bring, but selling those resources means losing them forever.

In addition, developing nations use much of their export earnings to buy basics for their citizens. These nations are trying to industrialize, but they often lack the money to buy the technology needed to create environmentally friendly industries.

Schoolchildren wear masks in Malaysia to protect themselves from poor air quality.

Air Pollution

A variety of chemicals is released into the air every day. Among them are carbon monoxide and nitrogen oxide from car engines, factories, cigarette smoke, and jet planes. These and other chemicals create air pollution. Acid rain and global warming are two results of air pollution.

Acid rain contains high levels of acid from certain chemicals released into the air. Acid rain falling into rivers and lakes kills fish. It also kills trees and eats away marble on buildings.

Global warming is an increase in the temperature of the earth's surface. By the 1990s, the upward trend in temperature had become noticeable. Many scientists believe that human activity is responsible for global warming. The increase in world population and the industrialization of more nations result in the burning of more fossil fuels. These produce large quantities of greenhouse gases, which heat up the atmosphere.

To reduce air pollution, some nations are supporting efforts to develop other forms of energy. Among these alternative sources of power are solar, water, wind, and nuclear. In 1997, more than 150 nations negotiated the Kyoto Protocol, or agreement, to reduce the production of carbon dioxide and other greenhouse gases. The United States, Australia, and India, among other nations, have not ratified the treaty. The Bush administration agreed with business leaders that adding pollution controls would be expensive and put an unfair burden on U.S. industry. Developing nations gave similar reasons for not joining the agreement.

Rain Forests and Deforestation

The Amazon River Basin in South America is the largest rain forest in the world. Other areas with large rain forests are in Central America, Central Africa, and Southeast Asia. Rain forests are home to thousands of species, or types, of birds, insects, animals, and plants. Fifty percent of all trees in the world grow in the rain forests. It is estimated that the trees in the Amazon provide 40 percent of the world's oxygen exchange and are vitally important to the purification of the world's air and water vapor quality.

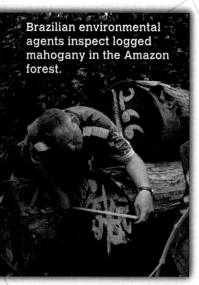

Brazilian environmental agents inspect logged mahogany in the Amazon forest.

The major danger to the rain forests is deforestation. This is the cutting down of forests without planting new trees. For example, the Amazon rain forest is 1.6 million square miles. However, every year ranchers, developers, and loggers illegally clear more and more of the land. Experts estimate that the area loses 6,600 square miles of rain forest each year. In all, 20 percent of the Amazon rain forest has disappeared.

The Brazilian government is often powerless against the armed gunmen who protect the wealthy cattle ranchers and loggers. However,

Soil Erosion and Desertification

Soil erosion is the wearing away of the thin layer of topsoil. This is the fertile soil that is needed to grow plants. Overfarming is the major reason for soil erosion. However, overgrazing by animals and cutting down trees also cause soil erosion and desertification. This occurs when land dries out so much that it becomes desert. The UN reports that about 15 million acres of land become desert every year.

The hardest hit area in the world is North Africa. Desertification, along with years of little or no rain, caused a famine in the region in the 1970s and 1980s. With no way to feed themselves, hundreds of thousands died. Survivors left their homes and became refugees.

in 2005, the murder of a Roman Catholic nun, Sister Dorothy Stang, forced the Brazilian government to act.

Sister Stang opposed the destruction of the rain forest and worked to protect the rights of the native population living there. Ranchers and loggers forced them into near slave-like work arrangements. After Sister Stang's murder, the Brazilian government sent in federal police to investigate and set up two new preserves in the Amazon rain forest. Some 9.2 million acres will now be protected.

Water: Fast Facts

- Only 45 percent of the people in developing nations have safe water, whereas 96 percent of the people in developed nations have safe water.
- 95 percent of cities around the world dump raw sewage into surface water (rivers, lakes, and oceans).
- Other forms of water pollution are solid wastes such as soda cans and plastic bottles, chemicals from factories, pesticides, fertilizers, and oil spills from oil tankers.
- 80 percent of water worldwide is used in farming, but 60 percent of that is wasted. Developing nations cannot afford the irrigation systems that use water efficiently.

What You Can Do for the Environment

1. You can write to local officials, state legislators, or members of Congress stating your position.

2. You can join a nongovernmental organizaion (NGO) that shares your viewpoint on environmental issues.

3. You can follow the 3Rs:

   Reduce: Cut down on what you use.

   - Use reusable containers for food instead of plastic bags.
   - Don't keep the water running while you brush your teeth.
   - Turn off the lights when you leave a room.

   Reuse: Figure out ways to reuse things.

   - Don't throw away the plastic bags from the grocery store. Use them as trash bags.
   - Use the blank side of school assignment sheets for scratch paper.

   Recycle: Recycle everything that you can.

   - Many communities have curbside pickup to recycle paper, cans and bottles, cardboard, and clothes.
   - Cartridges from printers and fax machines can be sent back free to the manufacturer to be recycled.
   - Cell phones, computers, and printers can be recycled. Contact your community to find out where and how to recycle them.

4. If you live in a place where you can have a garden, you can add a fourth R: *Rot.* Rot? Those banana peels and wilted lettuce leaves along with grass clippings and tree leaves make good compost. Compost is a natural fertilizer. You can spread it around trees and bushes and on your garden to help trees and plants grow.

NGOs and the Environment

There are a number of nongovernmental organizations (NGOs) that work to save the environment. These organizations are often described as "green." Among the well-known U.S. conservation and environmental NGOs are the World Wildlife Fund, Audubon Society, Nature Conservancy, and Sierra Club.

Sustainable Development

Sustainable development is economic development that uses natural resources to meet present needs without endangering supplies for the future. In other words, those who favor sustainable development believe people must make better use of resources. They believe that each generation must ensure that there are natural resources left for future generations.

Those who support sustainable development ask people to use less natural resources. For example, an advocate for sustainable development would not call for more oil drilling. Instead, he or she would try to influence automakers to produce—and consumers to buy—smaller, more fuel-efficient cars.

investigative reporting

With a partner, choose one of the following topics to learn more about. Create a poster to explain the issue and what is being done about it on the national or international level.

- air pollution
- water pollution (rivers or oceans)
- desertification
- deforestation
- energy use
- building dams

Human Rights

▶ **What are human rights?**

▶ **Describe how human rights have been addressed globally.**

UN trained specialists clear land mines in Iraq.

You may be surprised to learn that not all nations agree on a definition of basic human rights. A nation's cultural values influence its ideas about human rights. For example, the United States values freedom of the individual. It grants rights to women, such as the right to vote and to own property. In a nation influenced by Islamic teachings, women have fewer rights. For example, women in Saudi Arabia are not allowed to drive. In many developing nations, marriages are arranged by parents when the future bride and groom are still children.

In 1948, the UN drafted the Universal Declaration of Human Rights. The document was an attempt to define basic human rights. (See pages 437–440 for the complete document.) However, it is not legally binding. Nations do not have to guarantee the rights outlined in the document.

In order to make nations responsible for guaranteeing these basic human rights, the UN over the years has written additional documents on areas of human rights. These conventions, or agreements, and treaties are legally binding for the nations that ratify them. However, not all nations ratify them. Some of the UN's human rights documents

- make genocide a crime
- describe how prisoners of war should be treated, banning torture
- guarantee political and civil rights
- eliminate discrimination against women
- guarantee freedoms and protections to children

Universal Declaration of Human Rights

In 1976, the Declaration became international law after being ratified by 35 countries. To date, 65 countries have ratified the document.

"Article 1 All human beings are born free and equal in dignity and rights. . . .

Article 2 Everyone is entitled to all the rights and freedoms set forth in this Declaration, without distinction of any kind, such as race, color, sex, language, religion, political or other opinion, national or social origin, property, birth or other status. . . .**"**

VIEWPOINT

Capital Punishment

One issue that many people do not agree about is capital punishment—or the use of death as a penalty. Many people consider it an abuse of human rights. More than 60 nations have banned the death penalty. However, a majority of states in the United States continue to impose the death sentence for certain crimes.

Human Rights Abuses

What specifically are human rights abuses? The following is a partial list of abuses that human rights organizations are working to end:

- murder of political opponents
- jailing of political opponents without fair trials
- torture of political prisoners
- censorship of the media
- slavery
- trafficking in (selling) women and children
- discrimination against women in education, employment, and the legal system
- the use of landmines
- discrimination against people with HIV/AIDS
- bombing of civilians in wartime
- discrimination against minorities in education, employment, and the legal system
- the use of threats and/or violence against workers attempting to unionize their workplaces

How successful are efforts to protect human rights around the world? The answer to that question varies greatly. A great deal has been done by governments, the United Nations, and nongovernmental organizations to highlight human rights violations and end them, but much remains to be done.

The True Story of a Child Slave

Francis Bok writes and lectures against slavery. He captivates his audience because he tells a true story. It is the story of his 10 years as a slave—not 100 years ago, but from 1986 to 1996.

Bok was born in Sudan in North Africa. One day when he was seven, he was seized by Arab militiamen near his home village. He and other young children who were in the market that day were tied up and taken away. They were sold for forced labor. Bok's family and everyone in his village were killed the day he was taken captive. The militiamen forced them into an auditorium and set fire to it.

A rich farmer and his family took Bok as a slave. Bok's job was to take care of the family's goats and cattle. He lived in a shed with the animals and ate scraps of food the family gave him. The farmer's children beat him for fun.

"I never complained, because I knew that if I complained I would get hurt," Bok says.

When he was fourteen, Bok tried to escape. He was caught and beaten. The farmer threatened to kill him if he tried to escape again. Bok tried again and was caught. The farmer aimed his gun at Bok while the farmer's family laughed. Bok thought he was going to die. However, the farmer did not shoot him. He untied him, and Bok spent another three years as a slave.

When he was seventeen, Bok made a successful escape. With help from a Muslim truck driver, Bok was able to reach Khartoum, the capital of Sudan. He was sent to refugee camps and finally, with UN help, made his way to the United States. Bok now works to end slavery.

Child Labor

Slavery, or forced labor, is just one way that children are the victims of human rights abuse. The International Labour Organization (ILO), an agency of the UN, investigates child labor around the world. The agency has found that domestic labor is "one of the worst forms of child labour." Domestic laborers work in someone's home, often doing the cooking and cleaning. There is little regulation for this form of work, and more than 200 million children around the world work in domestic labor. Some are as young as five years old.

World Day Against Child Labor — June 12

The goal of this day is to raise people's awareness about the worldwide abuses of children through labor.

Burma has yet to institute child labor laws.

ILO studies find that domestic labor exploits, or takes advantage of, children. It may include the selling of children as slaves, or employing them in work that is hazardous or harmful to their health, such as in factories. Some employers pay the children nothing for their work, but give them a place to sleep and a little food to eat.

Child Soldiers

The ILO also investigates the use of children as soldiers. In the early 2000s, the ILO conservatively estimated that 300,000 children were serving in armed conflicts worldwide. The ILO bans the use of child soldiers, as do many international documents. However, guerrilla groups often recruit children for their forces. Governments who fight the guerrillas also use child soldiers.

Child soldiers fought in the Liberian Civil War.

Some children are kidnapped and forced into fighting. Other groups recruit children by promising them food and protection in the midst of civil war.

Children are considered good soldiers because they obey orders. Also, they are more willing to take risks than adult soldiers. Both paramilitary units and guerrillas use children as decoys. Children can be sent into an area to distract victims. Then adult soldiers move in and open fire.

When the fighting is over, or when children are removed from the armed groups, they have a difficult time adjusting to normal life. They have never had a childhood. They have been denied an education. As a result, they lack the skills to earn a living.

Convention on the Rights of the Child

"Article 2—[Nations] shall respect and ensure the rights set forth in the present Convention to each child within their jurisdiction without discrimination of any kind irrespective of the child's or his or her parent's or legal guardian's race, colour, sex, language, religion, political or other opinion, national, ethnic or social origin, property, disability, birth or other status.**"

Refugees in Search of a Home

What happens to the victims of human rights abuses, genocide, and war crimes? The United Nations High Commissioner for Refugees (UNHCR), the UN's refugee agency, estimates that there are 50 million refugees in the world today. About half of them are children.

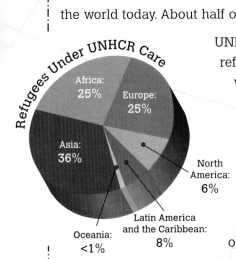

Refugees Under UNHCR Care

- Africa: 25%
- Europe: 25%
- Asia: 36%
- North America: 6%
- Latin America and the Caribbean: 8%
- Oceania: <1%

UNHCR defines a refugee as "someone who flees his or her country because of a well-founded fear of persecution for reasons of race, religion, nationality, political opinion or membership in a particular social group; a refugee either cannot return home or is afraid to do so."

The Universal Declaration of Human Rights guarantees refugees the right to seek asylum. This is a safe place with food, water, shelter, and medical care. UNHCR protects and assists more than 17 million refugees in 115 countries. Many of these people live in refugee camps while they wait for a safe return to their home countries. Most, however, will never return home and are waiting for resettlement in another country.

NAMES IN THE NEWS

Nongovernmental Organization (NGO): An NGO is a private organization that usually does not receive any government funding. NGOs work to achieve specific goals. Labor unions, conservation groups, and women's rights organizations are NGOs.

Amnesty International (AI): AI is a global NGO with over 1.8 million members in 150 countries and territories. It campaigns to have a single set of human rights recognized by all nations. Its members want all people everywhere to be protected by the UN's Universal Declaration of Human Rights.

Human Rights Watch (HRW): HRW is also a global NGO dedicated to protecting human rights. It publicizes human rights abuses "to shame abusers and . . . put pressure on them to reform their conduct." It also pressures groups such as the UN and the European Union to remove military and economic aid from governments violating their citizens' human rights.

investigative reporting

With a partner, conduct research and prepare a report on one of the following organizations:

- Amnesty International
- Human Rights Watch
- International Labour Organization (ILO)
- International Programme on the Elimination of Child Labour (IPEC)
- United Nations Refugee Agency (UNHCR)
- UNICEF

Case Study 4:
Genocide and Other Crimes Against Humanity

▶ **What is genocide?**

▶ **What are crimes against humanity?**

▶ **What is being done to stop genocide and crimes against humanity?**

It is estimated that 174 million people died in the 20th century as a result of genocide and other crimes against humanity. Genocide is the deliberate, systematic killing "in whole or in part, [of] a national, ethnical, racial or religious group." Hitler's campaign to rid Europe of Jews in the 1930s and 1940s is the best known example, but genocide has happened before and continues to happen.

Genocide is a crime against humanity. These crimes involve "the multiple commission of one or more acts such as . . . murder, extermination, enslavement, the forcible transfer of a population, torture, or rape."

The UN found evidence of crimes against humanity by both government and rebel forces in the Darfur region of Sudan in the early 2000s. The UN listed "killing of civilians, enforced disappearances, destruction of villages, rape and other forms of sexual violence, pillaging, and forced displacement." In the space of two years, more than 70,000 people were killed. Another 2 million escaped the region rather than stay and die.

Genocide and crimes against humanity are not inventions of the 20th century. As early as the 1300s B.C., Egyptians enslaved the Israelites. In 148 B.C., the Roman Empire defeated Carthage and burned the city to the ground. Any Carthaginian who survived was sold into slavery.

In the 1840s, the British did little to help as over 1 million Irish starved to death. Another 1.5 million emigrated when disease struck Ireland's crops.

The memorial to the Khmer Rouge victims at Choeung Ek, often known as the Killing Fields.

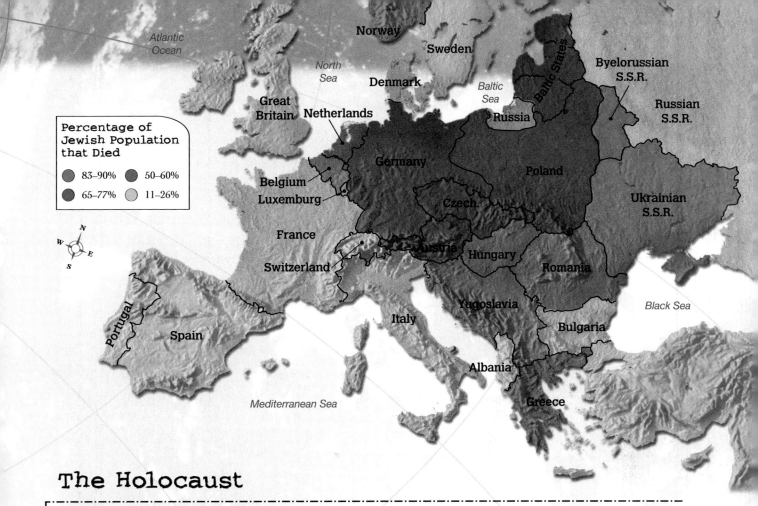

Percentage of
Jewish Population
that Died

- 83–90%
- 50–60%
- 65–77%
- 11–26%

The Holocaust

Beginning with the Nuremberg Laws in 1935, Adolph Hitler tried to force Jews to leave Germany. He took away their German citizenship and forbade them to marry non-Jewish Germans. They had to wear a yellow Star of David to show they were Jews. After November 9, 1938, and the violence of Kristallnacht, the persecution against Jews increased.

In 1942, Hitler decided on a "final solution." He decreed that all Jews were to be exterminated, or killed. The Holocaust was not limited to Germany. In every nation that Germany occupied, Jews were rounded up and shipped to concentration camps and forced labor camps.

Experts estimate that 6 million Jews were murdered in the Holocaust. Another 3 million to 6 million Gypsies, the mentally ill, and the disabled died in Hitler's campaign to purify Europe. Examine the map and table to learn how the Holocaust affected the Jewish population of Europe.

Jewish Deaths, 1939–1945

Belgium	40,000
Bulgaria	14,000
Czechoslovakia	155,000
Denmark	500
Baltic States (Estonia, Latvia, Lithuania)	228,000
France	90,000
Germany and Austria	210,000
Greece	54,000
Hungary	450,000
Italy	8,000
Poland	3,000,000
Romania	300,000
Soviet Union	
Russia	107,000
Byelorussia	245,000
Ukraine	900,000

Checking the Facts:
Which nation lost the largest number of Jews? How many Jews were murdered in the German-occupied part of the Soviet Union?

Major Genocides Since 1975

1975 to 1979 — Cambodia

The Khmer Rouge, under Pol Pot's leadership, murdered about 1.8 million people—or about 20 percent of the nation's population. The goal was to turn Cambodia into a Communist agrarian state.

1975 to 1999 — East Timor

Until 1975, East Timor was a Portuguese colony. In 1974, the dictator of Portugal was overthrown, and the following year East Timor declared independence. Indonesia quickly invaded the new nation in a brutal campaign of torture and murder. About 16 percent of the population of 600,000 was killed. By 1999, about 25 percent had been murdered. Most were Roman Catholics. The UN stepped in and took control.

1992 to 1995 — Bosnia-Herzegovina

This genocide was about religion. Bosnian Serbs who belonged to the Bosnian Orthodox Church began a program of ethnic cleansing. Their goal was to remove Catholics and Muslims from much of Bosnia. However, the forcible removals soon turned into genocide. About 200,000 non-Serbs were killed before troops from the North Atlantic Treaty Organization (NATO) were sent in as peacekeepers.

1994 — Rwanda

In this ethnic conflict, the majority Hutus (85 percent of the population) massacred the minority Tutsis (about 12 percent). Some moderate Hutu politicians were also killed. This program of genocide was initiated by the Rwandan government. In the 100-day massacre, the Rwandan army and militia murdered about 800,000 Tutsis. This was approximately 75 percent of the entire Tutsi population of Rwanda.

1997 to present — Democratic Republic of the Congo

To gain power, Laurent-Desire Kabila and his allies killed thousands of Congolese. Kabila then used various illegal means, such as torture and imprisonment, to keep control over the nation. Then Kabila's former allies joined Congolese rebels to attack him. The Congolese people were again the innocent victims of brutal murders, rapes, and executions. More than 1.7 million people are estimated to have been killed.

1998 to 1999 — Kosovo

Kosovo is a province within Serbia and Montenegro. Ethnic Muslim Albanians made up the largest population in Kosovo. In 1998, they began attacks against the government. They wanted to join Kosovo with Albania. The Serbian government fought back with "excessive force" and launched a campaign of ethnic cleansing. Some 400,000 ethnic Albanians were displaced. That was almost 20 percent of the population. NATO planes bombed government forces for 72 days before the government surrendered.

Armenian Genocide

Between 1915 and 1918, the government of the Ottoman Empire systematically murdered 1.5 million Armenian Christians. Another 500,000 were forced to leave their homeland. Why? Armenians were non-Turks and Christians. The new government of the Ottoman Empire, known as Young Turks, consisted of strong nationalists. They wanted to create a pure "Turkish" state. There was no place for non-Turks and non-Muslims.

U.S. ambassador to the Ottoman Empire, Henry Morgenthau, Sr., reported: "When the Turkish authorities gave the orders for deportations, they were merely giving the death warrant to the whole race; they understood this well, and, in their conversations with me, they made no particular attempt to conceal the fact."

UN Convention on Genocide, 1948

"Article I: The Contracting Parties [the nations that agree to the document] confirm that genocide, whether committed in time of peace or in time of war, is a crime under international law which they undertake to prevent and to punish.

Article IV: Persons committing genocide or any other of the acts . . . shall be punished, whether they are . . . rulers, public officials or private individuals."

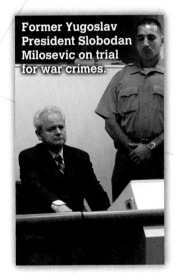

Former Yugoslav President Slobodan Milosevic on trial for war crimes.

International Criminal Court

The world did nothing to stop the Armenian genocide and little to help Jews against Hitler. After World War II, the Allies tried officials of Germany, Japan, and Italy as war criminals. Yet, genocide and crimes against humanity continued. As new horrors came to the attention of the world community, nations began calling for some way to punish such crimes.

The UN Security Council created International Criminal Tribunals to try people accused of war crimes in Rwanda and Kosovo. However, nations began to look for a permanent way to deal with crimes against humanity. In 1989, the UN Security Council first debated the idea of setting up an International Criminal Court (ICC).

The ICC began work on July 1, 2002. It took many years of negotiation to ensure that nations did not give up any of their rights. Another concern was that the ICC would not have enough authority to operate. By 2004, 96 nations had ratified the treaty officially forming the ICC. The United States has not ratified the treaty.

The ICC is not an agency of the UN. Its financial support comes from the nations that ratify the treaty that created the ICC. However, the ICC works closely with the UN, and the UN Security Council refers cases to the ICC.

investigative reporting

With a partner, conduct research to find out the latest developments

- about current events that may include crimes against humanity
- in the work of the International Criminal Court

Case Study 5:
Terrorism

▶ **What is terrorism?**

▶ **Who are terrorists?**

▶ **Explain the different types of terrorism that exist today.**

A terrorist is a person who uses force or the threat of force to frighten and demoralize an enemy. Terrorism is a political strategy that uses violence against people or property to achieve a goal. Often the goal of terrorism is to force a change in government or society.

The first awareness of terrorism for many Americans came on September 11, 2001. Two airplanes piloted by terrorists flew into the World Trade Center in New York City on that morning. A third plane flew into the Pentagon in Washington, D.C. Passengers in a fourth airliner caused the terrorists to crash the plane in a cornfield in Pennsylvania. Close to 3,000 people died that morning in the planes and on the ground in New York City and Washington, D.C.

Investigations showed that Al-Qaeda was responsible for what Americans call 9/11. Al-Qaeda is a terrorist organization founded by Osama bin Laden. Bin Laden is a militant, radical Muslim. He created Al-Qaeda after the first Gulf War ended in 1991. His original aim was to force the United States to remove its troops from Saudi Arabia, the home of the prophet Muhammad, founder of Islam. Bin Laden continues to target the U.S. and other free countries.

However, these were not the first strikes against U.S. property and citizens. In 1993, terrorists planted a car bomb in the parking garage under the World Trade Center towers. The U.S. embassies in Kenya and Tanzania were bombed by terrorists in 1998. In 2000, terrorists bombed the USS *Cole* while it lay at anchor in Adan Harbor, Yemen.

The U.S. State Department lists 37 major terrorist organizations around the world. There are other smaller groups as well. Read the section "Terrorist Organizations" to identify some current terrorist groups.

The remains of a bus after a Palestinian suicide bombing in Jerusalem.

Who Are Terrorists?

Terrorists operate in all regions of the world. They use many of the same tactics to create fear. However, their goals vary. The following are the four main categories of terrorist organizations:

1. nationalist groups who want to create their own nations
2. urban guerrillas who want to overthrow the government in power
3. Islamic militants who want to create a nation of Palestine
4. Islamic militants who are fighting Western, especially U.S., influences in the Middle East

Al-Qaeda fits the last group. Islamic fundamentalists want all Western influences to be removed from nations with large Islamic populations. They believe that Islamic nations should be theocracies. A theocracy is a government based on religious principles and run by religious teachers. Muslim terrorist groups in the Philippines and Southeast Asia have a similar goal of setting up Islamic nations.

The Basque Fatherland is a nationalist group. Members of this organization want to set up a separate nation by combining areas in Spain and France that have large populations of Basque people.

In Peru and Colombia, urban guerrillas want to overturn the governments in power. They believe government officials favor the wealthy and ignore the problems of the poor. Many of the poor have moved from rural areas to cities hoping to make a better life for themselves. Instead, they find few jobs, little or no public services, such as schools, medical care, and sanitation, and corrupt public officials.

The Middle East has been an area of conflict since Israel was founded in 1948. Militant groups such as HAMAS and Hizballah have been attacking Israel since the 1980s. Their aim and that of similar Islamic militants is to establish an independent nation of Palestine. They want to force the Israeli government to recognize Palestinian claims to a homeland and to negotiate with the Palestinians on setting up that homeland.

Terrorist Organizations

The following are some of the more notorious terrorist organizations operating today.

Nationalist Groups

- Harakat ul Mujahidin (HUM)
  Goal: to unite the Indian state of Kashmir with Pakistan
- Liberation Tigers of Tamil Eelam
  Goal: to set up a separate state for Tamil people by taking land from Sri Lanka

Urban Guerrillas

- Sendero Luminoso (Shining Path) [Peru]
- National Liberation Army of Colombia

Palestinian Militants

- HAMAS (Islamic Resistance Movement)
- Hizballah (Party of God)
- Palestine Islamic Jihad
- Palestine Liberation Front
- Popular Front for the Liberation of Palestine

Anti-Western Terrorists

- Al-Qaeda
- Al-Jihad (Egyptian Islamic Jihad) [Egypt]
- Jemaah Islamiya [Philippines and Southeast Asia]

These terrorist groups use suicide bombing (sometimes called homicide bombings), airplane hijacking, kidnapping, car bombing, and assassination as weapons of terror.

The World Trade Center, September 11, 2001

U.S. Response to Terrorism

According to the U.S. Department of State, "The global war on terrorism is being fought by many means—through diplomatic, military, financial, intelligence, investigative, and law enforcement actions—at home and abroad."

On October 24, 2001, the USA Patriot Act was signed into law. The law allows the United States government to:

- detain foreigners who are suspected of terrorism for seven days without charging them with a crime
- monitor e-mail and Internet use and tap telephones of suspects
- make search warrants valid across states
- order United States banks to investigate sources of large foreign bank accounts
- prosecute terrorist crimes without any limitations or time restrictions

State Sponsors of Terrorism

Terrorist organizations need financial support and safe havens in order to operate. The United States has identified six nations that it calls state sponsors of terrorism. The six are Cuba, Iran, Libya, North Korea, Sudan, and Syria. These nations provide money to terrorist organizations. They also allow these groups to live in and operate from their territory.

The U.S. government has placed economic sanctions on these six nations. Sanctions are restrictions placed on a nation because it has not obeyed international law. Among the sanctions are a ban on selling military equipment and giving foreign aid. In addition, the sanctions limit the type of nonmilitary goods that can be sold.

Chechen Terrorists

The region of Chechnya broke away from Russia in 1991 and declared itself an independent nation. Russia refused to recognize Chechen independence and sent troops to take control. Fighting lasted from 1994 to 1996.

In the late 1990s, Chechen rebels began to use terrorism to achieve their goal of independence. A series of bombings in Moscow and other Russian cities was blamed on Chechens. Militants took over a theater in Moscow in demanding freedom for Chechnya. Hundreds of innocent people died as the government tried to free them.

In 2004, at least 32 Chechen terrorists seized a school in Beslan, Russia. They demanded that Russia remove its troops from Chechnya. After 52 hours, troops moved in to free the hostages. More than half of the 339 people killed were children.

Survivors of the Beslan school siege

UN Actions Against Terrorism

The UN has 19 global or regional treaties relating to international terrorism. Many of them date to the 1970s and the beginning of airplane hijackings. After 9/11, the UN adopted Resolution 1373 that binds UN member nations to act to end terrorism.

The UN also set up a Counter-Terrorism Committee (CTC) made up of the 15 member nations of the Security Council. The CTC's role is to make sure that member nations "deny opportunities for the commission of acts of terrorism." The CTC also seeks to build cooperation among member nations in the fight against terrorism.

UN Resolution 1373

UN member nations must

- deny all forms of financial support to terrorist groups . . . ;
- suppress . . . safe haven . . . or support for terrorists . . . ;
- share information with other governments . . . ;
- cooperate with other governments in the investigation, detection, arrest, and prosecution of those involved . . . ; and
- criminalize active and passive assistance for terrorism in domestic laws and bring violators of these laws to justice . . .

U.S. Counterterrorism Policy

First, make no concessions to terrorists and strike no deals;

Second, bring terrorists to justice for their crimes;

Third, isolate and apply pressure on states that sponsor terrorism to force them to change their behavior; and

Fourth, bolster the counterterrorism capabilities of those countries that work with the U.S. and require assistance.

investigative reporting

With a partner find the latest information on the war on terror. Choose one topic and prepare a presentation about it.

- Check newspapers and newsmagazines for information about the activities of terrorist groups listed in this Case Study.
- Check the Web sites of the U.S. Departments of Homeland Security, State, Justice, and Defense and the UN for updates on counterterrorism activities and policies.

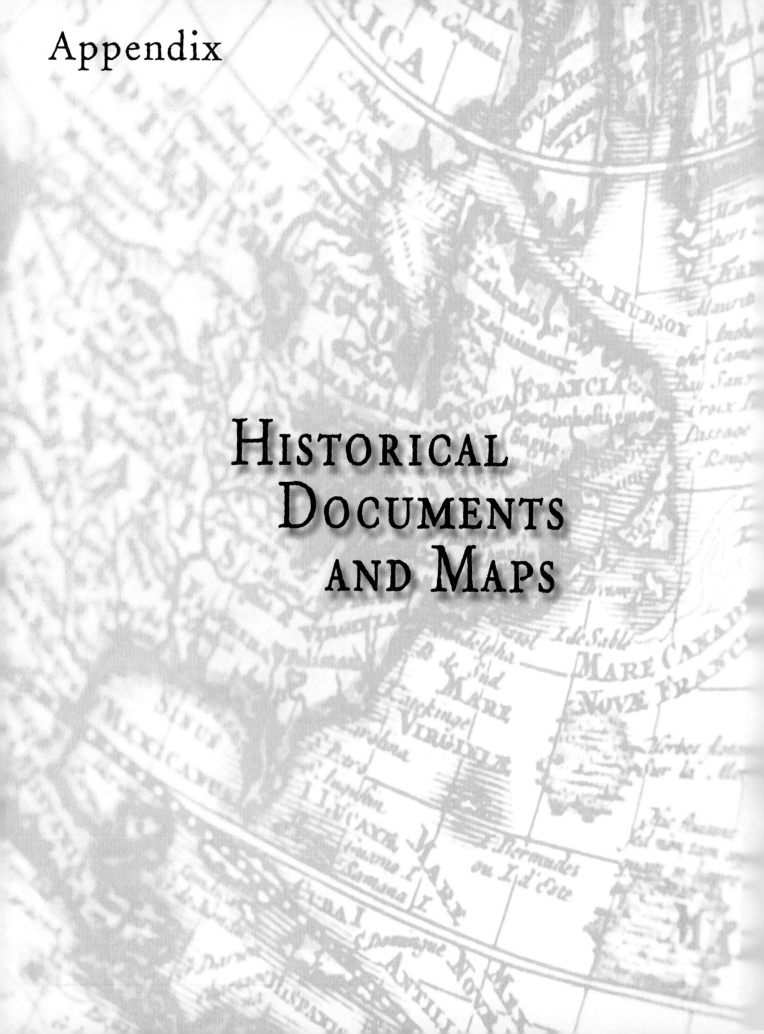

Appendix

Historical Documents and Maps

The Declaration of Independence

Action of Second Continental Congress, July 4, 1776

The unanimous Declaration of the thirteen United States of America

WHEN in the Course of human Events, it becomes necessary for one People to dissolve the Political Bands which have connected them with another, and to assume among the Powers of the Earth, the separate and equal Station to which the Laws of Nature and of Nature's God entitle them, a decent Respect to the Opinions of Mankind requires that they should declare the causes which impel them to the Separation.

WE hold these Truths to be self-evident, that all Men are created equal, that they are endowed by their Creator with certain unalienable Rights, that among these are Life, Liberty and the Pursuit of Happiness — That to secure these Rights, Governments are instituted among Men, deriving their just Powers from the Consent of the Governed, that whenever any Form of Government becomes destructive of these Ends, it is the Right of the People to alter or to abolish it, and to institute new Government, laying its Foundation on such Principles, and organizing its Powers in such Form, as to them shall seem most likely to effect their Safety and Happiness. Prudence, indeed, will dictate that Governments long established should not be changed for light and transient Causes; and accordingly all Experience hath shewn, that Mankind are more disposed to suffer, while Evils are sufferable, than to right themselves by abolishing the Forms to which they are accustomed. But when a long Train of Abuses and Usurpations, pursuing invariably the same Object, evinces a Design to reduce them under absolute Despotism, it is their Right, it is their Duty, to throw off such Government, and to provide new Guards for their future Security. Such has been the patient Sufferance of these Colonies; and such is now the Necessity which constrains them to alter their former Systems of Government. The History of the present King of Great- Britain is a History of repeated Injuries and Usurpations, all having in direct Object the Establishment of an absolute Tyranny over these States. To prove this, let Facts be submitted to a candid World.

HE has refused his Assent to Laws, the most wholesome and necessary for the public Good.

HE has forbidden his Governors to pass Laws of immediate and pressing Importance, unless suspended in their Operation till his Assent should be obtained; and when so suspended, he has utterly neglected to attend to them.

HE has refused to pass other Laws for the Accommodation of large Districts of People, unless those People would relinquish the Right of Representation in the Legislature, a Right inestimable to them, and formidable to Tyrants only.

419

HE has called together Legislative Bodies at Places unusual, uncomfortable, and distant from the Depository of their public Records, for the sole Purpose of fatiguing them into Compliance with his Measures.

HE has dissolved Representative Houses repeatedly, for opposing with manly Firmness his Invasions on the Rights of the People.

HE has refused for a long Time, after such Dissolutions, to cause others to be elected; whereby the Legislative Powers, incapable of the Annihilation, have returned to the People at large for their exercise; the State remaining in the mean time exposed to all the Dangers of Invasion from without, and the Convulsions within.

HE has endeavoured to prevent the Population of these States; for that Purpose obstructing the Laws for Naturalization of Foreigners; refusing to pass others to encourage their Migrations hither, and raising the Conditions of new Appropriations of Lands.

HE has obstructed the Administration of Justice, by refusing his Assent to Laws for establishing Judiciary Powers.

HE has made Judges dependent on his Will alone, for the Tenure of their Offices, and the Amount and Payment of their Salaries.

HE has erected a Multitude of new Offices, and sent hither Swarms of Officers to harrass our People, and eat out their Substance.

HE has kept among us, in Times of Peace, Standing Armies, without the consent of our Legislatures.

HE has affected to render the Military independent of and superior to the Civil Power.

HE has combined with others to subject us to a Jurisdiction foreign to our Constitution, and unacknowledged by our Laws; giving his Assent to their Acts of pretended Legislation:

FOR quartering large Bodies of Armed Troops among us;

FOR protecting them, by a mock Trial, from Punishment for any Murders which they should commit on the Inhabitants of these States:

FOR cutting off our Trade with all Parts of the World:

FOR imposing Taxes on us without our Consent:

FOR depriving us, in many Cases, of the Benefits of Trial by Jury:

FOR transporting us beyond Seas to be tried for pretended Offences:

FOR abolishing the free System of English Laws in a neighbouring Province, establishing therein an arbitrary Government, and enlarging its Boundaries, so as to render it at once an Example and fit Instrument for introducing the same absolute Rules into these Colonies:

FOR taking away our Charters, abolishing our most valuable Laws, and altering fundamentally the Forms of our Governments:

FOR suspending our own Legislatures, and declaring themselves invested with Power to legislate for us in all Cases whatsoever.

HE has abdicated Government here, by declaring us out of his Protection and waging War against us.

HE has plundered our Seas, ravaged our Coasts, burnt our Towns, and destroyed the Lives of our People.

HE is, at this Time, transporting large Armies of foreign Mercenaries to compleat the Works of Death, Desolation, and Tyranny, already begun with circumstances of Cruelty and Perfidy, scarcely paralleled in the most barbarous Ages, and totally unworthy the Head of a civilized Nation.

HE has constrained our fellow Citizens taken Captive on the high Seas to bear Arms against their Country, to become the Executioners of their Friends and Brethren, or to fall themselves by their Hands.

HE has excited domestic Insurrections amongst us, and has endeavoured to bring on the Inhabitants of our Frontiers, the merciless Indian Savages, whose known Rule of Warfare, is an undistinguished Destruction, of all Ages, Sexes and Conditions.

IN every stage of these Oppressions we have Petitioned for Redress in the most humble Terms: Our repeated Petitions have been answered only by repeated Injury. A Prince, whose Character is thus marked by every act which may define a Tyrant, is unfit to be the Ruler of a free People.

NOR have we been wanting in Attentions to our British Brethren. We have warned them from Time to Time of Attempts by their Legislature to extend an unwarrantable Jurisdiction over us. We have reminded them of the Circumstances of our Emigration and Settlement here. We have appealed to their native Justice and Magnanimity, and we have conjured them by the Ties of our common Kindred to disavow these Usurpations, which, would inevitably interrupt our Connections and Correspondence. They too have been deaf to the Voice of Justice and of Consanguinity. We must, therefore, acquiesce in the Necessity, which denounces our Separation, and hold them, as we hold the rest of Mankind, Enemies in War, in Peace, Friends.

WE, therefore, the Representatives of the UNITED STATES OF AMERICA, in GENERAL CONGRESS, Assembled, appealing to the Supreme Judge of the World for the Rectitude of our Intentions, do, in the Name, and by Authority of the good People of these Colonies, solemnly Publish and Declare, That these United Colonies are, and of Right ought to be, FREE AND INDEPENDENT STATES; that they are absolved from all Allegiance to the British Crown, and that all political Connection between them and the State of Great-Britain, is and ought to be totally dissolved; and that as FREE AND INDEPENDENT STATES, they have full Power to levy War, conclude Peace, contract Alliances, establish Commerce, and to do all other Acts and Things which INDEPENDENT STATES may of right do. And for the support of this Declaration, with a firm Reliance on the Protection of divine Providence, we mutually pledge to each other our Lives, our Fortunes, and our sacred Honor.

John Hancock	Charles Carroll	Geo. Taylor	Josiah Bartlett
Button Gwinnett	Of Carrollton	James Wilson	Wm. Whipple
Lyman Hall	George Wythe	Geo. Ross	Saml Adams
Geo Walton	Richard Henry Lee	Caesar Rodney	John Adams
Wm Hooper	Th Jefferson	Geo Read	Robt Treat Paine
Joseph Hewes	Benja Harrison	Tho M. Kean	Elbridge Gerry
John Penn	Thos Nelson Jr.	Wm Floyd	Step Hopkins
Edward Rutledge	Francis Lightfoot Lee	Phil. Livingston	William Ellery
Thos Heyward Junr.	Carter Braxton	Frans. Lewis	Roger Sherman
Thomas Lynch Junr.	Robt Morris	Lewis Morris	Samel Huntington
Arthur Middleton	Benjamin Rush	Richd. Stockton	Wm. Williams
Samuel Chase	Benja. Franklin	Jno Witherspoon	Oliver Wolcott
Wm. Paca	John Morton	Fras. Hopkinson	Matthew Thornton
Thos. Stone	Geo Clymer	John Hart	
	Jas. Smith	Abra Clark	

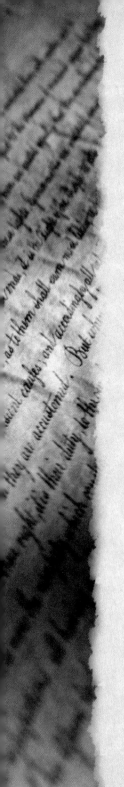

The United States Constitution

The pages that follow contain the original text of the United States Constitution. Sections that are no longer enforced have been crossed out. The spelling and punctuation of the document remain in their original format. The headings are not part of the original Constitution.

We the People of the United States, in Order to form a more perfect Union, establish Justice, insure domestic Tranquility, provide for the common defence, promote the general Welfare, and secure the Blessings of Liberty to ourselves and our Posterity, do ordain and establish this Constitution for the United States of America.

Article I
Legislative Branch

Section 1
Congress

All legislative Powers herein granted shall be vested in a Congress of the United States, which shall consist of a Senate and House of Representatives.

Section 2
House of Representatives

Clause 1: The House of Representatives shall be composed of Members chosen every second Year by the People of the several States, and the Electors in each State shall have the Qualifications requisite for Electors of the most numerous Branch of the State Legislature.

Clause 2: No Person shall be a Representative who shall not have attained to the Age of twenty five Years, and been seven Years a Citizen of the United States, and who shall not, when elected, be an Inhabitant of that State in which he shall be chosen.

Clause 3: Representatives and direct Taxes shall be apportioned among the several States which may be included within this Union, according to their respective Numbers, ~~which shall be determined by adding to the whole Number of free Persons, including those bound to Service for a Term of Years, and excluding Indians not taxed, three fifths of all other Persons.~~

The actual Enumeration shall be made within three Years after the first Meeting of the Congress of the United States, and within every subsequent Term of ten Years, in such Manner as they shall by Law direct.

The Number of Representatives shall not exceed one for every thirty Thousand, but each State shall have at Least one Representative; ~~and until such enumeration shall be made, the State of New-Hampshire shall be entitled to chuse three, Massachusetts eight, Rhode-Island and Providence Plantations one, Connecticut five, New-York six, New-Jersey four, Pennsylvania eight, Delaware one, Maryland six, Virginia ten, North Carolina five, South Carolina five, and Georgia three.~~

Clause 4: When vacancies happen in the Representation from any State, the Executive Authority thereof shall issue Writs of Election to fill such Vacancies.

Clause 5: The House of Representatives shall chuse their Speaker and other Officers; and shall have the sole Power of Impeachment.

Section 3
Senate

Clause 1: The Senate of the United States shall be composed of two Senators from each State, chosen ~~by the Legislature thereof,~~ for six Years; and each Senator shall have one Vote.

Clause 2: Immediately after they shall be assembled in Consequence of the first Election, they shall be divided as equally as may be into three Classes. The Seats of the Senators of the first Class shall be vacated at the Expiration of the second Year, of the second Class at the Expiration of the fourth Year, and of the third Class at the Expiration of the sixth Year, so that one third may be chosen every second Year; ~~and if Vacancies happen by Resignation, or otherwise, during the Recess of the Legislature of any State, the Executive thereof may make temporary Appointments until the next Meeting of the Legislature, which shall then fill such Vacancies.~~

Clause 3: No Person shall be a Senator who shall not have attained to the Age of thirty Years, and been nine Years a Citizen of the United States, and who shall not, when elected, be an Inhabitant of that State for which he shall be chosen.

Clause 4: The Vice President of the United States shall be President of the Senate, but shall have no Vote, unless they be equally divided.

Clause 5: The Senate shall chuse their other Officers, and also a President pro tempore, in the Absence of the Vice President, or when he shall exercise the Office of President of the United States.

Clause 6: The Senate shall have the sole Power to try all Impeachments. When sitting for that Purpose, they shall be on Oath or Affirmation. When the President of the United States is tried, the Chief Justice shall preside: And no Person shall be convicted without the Concurrence of two thirds of the Members present.

Clause 7: Judgment in Cases of Impeachment shall not extend further than to removal from Office, and disqualification to hold and enjoy any Office of honor, Trust or Profit under the United States: but the Party convicted shall nevertheless be liable and subject to Indictment, Trial, Judgment and Punishment, according to Law.

Section 4
Elections and Meetings

Clause 1: The Times, Places and Manner of holding Elections for Senators and Representatives, shall be prescribed in each State by the Legislature thereof; but the Congress may at any time by Law make or alter such Regulations, ~~except as to the Places of chusing Senators.~~

Clause 2: The Congress shall assemble at least once in every Year, ~~and such Meeting shall be on the first Monday in December, unless they shall by Law appoint a different Day.~~

Section 5
Rules of Procedure

Clause 1: Each House shall be the Judge of the Elections, Returns and Qualifications of its own Members, and a Majority of each shall constitute a Quorum to do Business; but a smaller Number may adjourn from day to day, and may be authorized to compel the Attendance of absent Members, in such Manner, and under such Penalties as each House may provide.

Clause 2: Each House may determine the Rules of its Proceedings, punish its Members for disorderly Behaviour, and, with the Concurrence of two thirds, expel a Member.

Clause 3: Each House shall keep a Journal of its Proceedings, and from time to time publish the same, excepting such Parts as may in their Judgment require Secrecy; and the Yeas and

Nays of the Members of either House on any question shall, at the Desire of one fifth of those Present, be entered on the Journal.

Clause 4: Neither House, during the Session of Congress, shall, without the Consent of the other, adjourn for more than three days, nor to any other Place than that in which the two Houses shall be sitting.

Section 6
Privileges and Restrictions

Clause 1: The Senators and Representatives shall receive a Compensation for their Services, to be ascertained by Law, and paid out of the Treasury of the United States. They shall in all Cases, except Treason, Felony and Breach of the Peace, be privileged from Arrest during their Attendance at the Session of their respective Houses, and in going to and returning from the same; and for any Speech or Debate in either House, they shall not be questioned in any other Place.

Clause 2: No Senator or Representative shall, during the Time for which he was elected, be appointed to any civil Office under the Authority of the United States, which shall have been created, or the Emoluments whereof shall have been encreased during such time; and no Person holding any Office under the United States, shall be a Member of either House during his Continuance in Office.

Section 7
How Bills Become Laws

Clause 1: All Bills for raising Revenue shall originate in the House of Representatives; but the Senate may propose or concur with Amendments as on other Bills.

Clause 2: Every Bill which shall have passed the House of Representatives and the Senate, shall, before it become a Law, be presented to the President of the United States; If he approve he shall sign it, but if not he shall return it, with his Objections to that House in which it shall have originated, who shall enter the Objections at large on their Journal, and proceed to reconsider it. If after such Reconsideration two thirds of that House shall agree to pass the Bill, it shall be sent, together with the Objections, to the other House, by which it shall likewise be reconsidered, and if approved by two thirds of that House, it shall become a Law. But in all such Cases the Votes of both Houses shall be determined by yeas and Nays, and the Names of the Persons voting for and against the Bill shall be entered on the Journal of each House respectively.

If any Bill shall not be returned by the President within ten Days (Sundays excepted) after it shall have been presented to him, the Same shall be a Law, in like Manner as if he had signed it, unless the Congress by their Adjournment prevent its Return, in which Case it shall not be a Law.

Clause 3: Every Order, Resolution, or Vote to which the Concurrence of the Senate and House of Representatives may be necessary (except on a question of Adjournment) shall be presented to the President of the United States; and before the Same shall take Effect, shall be approved by him, or being disapproved by him, shall be repassed by two thirds of the Senate and House of Representatives, according to the Rules and Limitations prescribed in the Case of a Bill.

Section 8
Powers of Congress

Clause 1: The Congress shall have Power To lay and collect Taxes, Duties, Imposts and Excises, to pay the Debts and provide for the common Defence and general Welfare of the United States; but all Duties, Imposts and Excises shall be uniform throughout the United States;

Clause 2: To borrow Money on the credit of the United States;

Clause 3: To regulate Commerce with foreign Nations, and among the several States, and with the Indian Tribes;

Clause 4: To establish an uniform Rule of Naturalization, and uniform Laws on the subject of Bankruptcies throughout the United States;

Clause 5: To coin Money, regulate the Value thereof, and of foreign Coin, and fix the Standard of Weights and Measures;

Clause 6: To provide for the Punishment of counterfeiting the Securities and current Coin of the United States;

Clause 7: To establish Post Offices and post Roads;

Clause 8: To promote the Progress of Science and useful Arts, by securing for limited Times to Authors and Inventors the exclusive Right to their respective Writings and Discoveries;

Clause 9: To constitute Tribunals inferior to the supreme Court;

Clause 10: To define and punish Piracies and Felonies committed on the high Seas, and Offences against the Law of Nations;

Clause 11: To declare War, grant Letters of Marque and Reprisal, and make Rules concerning Captures on Land and Water;

Clause 12: To raise and support Armies, but no Appropriation of Money to that Use shall be for a longer Term than two Years;

Clause 13: To provide and maintain a Navy;

Clause 14: To make Rules for the Government and Regulation of the land and naval Forces;

Clause 15: To provide for calling forth the Militia to execute the Laws of the Union, suppress Insurrections and repel Invasions;

Clause 16: To provide for organizing, arming, and disciplining, the Militia, and for governing such Part of them as may be employed in the Service of the United States, reserving to the States respectively, the Appointment of the Officers, and the Authority of training the Militia according to the discipline prescribed by Congress;

Clause 17: To exercise exclusive Legislation in all Cases whatsoever, over such District (not exceeding ten Miles square) as may, by Cession of particular States, and the Acceptance of Congress, become the Seat of the Government of the United States, and to exercise like Authority over all Places purchased by the Consent of the Legislature of the State in which the Same shall be, for the Erection of Forts, Magazines, Arsenals, dock-Yards, and other needful Buildings;—And

Clause 18: To make all Laws which shall be necessary and proper for carrying into Execution the foregoing Powers, and all other Powers vested by this Constitution in the Government of the United States, or in any Department or Officer thereof.

Section 9
Powers Denied to the Federal Government

Clause 1: ~~The Migration or Importation of such Persons as any of the States now existing shall think proper to admit, shall not be prohibited by the Congress prior to the Year one thousand eight hundred and eight, but a Tax or duty may be imposed on such Importation, not exceeding ten dollars for each Person.~~

Clause 2: The Privilege of the Writ of Habeas Corpus shall not be suspended, unless when in Cases of Rebellion or Invasion the public Safety may require it.

Clause 3: No Bill of Attainder or ex post facto Law shall be passed.

Clause 4: No Capitation, or other direct, Tax shall be laid, unless in Proportion to the Census or Enumeration herein before directed to be taken.

Clause 5: No Tax or Duty shall be laid on Articles exported from any State.

Clause 6: No Preference shall be given by any Regulation of Commerce or Revenue to the Ports of one State over those of another: nor shall Vessels bound to, or from, one State, be obliged to enter, clear, or pay Duties in another.

Clause 7: No Money shall be drawn from the Treasury, but in Consequence of Appropriations made by Law; and a regular Statement and Account of the Receipts and Expenditures of all public Money shall be published from time to time.

Clause 8: No Title of Nobility shall be granted by the United States: And no Person holding any Office of Profit or Trust under them, shall, without the Consent of the Congress, accept of any present, Emolument, Office, or Title, of any kind whatever, from any King, Prince, or foreign State.

Section 10
Powers Denied to the States

Clause 1: No State shall enter into any Treaty, Alliance, or Confederation; grant Letters of Marque and Reprisal; coin Money; emit Bills of Credit; make any Thing but gold and silver Coin a Tender in Payment of Debts; pass any Bill of Attainder, ex post facto Law, or Law impairing the Obligation of Contracts, or grant any Title of Nobility.

Clause 2: No State shall, without the Consent of the Congress, lay any Imposts or Duties on Imports or Exports, except what may be absolutely necessary for executing it's inspection Laws: and the net Produce of all Duties and Imposts, laid by any State on Imports or Exports, shall be for the Use of the Treasury of the United States; and all such Laws shall be subject to the Revision and Controul of the Congress.

Clause 3: No State shall, without the Consent of Congress, lay any Duty of Tonnage, keep Troops, or Ships of War in time of Peace, enter into any Agreement or Compact with another State, or with a

foreign Power, or engage in War, unless actually invaded, or in such imminent Danger as will not admit of delay.

Article II Executive Branch

Section 1
President and Vice-President

Clause 1: The executive Power shall be vested in a President of the United States of America. He shall hold his Office during the Term of four Years, and, together with the Vice President, chosen for the same Term, be elected, as follows

Clause 2: Each State shall appoint, in such Manner as the Legislature thereof may direct, a Number of Electors, equal to the whole Number of Senators and Representatives to which the State may be entitled in the Congress: but no Senator or Representative, or Person holding an Office of Trust or Profit under the United States, shall be appointed an Elector.

Clause 3: ~~The Electors shall meet in their respective States, and vote by Ballot for two Persons, of whom one at least shall not be an Inhabitant of the same State with themselves. And they shall make a List of all the Persons voted for, and of the Number of Votes for each; which List they shall sign and certify, and transmit sealed to the Seat of the Government of the United States, directed to the President of the Senate. The President of the Senate shall, in the Presence of the Senate and House of Representatives, open all the Certificates, and the Votes shall then be counted. The Person having the greatest Number of Votes shall be the President, if such Number be a Majority of the whole Number of Electors appointed; and if there be more than one who have such Majority, and have an equal Number of Votes, then the House of Representatives shall immediately chuse by Ballot one of them for President; and if no Person have a Majority, then from the five highest on the~~

~~List the said House shall in like Manner chuse the President. But in chusing the President, the Votes shall be taken by States, the Representation from each State having one Vote; A quorum for this Purpose shall consist of a Member or Members from two thirds of the States, and a Majority of all the States shall be necessary to a Choice. In every Case, after the Choice of the President, the Person having the greatest Number of Votes of the Electors shall be the Vice President. But if there should remain two or more who have equal Votes, the Senate shall chuse from them by Ballot the Vice President.~~

Clause 4: The Congress may determine the Time of chusing the Electors, and the Day on which they shall give their Votes; which Day shall be the same throughout the United States.

Clause 5: No Person except a natural born Citizen, or a Citizen of the United States, at the time of the Adoption of this Constitution, shall be eligible to the Office of President; neither shall any Person be eligible to that Office who shall not have attained to the Age of thirty five Years, and been fourteen Years a Resident within the United States.

Clause 6: ~~In Case of the Removal of the President from Office, or of his Death, Resignation, or Inability to discharge the Powers and Duties of the said Office, the Same shall devolve on the Vice President, and~~ the Congress may by Law provide for the Case of Removal, Death, Resignation or Inability, both of the President and Vice President, declaring what Officer shall then act as President, and such Officer shall act accordingly, until the Disability be removed, or a President shall be elected.

Clause 7: The President shall, at stated Times, receive for his Services, a Compensation, which shall neither be encreased nor diminished during the Period for which he shall have been elected, and he shall not receive within that Period any other Emolument from the United States, or any of them.

Clause 8: Before he enter on the Execution of his Office, he shall take the following Oath or Affirmation:—"I do solemnly swear (or affirm) that I will faithfully execute the Office of President of the United States, and will to the best of my Ability, preserve, protect and defend the Constitution of the United States."

Section 2
Powers of the President

Clause 1: The President shall be Commander in Chief of the Army and Navy of the United States, and of the Militia of the several States, when called into the actual Service of the United States; he may require the Opinion, in writing, of the principal Officer in each of the executive Departments, upon any Subject relating to the Duties of their respective Offices, and he shall have Power to grant Reprieves and Pardons for Offences against the United States, except in Cases of Impeachment.

Clause 2: He shall have Power, by and with the Advice and Consent of the Senate, to make Treaties, provided two thirds of the Senators present concur; and he shall nominate, and by and with the Advice and Consent of the Senate, shall appoint Ambassadors, other public Ministers and Consuls, Judges of the supreme Court, and all other Officers of the United States, whose Appointments are not herein otherwise provided for, and which shall be established by Law: but the Congress may by Law vest the Appointment of such inferior Officers, as they think proper, in the President alone, in the Courts of Law, or in the Heads of Departments.

Clause 3: The President shall have Power to fill up all Vacancies that may happen during the Recess of the Senate, by granting Commissions which shall expire at the End of their next Session.

Section 3
Duties of the President

He shall from time to time give to the Congress Information of the State of the Union, and recommend to their Consideration such Measures as he shall judge necessary and expedient; he may, on extraordinary Occasions, convene both Houses, or either of them, and in Case of Disagreement between them, with Respect to the Time of Adjournment, he may adjourn them to such Time as he shall think proper; he shall receive Ambassadors and other public Ministers; he shall take Care that the Laws be faithfully executed, and shall Commission all the Officers of the United States.

Section 4
Impeachment

The President, Vice President and all civil Officers of the United States, shall be removed from Office on Impeachment for, and Conviction of, Treason, Bribery, or other high Crimes and Misdemeanors.

Article III
Judicial Branch

Section 1
Federal Courts

The judicial Power of the United States, shall be vested in one supreme Court, and in such inferior Courts as the Congress may from time to time ordain and establish. The Judges, both of the supreme and inferior Courts, shall hold their Offices during good Behaviour, and shall, at stated Times, receive for their Services, a Compensation, which shall not be diminished during their Continuance in Office.

Section 2
Extent of Judicial Powers

Clause 1: The judicial Power shall extend to all Cases, in Law and Equity, arising under this Constitution, the Laws of the United States, and Treaties made, or which shall be made, under their Authority;—to all Cases affecting Ambassadors, other public Ministers and Consuls;—to all Cases of admiralty and maritime Jurisdiction;—to Controversies to which the United States shall be a Party;—to Controversies between two or more States;—between a State and Citizens of another State; —between Citizens of different States, —between Citizens of the same State claiming Lands under Grants of different States, and between a State, or the Citizens thereof, and foreign States, Citizens or Subjects.

Clause 2: In all Cases affecting Ambassadors, other public Ministers and Consuls, and those in which a State shall be Party, the supreme Court shall have original Jurisdiction. In all the other Cases before mentioned, the supreme Court shall have appellate Jurisdiction, both as to Law and Fact, with such Exceptions, and under such Regulations as the Congress shall make.

Clause 3: The Trial of all Crimes, except in Cases of Impeachment, shall be by Jury; and such Trial shall be held in the State where the said Crimes shall have been committed; but when not committed within any State, the Trial shall be at such Place or Places as the Congress may by Law have directed.

Section 3
Treason

Clause 1: Treason against the United States, shall consist only in levying War against them, or in adhering to their Enemies, giving them Aid and Comfort. No Person shall be convicted of Treason unless on the Testimony of two Witnesses to the same overt Act, or on Confession in open Court.

Clause 2: The Congress shall have Power to declare the Punishment of Treason, but no Attainder of Treason shall work Corruption of Blood, or Forfeiture except during the Life of the Person attainted.

Article IV
The States

Section 1
Recognition of Each Other's Acts

Full Faith and Credit shall be given in each State to the public Acts, Records, and judicial Proceedings of every other State. And the Congress may by general Laws prescribe the Manner in which such Acts, Records and Proceedings shall be proved, and the Effect thereof.

Section 2
Citizens' Rights in Other States

Clause 1: The Citizens of each State shall be entitled to all Privileges and Immunities of Citizens in the several States.

Clause 2: A Person charged in any State with Treason, Felony, or other Crime, who shall flee from Justice, and be found in another State, shall on Demand of the executive Authority of the State from which he fled, be delivered up, to be removed to the State having Jurisdiction of the Crime.

Clause 3: ~~No Person held to Service or Labour in one State, under the Laws thereof, escaping into another, shall, in Consequence of any Law or Regulation therein, be discharged from such Service or Labour, but shall be delivered up on Claim of the Party to whom such Service or Labour may be due.~~

Section 3
New States and Territories

Clause 1: New States may be admitted by the Congress into this Union; but no new State shall be formed or erected within the Jurisdiction of any other State; nor any State be formed by the Junction of two or more States, or Parts of States, without the Consent of the Legislatures of the States concerned as well as of the Congress.

Clause 2: The Congress shall have Power to dispose of and make all needful Rules and Regulations respecting the Territory or other Property belonging to the United States; and nothing in this Constitution shall be so construed as to Prejudice any Claims of the United States, or of any particular State.

Section 4
Guarantees to the States

The United States shall guarantee to every State in this Union a Republican Form of Government, and shall protect each of them against Invasion; and on Application of the Legislature, or of the Executive (when the Legislature cannot be convened) against domestic Violence.

Article V
Amending the Constitution

The Congress, whenever two thirds of both Houses shall deem it necessary, shall propose Amendments to this Constitution, or, on the Application of the Legislatures of two thirds of the several States, shall call a Convention for proposing Amendments, which, in either Case, shall be valid to all Intents and Purposes, as Part of this Constitution, when ratified by the Legislatures of three fourths of the several States, or by Conventions in three fourths thereof, as the one or the other Mode of Ratification may be proposed by the Congress; Provided ~~that no Amendment which may be made prior to the Year One thousand eight hundred and eight shall in any Manner affect the first and fourth Clauses in the Ninth Section of the first Article; and~~ that no State, without its Consent, shall be deprived of its equal Suffrage in the Senate.

Article VI
National Supremacy

Clause 1: All Debts contracted and Engagements entered into, before the Adoption of this Constitution, shall be as

valid against the United States under this Constitution, as under the Confederation.

Clause 2: This Constitution, and the Laws of the United States which shall be made in Pursuance thereof; and all Treaties made, or which shall be made, under the Authority of the United States, shall be the supreme Law of the Land; and the Judges in every State shall be bound thereby, any Thing in the Constitution or Laws of any State to the Contrary notwithstanding.

Clause 3: The Senators and Representatives before mentioned, and the Members of the several State Legislatures, and all executive and judicial Officers, both of the United States and of the several States, shall be bound by Oath or Affirmation, to support this Constitution; but no religious Test shall ever be required as a Qualification to any Office or public Trust under the United States.

Article VII
Ratification

The Ratification of the Conventions of nine States, shall be sufficient for the Establishment of this Constitution between the States so ratifying the Same. Done in Convention by the Unanimous Consent of the States present the Seventeenth Day of September in the Year of our Lord one thousand seven hundred and Eighty seven and of the Independence of the United States of America the Twelfth In witness whereof We have hereunto subscribed our Names,

---

George Washington, President and Deputy from Virginia

Delaware
George Read
Gunning Bedford, Junior
John Dickinson
Richard Bassett
Jacob Broom

Maryland
James McHenry
Daniel of St. Thomas Jenifer
Daniel Carroll

Virginia
John Blair
James Madison, Junior

North Carolina
William Blount
Richard Dobbs Spaight
Hugh Williamson

South Carolina
John Rutledge
Charles Cotesworth Pinckney
Charles Pinckney
Pierce Butler.

Georgia
William Few
Abraham Baldwin

New Hampshire
John Langdon
Nicholas Gilman

Massachusetts
Nathaniel Gorham
Rufus King

Connecticut
William Samuel Johnson
Roger Sherman

New York
Alexander Hamilton

New Jersey
William Livingston
David Brearley
William Paterson.
Jonathan Dayton

Pennsylvania
Benjamin Franklin
Thomas Mifflin
Robert Morris
George Clymer
Thomas FitzSimons
Jared Ingersoll
James Wilson
Gouverneur Morris
Attest: William Jackson, Secretary

Ammendments to the Constitution

The pages that follow contain the original text of the Amendments to the United States Constitution. Sections that are no longer enforced have been crossed out. The spelling and punctuation of the document remain in their original format. The headings are not part of the original Amendments.

Amendment 1 (1791)
Religious and Political Freedom

Congress shall make no law respecting an establishment of religion, or prohibiting the free exercise thereof; or abridging the freedom of speech, or of the press; or the right of the people peaceably to assemble, and to petition the Government for a redress of grievances.

Amendment 2 (1791)
Right to Bear Arms

A well regulated Militia, being necessary to the security of a free State, the right of the people to keep and bear Arms, shall not be infringed.

Amendment 3 (1791)
Quartering of Soldiers

No Soldier shall, in time of peace be quartered in any house, without the consent of the Owner, nor in time of war, but in a manner to be prescribed by law.

Amendment 4 (1791)
Search and Seizure

The right of the people to be secure in their persons, houses, papers, and effects, against unreasonable searches and seizures, shall not be violated, and no Warrants shall issue, but upon probable cause, supported by Oath or affirmation, and particularly describing the place to be searched, and the persons or things to be seized.

Amendment 5 (1791)
Life, Liberty, and Property

No person shall be held to answer for a capital, or otherwise infamous crime, unless on a presentment or indictment of a Grand Jury, except in cases arising in the land or naval forces, or in the Militia, when in actual service in time of War or public danger; nor shall any person be subject for the same offence to be twice put in jeopardy of life or limb; nor shall be compelled in any criminal case to be a witness against himself, nor be deprived of life, liberty, or property, without due process of law; nor shall private property be taken for public use, without just compensation.

Amendment 6 (1791)
Rights of the Accused

In all criminal prosecutions, the accused shall enjoy the right to a speedy and public trial, by an impartial jury of the State and district wherein the crime shall have been committed, which district shall have been previously ascertained by law, and to be informed of the nature and cause of the accusation; to be confronted with the witnesses against him; to have compulsory process for obtaining witnesses in his favor, and to have the Assistance of Counsel for his defence.

Amendment 7   (1791)
Right to Trial by Jury

In Suits at common law, where the value in controversy shall exceed twenty dollars, the right of trial by jury shall be preserved, and no fact tried by a jury, shall be otherwise re-examined in any Court of the United States, than according to the rules of the common law.

Amendment 8   (1791)
Bail and Punishment

Excessive bail shall not be required, nor excessive fines imposed, nor cruel and unusual punishments inflicted.

Amendment 9   (1791)
All Other Rights

The enumeration in the Constitution, of certain rights, shall not be construed to deny or disparage others retained by the people.

Amendment 10   (1791)
Rights of States and the People

The powers not delegated to the United States by the Constitution, nor prohibited by it to the States, are reserved to the States respectively, or to the people.

Amendment 11   (1795)
Suits Against a State

The Judicial power of the United States shall not be construed to extend to any suit in law or equity, commenced or prosecuted against one of the United States by Citizens of another State, or by Citizens or Subjects of any Foreign State.

Amendment 12   (1804)
Election of President

The Electors shall meet in their respective states, and vote by ballot for President and Vice-President, one of whom, at least, shall not be an inhabitant of the same state with themselves; they shall name in their ballots the person voted for as President, and in distinct ballots the person voted for as Vice-President, and they shall make distinct lists of all persons voted for as President, and of all persons voted for as Vice-President, and of the number of votes for each, which lists they shall sign and certify, and transmit sealed to the seat of the government of the United States, directed to the President of the Senate;

The President of the Senate shall, in the presence of the Senate and House of Representatives, open all the certificates and the votes shall then be counted;

The person having the greatest number of votes for President, shall be the President, if such number be a majority of the whole number of Electors appointed; and if no person have such majority, then from the persons having the highest numbers not exceeding three on the list of those voted for as President, the House of Representatives shall choose immediately, by ballot, the President. But in choosing the President, the votes shall be taken by states, the representation from each state having one vote; a quorum for this purpose shall consist of a member or members from two-thirds of the states, and a majority of all the states shall be necessary to a choice.

~~And if the House of Representatives shall not choose a President whenever the right of choice shall devolve upon them, before the fourth day of March next following, then the Vice-President shall act as President, as in the case of the death or other constitutional disability of the President.~~

The person having the greatest number of votes as Vice-President, shall be the Vice-President, if such number be a majority of the whole number of Electors appointed, and if no person have a majority, then from the two highest numbers on the list, the Senate shall choose the Vice-President; a quorum for the purpose shall consist of two-thirds of the whole number of Senators, and a majority of the whole number shall be necessary to a choice. But no person constitutionally ineligible to the office of

President shall be eligible to that of Vice-President of the United States.

Amendment 13 (1865)
Abolition of Slavery

Section 1 Neither slavery nor involuntary servitude, except as a punishment for crime whereof the party shall have been duly convicted, shall exist within the United States, or any place subject to their jurisdiction.

Section 2 Congress shall have power to enforce this article by appropriate legislation.

Amendment 14 (1868)
Civil Rights in the States

Section 1 All persons born or naturalized in the United States, and subject to the jurisdiction thereof, are citizens of the United States and of the State wherein they reside. No State shall make or enforce any law which shall abridge the privileges or immunities of citizens of the United States; nor shall any State deprive any person of life, liberty, or property, without due process of law; nor deny to any person within its jurisdiction the equal protection of the laws.

Section 2 Representatives shall be apportioned among the several States according to their respective numbers, counting the whole number of persons in each State, excluding Indians not taxed. But when the right to vote at any election for the choice of electors for President and Vice President of the United States, Representatives in Congress, the Executive and Judicial officers of a State, or the members of the Legislature thereof, is denied to any of the male inhabitants of such State, being twenty-one years of age, (See Note 15) and citizens of the United States, or in any way abridged, except for participation in rebellion, or other crime, the basis of representation therein shall be reduced in the proportion which the number of such male citizens shall bear to the whole number of male citizens twenty-one years of age in such State.

Section 3 No person shall be a Senator or Representative in Congress, or elector of President and Vice President, or hold any office, civil or military, under the United States, or under any State, who, having previously taken an oath, as a member of Congress, or as an officer of the United States, or as a member of any State legislature, or as an executive or judicial officer of any State, to support the Constitution of the United States, shall have engaged in insurrection or rebellion against the same, or given aid or comfort to the enemies thereof. But Congress may by a vote of two-thirds of each House, remove such disability.

Section 4 The validity of the public debt of the United States, authorized by law, including debts incurred for payment of pensions and bounties for services in suppressing insurrection or rebellion, shall not be questioned. But neither the United States nor any State shall assume or pay any debt or obligation incurred in aid of insurrection or rebellion against the United States, or any claim for the loss or emancipation of any slave; but all such debts, obligations and claims shall be held illegal and void.

Section 5 The Congress shall have power to enforce, by appropriate legislation, the provisions of this article.

Amendment 15 (1870)
Black Suffrage

Section 1 The right of citizens of the United States to vote shall not be denied or abridged by the United States or by any State on account of race, color, or previous condition of servitude.

Section 2 The Congress shall have power to enforce this article by appropriate legislation.

Amendment 16 (1913)
Income Tax

The Congress shall have power to lay and collect taxes on incomes, from whatever source derived, without apportionment among the several States, and without regard to any census or enumeration.

Amendment 17 (1919)
Direct Election of Senators

Section 1 The Senate of the United States shall be composed of two Senators from each State, elected by the people thereof, for six years; and each Senator shall have one vote. The electors in each State shall have the qualifications requisite for electors of the most numerous branch of the State legislatures.

Section 2 When vacancies happen in the representation of any State in the Senate, the executive authority of such State shall issue writs of election to fill such vacancies: Provided, That the legislature of any State may empower the executive thereof to make temporary appointments until the people fill the vacancies by election as the legislature may direct.

Section 3 This amendment shall not be so construed as to affect the election or term of any Senator chosen before it becomes valid as part of the Constitution.

Amendment 18 (1919)
National Prohibition

Section 1 After one year from the ratification of this article the manufacture, sale, or transportation of intoxicating liquors within, the importation thereof into, or the exportation thereof from the United States and all territory subject to the jurisdiction thereof for beverage purposes is hereby prohibited.

Section 2 The Congress and the several States shall have concurrent power to enforce this article by appropriate legislation.

Section 3 This article shall be inoperative unless it shall have been ratified as an amendment to the Constitution by the legislatures of the several States, as provided in the Constitution, within seven years from the date of the submission hereof to the States by the Congress.

Amendment 19 (1920)
Women's Suffrage

The right of citizens of the United States to vote shall not be denied or abridged by the United States or by any State on account of sex.

Congress shall have power to enforce this article by appropriate legislation.

Amendment 20 (1933)
"Lame-Duck" Amendment

Section 1 The terms of the President and Vice President shall end at noon on the 20th day of January, and the terms of Senators and Representatives at noon on the 3d day of January, of the years in which such terms would have ended if this article had not been ratified; and the terms of their successors shall then begin.

Section 2 The Congress shall assemble at least once in every year, and such meeting shall begin at noon on the 3d day of January, unless they shall by law appoint a different day.

Section 3 If, at the time fixed for the beginning of the term of the President, the President elect shall have died, the Vice President elect shall become President. If a President shall not have been chosen before the time fixed for the beginning of his term, or if the President elect shall have failed to qualify, then the Vice President elect shall act as President until a President shall have qualified; and the Congress may by law provide for the case wherein neither a President elect nor a Vice President elect shall have qualified, declaring who shall then act as President, or the manner in which one who is to act shall be selected, and such person shall act accordingly until a President or Vice President shall have qualified.

Section 4 The Congress may by law provide for the case of the death of any of the persons from whom the House of Representatives may choose a President whenever the right of choice shall have devolved upon them, and for the case of the death of any of the persons from whom the Senate may choose a Vice President whenever the right of choice shall have devolved upon them.

Section 5 Sections 1 and 2 shall take effect on the 15th day of October following the ratification of this article.

Section 6 This article shall be inoperative unless it shall have been ratified as an amendment to the Constitution by the legislatures of three-fourths of the several States within seven years from the date of its submission.

Amendment 21 (1933)
Repeal of Prohibition

Section 1 The eighteenth article of amendment to the Constitution of the United States is hereby repealed.

Section 2 The transportation or importation into any State, Territory, or possession of the United States for delivery or use therein of intoxicating liquors, in violation of the laws thereof, is hereby prohibited.

Section 3 This article shall be inoperative unless it shall have been ratified as an amendment to the Constitution by conventions in the several States, as provided in the Constitution, within seven years from the date of the submission hereof to the States by the Congress.

Amendment 22 (1951)
Presidential Term of Office

Section 1 No person shall be elected to the office of the President more than twice, and no person who has held the office of

President, or acted as President, for more than two years of a term to which some other person was elected President shall be elected to the office of the President more than once. ~~But this article shall not apply to any person holding the office of President when this article was proposed by the Congress, and shall not prevent any person who may be holding the office of President, or acting as President, during the term within which this article becomes operative from holding the office of President or acting as President during the remainder of such term.~~

Section 2 This article shall be inoperative unless it shall have been ratified as an amendment to the Constitution by the legislatures of three-fourths of the several states within seven years from the date of its submission to the states by the Congress.

Amendment 23 (1961)
Voting in the District of Columbia

Section 1 The District constituting the seat of government of the United States shall appoint in such manner as the Congress may direct:

A number of electors of President and Vice President equal to the whole number of Senators and Representatives in Congress to which the District would be entitled if it were a state, but in no event more than the least populous state; they shall be in addition to those appointed by the states, but they shall be considered, for the purposes of the election of President and Vice President, to be electors appointed by a state; and they shall meet in the District and perform such duties as provided by the twelfth article of amendment.

Section 2 The Congress shall have power to enforce this article by appropriate legislation.

Amendment 24 (1964)
Abolition of Poll Taxes

Section 1 The right of citizens of the United States to vote in any primary or other election for President or Vice President, for

electors for President or Vice President, or for Senator or Representative in Congress, shall not be denied or abridged by the United States or any state by reason of failure to pay any poll tax or other tax.

Section 2 The Congress shall have power to enforce this article by appropriate legislation.

Amendment 25 (1967)
Presidential Disability and Succession

Section 1 In case of the removal of the President from office or of his death or resignation, the Vice President shall become President.

Section 2 Whenever there is a vacancy in the office of the Vice President, the President shall nominate a Vice President who shall take office upon confirmation by a majority vote of both Houses of Congress.

Section 3 Whenever the President transmits to the President pro tempore of the Senate and the Speaker of the House of Representatives his written declaration that he is unable to discharge the powers and duties of his office, and until he transmits to them a written declaration to the contrary, such powers and duties shall be discharged by the Vice President as Acting President.

Section 4 Whenever the Vice President and a majority of either the principal officers of the executive departments or of such other body as Congress may by law provide, transmit to the President pro tempore of the Senate and the Speaker of the House of Representatives their written declaration that the President is unable to discharge the powers and duties of his office, the Vice President shall immediately assume the powers and duties of the office as Acting President.

Thereafter, when the President transmits to the President pro tempore of the Senate and

the Speaker of the House of Representatives his written declaration that no inability exists, he shall resume the powers and duties of his office unless the Vice President and a majority of either the principal officers of the executive department or of such other body as Congress may by law provide, transmit within four days to the President pro tempore of the Senate and the Speaker of the House of Representatives their written declaration that the President is unable to discharge the powers and duties of his office. Thereupon Congress shall decide the issue, assembling within forty-eight hours for that purpose if not in session. If the Congress, within twenty-one days after receipt of the latter written declaration, or, if Congress is not in session, within twenty-one days after Congress is required to assemble, determines by two-thirds vote of both Houses that the President is unable to discharge the powers and duties of his office, the Vice President shall continue to discharge the same as Acting President; otherwise, the President shall resume the powers and duties of his office.

Amendment 26 (1971)
Eighteen-Year-Old Vote

Section 1 The right of citizens of the United States, who are 18 years of age or older, to vote, shall not be denied or abridged by the United States or any state on account of age.

Section 2 The Congress shall have the power to enforce this article by appropriate legislation.

Amendment 27 (1992)
Congressional Salaries

No law varying the compensation for the services of the Senators and Representatives shall take effect until an election of Representatives shall have intervened.

Universal Declaration of Human Rights

On December 10, 1948, the General Assembly of the United Nations adopted and proclaimed the Universal Declaration of Human Rights, the full text of which appears in the following pages. The Assembly then called upon all member nations to publicize the text of the Declaration and "to cause it to be disseminated, displayed, read and expounded principally in schools and other educational institutions, without distinction based on the political status of countries or territories."

PREAMBLE

Whereas recognition of the inherent dignity and of the equal and inalienable rights of all members of the human family is the foundation of freedom, justice and peace in the world,

Whereas disregard and contempt for human rights have resulted in barbarous acts which have outraged the conscience of mankind, and the advent of a world in which human beings shall enjoy freedom of speech and belief and freedom from fear and want has been proclaimed as the highest aspiration of the common people,

Whereas it is essential, if man is not to be compelled to have recourse, as a last resort, to rebellion against tyranny and oppression, that human rights should be protected by the rule of law,

Whereas it is essential to promote the development of friendly relations between nations,

Whereas the peoples of the United Nations have in the Charter reaffirmed their faith in fundamental human rights, in the dignity and worth of the human person and in the equal rights of men and women and have determined to promote social progress and better standards of life in larger freedom,

Whereas Member States have pledged themselves to achieve, in co-operation with the United Nations, the promotion of universal respect for and observance of human rights and fundamental freedoms,

Whereas a common understanding of these rights and freedoms is of the greatest importance for the full realization of this pledge,

Now, Therefore THE GENERAL ASSEMBLY proclaims THIS UNIVERSAL DECLARATION OF HUMAN RIGHTS as a common standard of achievement for all peoples and all nations, to the end that every individual and every organ of society, keeping this Declaration constantly in mind, shall strive by teaching and education to promote respect for these rights and freedoms and by progressive measures, national and international, to secure their universal and effective recognition and observance, both among the peoples of Member States themselves and among the peoples of territories under their jurisdiction.

Article 1.

All human beings are born free and equal in dignity and rights. They are endowed with reason and conscience and should act towards one another in a spirit of brotherhood.

Article 2.

Everyone is entitled to all the rights and freedoms set forth in this Declaration, without distinction of any kind, such as race, colour, sex, language, religion, political or other opinion, national or social origin, property, birth or other status. Furthermore, no distinction shall be made on the basis of the political, jurisdictional or international status of the country or territory to which a person belongs, whether it be independent, trust, non-self-governing or under any other limitation of sovereignty.

Article 3.

Everyone has the right to life, liberty and security of person.

Article 4.

No one shall be held in slavery or servitude; slavery and the slave trade shall be prohibited in all their forms.

Article 5.

No one shall be subjected to torture or to cruel, inhuman or degrading treatment or punishment.

Article 6.

Everyone has the right to recognition everywhere as a person before the law.

Article 7.

All are equal before the law and are entitled without any discrimination to equal protection of the law. All are entitled to equal protection against any discrimination in violation of this Declaration and against any incitement to such discrimination.

Article 8.

Everyone has the right to an effective remedy by the competent national tribunals for acts violating the fundamental rights granted him by the constitution or by law.

Article 9.

No one shall be subjected to arbitrary arrest, detention or exile.

Article 10.

Everyone is entitled in full equality to a fair and public hearing by an independent and impartial tribunal, in the determination of his rights and obligations and of any criminal charge against him.

Article 11.

(1) Everyone charged with a penal offence has the right to be presumed innocent until proved guilty according to law in a public trial at which he has had all the guarantees necessary for his defence.
(2) No one shall be held guilty of any penal offence on account of any act or omission which did not constitute a penal offence, under national or international law, at the time when it was committed. Nor shall a heavier penalty be imposed than the one that was applicable at the time the penal offence was committed.

Article 12.

No one shall be subjected to arbitrary interference with his privacy, family, home or correspondence, nor to attacks upon his honour and reputation. Everyone has the right to the protection of the law against such interference or attacks.

Article 13.

(1) Everyone has the right to freedom of movement and residence within the borders of each state.
(2) Everyone has the right to leave any country, including his own, and to return to his country.

Article 14.

(1) Everyone has the right to seek and to enjoy in other countries asylum from persecution.

(2) This right may not be invoked in the case of prosecutions genuinely arising from non-political crimes or from acts contrary to the purposes and principles of the United Nations.

Article 15.

(1) Everyone has the right to a nationality.

(2) No one shall be arbitrarily deprived of his nationality nor denied the right to change his nationality.

Article 16.

(1) Men and women of full age, without any limitation due to race, nationality or religion, have the right to marry and to found a family. They are entitled to equal rights as to marriage, during marriage and at its dissolution.

(2) Marriage shall be entered into only with the free and full consent of the intending spouses.

(3) The family is the natural and fundamental group unit of society and is entitled to protection by society and the State.

Article 17.

(1) Everyone has the right to own property alone as well as in association with others.

(2) No one shall be arbitrarily deprived of his property.

Article 18.

Everyone has the right to freedom of thought, conscience and religion; this right includes freedom to change his religion or belief, and freedom, either alone or in community with others and in public or private, to manifest his religion or belief in teaching, practice, worship and observance.

Article 19.

Everyone has the right to freedom of opinion and expression; this right includes freedom to hold opinions without interference and to seek, receive and impart information and ideas through any media and regardless of frontiers.

Article 20.

(1) Everyone has the right to freedom of peaceful assembly and association.

(2) No one may be compelled to belong to an association.

Article 21.

(1) Everyone has the right to take part in the government of his country, directly or through freely chosen representatives.

(2) Everyone has the right of equal access to public service in his country.

(3) The will of the people shall be the basis of the authority of government; this will shall be expressed in periodic and genuine elections which shall be by universal and equal suffrage and shall be held by secret vote or by equivalent free voting procedures.

Article 22.

Everyone, as a member of society, has the right to social security and is entitled to realization, through national effort and international co-operation and in accordance with the organization and resources of each State, of the economic, social and cultural rights indispensable for his dignity and the free development of his personality.

Article 23.

(1) Everyone has the right to work, to free choice of employment, to just and favourable conditions of work and to protection against unemployment

(2) Everyone, without any discrimination, has the right to equal pay for equal work.

(3) Everyone who works has the right to just and favourable remuneration ensuring for himself and his family an existence worthy of human dignity, and supplemented, if necessary, by other means of social protection.

(4) Everyone has the right to form and to join trade unions for the protection of his interests.

Article 24.

Everyone has the right to rest and leisure, including reasonable limitation of working hours and periodic holidays with pay.

Article 25.

(1) Everyone has the right to a standard of living adequate for the health and well-being of himself and of his family, including food, clothing, housing and medical care and necessary social services, and the right to security in the event of unemployment, sickness, disability, widowhood, old age or other lack of livelihood in circumstances beyond his control.

(2) Motherhood and childhood are entitled to special care and assistance. All children, whether born in or out of wedlock, shall enjoy the same social protection.

Article 26.

(1) Everyone has the right to education. Education shall be free, at least in the elementary and fundamental stages. Elementary education shall be compulsory. Technical and professional education shall be made generally available and higher education shall be equally accessible to all on the basis of merit.

(2) Education shall be directed to the full development of the human personality and to the strengthening of respect for human rights and fundamental freedoms. It shall promote understanding, tolerance and friendship among all nations, racial or religious groups, and shall further the activities of the United Nations for the maintenance of peace.

(3) Parents have a prior right to choose the kind of education that shall be given to their children.

Article 27.

(1) Everyone has the right freely to participate in the cultural life of the community, to enjoy the arts and to share in scientific advancement and its benefits.

(2) Everyone has the right to the protection of the moral and material interests resulting from any scientific, literary or artistic production of which he is the author.

Article 28.

Everyone is entitled to a social and international order in which the rights and freedoms set forth in this Declaration can be fully realized.

Article 29.

(1) Everyone has duties to the community in which alone the free and full development of his personality is possible.

(2) In the exercise of his rights and freedoms, everyone shall be subject only to such limitations as are determined by law solely for the purpose of securing due recognition and respect for the rights and freedoms of others and of meeting the just requirements of morality, public order and the general welfare in a democratic society.

(3) These rights and freedoms may in no case be exercised contrary to the purposes and principles of the United Nations.

Article 30.

Nothing in this Declaration may be interpreted as implying for any State, group or person any right to engage in any activity or to perform any act aimed at the destruction of any of the rights and freedoms set forth herein.

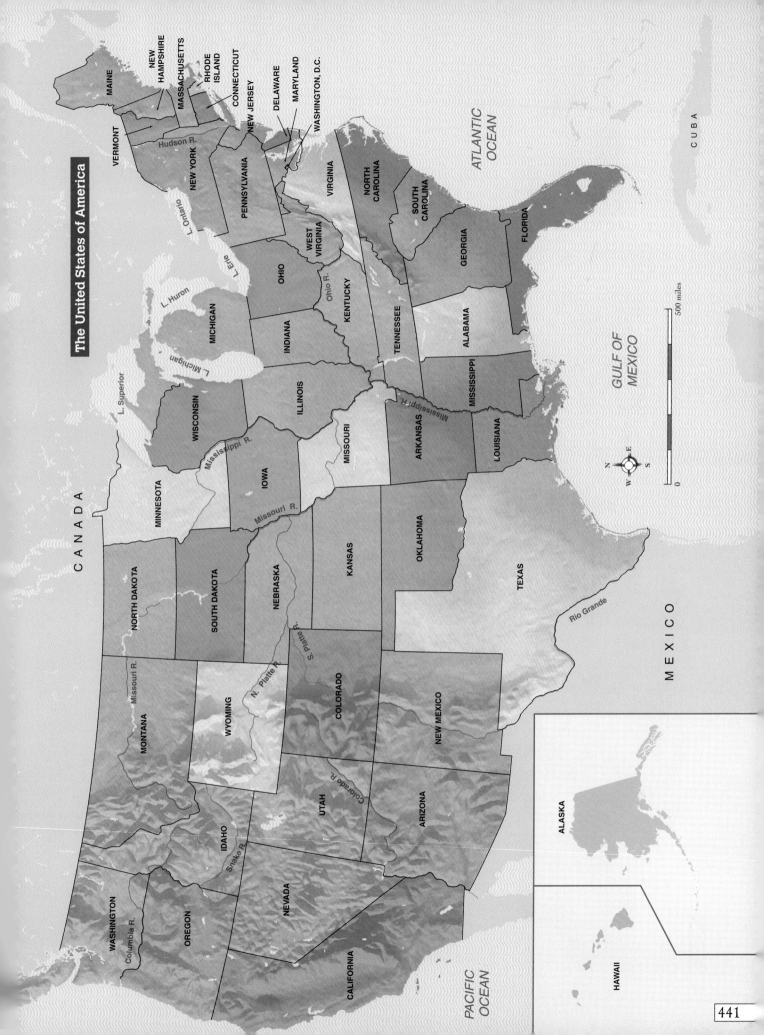

The United States of America

CANADA

MAINE

VERMONT
NEW HAMPSHIRE
MASSACHUSETTS
RHODE ISLAND
CONNECTICUT
NEW JERSEY
DELAWARE
MARYLAND
WASHINGTON, D.C.

Hudson R.

L. Ontario

L. Erie

NEW YORK

PENNSYLVANIA

WEST VIRGINIA

VIRGINIA

NORTH CAROLINA

SOUTH CAROLINA

GEORGIA

FLORIDA

ATLANTIC OCEAN

CUBA

L. Huron

MICHIGAN

L. Michigan

OHIO

KENTUCKY

Ohio R.

TENNESSEE

ALABAMA

WISCONSIN

ILLINOIS

INDIANA

MISSOURI

Mississippi R.

ARKANSAS

MISSISSIPPI

LOUISIANA

GULF OF MEXICO

L. Superior

Mississippi R.

MINNESOTA

IOWA

Missouri R.

KANSAS

OKLAHOMA

TEXAS

Rio Grande

MEXICO

500 miles

N
W E
S

0

NORTH DAKOTA

SOUTH DAKOTA

NEBRASKA

S. Platte R.

N. Platte R.

COLORADO

NEW MEXICO

Missouri R.

MONTANA

WYOMING

UTAH

Colorado R.

ARIZONA

IDAHO

Snake R.

NEVADA

WASHINGTON

OREGON

Columbia R.

CALIFORNIA

PACIFIC OCEAN

ALASKA

HAWAII

441

The World

442

PACIFIC OCEAN

ARCTIC OCEAN

NORTH ATLANTIC OCEAN

SOUTH ATLANTIC OCEAN

PACIFIC OCEAN

INDIAN OCEAN

Tropic of Cancer

Equator

Tropic of Capricorn

GREENLAND

ICELAND

CANADA

UNITED STATES OF AMERICA

MEXICO

GUATEMALA
EL SALVADOR
COSTA RICA
NICARAGUA
HONDURAS
BELIZE
PANAMA
COLOMBIA
ECUADOR
PERU

CUBA
HAITI
DOMINICAN REPUBLIC
PUERTO RICO
VENEZUELA
GUYANA
SURINAME
FRENCH GUIANA

BRAZIL

BOLIVIA

PARAGUAY

CHILE

ARGENTINA

URUGUAY

FALKLAND/MALVINAS ISLANDS

RUSSIA

UNITED KINGDOM
IRELAND
NETHERLANDS
BELGIUM
LUXEMBURG
CZECH REP.
SWITZERLAND
FRANCE
AUSTRIA
PORTUGAL
SPAIN
ANDORRA
MOROCCO
WESTERN SAHARA
MAURITANIA
SENEGAL
GAMBIA
GUINEA-BISSAU
GUINEA
SIERRA LEONE
LIBERIA
IVORY COAST
BURKINA FASO
GHANA
TOGO
BENIN
ALGERIA
MALI
NIGER
NIGERIA
CAMEROON
EQUATORIAL GUINEA
GABON
CONGO

NORWAY
DENMARK
GERMANY
SWEDEN
FINLAND
ESTONIA
LATVIA
LITHUANIA
BELARUS
RUSSIA
POLAND
UKRAINE
SLOVAKIA
HUNGARY
MOLDOVA
ROMANIA
BULGARIA
GREECE
MACEDONIA
ALBANIA
SERBIA
BOSNIA
CROATIA
SLOVENIA
ITALY
TUNISIA
LIBYA
CHAD
TURKEY
CYPRUS
SYRIA
LEBANON
ISRAEL
JORDAN
EGYPT
SUDAN
IRAQ
SAUDI ARABIA
YEMEN
ERITREA
ETHIOPIA
DJIBOUTI
CENTRAL AFRICAN REPUBLIC
UGANDA
KENYA
RWANDA
BURUNDI
DEM. REP. OF THE CONGO
TANZANIA
ANGOLA
ZAMBIA
MALAWI
MOZAMBIQUE
ZIMBABWE
NAMIBIA
BOTSWANA
SWAZILAND
LESOTHO
SOUTH AFRICA
MADAGASCAR
MAURITIUS

GEORGIA
ARMENIA
AZERBAIJAN
IRAN
OMAN
QATAR
UNITED ARAB EMIRATES

KAZAKHSTAN
UZBEKISTAN
KYRGYZSTAN
TAJIKISTAN
TURKMENISTAN
AFGHANISTAN
PAKISTAN
INDIA
NEPAL
BHUTAN
BANGLADESH
SRI LANKA

MONGOLIA

CHINA

NORTH KOREA
SOUTH KOREA
JAPAN
TAIWAN

MYANMAR (BURMA)
LAOS
THAILAND
VIETNAM
CAMBODIA
BRUNEI
MALAYSIA
PHILIPPINES
INDONESIA

PAPUA NEW GUINEA

AUSTRALIA

NEW ZEALAND

ANTARCTICA

0   2000   4000   6000   8000 miles (at Equator)

N
W   E
S

North America

GREENLAND

ATLANTIC
OCEAN

CANADA

YUKON
TERRITORY

NORTHERN TERRITORIES

BRITISH
COLUMBIA

ALBERTA

SASKATCHEWAN

MANITOBA

ONTARIO

QUEBEC

NEWFOUNDLAND

NEW
BRUNSWICK

Hudson
Bay

AK

UNITED STATES
OF AMERICA

WA
OR
ID
NV
CA
UT
AZ
MT
WY
CO
NM
ND
SD
NE
KS
OK
TX
MN
IA
MO
AR
LA
WI
IL
IN
MI
OH
KY
TN
MS
AL
GA
FL
SC
NC
VA
WV
PA
NY
VT
NH
ME
MA
RI
CT
NJ
DE
MD

PACIFIC
OCEAN

Gulf of
Mexico

MEXICO

BELIZE
GUATEMALA
EL SALVADOR
HONDURAS
NICARAGUA
COSTA RICA
PANAMA

CUBA

BAHAMAS

JAMAICA

HAITI

DOMINICAN
REPUBLIC

PUERTO
RICO

Caribbean Sea

SOUTH
AMERICA

N
W   E
S

0   500   1000   1500   2000 miles

443

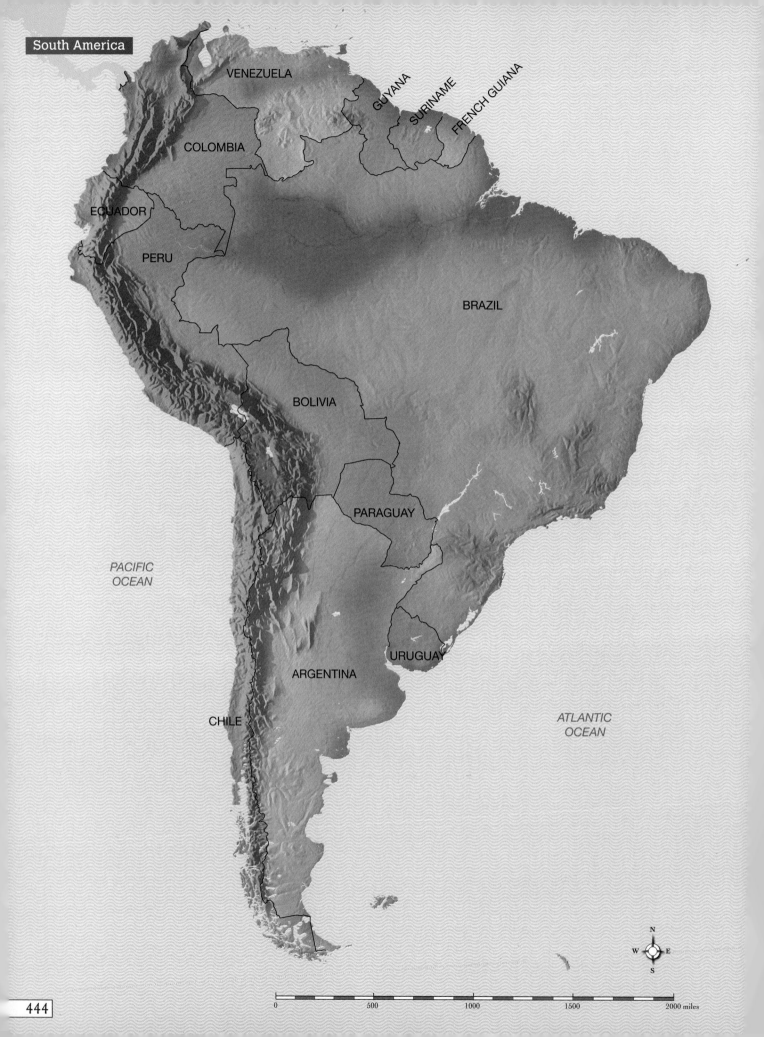

South America

VENEZUELA
GUYANA
SURINAME
FRENCH GUIANA
COLOMBIA
ECUADOR
PERU
BRAZIL
BOLIVIA
PARAGUAY
PACIFIC
OCEAN
URUGUAY
ARGENTINA
CHILE
ATLANTIC
OCEAN

N
W E
S

0   500   1000   1500   2000 miles

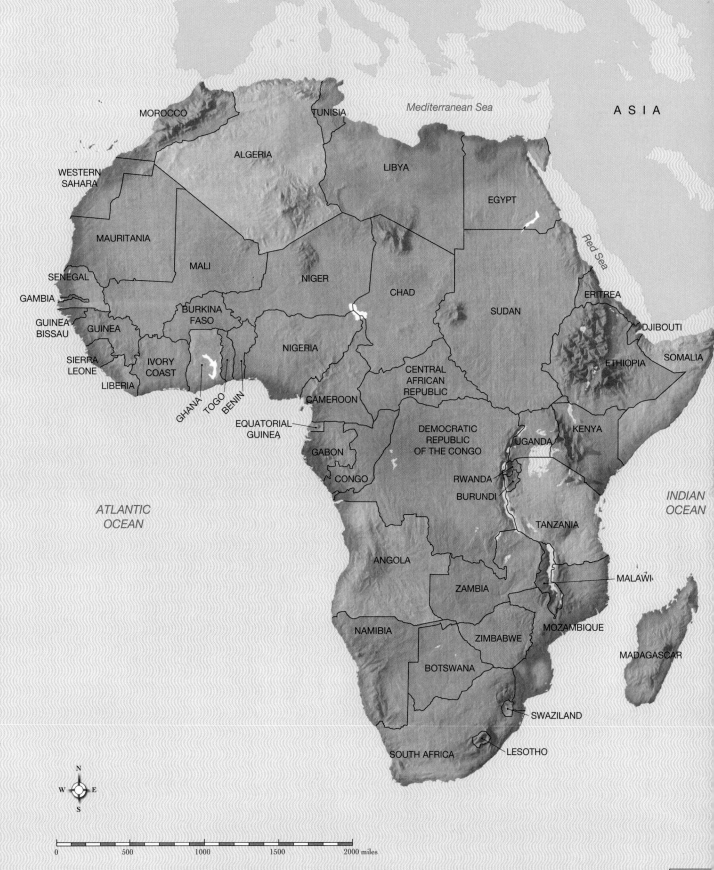

Africa

EUROPE

ASIA

Mediterranean Sea

MOROCCO

TUNISIA

ALGERIA

LIBYA

EGYPT

WESTERN
SAHARA

Red Sea

MAURITANIA

MALI

NIGER

CHAD

SUDAN

ERITREA

SENEGAL

DJIBOUTI

GAMBIA

BURKINA
FASO

NIGERIA

CENTRAL
AFRICAN
REPUBLIC

ETHIOPIA

SOMALIA

GUINEA
BISSAU

GUINEA

SIERRA
LEONE

IVORY
COAST

LIBERIA

GHANA

TOGO

BENIN

EQUATORIAL
GUINEA

CAMEROON

GABON

CONGO

DEMOCRATIC
REPUBLIC
OF THE CONGO

UGANDA

KENYA

RWANDA

BURUNDI

TANZANIA

INDIAN
OCEAN

ATLANTIC
OCEAN

ANGOLA

ZAMBIA

MALAWI

NAMIBIA

ZIMBABWE

MOZAMBIQUE

MADAGASCAR

BOTSWANA

SWAZILAND

SOUTH AFRICA

LESOTHO

N
W E
S

0   500   1000   1500   2000 miles

445

Europe

1000 miles

500

0

N
W · E
S

446

GREENLAND

ATLANTIC
OCEAN

ICELAND

IRELAND
N. IRELAND
SCOTLAND
WALES
ENGLAND

PORTUGAL

SPAIN

ANDORRA

FRANCE

LUXEMBURG

BELGIUM

NETHERLANDS

North
Sea

DENMARK

NORWAY

SWEDEN

FINLAND

ESTONIA
LATVIA
LITHUANIA
Baltic
Sea

RUSSIA

POLAND

GERMANY

SWITZERLAND

ITALY

SLOVENIA

CROATIA

BOSNIA-
HERZEGOVINA

SERBIA AND
MONTENEGRO

ALBANIA

GREECE

MACEDONIA

Mediterranean Sea

AUSTRIA

CZECH REP.

SLOVAKIA

HUNGARY

ROMANIA

BULGARIA

TURKEY

Black Sea

MOLDOVA

UKRAINE

BELARUS

U   S   S   R

Ural Mts.

Ural Mts.

Caucasus Mts.

Caspian Sea

Aral
Sea

KAZAKHSTAN

A S I A

A S I A

AFRICA

Asia

N W E S

EUROPE

RUSSIA

PACIFIC OCEAN

JAPAN

N. KOREA

S. KOREA

MONGOLIA

CHINA

E. China Sea

TAIWAN

S. China Sea

PHILIPPINES

KAZAKHSTAN

KYRGYZSTAN

TAJIKISTAN

KASHMIR

NEPAL

BHUTAN

MYANMAR (BURMA)

LAOS

VIETNAM

THAILAND

CAMBODIA

MALAYSIA

INDONESIA

BANGLADESH

INDIA

Aral Sea

UZBEKISTAN

TURKMENISTAN

AFGHANISTAN

PAKISTAN

AZERBAIJAN

ARMENIA

GEORGIA

Caspian Sea

IRAN

OMAN

SRI LANKA

INDIAN OCEAN

Arabian Sea

Black Sea

TURKEY

SYRIA

IRAQ

KUWAIT

Persian Gulf

UNITED ARAB EMIRATES

LEBANON

ISRAEL

JORDAN

SAUDIA ARABIA

YEMEN

Red Sea

Mediterranean Sea

AFRICA

AUSTRALIA

0   1000   2000   3000   4000 miles

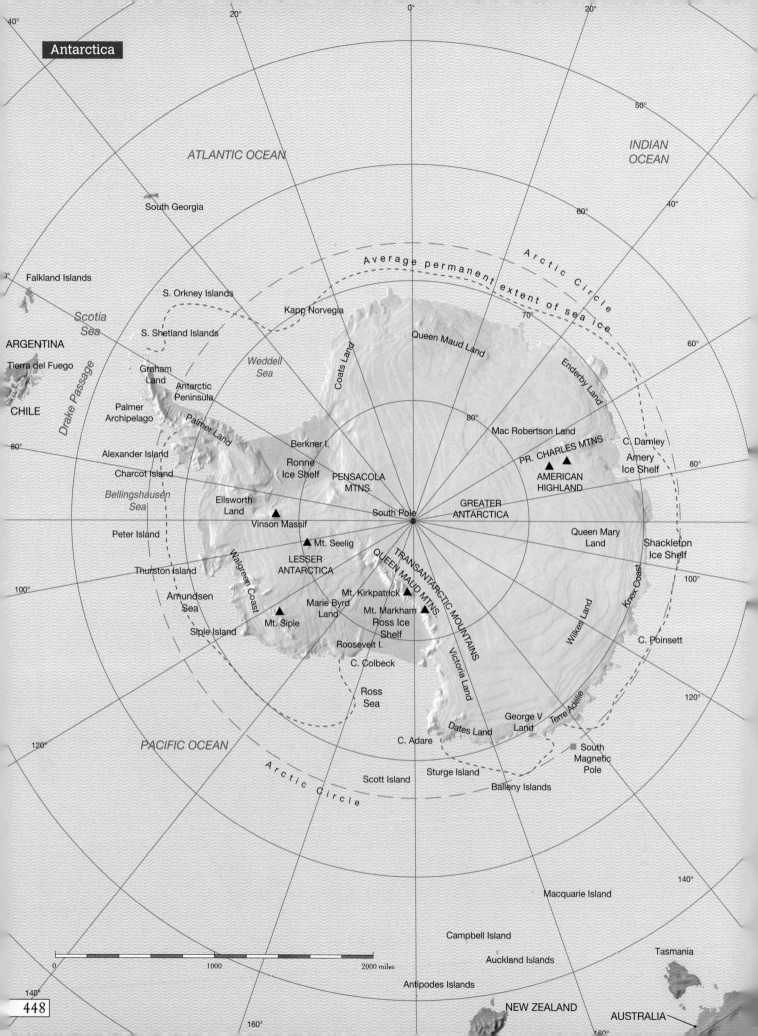

Antarctica

ATLANTIC OCEAN

INDIAN OCEAN

20° 0° 20° 40° 50° 60°

South Georgia

Arctic Circle

Average permanent extent of sea ice

Falkland Islands

Scotia Sea

S. Orkney Islands

Kapp Norvegia

Queen Maud Land

70°

Enderby Land

60°

ARGENTINA

Tierra del Fuego

S. Shetland Islands

Weddell Sea

Coats Land

CHILE

Graham Land

Antarctic Peninsula

Palmer Archipelago

Palmer Land

Mac Robertson Land

PR. CHARLES MTNS ▲ ▲

C. Damley

80°

Alexander Island

Berkner I.

Ronne Ice Shelf

PENSACOLA MTNS.

AMERICAN HIGHLAND

Amery Ice Shelf

80°

Charcot Island

Drake Passage

Bellingshausen Sea

Ellsworth Land ▲

Vinson Massif

South Pole

GREATER ANTARCTICA

Peter Island

Mt. Seelig ▲

Queen Mary Land

Shackleton Ice Shelf

Thurston Island

LESSER ANTARCTICA

QUEEN MAUD MTNS.

TRANSANTARCTIC MOUNTAINS

100°

Amundsen Sea

Walgreen Coast

Marie Byrd Land

Mt. Kirkpatrick ▲

Mt. Markham ▲

Ross Ice Shelf

Wilkes Land

Knox Coast

C. Poinsett

Siple Island

Mt. Siple ▲

Roosevelt I.

C. Colbeck

Victoria Land

120°

120°

PACIFIC OCEAN

Ross Sea

Dates Land

George V Land

Terre Adélie

South Magnetic Pole

Arctic Circle

C. Adare

Scott Island

Sturge Island

Balleny Islands

140°

Macquarie Island

140°

Campbell Island

Auckland Islands

Tasmania

Antipodes Islands

NEW ZEALAND

AUSTRALIA

0 1000 2000 miles

448

Glossary/Index

Vocabulary definitions are shown in bold type.

Acknowledgements

Cover Images: (left to right) ©Gideon Mendel/CORBIS; ©Stefano Bianchetti/Corbis; ©Mary Evans Picture Library; ©Bettmann/CORBIS; ©Wilson Koh www.wilsonkoh.com; (bottom) ©Bettman/CORBIS

Margin Images: Magna Carta ©Bettmann/CORBIS; The Scroll of Rule ©West Semitic Research/Dead Sea Scrolls Foundation/CORBIS

3 (t)©Hulton Archive/Getty Images, (b)©Nik Wheeler/CORBIS, (l)©Gianni Dagli Orti/CORBIS; 4 ©Taxi/Getty Images; 5 ©Ron Watts/CORBIS; 6 ©Reuters/CORBIS; 7 (tl)©John Reader/Photo Researcher, Inc., (br)©John Reader/ Photo Researchers, Inc.; 8 (t)©Dewitt Jones/CORBIS, (b)©Richard T. Nowitz/Photo Researchers, Inc.; 9 ©Des Bartlett/Photo Researchers, Inc.; 10 ©CORBIS; 12 (t)©Chris R. Sharp/Photo Researchers, Inc., (bl)©Jonathan Blair/CORBIS; 13 ©Roger Wood/CORBIS; 16 ©Georg Gerster/Photo Researcher's, Inc.; 17 ©The Granger Collection; 19 (t)©Diego Lezama/CORBIS, (b)©Dean Conger/CORBIS; 20 (t)©Swiss Erlenmeyer Collection, (bl)©JupiterImages Corporation; 23 ©The Rhodes Jewish Museum; 24 ©Bettmann/CORBIS; 29 (t)©ML Sinibaldi/CORBIS, (br)©Keren Su/CORBIS, (bl)©Historical Picture Archive/CORBIS; 32 ©Sandro Vannini/CORBIS; 33 (t)©Roger Wood/CORBIS, (b)©Christine Osborne/CORBIS, (b)©Roger Wood/CORBIS; 34 (t)©JupiterImages Corporation, (b)©Sandro Vannini/CORBIS; 35 (t)©Bojan Brecelj/CORBIS, (r)©Gianni Dagli Orti/CORBIS; 36 ©Charles & Josette Lenars/CORBIS; 37 (t)©Jonathan Blair/CORBIS, (br)©Archivo Iconografico, S.A./CORBIS; 40 ©Michael Freeman/CORBIS; 42 ©Reuters/CORBIS; 43 (t)©Diago Lezama Orezzoli/CORBIS, (b)©CORBIS; 45 ©Michael Freeman/CORBIS; 46 ©Roman Soumar/CORBIS; 47 (t)©Bettmann/CORBIS, (b)©Bettmann/CORBIS, (r)©Luca I. Tettoni/CORBIS; 49 ©Leonard de Selva/CORBIS; 50 (t)©Macduff Everton/CORBIS, (t)©Archivo Iconografico, S.A./CORBIS, (t)©Pierre Vauthey/CORBIS, (t)©Nik Wheeler; 52 (t)©Adam Woolfitt/CORBIS, (b)©Lindsey Hebberd/CORBIS; 53 Primary Source from "Arthashastra", *Classical India*, edited by William H. McNeill and Jean W. Sedlar, New York: Oxford University Press, 1969.; 56 ©Lonely Planet Images/Getty Images; 58 ©Asian Art & Archeology, Inc./CORBIS; 60 ©Bettmann/CORBIS; 61 ©Archivo Iconografico, S.A./CORBIS; 63 ©The Granger Collection; 64 ©Bettmann/CORBIS; 65 ©University of Purdue; 66 (t)©The Trustees of the British Museum, (b)©University of Maryland; 72 (t)©Gianni Dagli Orti/CORBIS, (l)©Archivo Iconografico, S.A./CORBIS, (bl)©Bettmann/CORBIS, (br)©Peter M. Wilson/CORBIS; 74 (l)©Araldo de Luca/CORBIS, (b)©The Granger Collection; 75 ©Araldo de Luca/CORBIS; 76 ©Christie's Images/CORBIS; 77 (t)©Mary Evans Picture Library, (b)©John Hios/akg-images; 79 ©The Granger Collection; 80 ©Fotosearch; 81 ©The Granger Collection; 82 ©Araldo de Luca/CORBIS; 83 ©Wolfgang Kaehler; 86 ©Robert Harding World Imagery/Getty Images; 87 ©Charles & Josette Lenars/CORBIS; 88 ©Photodisc Green/Getty Images; 91 ©Free Agents Limited/CORBIS; 92 ©Giraudon/Art Resource, NY; 93 (t)©Bettmann/CORBIS, (b)©Musee d'Orsay, Paris, France, Giraudon;/Bridge; 95 ©Robert Harding World Imagery/Getty Images; 96 ©Taxi/Getty Images; 97 ©Scala/Art Resource, NY; 98 ©Mary Evans Picture Library; 99 ©Mary Evans Picture Library and ©Bettmann/CORBIS; 100 (t)©The Bridgeman Art Library/Getty Images, (b)©Mary Evans Picture Library; 105 (bl)©Christine Osborne/CORBIS, (t)©Wolfgang Kaehler; 106 ©Francesco Venturi/CORBIS; 107 ©Courtesy of the Museum of Antiquities, University of Sasktchewan; 108 ©Adam Woolfitt/CORBIS; 110 (b)©Catholic University of America, (t)©Scala/Art Resource, NY; 112 (t)©Art Resource, NY, (b)©Paul H. Kuiper/CORBIS; 114 ©José F. Poblete/CORBIS; 115 ©Diego Lezama/CORBIS; 118 ©Reuters/CORBIS; 120 ©www.artislamic.com; 122 ©Bojan Brecelj; 123 ©Aaron Horowitz/CORBIS; 126 (t)©Michael Busselle/CORBIS, (b)©M. Burgess/Robertstock.com; 127 Primary Source from "One Who Wraps Himself" from *The Essential Rumi* translated by Coleman Barks, HarperSanFrancisco, 1995.; 128 ©Sheldan Collins/CORBIS; 129 (l)©David Lees/CORBIS, (b)©www.artislamic.com; 132 ©Wolfgang Kaehler 20_www.wkaehlerphoto.com; 133 ©Museum of Mankind, London, UK/www.bridgeman.co.uk; 134 (l)©Getty Images, Inc., (r)©Getty Images, Inc.; 136 (t)©Jason Laure, (r)©Brooklyn Museum of Art, New York, USA/www.bridgeman.co.uk, (l)©Private Collection, Heidi Schneebeli/Bridgeman Art Library; 137©Roger De La Harpe; Gallo Images/CORBIS; 138 ©Carmen Redondo/CORBIS; 139 ©Jason Laure; 140 ©Jason Laure; 141 ©Jeffrey L. Rotman/CORBIS; 143 ©Sandro Vannini/CORBIS; 144 ©Horniman Museum, London, UK, Heini Schneebli/www.bridgeman.co.uk; 145 Primary Source from *African Cities and Towns Before the European Conquest* by Richard W. Hull. Copyright ©1976 by W.W. Norton & Company, Inc. Used by permission of W.W. Norton & Company, Inc.; 148 ©Getty Images, Inc.; 150 ©Gianni Dagli Orti/CORBIS; 151 (t)©Werner Forman/CORBIS, (b)©Mary Evans/Edwin Wallace; 152 ©Nik Wheeler/CORBIS; 153 ©New York Historical Society, New York, NY, USA; 154 (l)©J. C. Kanny/Lorpresse/CORBIS SYGMA, (r)©Gianni Dagli Orti/CORBIS; 155 ©Werner Forman/CORBIS; 156 ©John McAnulty/CORBIS; 157 (b)©Richard A. Cooke/CORBIS, (t)©Richard A. Cooke/CORBIS; 158 ©CORBIS; 159 ©Nathan Benn/CORBIS; 162 ©Lin Liqun/CORBIS; 164 (b)©Giraudon/Art Resource, NY, (t)©Private Collection/Bridgeman Art Library; 166 ©Burstein Collection/CORBIS, Primary Source from *The Travels of Marco Polo* edited by Milton Rugoff, New York: New American Library, 1961.; 167 ©Brian A. Vikander/CORBIS; 170 ©Free Agents Limited/CORBIS; 171 (r)©Scala/Art Resource, NY, (l)©Burstein Collection/CORBIS; 172 ©John Van Hasselt/CORBIS; 173 ©Peter Harholdt/CORBIS; 176 ©Ancient Art & Architecture/DanitaDelimont.com; 177 (t)©Getty Images, Inc., (b)©Musee Royaux des Beaux-Arts de Beliguque, Brussels, Belgium/Bridge; 181 (t)©Gianni Dagli Orti/CORBIS, (l)©Gianni Dagli Orti/CORBIS, (r)©Hulton Archives/Getty Images, Inc.; 182 ©Paul Almasy/CORBIS; 183 ©Archivo Iconografico, S.A./CORBIS; 184 ©Archivo Iconografico, S.A./CORBIS; 185 ©NPTL/The Images Works; 186 (tl)©Tibor Bognar/CORBIS, (bl)©Historical Picture Archive/CORBIS, (r)©Elio Ciol/CORBIS; 187 ©Archivo Iconografico, S.A./CORBIS; 188 ©The Granger Collection, New York; 191 ©Bettmann/CORBIS; 192 ©Historical Picture Archive/CORBIS; 193 (b)©Castello di Issogne, Val d'Aosta, Italy, Giraudon;/www.bridgeman.co.uk, (t)©Gianni Dagli Orti/CORBIS; 195 ©Bettmann/CORBIS; 196 (r)©Bettmann/CORBIS, (l)©2005 JupiterImages Corporation; 197 ©Stefano/Bianchetti/CORBIS; 200 ©David Lees/CORBIS; 202 (l)©Robert Harding World Imagery/Getty Images, Inc., (r)©The Bridgeman Art Library/Getty Images, Inc.;

(t) top, (b) bottom, (l) left, (r) right